Managing4Good:

Kaplan's Guide to Responsible and Sustainable Business

by John Fagan

KAPLAN
PUBLISHING

British library cataloguing-in-publication data
A catalogue record for this book is available from the British Library.
Published by:
Kaplan Publishing UK
Unit 2 The Business Centre
Molly Millars Lane
Wokingham
Berkshire
RG41 2QZ
ISBN 978-0-85732-206-7

First edition published 2010

Printed and bound in Great Britain.

Contents

We can't solve problems by using the same kind of thinking we used when we created them.

Albert Einstein

Preamble ●●●

Why read this book?

Responsible business management, or corporate responsibility, is becoming a mainstream part of company activity. Understanding the wide range of issues this incorporates will be crucial for the next generation of business leaders, as business operations will need to adapt if they are to thrive in changing economic and environmental climates.

Businesses in the UK and beyond are concerning themselves with responsible business management, to a greater or lesser extent, and they are generally aware of the impact legislation has on their operations, both now and increasingly in the future.

This book is essential reading for anyone studying business, management, accounting, strategy, operations and marketing to familiarise themselves with the breadth of issues in this evolving sphere. Knowledge in this field will enhance career opportunities.

> *I'm happy to do projects around sustainability because I can see this will help my career prospects.*
>
> **BA Business Administration student 2008**

All businesses operating in the present climate need to be aware of the changing world of which they are now a part. Businesses are facing new challenges from all angles: challenging legislation and energy targets from the government; specific demands from investors; expectations from employees; requests for transparency from customers. All these issues are interlinked, and an understanding of the connections is essential. It will become apparent that many of the problems and solutions will be common to all industries and sectors.

Managing4Good attempts to bring together these complex and varied issues in one handy student guide. Each section will guide you through the definition and common understandings of the issues and utilise current research and real case studies to aid learning.

Who the book is for?

Whatever subject area you are studying, you will find that responsibility and sustainability are terms that are becoming more commonly used and relevant in day to day work. Below are various examples of how professional bodies view their industry's role in delivering responsible and sustainable business management.

Accountancy

The International Federation of Accountants (IFAC) recognises the role that professional accountants have "at the heart of sustainability"[1] with the belief that "the role of professional accountants has ... expanded beyond that of preparers or assurers of financial and sustainability reports. Professional accountants need to adapt to a world in which sustainability is the key to long-term business performance, and need to understand how, in their diverse roles in organisations, they play a significant role"[2]. IFAC maintains that accountants have the necessary qualities to support wider business understanding, and lead the sustainability agenda.

> *Unless the accounting profession embraces sustainability, we will become less and less relevant to society.*
>
> **Nick Shepherd, President, EduVision (IFAC, 2009)**

The Chartered Institute of Management Accountants (CIMA) "believes that finance professionals have an important role to play in ensuring organisations consider climate change in a strategic context and integrating sustainability issues into their long-term decision making processes"[3]. CIMA has undertaken research into the role of the finance team in climate change projects[4], dedicated an *Excellence in Leadership* journal to *Responsible Business*[5] and produced a ten point climate control action plan "aimed at boards, management accountants and the wider management team working together to incorporate climate change into their organisations' strategies and into day-to-day business life"[6].

The Association of Chartered Certified Accountants (ACCA) has produced the report *Going Concern? A Sustainability Agenda for Action*[7]. In this, ACCA urges that "the accountancy profession has an important role in defining and delivering the means by which sustainable development is measured and reported"[8], and sets out how all organisations should incorporate corporate social responsibility (CSR) and sustainable development in their strategies.

1 IFAC. (August 2009). Professional Accountants in Business - at the Heart of Sustainability? New York.

2 IFAC. (2009, November). IFAC Sustainability Framework. Retrieved November 2009, from IFAC: http://web.ifac.org/sustainability-framework/overview

3 CIMA. (2009). Climate change: the role of the finance professional. London: CIMA. Pp3.

4 CIMA. (2009). Climate change: the role of the finance professional. London: CIMA.

5 CIMA. (2008, August). Excellence in Leadership. Retrieved from http://www.excellence-leadership.com/book-plan-08-06.html

6 CIMA. (2008, June). Excellence in Leadership: Responsible Leadership. Retrieved from http://www.excellence-leadership.com/book-plan-08-06.html pp9

7 ACCA. (2008). Going Concern? A Sustainability Agenda for Action. London: ACCA.

8 ACCA. (2008). Going Concern? A Sustainability Agenda for Action. London: ACCA. Pp 3.

The Institute of Charted Accountants in England and Wales (ICAEW) has introduced *The Business Sustainability* e-learning programme[9], an on-line course which aims to raise awareness of the business case for corporate responsibility and the issues which face companies in adopting sustainable practices.

Business and Economics

The Confederation of British Industry (CBI) works with over 200,000 British businesses, a figure which includes some 70% of FTSE 100 companies and around 50% of FTSE 350 companies. The CBI report *Climate Change - Everyone's Business*[10] identifies that, in order to achieve a competitive low-carbon economy, climate change has to become a priority at national and international levels involving partnerships between government, consumers and businesses. They suggest that businesses need to be given more information and incentives to help them take action on climate change, and could save an average of 30% energy through improved energy efficiency in buildings, transport and equipment.

The CBI predicts that there will be a range of new business opportunities presented by action on climate change and UK businesses should be planning now to capture these opportunities.

Human Resources

The Chartered Institute of Personnel and Development (CIPD) produced a report *Making CSR happen: the contribution of people management*[11] which involved building several case studies on a variety of companies. The study concludes that both CSR and HR activities are major contributors to the creation of long-term or sustainable success in organisations and this reinforces findings from other research that CIPD had carried out in recent years. They realised that in an increasingly knowledge and service based economy employees will become the key stakeholders. Many of the CSR activities reported in the study were aimed at sustaining and improving the employment relationship.

Law

The Law Society is committed to operating as a responsible and sustainable organisation, and to helping their members do the same. Some aspects of corporate responsibility work have been embraced by the profession for many decades. Their aim is to develop, adopt and promote best practice across the board.

9 ICAEW. (2009). Business Sustainability Programme. Retrieved November 2009, from ICAEW: http://www.icaew.com/index.cfm/route/154476/icaew_ga/en/Qualifications/Specialist_qualifications_and_programmes/Business_Sustainability_Programmes/Business_Sustainability_Programme

10 CBI. (2007). Climate change: Everyone's business. London: CBI.

11 CIPD. (2005). Making CSR happen: the contribution of people management. Retrieved November 2009, from CIPD: http://www.cipd.co.uk/subjects/corpstrtgy/corpsocres/_mkngcsrhpn.htm?IsSrchRes=1

The Law Society supports solicitors who go greener through the Legal Sector Alliance (LSA). The LSA is a collection of law firms and organisations working collaboratively on climate change by reducing their carbon footprint and adopting environmentally sustainable practices. The LSA has over 100 members representing over 20 per cent of solicitors in private practice in England and Wales, ranging from sole practitioners to global law firms.

Management

The Chartered Management Institute's report *Lean and Green: Leadership for a low-carbon future*[12] suggests that while the importance of the green agenda is increasingly well-recognised, too few organisations are taking the urgent action needed to transform the UK economy for a low-carbon future. The report identifies a failure of boardroom leadership as a significant block to progress, which in turn risks quelling employee enthusiasm for the action needed to build low-carbon businesses. The report calls for managers to do more to cut emissions by making green issues part of the mainstream of management activities, and the authors specifically urge the professional bodies to support senior management in embracing a low-carbon future.

Marketing

The Chartered Institute of Marketing have identified that more than 75% of marketers believe that a company's sustainability practices will increasingly affect customers' buying decisions[13]. The Institute believes that marketers have an important role to play in ensuring that sustainability can be used to gain a competitive advantage in successful relationships and brand reputation.

Not just for students

This book is also for those in business who would like to know more about responsible business management – what is this CSR? What could our company do to behave more responsibly? What would attract and retain top level, innovative employees? How do global issues affect our business? What role can individuals, employees and managers play in achieving more responsible business practice? This guide will answer the above questions and many more.

All the organisations mentioned above provide seminars, training events and continuing professional development (CPD) for their members on many of the issues to be explored in this book.

Many larger businesses rely on shareholder investment either from institutional or retail investors and it is becoming apparent that these investors are becoming much more discerning and will only invest in companies that demonstrate good standards in corporate responsibility. The FTSE4Good Index series was launched in 2001 to help responsible investors make more informed decisions which will minimise social and environmental risks.

12 Chartered Management Institute. (2009). Lean and Green: Leadership for a low-carbon future. London: Chartered Management Institute.

13 Chartered Institute of Marketing. (2007). Shape the Agenda: The good, the bad and the indifferent - marketing and the triple bottom line. Chartered Institute of Marketing. Pp 11.

The companies wishing to be included in the indices need to demonstrate that they are working towards[14]:

- environmental management
- climate change mitigation and adaptation
- countering bribery
- upholding human and labour rights
- supply chain labour standards.

The above issues will be covered in later sections of the book where it will be seen that these factors influence stakeholders involved with any given business, large or small. It is probably true to say that where large companies lead today, small and medium sized enterprises (SMEs) will follow tomorrow and therefore it is in the best interest of every business owner or manager to ensure that in the future they are **Managing4Good**.

And there is more...

Once you have purchased this book you will have access to additional materials on its themes together with updates and other information. Please go to http://kaplan-publishing.kaplan.co.uk/managing4good.

Acknowledgements

We are extremely grateful to many organisations for their permission to incorporate extracts into this book and to draw on other content.

Every effort has been made to contact the holders of copyright material but if any have been inadvertently overlooked the author will be pleased to make the necessary arrangements at the first opportunity.

14 FTSE4Good. (2008). FTSE4Good index series factsheet. Retrieved November 2009, from FTSE: http://www.ftse.com/Indices/FTSE4Good_Index_Series/Downloads/FTSE4Good_Factsheet.pdf

SECTION 1

Introduction

- What we mean by Responsible and Sustainable
- Sphere of Influence

CHAPTER 1

What we mean by Responsible and Sustainable

- Looking Back to Look Forward
- Breadth and Boundaries of Responsibility
- Stakeholders' Needs
- Sustaining Business
- Sustaining the Planet

There is increasing acceptance that the role of business is not just to do business, but to do business in a responsible manner, accepting responsibilities to the workforce, the marketplace, the wider community and the environment. In an ideal situation, these responsibilities would be at the heart of an organisation from its inception, but in more recent years, it has become increasingly common for previously more traditional, inward-looking organisations to be seen flying the "CSR" flag with great vigour. Some of these are genuine efforts to bring heart into an organisation, and others regarded as more of an "add-on" to business operations. Either way, the fact that so many organisations are now participating in various CSR activities is evidence in itself that it makes good business sense with regard to the bottom line. In addition, CSR will become increasingly important and will not go away.

Looking Back to Look Forward ●●●

Behaving responsibly is nothing new. In the late 1800s, factory workers for Cadbury were provided with housing on the Bourneville estate, education and training. Treating the workforce as part of their family, the owners also provided medical facilities and pension schemes. The Cadbury family recognised that the business would also benefit from these, ensuring a healthy and dedicated workforce.

Clarks, makers of Clarks Shoes, started out as a sheepskin and shoe making business set up by brothers Cyrus and James Clark, Somerset farmers and Quakers. Workers made the products in their homes in the village, yet the business soon grew to become known as a global shoe brand, with several factories in Somerset. The company had a paternalistic attitude towards its workers and provided them with housing, education and leisure activities including a civic hall, library, open-air swimming pool and theatre.

William Lever, founder of Lever Brothers which has since become Unilever, decided that his soap works was not big enough and started looking for a new site. He would need a large amount of land as he wanted a new village as well as a factory which became known as Port Sunlight. Sunlight was one of the brands of soap that Lever Brothers made. The plans ensured that his workers would be in decent housing with plenty of room and each having a garden or allotment. Lever was very concerned about the welfare of his workers so this new village and lifestyle offered medical facilities, insurance, social clubs, churches and other facilities. He wanted what was called a 'garden suburb' that also had other buildings such as a post office, a bank and a village hall.

The overriding commonality of these examples is their concern for the well-being and conditions of their workers. They all felt that as responsible employers running responsible businesses the welfare of their employees and their families was paramount. The responsible practices displayed by these businesses in these examples may well have stood them in good stead for their subsequent successes. Employees would have been loyal and motivated by their good treatment, and customers and suppliers alike would trust that they were being treated fairly because of this reputation.

Present day businesses can do well from looking back to the past to see how benefits can be made from not only incorporating, but fully embedding good CSR practices into their operations. This enhances relationships with the employees, customers, suppliers and the community, as well as ensuring that good business practices are maintained. In turn this enhances the reputation and performance of the business, which has positive results on the bottom line, and long-term success.

Breadth of Responsibility ●●●

The breadth of issues that can fall under "business responsibilities" can be overwhelming. This book brings together issues that businesses are considering today. This is continually evolving, as an objective for a business to be fully responsible for all its actions is, as IKEA state, "never ending"[1]. Different stakeholders will have different arguments as to what is responsible. Those that manage the business need to balance these carefully.

As far as each of the following stakeholders is concerned, a traditional view of responsibilities of a business would be:

Stakeholder	Responsibility to the stakeholder
Shareholder	Good return on investment
Employee	Fair pay and working conditions; job security
Customers	Value for money
Suppliers	Regular, guaranteed orders and prompt payment
Local community	Employment opportunities and limited impact from operations
Government	Source of tax

Each of these stakeholders would argue that their needs are the most important and in fact the only genuine responsibility of the business. For example, shareholders may argue that the company has a responsibility to ensure that their dividends are maximised, so the allocation of any monies to other purposes such as charitable donations or environmental research is taking potential dividends from them, the owners. On the other hand, trade unions, working on behalf of the employees, may argue that profits made should be put back into the business to maintain job security and any dividend paid to shareholders is a leakage of cash flow that would be better spent on wages. A business has to balance any conflicts in responsibility to ensure that the business works in the interest of all stakeholders over the long-term.

The traditional view of responsibilities is fast being seen as limited in its perspective as stakeholders are expecting more of organisations. In addition to the expectations

1 IKEA. (2009). The Never Ending Job. Retrieved November 2009, from IKEA: http://www.ikea.com/ms/en_CN/about_ikea/our_responsibility/the_never_ending_list/about.html

The Never Ending Job is the name IKEA have given to their work towards becoming more sustainable.

in the above table, shareholders are expecting companies to embrace environmental and social issues to ensure the value of the company is maintained or improved; employees are expecting to see some extension of their personal values within the workplace; the local community is expecting organisations to have positive impacts in the community, rather than just limiting their negative impacts; and organisations are expected to consider the wider impacts of their operations, including the welfare of the employees of the suppliers; and the disposal of any final product.

The Boundaries of Responsibility ●●●

Where responsibility ends is ever debatable, even when a venture is tackled in a "responsible manner" as claimed by the BBC[2] when pupils in Waterloo Road, a popular series set in a school, drank ethanol in a science lesson because it was like alcohol. The day after the programme was aired six teenage pupils in the West Midlands were hospitalised after copying the pupils on the programme. This is not just a debate about the role of television in influencing children, but the BBC, as a business selling programmes worldwide, reconsidering how they present issues depending on the level of responsibility they feel they should take.

Boundaries of responsibility do not even stop at geographical boundaries.

> A major pushchair manufacturer has been publicly questioned about the different levels of consumer care it offers in different countries, for the same product[3]. At the end of 2009, owners of one million pushchairs in the US were told to stop using them after twelve children had their fingers amputated by a hinge. Those with pushchairs in the US were sent a safety kit, but UK owners of identical models simply received extra guidance on using the pushchair. The pushchair's manufacturers argued the case that, "there are a lower number of similar reported incidents among the considerably higher number of pushchairs sold in Europe annually relative to the US market." However, it later became apparent that children in the UK were also injured but parents had not reported it. This incident raises questions about the ethics of using different standards across business operations and between countries.

All businesses above a certain size must comply with a range of employment and consumer protection legislation. In 2008 the Crown Prosecution Service brought the country's first corporate manslaughter case against a Cotswold based company over the death of a young geologist during his work. A director of the company was charged with gross negligence, manslaughter, and with an offence contrary to the Health and Safety at Work Act 1974. The company face unlimited fines and the director himself faces the possibility of the maximum sentence of life imprisonment. The reviewing lawyer from the CPS Special Crime Division explained that, "under the Corporate Manslaughter and Corporate Homicide Act 2007 an organisation is guilty

2 BBC News. (2009, November 19). Pupils ill after drinking ethanol. Retrieved November 22, 2009, from BBC News online: http://news.bbc.co.uk/1/hi/england/beds/bucks/herts/8368346.stm

3 BBC News. (2009, November 12). Climbdown over pushchair safety. Retrieved November 2009, from BBC News: http://news.bbc.co.uk/1/hi/business/8357611.stm

of corporate manslaughter if the way in which its activities are managed or organised causes a death and amounts to a gross breach of a duty of care to the person who died. A substantial part of the breach must have been in the way activities were organised by senior management. I have concluded that there is sufficient evidence for a realistic prospect of conviction for this offence."[4] The director appeared before local Magistrates in June 2009. No pleas were entered, and at the time of writing, the case has been committed to Bristol Crown Court.

This legislation covers all individuals affected detrimentally by the actions of any business organisation, and puts the burden of responsibility on company directors in particular. All businesses are required to take out Employer and Public Liability insurance cover but this only deals with compensation to the victims. For the first time, managers and owners can now be imprisoned for negligent actions that lead to the death of an individual.

A business trying to decide where its boundaries of responsibility can be found might consider the concept found in law relating to negligence which utilises the notion of "reasonable foreseeability," and carry out the equivalent of risk assessments on all its current operations and future plans.

Responsible businesses do not rely on legislation to set the boundaries of what is and isn't acceptable. Companies such as Tesco and BT are trying to take a leadership role in pushing the boundaries of their sectors in terms of sustainable operations, and have been recognised for this in the Sunday Times Best Green Companies[5] league table. This is ahead of any pressure from government or industry and has the immediate benefit of keeping a competitive edge as well as enhancing reputation. By keeping at the forefront of industry developments, these leaders will ensure that they are driving the change, and therefore will be likely to influence future legislation, and industry directives.

Sustainable Business ●●●

"Sustainable Business" can be interpreted in two ways. A literal interpretation would be to ensure that a business exists in the long-term, using the term "sustain" to mean nurture, manage and maintain. A key accounting concept is "Going Concern", which identifies that many of the accounting procedures and systems are based on the notion that the business will be here next year and the year after. Businesses would not borrow long term or depreciate assets over a period of time if they did not make this basic assumption. Sustaining a business is necessary to fulfil responsibilities to stakeholders.

4 CPS. (2009, April 23). CPS advises first corporate manslaughter charge under new act. Retrieved November 30, 2009, from CPS: http://www.cps.gov.uk/news/press_releases/124_09/

5 Sunday Times. (2009, May). Sunday Times 60 Best Green Companies. Retrieved November 2009, from Sunday Times.

> *Sustainability is quite simply a vital issue for business and the concept, quite simply, is about developing a corporate strategy that responds to stakeholders' expectations while ensuring long term performance and profitability.*

IFAC, 2006[6]

A more current interpretation of a "sustainable business" is one that is looking to reduce its environmental impacts. It is recognition that if the business is to be here next year then it has to maintain the environment in which it operates as well as the business itself. There is a pressing realisation that many of the resources used by businesses are finite and that endless consumption will not be possible. Where a business needs raw materials, they will need to be adaptable to cope with future shortages through planned replenishment, finding alternative sources of raw materials, or adapting their business model to recover and reuse components. In addition, resources are not only threatened by over consumption, but also burning fossil fuels to power production is itself having a detrimental effect on the environment, with consequences such as flooding, drought and forest fires, further reducing the availability of these scarce resources.

The accounting sector is making the links between these two interpretations of a "sustainable business". In their report Going Concern? A Sustainability Agenda for Action, for example ACCA outline their public position on, and commitment to, the sustainable development and CSR agenda.

Driving Responsible and Sustainable Business Management

As more organisations adopt responsible business practices, so they demand the same of their business peers, suppliers, and customers; and so those organisations that lag behind will be asked why they too are not adopting best practice.

Expectations of various stakeholders may bring CSR into the senior management's line of vision, but it will be legislation that will firmly hold it there. The CRC Energy Efficiency Scheme[7] is one such piece of legislation. It is a mandatory scheme, central to the UK strategy for improving energy efficiency and reducing carbon dioxide (CO2) emissions, as set out in the Climate Change Act 2008. The scheme came into effect in April 2010 and requires a company director for each of around 5,000 of the highest energy consuming organisations in the UK to take responsibility for submitting carbon emission data to the Environment Agency each year. Not only does the scheme require senior level sign-off, it also brings in an element of reputational risk, with a public league table, and a financial aspect as carbon emission allowances need to be

6 IFAC (2006) Professional Accountants in Business – At the Heart of Sustainability? New York. Information paper August 2006.

7 CRC Energy Efficiency Scheme, originally named the Carbon Reduction Commitment.

purchased. Under the CRC, organisations will be required to buy CO2 "allowances" for each tonne of CO2 they emit. The revenue raised from selling allowances will be "recycled" back to participants according to the progress they make in reducing emissions.

As well as gaining the senior level attention, the responsibility within organisations for compliance with the CRC Energy Efficiency Scheme will most likely fall to the Energy Manager and Financial Manager.

Forget beans, accountants are now required to count carbon too.

> *Companies will suffer financial consequences if they fail to address CSR, not least from increasingly demanding institutional investors.*

CIMA, June 2008[8]

8 CIMA. (2008, June). Excellence in Leadership: Responsible Leadership. Retrieved from http://www.excellence-leadership.com/book-plan-08-06.html

CHAPTER 2

Sphere of Influence

- What is a Sphere of Influence
- The Sphere of Influence and Responsible Business
- Using the Sphere of Influence

What is a Sphere of Influence

Individuals may be daunted by the prospect of the issues to be looked at in this book and may well feel that they have no real power to make significant changes to any of the threats to society and the planet. However, using the simple notion of the ability to influence events and people in one's own life by making changes and discussing with colleagues, friends and family, the influence or impact an individual can have grows exponentially.

Case Study

A senior lecturer in a further education college who was set the task of rewriting a Foundation Degree with the title "Responsible Business" attended a four-day course on "Business Response to Climate Change", and as a result realised that his sphere of influence in terms of responsible business practice was as follows:

- current students (both full-time and part-time)
- college management
- colleagues (within college, and other institutions)
- curriculum
- friends and family
- future students when new programme is launched
- employers (of students; and some who are students)
- awarding bodies and external moderators.

Within the same academic year he worked with 150 students from various levels on a range of projects involving a more sustainable approach to business operations in hair salons, sports centres and offices. In all cases the students really enjoyed the work and at the same time the organisations involved benefited through significant cost savings and also emitted less carbon.

One part-time student, a hotel manager, through a sustainability assignment, cut the cost of the hotel's waste management system by 66%. In the process of her research, she discovered that all 50 staff were keen to be involved in such a project and this message was passed on to the regional manager who in turn planned to include this in staff development across the region and ultimately throughout the UK chain. The influence the lecturer has had on this one student has affected a national chain of hotels.

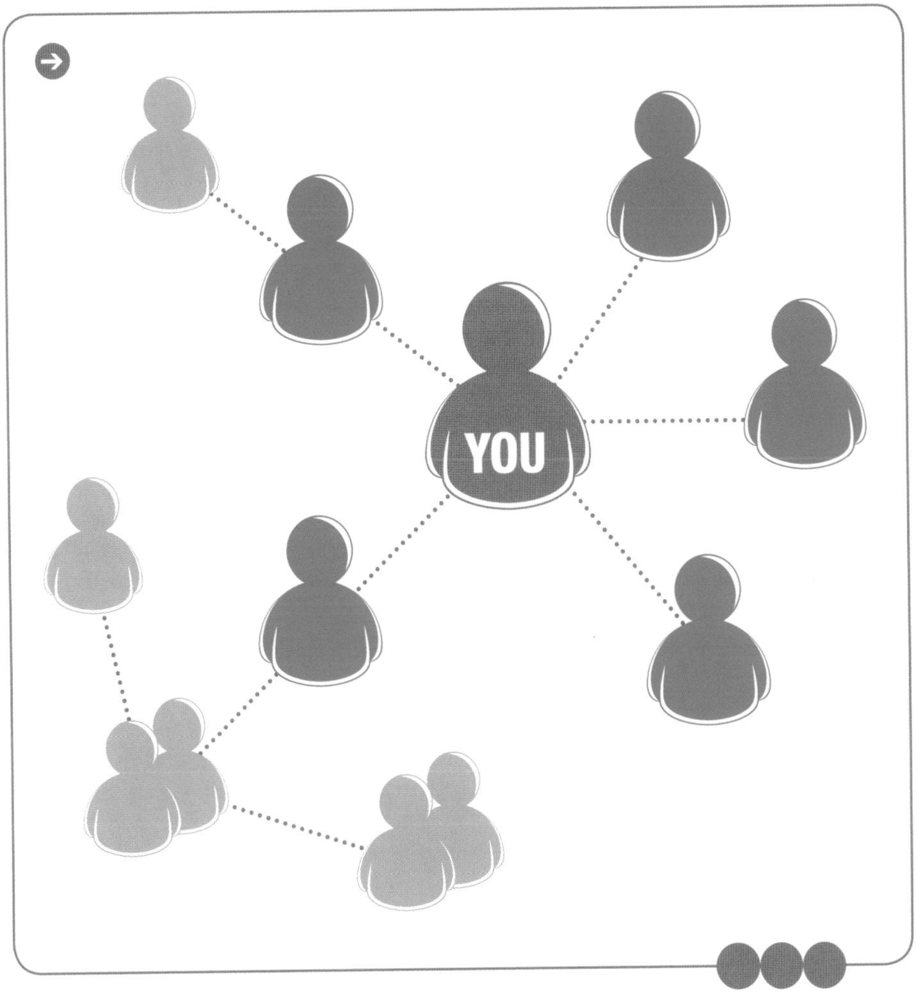

The lecturer may not have fully realised how powerful his sphere of influence was. As well as immediate influence and change brought about by his curriculum decisions, an annual survey of public trust in professionals found that teachers were second only to doctors in the level of trust placed on them by the public. In response to the question "would you generally trust them to tell the truth or not" 88% of those asked said that they would trust a teacher to tell them the truth. In the case of doctors it was 92% but unfortunately for business leaders it was only 25% and for journalists 22%. Government ministers and politicians fared the worst in achieving only 16% and 13% respectively. This may be related to a backlash over the controversy of MPs' expenses at the time of the survey[1].

This lack of trust will obviously make it harder for business leaders to persuade the

1 Ipsos Mori. (2009, June 19). Only one in five say they trust journalist to tell the truth. Retrieved November 11, 2009, from ipsos-mori.com: http://www.ipsos-mori.com/newsevents/ca/ca.aspx?oItemId=32

public that they are acting responsibly, particularly if they are involved in an initiative within a government ministry!

The Sphere of Influence and Responsible Business

The concept can be applied to any business (see Figure 1). The initial sphere of influence is the workplace, and those within it, and so in the first instance, it is the responsible management of that workplace that will have the most immediate impact. The treatment and engagement of the employees is of paramount importance to running a successful and sustainable business.

At the same time, the management and employees will also be interacting with customers, suppliers, shareholders, trade unions and government agencies. This is the next sphere of influence, as can be seen in the diagram, the business ripple. It has already been stated that a truly responsible business will not be waiting for the government to take the lead and therefore only be prepared to react to legislation as and when it happens. There is a danger that many organisations have limited horizons when it comes to planning for the future. Organisations acting responsibly in this sphere take the lead in initiatives relating to ethical products or services, sustainable supply chain management, ethical investment and borrowing, employee and trade union engagement, and the ability to influence future legislation.

Businesses don't operate in isolation from the community, and so the ripple continues into the community with the effect on employment opportunities, sponsorship and charitable donations, other businesses thriving in the area, infrastructure and travel provision, involvement with education, and businesses encouraging their staff to work as volunteers within community projects.

All three inner circles affect the environment as energy is used to operate the business, materials are used, and waste is produced.

Figure 1

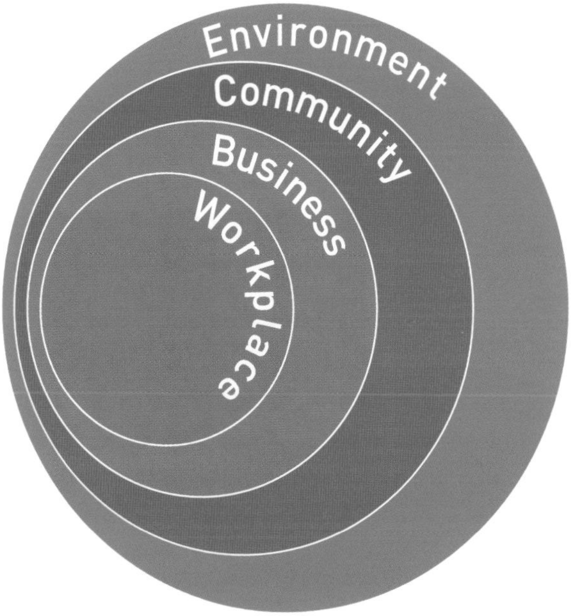

Looking at the model from the outside it shows how the inner layers are restricted in operation by the outer layers. The community is limited by the state of the environment as without materials, energy and places to dispose of waste, the community is limited in its function. In turn, the business relies on a functioning community to purchase products and services, and provide the source of the workforce to the business. The workplace relies on business operations in order for jobs to be created and maintained. Without the outer sphere each time, the inner cannot function. This emphasises the importance of taking responsibility for these four areas for a prosperous business.

Throughout the book, this model will be referred to, and particularly with regard to how a business can have a responsible influence in the four spheres of workplace, business, community and environment.

Using the Sphere of Influence ●●●

BT's Sphere of Influence can be mapped into this model. Taking figures from the BT Annual Report and Accounts 2009, Figure 2 shows the different areas in which the company has a direct influence.

Figure 2

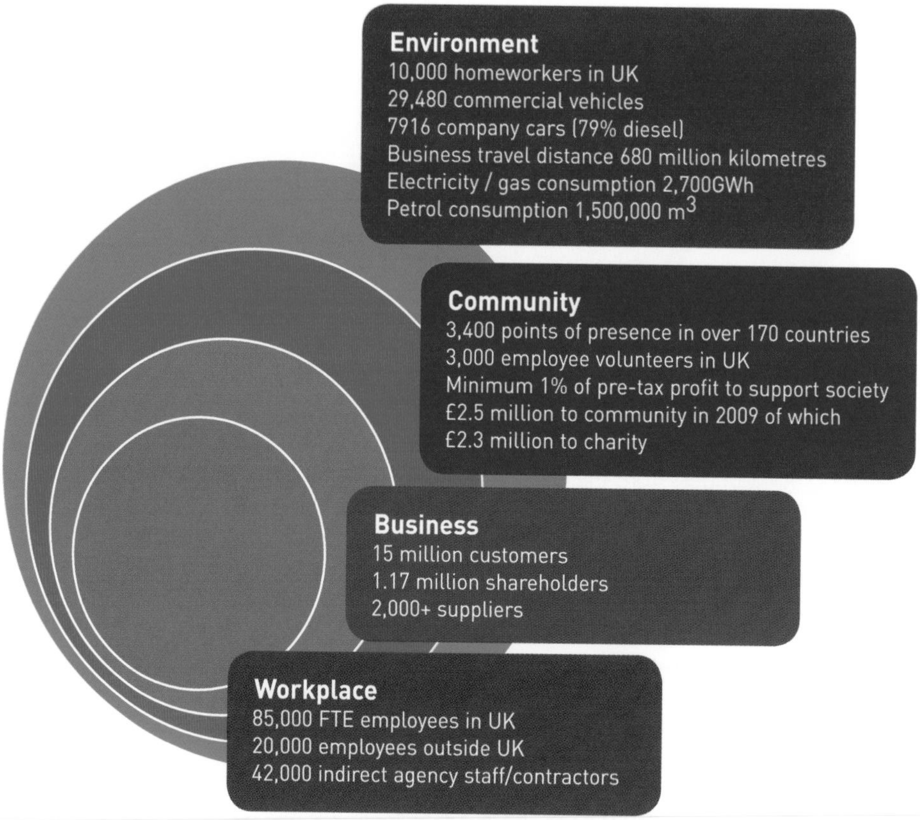

Environment
10,000 homeworkers in UK
29,480 commercial vehicles
7916 company cars (79% diesel)
Business travel distance 680 million kilometres
Electricity / gas consumption 2,700GWh
Petrol consumption 1,500,000 m3
Community
3,400 points of presence in over 170 countries
3,000 employee volunteers in UK
Minimum 1% of pre-tax profit to support society
£2.5 million to community in 2009 of which
£2.3 million to charity
Business
15 million customers
1.17 million shareholders
2,000+ suppliers
Workplace
85,000 FTE employees in UK
20,000 employees outside UK
42,000 indirect agency staff/contractors

The ripple effect of influence from these different contact points should also be appreciated. BT has put a lot of effort into reducing their carbon footprint. The 85,000 employees, many of whom will have been encouraged to join Carbon Clubs within the organisation, will then be discussing these initiatives with their own family and friends. The 3,000 local community volunteers will be having environment-related conversations as they go about their community work.

BT only trade with "ethical" suppliers, which will then influence the business practices of those organisations, and result in further conversations amongst their staff, family and friends. As in many other PLCs, the majority of shares owned in BT are held by institutional investors. 38% of shareholders own fewer than 400 shares, which amounts to only 1.14% of total shares. In comparison, a tiny 0.2% of shareholders own over 5 million shares. These shareholders own 74.25% of issued shares[2]. The most substantial shareholders are Invesco Limited, Legal & General Group PLC and Barclays PLC representing holdings of 5.08%, 4.65% and 4.66% of BT's voting rights respectively[3].

BT is a large consumer of energy and natural resources, and the amount of travel taken to carry out business functions has a major impact on carbon emissions. Even so, the figures in the environment sphere of the diagram are reductions from previous years and it is BT's intention to continue to reduce their environmental impacts year on year through self imposed targets.

Decisions that BT are making in the four areas of influence are immensely important not only to the UK but also the rest of the world because they operate on a global scale as can be seen by the number of countries in their community.

In the online BT Sustainability Report 2009, BT state that they are "running a responsible business" with the added message, "our goal is to transform our business in ways that benefit BT, our customers, society and the environment. In doing so, we are committed to maintaining responsible business practices and further integrating corporate responsibility into our business processes."[4]

Although not all organisations have the potential sphere of influence of BT, the above model is relevant to every business. The nature and sector of each organisation will determine the constituent parts of the workplace, business, community and environment and therefore the sphere of influence of that business.

2 BT Sustainability Report. (2009, December 4). BT Sustainability Report. Retrieved December 4, 2009, from BT: http://www.btplc.com/Societyandenvironment/Ourapproach/Sustainabilityreport/section/index.aspx?sectionid=2fd63b19-1de3-400c-8a04-911831011361 Pp 150.

3 BT Sustainability Report. (2009, December 4). BT Sustainability Report. Retrieved December 4, 2009, from BT: http://www.btplc.com/Societyandenvironment/Ourapproach/Sustainabilityreport/section/index.aspx?sectionid=2fd63b19-1de3-400c-8a04-911831011361 Pp 74.

4 BT. (2009). Running a responsible business. Retrieved November 2009, from BT Sustainability Report: http://www.btplc.com/Societyandenvironment/Ourapproach/Sustainabilityreport/section/index.aspx?name=running%20a%20responsible%20business

SECTION 2

Central Themes

- Corporate Social Responsibility
- Sustainable Development
- Globalisation
- New Economics
- Systemic Thinking
- Leadership in a Changing World

CHAPTER 3

Corporate Social Responsibility

- What is it?
- Why do Businesses Adopt it?
- What are Businesses Doing about CSR?

Figure 1

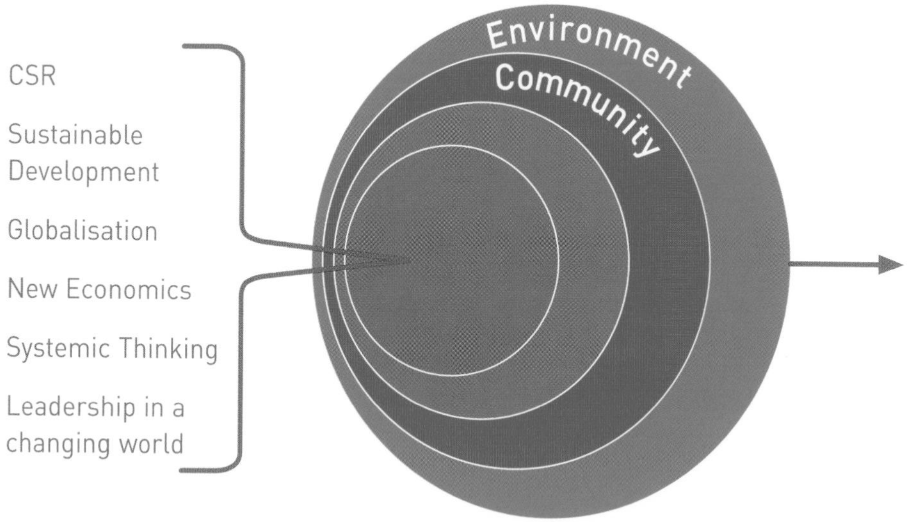

Corporate Social Responsibility

Over the last ten years, Corporate Social Responsibility (or CSR) has become a mainstream boardroom discussion topic, with two-thirds of the FTSE 500 companies in 2008 producing CSR reports and many having senior management with CSR responsibilities.

As yet there is no international definition of CSR. The World Business Council for Sustainable Development has defined it as "the commitment of business to contribute to sustainable economic development, working with employees, their families, the local community and society at large to improve their quality of life"[1] but it can generally be regarded as a business taking responsibility for its impact on society and the environment.

Typically the areas of impact are grouped under four headings, as outlined in Figure 2.

1 World Business Council for Sustainable Development (2000) Corporate Social Responsibility: making business sense, available from www.wbcsd.org

Figure 2 – outline of a typical CSR programme

Workplace:	Marketplace:
• diversity & inclusion • health & well-being • flexible working • employee voice • work-life balance • training	• customer relationships • supplier relationships • product & service impact • business integrity
Environment: • climate change • biodiversity • waste • travel • air, soil & water pollution	**Community:** • economic renewal • education • employability

Workplace

One of business's biggest positive impacts on society will be the jobs they provide, and the wealth put into the community through the payment of wages. However, this positive effect could be seriously reduced if discrimination of any sort is allowed to take place. The same would be true if the nature of the work is meaningless and soul destroying and takes no account of the work-life balance and the employee's rights to a private life. Businesses should consider that their employees are their greatest asset and as with other assets of the business the more invested in them the better the return. Employee's need to be developed, challenged and respected if they are to have the desire and motivation to achieve the goals the business has set for itself. Employee differences should be welcomed and appreciated.

Marketplace (or business)

One key factor is how a business shows responsibility in the way that it makes its money. How much value does its goods or services create and what are the possible costs they impose on society? Does the business provide its goods or services with integrity and honesty? Is the supplier relationship based on trust and ethical standards? Does the business insist that its suppliers share the same values ensuring acceptable practice on their part? As well as ethical buying and selling, the business should also be establishing a level of expectation that its customers, suppliers and shareholders can trust. Retaining that trust will depend on by how well the business delivers on its promises whilst also looking after the interests of others.

Environment

The threat of climate change has now been accepted by the vast majority of businesses and they see it as having a possible detrimental effect on their future success. Responsible businesses have realised that future generations will be affected by their actions today. Environmental good practice also brings about business efficiencies. It should be about making the best and most sustainable use of raw materials and feeding the benefits of these actions straight through to the bottom line.

The big question will be whether businesses can take their customers with them in their actions to reduce their environmental impact. The challenge will be to design successful businesses that will add value to society without the overconsumption of the natural resources of the world at great cost to the environment. A further related challenge will be to ensure that the business meets or even beats the government targets for huge cuts in carbon emissions over the next few years.

Community

A successful business needs to operate in a healthy, thriving community where the employees are happy to live and with an education system they want their children to be involved with. A business must also realise that it should be a good neighbour to the communities it operates within with the ability to expand or change without affecting the goodwill that it has generated by being an active supporter of community projects. The business should be a welcome guest not an unwelcome intruder.

The business should also be fully aware of the likely impact of its operations and processes on the local community ensuring that it minimises any effect its presence in the community might have. Employees will want to work-for-an-organisation that cares about its community and involving them in community projects and educational partnerships will help the business with long-term recruitment by creating a workforce locally which other people want to join.

This is the sphere of influence of a business, as outlined in Chapter 2, which brings the four areas together, recognising their *interconnectedness*.

Why do Businesses Adopt CSR

Those that adopt CSR do so for one of two reasons: to mitigate risk or to seize an opportunity. This can often reflect how CSR is managed within the business.

A number of companies have used CSR as a way of managing risk from potential threats such as the penalties from not operating within environmental legislation. Compliance would remove the risk of penalty but ultimately could be perceived as only achieving the minimum possible standard. This reactive strategy nullifies the organisation's own potential sphere of influence. Figure 3 represents a business where management react to external pressures.

Figure 3: Diagram by Mallen Baker

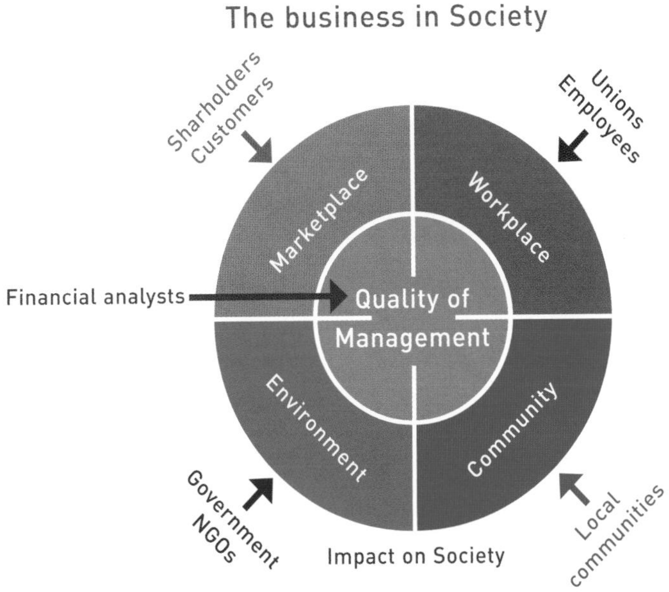

All the arrows are pointing inwards and would therefore appear to indicate that the quality of management is either affected by internal forces in terms of employees bringing pressure from "the bottom up" possibly because of dissatisfaction, or by external forces such as customers, communities and the government also bringing pressure to bear. The likely result of this approach would be a very unhappy management team who would not feel in control of the business and its future strategy operating as they do in a relatively hostile environment. It also goes against the notion of a responsible business making full use of its own sphere of influence to lead on change rather than react to change.

BT[2] as an organisation has decided that its CSR policy should provide opportunities and as a result has identified a series of mindsets that could be adopted from the compliant to the innovative. In the BT CSR model, they would label Figure 3 "mindset

2 BT.com. (2009, December 11). Sustainability Report 2009. Retrieved December 11, 2009, from btplc.com: http://www.btplc.com/Societyandenvironment/Ourapproach/Sustainabilityreport/index.aspx

1.0", with values drivers being simply "risk management" and "licence to operate" which provides protection against threats (see Figure 4). BT's model however moves through to "mindset 3.0", where the company's strategy is to innovate, i.e. utilise their sphere of influence to maximum effect.

Figure 4: BT

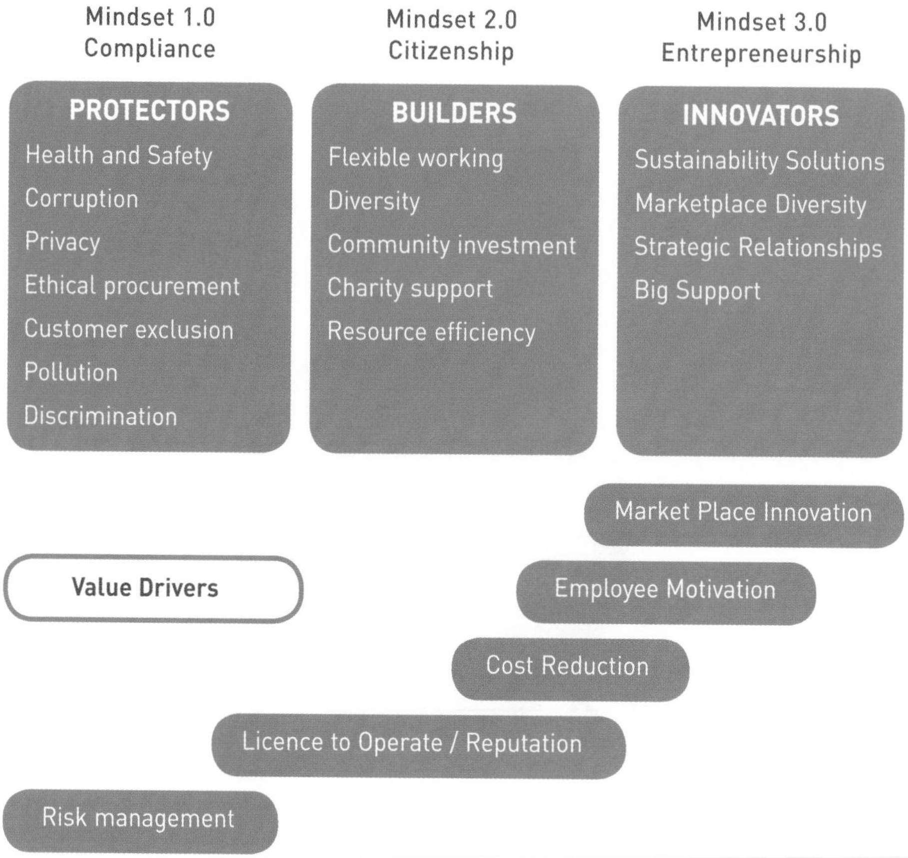

Using their influence in a very positive and ground breaking way BT are not satisfied to be considered simply as a reputable company based on good citizenship where they offer a range of best practice employment conditions and are heavily involved with charities, community projects and initiatives to maximise resource efficiency. Instead they have opted to be innovators under the mindset of entrepreneurship with the driving forces being employee motivation and market place innovation to reach for a level which will not only enhance their reputation and improve their marketing edge over their competitors but will also influence future legislation and other industry sectors to follow their example.

There are a number of benefits to businesses of adopting a CSR strategy.

- Employee recruitment and retention – with CSR reports being available on-line, potential employees can see more easily if this is the type of place where they wish to work. There is growing evidence that people wish to work for organisations that share their values, and CSR is an opportunity for businesses to display what values they have in addition to their prime product or service provision.

69% of BT employees asked stated that 'knowing about BT's social responsibility reputation makes me more proud to work for BT'.

BT.com, 2009

Often CSR programmes invite employees to get involved with fundraising or community volunteering. These activities can bring feelings of fulfilment that otherwise may be missing from their day-to-day work. This can make employees feel better motivated, more productive, and likely to stay longer with the organisation. This will save on recruitment and retraining costs.

- Building company reputation – a company may wish to either build its reputation on being "ethical" (such as the Body Shop), or wish to gain some ground in a competitive area. Increasingly contract tenders are asking for details of environmental best practice and any CSR initiatives, in addition to questions on quality and price. It makes business sense to look as favourable in a tender process as possible. Customers want to buy from businesses they respect and CSR strategies can be particularly effective when targeting ethical companies, public sector, and not-for-profit organisations.
- Press coverage and PR – innovative companies are likely to receive positive media coverage through working with the local community.
- New products & services – by understanding the environmental and social impacts of the business, new opportunities can be identified for future development.
- Marketing edge – in a competitive market, CSR can give a competitive edge over competition. Values-led customers will favour businesses that share their values.

BT plc believes that the reputation it has gained as a result of its Corporate Responsibility activities is maintaining and building its market share in a competitive market. It estimates that corporate (social) responsibility accounts for over 25% of image and reputation impact on customer satisfaction.

The Business Case for Corporate Responsibility (Arthur D Little: Business in the Community, 2003)

What are Businesses Doing about CSR? ●●●

Reporting on CSR

Companies incorporating CSR into their business typically produce an annual report outlining what they have achieved. This can be externally verified, and there is a growing trend to publish this with, or include it in, the annual financial accounts. In 2008, 750 reports out of 3,000 that were published globally included an external validation.

There are a number of reporting guidelines, although as yet there is no set standard that must be used. Most commonly found guidelines include:

AA1000

The AA1000 Series[3] 3 provides a multi-stakeholder approach to reporting performance against a framework that can be used by individual businesses and organisations. The Series is based on three principles.

1. **Materiality** - requires knowing all the areas of performance that stakeholders need to judge the organisation's sustainability performance against.
2. **Completeness** - requires understanding stakeholder concerns, and providing information accurate enough to assess the organisation's performance in all these areas.
3. **Responsiveness** - requires coherently responding to stakeholders' concerns and interests.

The Series can be used to achieve the Standard and undergo assurance or as a guide to inform and develop reporting processes and good practice.

It was the first international standard designed to ensure the credibility and quality of a company's reporting on its social, economic and environmental performance and it offers improved credibility and confidence in the published information.

Global Reporting Initiative

The Global Reporting Initiative (GRI)[4] was initially convened by the Coalition for Environmentally Responsible Economies (CERES) having a vision that all organisations will report on economic, environmental, and social performance as a matter of routine in a way that is comparable with other forms of financial reporting.

The GRI has developed a set of core performance indicators intended to be applicable to all business enterprises, but with variations for specific types of

3 AccountAbility. (2009, December 4). AA1000 What is it? Retrieved December 4, 2009, from AccountAbility: http://www.accountability21.net./aa1000/

4 The Global Reporting Iniative (GRI). (2009, December 4). Retrieved December 4, 2009, from Mallenbaker.net: http://www.mallenbaker.net/csr/gri.php

enterprises. However, there should be a uniform format for reporting information integral to a company's sustainability performance.

Revisions to the GRI are obtained through a set of committees and sub-committees made up of a variety of stakeholder groups and it is this multi-stakeholder approach which gives credibility and trust to this global framework.

The GRI Sustainability Reporting Guidelines recommend specific information be provided and that the report should be structured around the CEO's statement, key environmental, social and economic indicators, a profile of the reporting organisation, policies and systems, stakeholder relationships, operational performance, product performance and a sustainability overview.

SA8000

Social Accountability 8000[5] (SA8000) has been developed by Social Accountability International (SAI) and is promoted as a voluntary, universal standard for companies interested in auditing and certifying labour practices in their facilities and those of their suppliers and vendors. It is designed for independent third party certification.

SA8000 is based on the principles of international human rights best practice as described in International Labour Organisation conventions, the United Nations Convention on the Rights of the Child and the Universal Declaration of Human Rights. It measures the performance of companies in eight key areas: child labour, forced labour, health and safety, free association and collective bargaining, discrimination, disciplinary practices, working hours and compensation. SA8000 also provides for a social accountability management system to demonstrate ongoing conformance with the standard.

Global Compact

The United Nations Global Compact[6] is a strategic policy initiative for businesses that are committed to aligning their operations and strategies with ten universally accepted principles in the areas of human rights, labour, environment and anti-corruption.

The ten principles are:

Human Rights

1. Businesses should support and respect the protection of internationally proclaimed human rights; and

2. make sure that they are not complicit in human rights abuses.

5 Social Accountability SA8000. (2009, December 4). Retrieved December 4, 2009, from Mallenbaker.net: http://www.mallenbaker.net/csr/CSRfiles/SA8000.html

6 United Nations Global Compact. (2009, December 4). Retrieved December 4, 2009, from UN Global Compact: http://www.unglobalcompact.org/

Labour

3. Businesses should uphold the freedom of association and the effective recognition of the right to collective bargaining
4. the elimination of all forms of forced and compulsory labour
5. the effective abolition of child labour; and
6. the elimination of discrimination in respect of employment and occupation.

Environment

7. Businesses are asked to take a precautionary approach to environmental challenges
8. undertake initiatives to promote greater environmental responsibility; and
9. encourage the development and diffusion of environmentally friendly technologies.

Anti-Corruption

10. Businesses should work against corruption in all its forms including extortion and bribery.

United Nations Intergovernmental Working Group[7]

The International Standards of Accounting and Reporting (ISAR) working group is hosted by the United Nations Conference on Trade and Development (UNCTAD). ISAR was created in 1982 by the United Nations Economic and Social Council (ECOSOC). The mission of ISAR is to facilitate investment, development and economic stability by promoting good practices in corporate transparency and accounting

Useful websites

Business in the Community: www.bitc.org

Business Respect: www.businessrespect.net

Business for Social Responsibility: www.bsr.org

World Business Council for Sustainable Development: www.wbcsd.org

7 Intergovernmental working groups. (2009, December 4). Retrieved December 4, 2009, from Wikipedia: http://en.wikipedia.org/wiki/Intergovernmental_Working_Group_of_Experts_on_International_Standards_of_Accounting_and_Reporting_(ISAR)

CHAPTER 4

Sustainable Development

- Sustainable Development
- Sustainable Development Strategies
- The Triangle of Change
- The Triple Bottom Line

Sustainable Development

Sustainable Development is a widely used and recognised term, accepted by industry and government in the UK and worldwide. The 1992 Earth Summit in Rio brought the phrase "sustainable development" into common usage. The concept brings together people, planet and profit (or society, environment and economy), recognising that any activity in any of these areas will have an impact on the other two. Sustainable Development is about meeting the needs of the present while safeguarding the interests of future generations. In order to achieve development and growth that is environmentally sustainable, we need to find ways to achieve our current economic, social and environmental objectives whilst at the same time considering the longer-term, global implications.

There are a number of attempts to define Sustainable Development, but the most commonly used and accepted is the Bruntland Commission definition (1987):

Sustainable Development is development that meets the needs of the present without compromising the ability of future generations to meet their own needs.

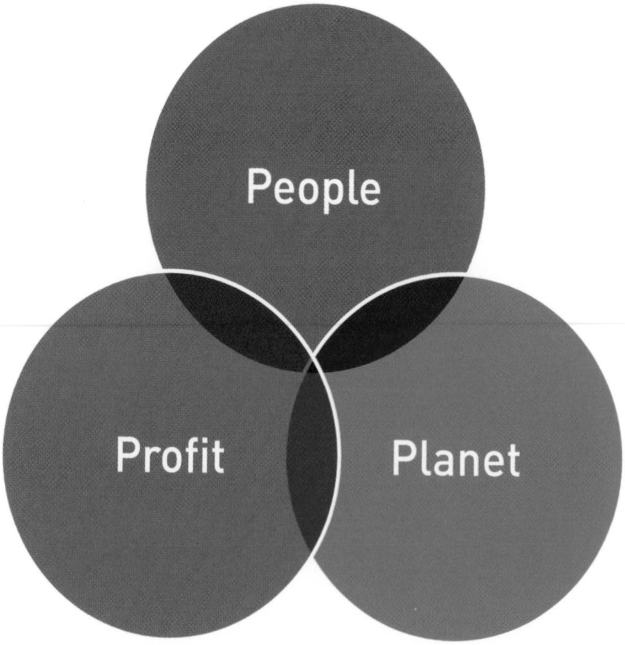

Sustainable Development Strategies ●●●

The UK government's Sustainable Development strategy has four main objectives:

- social progress which reinforces the needs of everyone
- effective protection of the environment
- the prudent use of natural resources, and
- the maintenance of high levels of economic growth and employment.

The Sustainable Development Commission (SDC) is the government's independent adviser on sustainable development, reporting to the Prime Minister and the First Ministers from Scotland, Wales and Northern Ireland. They put sustainable development at the heart of government policy through advice, advocacy and appraisal.

In February 2009, the Sustainable Development Commission (SDC) became an executive non-departmental body (Executive NDPB).

The SDC and UK government have agreed a common approach to assessing whether or not a policy delivery is sustainable - these are the 'Five principles of sustainable development'.

The principles were outlined in the UK Framework for Sustainable Development "One Future – different paths" agreed by the UK government and reflected in their strategies.

Living within environmental limits

Respecting the limits of the planet's environment, resources and biodiversity – to improve our environment and ensure that the natural resources needed for life are unimpaired and remain so for future generations.

Ensuring a strong, healthy and just society

Meeting the diverse needs of all people in existing and future communities, promoting personal well-being, social cohesion and inclusion, and creating equal opportunity.

Achieving a sustainable economy

Building a strong, stable and sustainable economy which provides prosperity and opportunities for all, and in which environmental and social costs fall on those who impose them (polluter pays), and efficient resource use is incentivised.

Using sound science responsibly

Ensuring policy is developed and implemented on the basis of strong scientific uncertainty (through the precautionary principle) as well as public attitudes and values.

Promoting good governance

Actively promoting effective, participative systems of governance in all levels of society - engaging people's creativity energy and diversity.

These principles form the basis of national sustainable development strategies and action plans. The UK government adopted the principles in "Securing the future" which was developed in parallel to the shared framework document in March 2005[1].

Consumption and Business

The Sustainable Development Commission (SDC) has stated that if everyone in the world consumed at the average rate we do in the UK, we would require the equivalent of three planets. They go on to say that globally we are already 'living beyond our means' by around 20% and this is despite the fact that a significant proportion of the world receives significantly less than their fair share.

To tackle this inequity and also the level of resource depletion, Sustainable Consumption and Production (SCP) was made a key commitment at the World Summit on Sustainable Development in Johannesburg in 2002. Accelerating the shift towards SCP is also a priority for EU and UK governments.

The challenge of SCP is to reduce the negative impact on society and the environment brought about by consumers and the producers of products and services. It is now up to consumers, businesses and governments to work together to bring about a shift towards sustainable consumption and production.

Business in the Triangle of Change

The SDC identified in their report "I will if you will" (May 2006) that a "critical mass" of people and businesses want to take action to reduce the impact on the environment through their consumption and production. However both consumer and business alike felt that government needed to be involved or they would have no confidence that matters might improve.

The diagram below, known as the "Triangle of Change," illustrates the fact that business, government and people share the responsibility in working towards a more sustainable future.

The SDC have created a Sustainable Consumption and Business team which ensures that advice given to the government is as informed as it can be by their connection with business. Where appropriate the team will challenge individual businesses to become involved in finding sustainable solutions alongside the government.

1 One Future - different paths. (2005, March). Our Principles. Retrieved December 11, 2009, from Sustainable Development Commission: http://www.sd-commission.org.uk/pages/our-principles.html

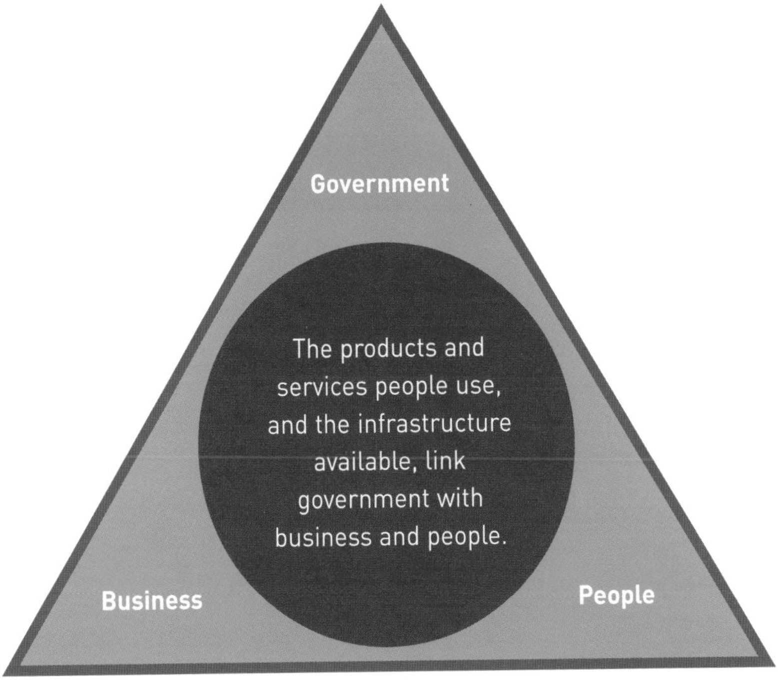

Sustainable Consumption

The UK government has been advised by the SDC that it would make sense to focus on those areas of consumption that have the biggest impact on people and the environment, and those are buildings, food and transport and as a result the SDC has put forward recommendations as follows:

- **The way people run their homes**[2]

  The way buildings are designed, constructed and managed will determine the UK's ability to achieve its sustainable development goals.

> Around 80% of the population live in urban areas. While new buildings add at most 1% a year to the existing stock, the other 99% of buildings are already built and produce 27% of all carbon emissions. At least 80% of the current housing stock will still be standing in 2050. Therefore tackling its energy efficiency is vital to our future.

Anne Power, SDC Commissioner

2 Built Environment. (2009, December 11). Built Environment. Retrieved December 11, 2009, from Sustainable Development Commission: http://www.sd-commission.org.uk/pages/built-environment.html

- **The food that people eat**

> *Government cannot resolve the problems of obesity, waste or climate change alone. Given the enormous influence wielded by supermarkets, working with them effectively is essential.*
>
> **Tim Lang, SDC Commissioner**

Specifically the SDC identify six key priority areas[3] for government and supermarket action on:

- climate change
- waste
- water
- ecosystems
- nutrition and obesity
- fair supply chains.

- **The methods of transport being used**

  Road transport now accounts for 22% of UK CO2 emissions, with road traffic rising by around 2% per year. Globally aviation is growing at around 5% per year.

  Transport has further environmental and social impacts. Air quality pollutants are associated with respiratory problems and there are in the region of 30,000 deaths or serious injuries from road accidents every year. Transport is the major source of noise in the UK. Congestion is estimated to cost the UK economy £20 billion per year[4].

- **The redefinition of prosperity**

  SDC's "Redefining Prosperity" project has looked into the connections and conflicts between sustainability, growth, and well-being[5].

The business challenge is to create higher outputs, with lower inputs (natural resources) and less waste. Sustainable development is an objective, to instil it into business an organisation needs to set strategies and translate this concept into a practical reality.

3 Green, Healthy and Fair report. (2008, February). Green, Healthy and Fair. Retrieved December 11, 2009, from Sustainable Development Commission: http://www.sd-commission.org.uk/publications.php?id=692

4 2009, Sustainable Development Commission. (2009, December 11). Transport. Retrieved December 11, from Sustainable Development Commission: http://www.sd-commission.org.uk/pages/transport.html

5 Prosperity without Growth. (2009, April). Prosperity without Growth. Retrieved December 11, 2009, from Sustainable Development Commission: http://www.sd-commission.org.uk/pages/redefining-prosperity.html

A business working on becoming more sustainable may do so by embracing CSR. Often this starts with getting a greater understanding of the environmental impacts of the business. This is done by undertaking an environmental review, or by assessing the organisation's carbon footprint.

As well as the clear ethical reasons for reducing the negative impacts of products and services there is also the added benefit that it makes good business sense to review a product's sustainability. Responsible and, as a result, successful businesses will be those that look to mitigate the risks of future resource and policy constraints on their supply chain by grabbing any opportunity that sustainability presents. By doing so these businesses are likely to save money, improve their brand and their reputation, manage their resource risk and grow and access new markets.

Business will be a crucial element in the achievement of sustainable development for the UK as a whole and the SDC is very keen to work with the business community as they see it as a two-way process. Business will have the opportunity to feed back information to government, and sustainable development advice and support can be given to the business world via the SDC. This advice will centre on the products or services of a business, its resource use, its travel arrangements and how it can work more closely with the community.

Case Study[6]

1. Solar Tower – Sustainable materials

When a tower block building in Manchester, home to a Financial Services business, started to lose mosaic tiles an urgent refurbishment was needed and the bold decision was made to clad three sides of the 400 ft tower with 7,000 solar panels which involved a further commitment to investing in renewable energy. The company received almost 20% of the overall cost in grants from government agencies. The solar panels produce enough electricity each year to power 1,000 computers (a saving of approximately £50,000) while at the same time reducing carbon emissions by 77 tonnes.

2. Roofing – Sustainable factory waste

A roofing materials company has instigated a program to reduce waste at source. Concrete waste is crushed and re-used as a partial replacement for the aggregate needed by the company and this not only reduces disposal to land-fill but also achieves savings of 15,000 tonnes of aggregate per year. This project is in addition to an earlier scheme to treat pigmented waste water which saved on tanker disposal of waste and allowed the water to be re-used. However, some filtered waste still had to go to land-fill. These solutions have seen the costs involved being reduced by 50%, saving £25,000 per year and diverting 288 tonnes of hazardous waste away from land-fill.

3. Publishing company – Business Travel

An international publishing PLC invested in new video-conferencing technology which enabled their Management Committee, the top level senior executive team, to hold eight of their ten annual meetings using the new facility. Previously all ten meetings were held face to face involving travel from New York to London or vice versa. The main benefits were greater operational efficiencies in terms of flexible decision making and the saving of much dead time travelling. They had also cut the costs involved by 80%. In terms of environmental impact the greatly reduced travelling has eliminated the emission of over 800 tonnes of CO_2. The impact on its workforce is that this video-conferencing technology allows the employees to choose whether to travel or not and therefore improve their work-life balance. Increasingly the system is being used by staff throughout the company as a viable alternative to travelling to meetings.

6 Sustainable Development Commission. (2009, December 11). Business case studies. Retrieved December 11, 2009, from Sustainable Development Commission: http://www.sd-commission.org.uk/pages/business-case-studies.html

ACCA recommends that "businesses should make sustainability issues a core part of their strategy, and that risk identification and management should be governed at board level."

Every business can implement sustainable practices that will improve the bottom line and the environment. Consideration should be given to the business's vision, values, or core mission statement, setting realistic, specific and measurable goals, how internal commitment is demonstrated by senior executives, how employees engagement will be achieved with all stakeholders at all levels of the business and what methods of communication will be employed to ensure that everyone understands the objectives. Introducing technologies and policies to reduce business travel and commuting is often a good place to begin and product life-cycle analysis that includes the carbon footprint could inform new designs. Working in partnership with others in the supply chain is likely to be critical to achieve sustainable and ethical procurement practices.

The Triple Bottom Line ●●●

Relatively few businesses have a strategy for sustainability or have even considered outlining how they may change their practices to become more sustainable. The Triple Bottom Line – Economic, Social and Environmental or Profit, People and Planet – is a practical framework for businesses wanting to become more sustainable. Sustainability can be a confusing and open-ended term whereas the Triple Bottom Line is an effective structure within which businesses can become sustainable without ignoring the importance of the financial bottom line.

The term Triple Bottom Line is attributed to John Elkington who co-founded SustainAbility and who also wrote the book Cannibals with Forks: The Triple Bottom Line of 21st Century Business (1999)[7].

The Triple Bottom Line is also referred to as "TBL" or "3BL" or even the "Three Pillars" with the pillars being People, Planet and Profit. This concept is well recognised and is increasingly being used by businesses as an acceptable way for them to demonstrate that they have strategies in place for sustainable growth. TBL is a form of reporting that will take into account the impact the business is having in terms of social and environmental values as well as highlighting the financial returns. More traditional models of reporting have simply concentrated on profits made but the Triple Bottom Line also recognises the importance of a happy and motivated workforce operating in a community and environment which will sustain the employees and their families as well as the resources needed for trade. Without this the business is simply unsustainable in the long-term.

Let us look at each of the three elements.

People

This has also been referred to as "human capital" and it basically pertains to the notion that the employees of the business should be treated with respect and fairness alongside the community within which the business operates. The TBL model not only guarantees the idea of a fair payment system for the employees but also that the business will be putting back money into the community through donations, sponsorship or projects that benefit the community as a whole.

Planet

Another term for this is "natural capital" and a business will be trying to minimise the impact it is having in ecological terms with regard to all areas from sourcing raw materials, processing those materials into finished goods, distributing the goods and completing all associated administrative tasks. This is sometimes described using the phrase "cradle to grave" and in some cases where the business offers a recycling or take-back facility it can be described as "cradle to cradle". A business utilising a TBL approach would also refrain from the production of toxic items.

7 Elkington, J. (1999). Cannibals with Forks: The Triple Bottom Line of 21st Century Business. In J. Elkington, Cannibals with Forks:The Triple Bottom Line of 21st Century Business (p. 1). Capstone.

Profit

This is about making honest and optimal profits rather than attempting to achieve all-out profit maximisation where there is a considerable danger of exploitation of both human and natural capital and consequently the environment.

In the past it may have been the case that many organisations would be cynical about the true benefits of TBL reporting but increasingly the business world is taking a much more positive stance. As supply chains will also be accountable to the overall impact of a business they will need to be scrutinised as part of TBL audits. This will mean that the business will demand a much greater say in the ingredients, components and packaging used by their suppliers.

The triple bottom line approach may look like this:

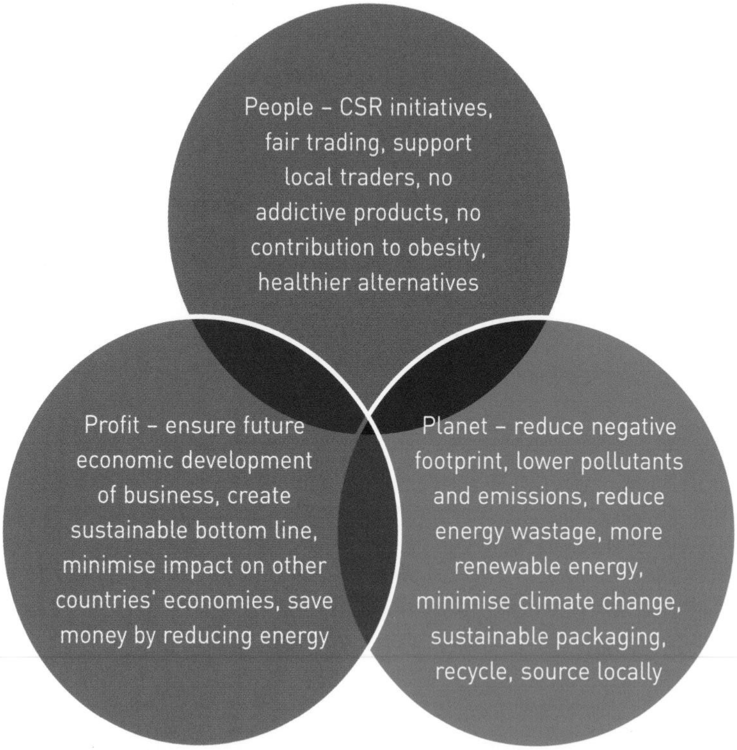
People – CSR initiatives, fair trading, support local traders, no addictive products, no contribution to obesity, healthier alternatives
Profit – ensure future economic development of business, create sustainable bottom line, minimise impact on other countries' economies, save money by reducing energy
Planet – reduce negative footprint, lower pollutants and emissions, reduce energy wastage, more renewable energy, minimise climate change, sustainable packaging, recycle, source locally

According to Corpwatch, of the 100 largest economies in the world only 49 are actual countries whereas the other 51 are businesses, so the impact on the world economy and the environment that these massive corporations can have is incalculable[8]. So it cannot just be about profits as the future of society and the environment is also at stake. TBL should be seen as an ongoing process that helps a business become sustainable and also ensures that it is seen by the community at large as not just about making profits but also working for the benefit of society and the environment. In the final analysis, without people and the planet there would be no profit.

8 Cavanagh, S. A. (2000). Top 200: The rise of Corporate Global Power. Institute of Policy Studies.

The Triple Bottom Line and SMEs

Smaller businesses may feel that their likely impact on society or the environment will be negligible in comparison to major corporations (this will also be failing to recognise their sphere of influence). All businesses should realise that they do have a role to play in shifting the balance in business from unsustainable to sustainable.

Over ninety nine per cent of UK businesses are small or medium sized enterprises[9]. With grants increasingly available to pay for energy saving initiatives and changes in working methods, businesses of every size have the opportunity and the responsibility to make sure they minimise their impact on the world around them.

There is a very strong business case for smaller businesses to implement TBL as it is now being realised that there is a definite competitive advantage to be had by communicating their sustainable credentials to increasingly "concerned customers". Also by switching to sustainable suppliers and sourcing locally they are more likely to be treated favourably by other like-minded sustainable businesses. One effect of climate change is the increasing amount of legislation imposed on business by government and this is only likely to continue. It therefore makes sense for small businesses to be compliant with such demands now rather than wait for specific legislation. Finally the cost savings brought about by a more sustainable approach can be proportionately larger in percentage terms for the smaller business.

Integrated Bottom Line[10]

This is a process for integrating financial, environmental, and social costs and benefits into a unified measure of business activity. Conventional objectives of profitability, competitive advantage, efficiency, and economic growth are judged successful by their compatibility with biodiversity, ecological sustainability, equity, community support, and maximized well-being for a variety of stakeholders.

An integrated bottom line differs from a triple bottom line in that all measures are combined into one balance sheet and income statement (rather than separated into three different ones).

The Fourth Bottom Line[11]

Very recently concern has been expressed about the Triple Bottom Line and it has been suggested that although a novel idea to many businesses its time may have already passed. A growing number of businesses have been making efforts to shrink their environmental footprint and, in some cases, make restitution for past negative

---

9 Department for Business Innovation and Skills. (2009, October). Statistical Press Release. Retrieved December 11, 2009, from National Statistics Office: http://stats.bis.gov.uk/ed/sme/smestats2008-ukspr.pdf

10 Integrated Triple Bottom Line. (2009, December 11). Retrieved December 11, 2009, from The Dictionary of Sustainable Management: http://www.sustainabilitydictionary.com/i/integrated_bottom_line.php

11 Kenney, S. (2009, November 5). The Fourth Bottom Line of Sustainability. Retrieved December 11, 2009, from Triple Pundit: http://www.triplepundit.com/2009/11/the-fourth-bottom-line-of-sustainability

impacts. But it has been argued that the time has come to add a fourth P to People, Planet and Profit and that is Perspective.

Steven Kenney argues that a truly future-focused perspective is the next step towards full sustainability and the objective should be much more than securing present conditions and making amends for past misdeeds. It should be about working today to make business, community and the environment stronger for tomorrow's conditions. It is important to identify and understand the forces that cause change and then to take advantage of them so that businesses, communities and ecosystems will be better equipped for the future.

An increase in profits is either brought about by cost savings by or growth but this reduction of costs will eventually reach a point where there are no more cuts to be made. The only long-term sustainable approach is to strengthen the production and competitive position of the business.

Kenney writes that the same reasoning can be applied to the People and Planet elements. The reduction of carbon emissions will greatly assist the battle against climate change but should more be done to strengthen the resilience of the environment through research and innovation. Many organisations are no longer working in isolation to create a sustainable future but are taking advantage of perspective by gaining ideas and systems from other experts and organisations worldwide.

This concept seems to fit very closely with BT's Mindset 3.0 Entrepreneurship and Innovation.

Further Reading

Murray, J (2008) How can you trust your CSR report? www.businessGreen.com news item 05 Aug 2008

World Business Council for Sustainable Development (2000) Corporate Social Responsibility: making business sense, available from www.wbcsd.org

CHAPTER 5

Globalisation

- A New Term for an Old Phenomenon
- What is Globalisation?
- The effects on Business
- The Influence of Multi-nationals

Until recently, the planet was a large world in which human activities and their effects were neatly compartmentalised within nations, within sectors (energy, agriculture, trade), and within broad areas of concern (environmental, social). These compartments have begun to dissolve. This applies in particular to the various global 'crises' that have seized public concern...These are not separate crises: an environmental crisis, a development crisis, an energy crisis. They are all one." (WCED, Our Common Future, 1987)

A New Term for an Old Phenomenon ●●●

The world's economies have developed ever-closer links since 1950, in trade, investment and production. Known as globalisation, this process is not new, but its pace and scope has accelerated in recent years, to embrace more industries and more countries. During the last decades of the 20th century many barriers to international trade fell and a wave of businesses began pursuing global strategies to gain competitive advantage. Rather than thinking in terms of national markets and national economies, leaders of business thought in terms of global markets.

Since 1955, the volume of the world trade has grown much faster than the world economy as a whole, and for many countries it has been the engine of growth. The gains of trade have been unevenly distributed as first Europe and then Asia joined the world trading system. Other poor regions, such as Africa, dependent on commodities, have been left behind. Trade talks helped boost trade in manufactured goods between rich countries as tariffs were cut. Countries which aimed at export-led growth, such as Japan, Korea, and China, have benefited.

As already stated globalisation is not a new phenomenon but over the last hundred years there have been three distinct phases and the trends that developed did not follow the same rationale in each phase. Up until the First World War the pattern of trade was largely between countries producing and exporting different goods and typically between manufacturing exporters and primary product exporters therefore based mainly on a non-competitive pattern dominated by comparative advantage. In other words these countries were specialising in producing only those goods that they could produce more efficiently than other goods which they would need to import. Comparative advantage results from a range of production factors such as capital, land, labour, entrepreneurial skills, power resources and technology. So it followed that free trade was beneficial to all countries because each country gained by specialising according to its comparative advantage.

The second phase happened after World War Two when the pattern and rationale for trade moved away from comparative advantage and on to flows between advanced industrial countries producing similar things. The size of the flow was determined by competitive advantages linked to specialisation and economies of size and scale. The competitive advantage was gained through providing the same value as competitors but either offering the goods at lower prices or through differentiation, in other words, through things that made the product or brand stand out as a provider of unique value to the customer in comparison with the competition. Sometimes this unique value was due to the history and reputation of the particular manufacturer or retailer.

In the last 30-40 years, beginning with the rise of Japan as a major exporter, the dominant trade pattern has swung back along the developed-developing axis but this time developing country exports have been increasingly manufactured and not primary products. The way manufactured goods are produced has changed dramatically in the last 50 years as the cost of transport and communications has fallen.

The boundaries of what constitutes comparative advantage have changed and it became possible to exploit differences, for example, between labour intensive, low labour cost locations such as China and capital intensive, high labour cost countries such as the United States. Add into this mix technology transfer and multi-national companies' expertise and access to markets and a winning formula is created to enable the building of a successful export industry.

Case Study[1]

In early September 2008 the BBC started a year-long project to illustrate the growth in world trade by launching their own freight container known as the "BBC Box" equipped with a GPS satellite transmitter. It s voyages were then tracked for the next twelve months until its return in November 2009. The aim of the project was to lift the veil on the complex patterns of global trade.

It left Southampton heading for Scotland to collect whiskey which was destined for Shanghai, a journey of approximately 6000 miles. In Shanghai it was partially loaded with goods such as measuring tapes and then was transported to Sendai, Japan where further goods were added including plastic spray bottles and bathroom scales and the box was then shipped to Los Angeles a total journey of over 6500 miles. The ultimate destination of these goods was New York a further 2450 miles across the width of the country. The box then travelled 6560 miles from New York to Santos in Brazil where it was loaded with foodstuffs heading for one of Japan's biggest food manufacturers which meant a travelling distance of a further 11400 miles. After months of lying idle in Japan the box made the final leg of its journey arriving back to the UK in November 2009.

1 BBC News. (2009, November 4). Lessons learned as the box returns. Retrieved January 6, 2010, from news.bbc.co.uk: http://www.news.bbc.co.uk/1/hi/business/8314116.stm

The Box in numbers

Duration: **421** days

Distance travelled: approx **51,654** miles

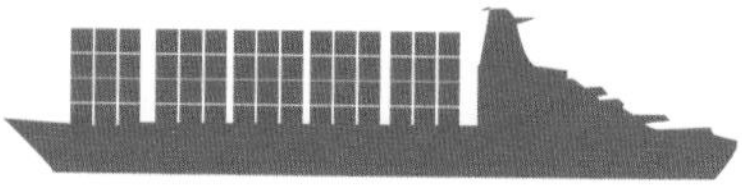

47,076
miles by ship

3,229
miles by train

1,349
miles by road

2.08
laps of the earth

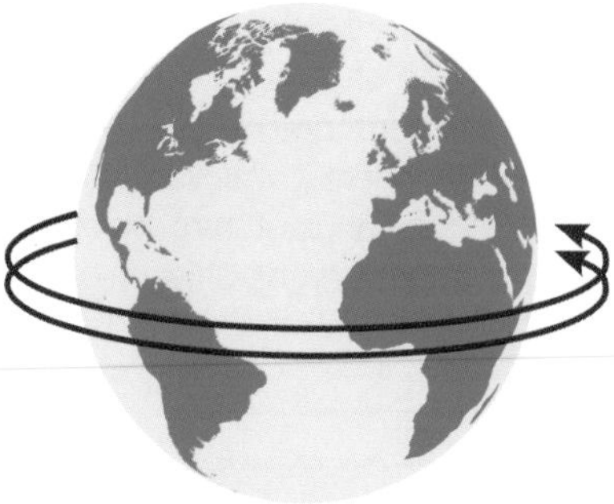

Cargos include:

15,120
bottles of whisky

4,320
bathroom scales

95,940
tins of cat food

Strange but true[2]

- We export 5,000 tonnes of toilet paper from the UK to Germany, but then import over 4,000 tonnes back again
- 4,400 tonnes of ice cream gets exported from the UK to Italy, and 4,200 tonnes is then imported back
- We import 22,000 tonnes of potatoes from Egypt and export 27,000 tonnes back the other way
- 116 tonnes of 'sweet biscuits' (the official category for trade statistics) comes into the UK, passing 106 tonnes headed in the opposite direction.

In 2008 China became the largest exporter of manufactured goods in the world by outperforming Germany. Between 2000 and 2008 the exports of manufactured goods from China rose by an annual average of 25.2% which was twice the rate of Germany. EU exports of manufactured goods to countries outside the EU still topped the table but the gap between the EU and China had closed from 67% in 2000 to 15% in 2008. On the import side the three major importers of manufactures – United States, Germany and China – has not changed[3].

What is Globalisation?

Globalisation is a business philosophy based on the belief that the world is becoming more homogeneous - national distinctions are fading and will eventually disappear. Globalisation is an increase in interconnectedness and interdependence of economic activity and social relations. If the world is homogeneous then companies need to think globally and standardise their strategy across national boundaries.

More and more goods are produced by global multi-national companies with production plants around the world. This set-up enables them to take advantage of cheaper labour and gives them better access to local markets. However, as well as in the "real economy" of goods and services, globalisation has also happened in the "non-real" world of financial capital flows, technology transfer, human capital enhancement and skills/education transfer. This could be described as finance and knowledge globalisation. As already indicated the real international transfer of goods and services has grown greatly but still changes relatively slowly. What particularly distinguishes the present period of greater global integration is the speed with which finance and knowledge globalisation has increased.

As well as the free movement of goods, there has also been a dramatic increase in the flows of money (capital) around the world. Banks and private investors now hold trillions of assets invested overseas since the liberalisation of world capital markets in the l980s. These capital flows are highly concentrated among rich countries and a few developing countries, and can fluctuate from year to year. While some big

2 http://neweconomics.org/press-releases/world-enters-%E2%80%98ecological-debt%E2%80%99-250909

3 December 11, 2009, from World Trade Organisation: http://www.wto World Trade Organisation. (2009, December 11). International Trade Statistics 2009. Retrieved.org/english/res_e/statis_e/its2009_e/its09_toc_e.htm

developing countries like China have benefited from capital flows, smaller countries have been vulnerable when capital flows suddenly reversed, as in the 1997-8 Asian crisis. The world distribution of wealth and income is highly unequal. The richest 10% of households in the world have as much yearly income as the bottom 90%. Wealth - total assets rather than yearly income – is even more unequal. The rich are concentrated in the US, Europe and Japan, with the richest 1% alone owning 40% of the world's wealth. Poverty, on the other hand, is widespread across the developing countries - which have five-sixths of the world's population. But it has fallen sharply in China.

But liberalising trade in services - such as accounting - or agriculture has proved harder.

More recently, "virtual companies" have outsourced their production to other firms around the world. These use the internet to manage their global supply chain, or their IT services like billing.

Outsourcing – getting someone else to do your work.

	% of all outsourced jobs	Most popular destinations
Information Technology	28	1. India
Human Resources	15	2. China
Sales and Marketing	14	3. Philippines

Why Outsource?[4]

Successful companies are often faced with personnel shortages or wish to reduce their labour costs at home in order to maintain their profitability. Staff shortages may be caused by several factors such as a new product launch, increased customer service demands or expanding debt collection requirements. In some cases it is difficult to recruit staff in the business's home country because the working population are unwilling to take on work of that nature or the rates of pay offered are unacceptable to them. Cyber Futuristics list some possible benefits of outsourcing as:

- it allows the company to focus on its core business
- it reduces the capital cost of the infrastructure
- it improves employee satisfaction with higher value jobs
- it makes the best use of competitive resources available worldwide
- it reduces the costs associated with recruitment.

4 Cyber Futuristics. (2009, December 11). Case Studies - Why Outsource? Retrieved December 11, 2009, from Cyber Futuristics: http://cyfuture.com/case-studies.htm

Cyber Futuristics note that India is proving to be the number one choice at the moment because it has inherent strengths, which have made it a major success as an outsourcing destination. The major ones are:

- a booming IT industry with IT strengths recognised worldwide
- the largest English speaking population outside of the USA
- cost effective manpower resources
- the Indian government is very supportive of such activities
- an excellent training infrastructure
- an excellent telecom infrastructure in the major cities.

The Effects of Globalisation on Business

The effects of globalisation can vary considerably from one part of the world to another and also from one area of business to another. A good communications infrastructure is very important to modern businesses, but not all countries will have one. There is also the 'non-traded' sector where particular goods or services are not traded internationally, for example domestic cleaning services. The main areas of impact on business brought about by globalisation will be as follows.

Competition - A combination of foreign businesses buying into or investing in domestic markets and increasing deregulation will open up these domestic markets to increased competition for both local and foreign companies alike, but obviously at the same time it improves the choices available to the consumer. Deregulation also encourages innovation in new products and markets which challenges traditional market leaders.

Meeting customer expectations and taste - Generally, consumers all over the world are better informed, have higher incomes and therefore have higher and more exacting expectations. Possibly where this is most noticeable is with regard to the choices available to UK consumers in the supermarket. The fact that there is an expectation that all typical food choices will be available all year round has forced UK supermarkets to buy stock from all parts of the world. As a result the notion of locally sourced goods has largely disappeared and because of this many concerned consumers and organisations have been critical of the "food miles" involved and the potentially bad impact on the environment?

Case Study

When researchers purchased a basket of foodstuffs from several supermarkets and then tracked the food miles for those products this is the summary of their findings.

Product	Country of Origin	Food miles
Apples	USA	10,133
Sugar snap peas	Guatemala	5,457
Asparagus	Peru	6,886
Grapes	Chile	7,247
Lettuce, strawberries, broccoli and spinach	Spain	958
Potatoes	Israel	2,187
Tomatoes	Saudi Arabia	3,086
Chicken	Thailand	6,643
Prawns	Indonesia	7,287
Brussels sprouts	Australia	10,562
Wine	New Zealand	14,287
Carrots and peas	South Africa	5,979

All imported products result in the emission of carbon dioxide from the planes and ships that brought them to the UK. So a strong argument has developed that ethical consumers should only buy and eat local produce and also only when in season. Many thousands of individuals share this view whether in the UK or overseas and as a result have opted not to buy foods that have been transported long distances. There is even a newly created term for them which is "locavores".

However a recent article[5] casts serious doubt on this and even suggests that the "myth of food miles" may be harmful rather helpful to the environment.

> There is growing evidence that some air-freighted food is greener than food grown in the UK and therefore the concept of food miles is too simplified and possibly damaging to the environment.
>
> Two staple foods that are in the supermarkets all year round are apples and lettuce and these both provide good examples of why food miles may be misleading. In the UK apples are harvested in September and October and so have to be kept in chilled storage for the other 10 months of the year. The amount of energy used to keep them fresh until August will overtake the carbon cost of shipping them from New Zealand. Lettuces in Britain are grown in winter, in greenhouses or polytunnels which require heating. Picking the right sources for your apples and lettuces depends on the time of year.

It can be seen that trying to reduce the carbon emissions produced by food is complicated and replacing food miles with a carbon footprint figure will only partly simplify the issue. The use of carbon footprint labelling and the concept of product miles will be looked at in far greater detail in the Business section of this book.

Meeting customer expectation will force businesses to meet higher standards. However the notion that globalisation is based on the simple idea that "one size fits all" in that if a product is very successful in its home country then automatically it will be popular in every other country is not necessarily going to be the case. There have been winners and losers when it comes to achieving global success.

Coca Cola did not at first succeed in their penetration of the Indian market because their standard products that are so successful elsewhere in the world were simply too expensive for the general Indian population. The company had to completely rethink its marketing strategy specifically for India and as result sold their drink in bottles which were much smaller than their normal size and at a greatly reduced price, in fact half the original price. The company also had to rebuild sales of a local brand which they had bought to deliberately phase out of the Indian Cola market. Sales also had to be focused on the countryside as well as the towns and cities. Coca Cola had to revise its employment strategy to employ local staff and to also use local advertising agencies.

5 Guardian Newspaper. (2008, March 23). How the myth of food miles hurts the planet. Retrieved January 6, 2010, from guardian.co.uk: http://www.guardian.co.uk/environment/2008/mar/23/food.ethicalliving

In the past the term "glocalisation" was just used to refer to internet sites that had to be translated into the language of the country in which it was operating, but now this same term has a much wider significance. Companies wishing to expand their global share of the market may have to be prepared to tailor their product or service to meets the needs and expectations of the target country or region. In the same way that employers are required to be aware of diversity and so recognise and value differences, then a responsible business wishing to export its goods or services worldwide must also allow for diversity.

Economies of scale - Selling into a global market allows for enormous economies of scale, although not all industries benefit from these.

Location of business - Businesses are now much freer to choose where they operate from, and can move to a cheaper and more efficient location. In the last decade the UK has been seen by many businesses as an attractive business location, especially in financial services, and many businesses have located in the UK which has boosted the UK economy but also provided increased competition for UK businesses. This increased movement of businesses and jobs has, to some extent, forced governments to compete with each other in providing an attractive and low-cost location. Manufacturing businesses are increasingly relocating to low-wage countries such as Indonesia. Inputs vary in price across the world, and businesses now have more freedom of movement to access those cheaper inputs, for example, labour in developing countries. One limitation on this is that managers won't always move to some countries if living conditions are unpleasant or even dangerous.

When a business does decide to relocate part or all of its operations to another country a term which is often used to describe this process is "moving offshore" or "offshoring".

A study carried out by Deloitte entitled "Global Financial Services Offshoring Report" highlighted that the shifting of UK financial services jobs to developing countries such as India has saved the sector about £1.5bn per year. The report went on to say that the number of financial jobs going overseas between 2003 and 2007 had increased 18-fold and that more than 75% of major financial institutions have operations overseas compared with fewer than 10% in 2001. The author also recommended that financial institutions thought through the revision of their systems to ensure that they avoid transferring inefficiencies from their old onshore processes. By 2007 the typical financial services team had 6% of its staff outside the host country a proportion which doubled since 2006[6 & 7].

6 BBC News. (2007, June 22). Offshoring has not hit UK jobs. Retrieved December 11, 2009, from BBC News: http://news.bbc.co.uk/go/pr/fr/-/1/hi/business/6229164.stm Gentle, C. (2007). Global Financial Services Offshoring Report. Deloitte.

7 Deloitte. (2007). Financial services companies increase overseas headcount 18-fold as offshoring accelerates and evolves. Retrieved January 7, 2010, from deloitte.com: http://www.deloitte.com/view/en_GB/uk/newsroom/newsreleases/press-release/4a5f5c968b0fb110VgnVCM100000ba42f00aRCRD.htm

The following arguments for and against moving offshore can be put forward.

For	Against
Cost	Security
Quality	Quality
Time to market	Employee concerns
Technical skills and expertise	Better onshore options
Strategy	Strategy
Market penetration	Customer support

Multi-national and multi-cultural management - this will be a major challenge for any global business and its managers. The very nature of a multi-national company is that it is very complex with many variables to contend with and as a result will be more difficult to manage. A multi-cultural employment policy will lead to many different nationalities, languages, religions and cultures in different offices, shops or factories across the globe. These employees are differently motivated and react in quite different ways to incentives, and it is very difficult to find managers who are sensitive to all these different factors. It is very easy to inadvertently give offence and de-motivate workers. Many multi-nationals have produced global worker rights for all their staff regardless of nationality but again diversity must allow for the right to be different.

Globalisation of markets - the notion of national borders to global businesses is becoming less and less important. Global markets stretch across borders and multi-national companies are usually well placed to take advantage of this. Issues of language and culture will arise but consumers are growing in similarity even if still not the same in each country. Many businesses have made expensive mistakes by not taking into account local variation as was the case with Coca Cola. Translation from one language to another is fraught with all sorts of danger particularly for the marketing section where product literal translation of a product name or brand may mean something completely different in another language.

Globalisation has brought about a growth in the number of multi-national enterprises and there have been various forces driving this growth, several of which have been mentioned already. Large companies are always looking to increase their market share and this ultimately will involve moving into new territories as the home market is finite and often legislation in that country is in place to remove the risk of monopoly. This will often prevent a company from achieving expansion of its market share through takeover in its own country. Other forces previously identified are cost reduction, cheaper transport costs, shifting production to other countries with lower wage costs, the avoidance of tariffs and duties, extension of product life cycles and the deregulation of capital markets.

The Influence of Multi-Nationals

Many large multi-national companies have become very powerful and as already stated some are worth more than the entire GDP of many countries. This means that these companies can have an enormous effect either positively or negatively on the countries in which they do business particularly in small or poor countries. The main areas of influence are as follows.

The balance of payments – multi-national companies import large amounts of capital to fund their new business investments. In economic terms this surplus on the capital account creates a deficit on the current account as the country is seen to be importing more goods and services than it is exporting. This lifts local standards of living until the import of capital stops for whatever reason and then standards fall again.

If the new business is to make goods that were previously imported then the current account will improve or if the new venture is developing local raw materials for export then again the current account would improve. If the company has to import large amounts of technical equipment which is not available locally this would worsen the current account. However, if the company re-invests its profits then this may well offset any imports and there will be no effect on the balance of payments. Alternatively if profits are transferred back to the parent company then the current account worsens. Further, the exchange market of a small country may not be well-developed, so any attempt by a business to buy or to sell large amounts of foreign exchange will send the price of that currency sharply up or down unless things are managed very carefully and responsibly.

Knowledge/technology transfer – multi-national companies invariably operate at a much higher standard of managerial and technical expertise than that which can be found in the local economy. This means that for those locally recruited employees there is a great deal they can learn which in turn can be passed on to the wider business community. This is particularly true in developing countries where technology transfer is very important and obviously this will depend on how willing the multi-national company is to employ and train local workers.

Social responsibility - a responsible business will always carry out its affairs taking full account of all standards and regulations that it must operate by even though that usually creates additional costs. Multi-national companies are constantly looking to reduce costs so, as already seen, there is a big advantage in locating in countries with few regulations. Those countries that are particularly poor are often prey to bribery and corruption, which also means any regulations they might have are ineffectual. The risk here is that it opens up the possibility for a relaxation in standards causing the company to fall below the levels considered acceptable in the company's home country. There have been many examples of large companies being criticised for using "sweat shop" or child labour in other parts of the world and this has often damaged their reputation sufficiently in their home and other markets to make them unattractive to ethical consumers and investors.

Employment – when a multi-national sets up a new business it will need new workers and so employment prospects are improved, new jobs are created and the transfer of skills and knowledge may also take place. Training will be needed if there is a mismatch between the skills required by the company and those available in the local employment market. The business may decide to set up a factory specifically designed to suit the local employment market. Sometimes the jobs are too demanding for the locals or it could be that they are considered too demeaning. There are many examples around the world where companies use huge numbers of expatriate workers to fill their vacancies and again this should be handled sensitively and responsibly. There is also a considerable risk that new business will prove to be too much competition for local businesses forcing them to close and ultimately have a detrimental effect on employment figures generally. Multi-nationals usually employ fewer workers as part of their greater efficiencies and there is also the distinct possibility that the company could always choose to re-locate in the future.

Government control – it is often very difficult for some governments to exercise effective control over multi-national companies because they are so large and powerful and any risk of them re-locating elsewhere could have a catastrophic effect on a country's economy and unemployment figures.

To summarise, globalisation in the past was concerned with finding cheap and plentiful supplies of commodities and this in turn lead to businesses also looking to find sources of cheap and plentiful labour. Allied to this was the growing trend to establish much cheaper manufacturing sites in other parts of the world, mostly Asia, but to continue to make products based on western research and development and western branding and marketing. A good example of this is Raleigh Bicycles which is a UK company with UK distribution but its products are made in China.

In the future globalisation will change as it is predicted that between now and 2030 75% of the world's growth will come from BRICM (Brazil, Russia, India, China and Mexico), the vast majority of which will come from China and India. Western companies need to find ways to break into these markets if they wish to continue their own global expansion.

There is a major problem associated with globalisation which needs to be addressed and that is the "globalisation of waste". The acts of production, consumption and disposal have been geographically separated like never before and whilst production may take place in one country, products are often consumed in another and then disposed of in a third. A computer might be manufactured in Asia, used in North America and disposed of in Africa. The term "E waste" is used to describe the disposal of computer components and although it may seem to be a "clean" type of waste it can prove to be very hazardous. Workers, typically children, will burn the plastic parts to gain access to copper wiring, for example, but the smoke from burning plastic is very toxic.

As the product life-cycle becomes global so does the trail of waste it leaves behind and many developed countries, in cleaning up their own act in terms of recycling, are using the underdeveloped countries of the world as dumping grounds for their waste. Despite various international conventions direct dumping still occurs and it is true to say that several major countries are not party to these conventions. With the globalisation of products, and an associated globalisation of waste, there has to be a "globalisation of responsibility". The producer has to tie in business advantage with responsibility for waste. Producer liability is possibly the only answer.

Many believe that the business world's hunger for growth and the consequent development of globalisation was a major contributing factor in climate change and global warming. So it does seem somewhat ironic that the vast majority of growth in the future will take place in countries such as India and China because they are also the parts of the world which may suffer most from the effects of global warming. In the longer term the environmental backlash of increased temperatures and water shortages may ultimately bring about the demise of globalisation.

CHAPTER 6

New Economics

- Global Ecological Debt
- Limitless Resources
- Endless Growth
- The New Economic System

> *The contrast between our bright hopes for the future of the information economy and the deterioration of Earth's ecosystem leaves us with a schizophrenic outlook*[1].

Global Ecological Debt

Forget credit crunches and national debts, we are talking global ecological debts. This should be fundamentally more worrying and more newsworthy than any banking crisis. The ecology is what the economy relies on to survive, and it is being used at a greater rate than it can be replenished.

Without the environment for energy, for resources, and as a sink for waste, society does not exist, and the economy does not function.

Limitless Resources

Traditional economics models have assumed limitless resources, and limitless economic growth. This theory of limitless resources – that what we want, we can have – put the environment firmly within the control of the economic system. It has been assumed that if demand increases, then supply will meet that demand. However, this broad assumption is fundamentally flawed, as the natural resources are indeed limited. Energy, created millions of years ago, is now being used (as oil, gas and coal) at rates that far exceed replenishment. Forests are being cut down at a faster rate than they can grow; fish stocks are being harvested at an unsustainable rate; air, water and soil are becoming more polluted. There is only a finite period of time that the economy can rely so heavily on the environment before the resources are used, and the model collapses.

Even if the energy were inexhaustible, the environment is struggling to retain a balance for ecosystems to survive with the rapid emissions of carbon dioxide into the atmosphere. The carbon has been captured millions of years ago, as oil, gas and coal. As these fossil fuels are extracted and burnt, the intense release of gases is causing the earth to warm. This is having knock-on effects, in weather patterns and biodiversity.

Biodiversity is not able to adapt at the rate required to keep up with changes in climate caused by this fast release of carbon dioxide. In addition, the loss of biodiversity due to other resource use, such as deforestation and fishing has knock-on effects in ecosystems. Puffin populations are declining in north-east Scotland as their food source is reduced by industrial scale fishing. Modern intensive farming reduces soil quality and the trend towards monocrops (single crops planted on large scales), further reduces biodiversity.

1 Brown, L. (2000). The State of the World: 2000. London: WW Norton & Co.

The loss of biodiversity is alarming considering the changing climate. Where diversity is lost, so potential for finding species that can survive in future climates is reduced. Biodiversity needs to be protected as a long-term strategy.

As well as being limitless, these resources, or natural capital, are regarded as free by the economy. The only cost is the physical extraction of the natural material – the actual oil, coal, wood, or diamonds do not have a cost. The UN's Millennium Ecosystem Assessment has been researching the consequences of ecosystem change for human well-being. They state that "the degradation of an ecosystem represents the loss of a capital asset, yet the economic impact of this loss is poorly reflected in financial measures, including national accounts"[2]. The Assessment uses an example of timber production (which bears an economic value) resulting in a loss of non-economic values such as the losses of watershed protection, recreational facility, non-timber forest products, and carbon sequestration, calculating that the "marketed values ... are less than one third of the total economic value". So not only is natural capital lost (the forest), but the economic gain from this (for the timber) is low compared to the lost value of the additional benefits that the forest previously brought (recreation, water retention, land and soil stability, and carbon sequestration).

It becomes clear that the true relationship between the economy and the environment is still being discovered. What is apparent though is that the economy is a subsystem of the environment, not the other way around. Without the environment, there is no economy. Without the economy, there is still the environment. The economy relies on the environment to both survive and thrive.

How does this impact on the way business does business?

The dramatic change that needs to happen in the way that the economy should relate to the environment is worthy of headline news worldwide but unfortunately that is not happening and so there is a great danger that this miscalculation on the part of society will go unchecked.

Endless Growth ●●●

The economic system is based on the belief of limitless growth. It is an embedded, unquestioned assumption, accepted worldwide, across countries and religions. Growth is synonymous with progress. If someone sets up in business, and purchases tools, materials, premises and transport to do this, they want to see these investments bring in more than the original cost, i.e. make a profit. This profit may be reinvested into the business, to improve it, or could be invested in other businesses. Either way, again, a return, or profit is expected of the investment. And so growth continues.

> *For the last five decades the pursuit of growth has been the single most important policy goal across the world.*
>
> **Professor Tim Jackson, 2009, p. 5**

2 Millennium Ecosystem Assessment. (2005). Ecosystems and Human Well-being: Opportunities and Challenges for Business and Industry. Washington, DC.: World Resources Institute.

Gross Domestic Product (GDP) is a key measure of growth, and is the total value of all goods and services produced in an economy. Increase in the GDP of a country is seen as a positive indication of an increase in living standards in a country. Any economic activity within a country adds to this national account, and is a sign of progress. However, millions of pounds a year is spent by motorists on petrol used to sit in traffic jams. This adds to the GDP, and if motorists sit in traffic jams for even longer and spend even more on fuel the following year, so the national GDP increases, and it would appear that the country's living standards have increased. Of course this example does not show an increase in living standards, rather a decline. This brings the use of GDP as an effective measure of progress into question.

Regardless of how it is measured, considering the relationships between the economy and the environment, can this growth realistically go on? The New Economics Foundation has calculated the World's Ecological Debt Day. This is the day each year that the world uses more resources, and creates more waste than ecosystems can produce and absorb. In 2009 this was the 25th September[3]. Beyond this date, the world is living on ecological debt. This debt day has been getting earlier year on year. In 2007, it fell on the 6th October. The UK's Ecological Debt Day in 2009 was 12th April. Beyond this date, the UK relied on the rest of the world. This would prove bad business sense in any business model. It suggests vulnerability for the country (that the UK relies on the rest of the world so heavily).

Unfortunately GDP figures are generally used without the caveat that they represent an income that cannot be sustained.

Current calculations ignore the degradation of the natural resource base and view the sale of non-renewable resources entirely as income.

A better way must be found to measure the prosperity and progress of mankind.

Barber Conable, former President of the World Bank, 1989[4]

3 BBC News. (2009, September 25). Recession barely dents 'eco-debt'. Retrieved November 2009, from BBC News: http://news.bbc.co.uk/1/hi/8273791.stm

4 http://www.foe.co.uk/community/tools/isew/annex1.html

Beyond the threats to ecological sustainability, the effects of growth on society do not fare much better. It would be simple to assume that higher economic growth resulted in greater well-being for the population, but this does not appear to hold true.

Figure 1

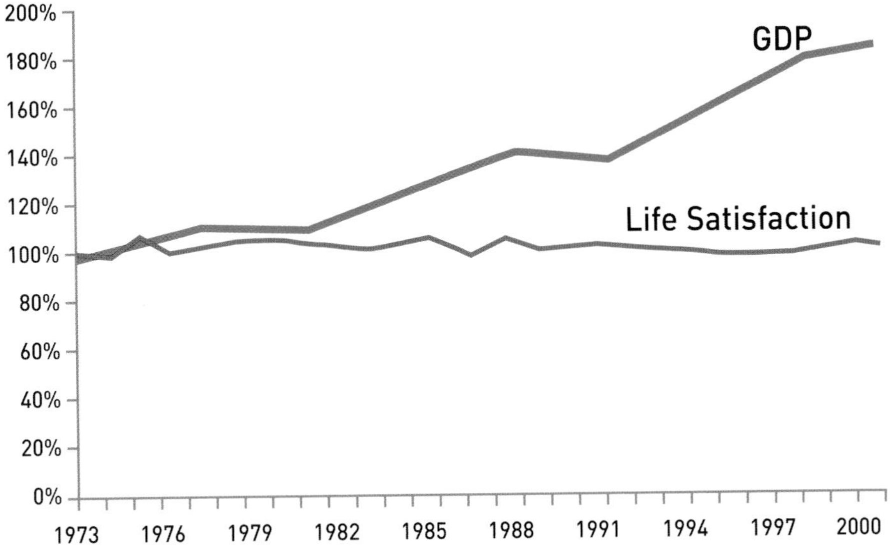

The UK has seen strong GDP growth and increase in consumer spending, but no real increase in life satisfaction in the last couple of decades.[5 and 6]

5 Sustainable Development Commission (2009) A prosperous nation: SDC e-bulletin. http://www.sd-commission.org.uk/pages/a-prosperous-nation-sdc-e-bulletin.html Accessed 11 December 2009.

6 Harding, S (2008) Intelligent Growth. In Resurgence, March 2008.

The New Economic System ●●●

The need for a new means of measuring is becoming more evident. And the principles of New Economics are slowly emerging, challenging the very notions of wealth and poverty, and instead using measurements of well-being and environmental sustainability as indicators of real wealth, rather than possessions and consumption. As well as new measures we may need new ways of doing business. Business with social and ecological benefits.

New measures	A central theme of New Economics is that we need to strive for good lives that do not cost the earth. A new indicator to guide societies is needed, rather than money. The UN Human Development Index is the most widely used metric of international development. It uses three indicators to characterise a nation's overall level of development: GDP per capita, life expectancy at birth, and educational attainment. Whilst recognising that these indicators do not give a complete picture of development, the UN uses these indicators to give an approximation. If all three are increasing, the development is being made. The Happy Planet Index[7] uses indicators to represent the amount of human well-being a country produces relative to its resources use. It is measured in terms of life expectancy and happiness, and is an efficiency index, measuring how much well-being is achieved per unit of environmental impact. The Happy Planet Index shows that high resource consumption is not synonymous with high levels of well-being, and that high levels of well-being are possible without high resource consumption. The Index shows that the UK is inefficient at converting natural capital (resources) into well-being. The UK lives far beyond its ecological means to achieve similar levels of life satisfaction and life expectancy as Costa Rica, where this is achieved with less than half the ecological footprint.

7 nef (the New Economics Foundation). (2009), from Happy Planet Index: http://www.happyplanetindex.org/

New business	There is a wealth of new business that would benefit the economy, society, and the environment. These include technologies such as solar and wind power, emerging technologies (such as low- and zero- waste manufacturing), investment in green infrastructure (such ecosystem based catchment management that would benefit water quality, flood risk, fishery and biodiversity as well as having a range of social benefits). It is argued that encouraging these new businesses would "create serious momentum, infrastructure and capacity for the novel and sustainable markets necessary to underpin the new economy that will be required for a secure, clean and fair future"[8].

Moving forward

Questioning the basis of economics brings yet more questions. The answers are less clear, but the main point that should be taken from this chapter is that *the old way is not sustainable* (in any sense of the word). The future of growth needs to be *intelligent growth,* learning to do more with less, utilising renewable energy sources, ensuring that business operations have positive social and environmental impacts, building communities, and restoring biodiversity; as opposed to the present course of *suicidal growth*, where business operations have largely negative environmental and, so social implications.

As someone who lives in a rich country I would prefer to live under the current system, but climate change means we don't have a choice... we can either design a slower-growth economy over the next few decades, or we'll get there suddenly, through environmental disaster.

Peter Victor[9]

8 Everard, D. M. (2009). Reanimating the corpse. the environmentalist , 10-11.

9 QUOTE REF Peter Victor FROM: http://www.guardian.co.uk/business/2009/mar/22/gdp-economic-growth-happiness-wellbeing

> *Anyone who believes exponential growth can go on forever in a finite world is either a madman or an economist.*

Kenneth Boulding.

The nef (the new economics foundation)[10] have produced a radical plan "The Great Transition: A tale of how it turned out right" in late 2009 which argues that adopting a "business as usual" approach to either a global or national economy is very short-sighted. A team of scientists and economists at the organisation have produced a blueprint or "greenprint" for how the UK could make step changes in delivering quality of life for all, whilst living within its collective environmental means. What may shock some is the fact that this can be achieved even as the UK economy stops growing in a conventional economic manner and GDP falls significantly.

The nef has calculated that between 2010 and 2050 the total cost of climate change combined with the cost of addressing social problems could be as much as £7 trillion. The Great Transition tackles climate and inequality at the same time. It puts the UK on a rapid course for a reduction in carbon emissions ensuring it meets its commitments in any global deal and avoiding up to £1.3 trillion in environmental costs. Simultaneously a "great re-distribution" will bring about a re-balancing that sets out a new productive relationship between markets, society and the state which builds a more effective "ecology of finance" so that money flows to where it is most needed such as to the low-carbon transition of the UK's energy, housing and transport systems. The nef also calculated that this progressive redistribution towards Danish levels of equality could generate £7.35 trillion of social value. The nef agrees that it is a "big bold plan that tears up business as usual" but "if the only navigation system you have keeps directing you over a cliff, it's time to reprogram it."

Further reading:

Boyle, D & Simms, A (2009) The New Economics: A bigger picture.

10 nef (the new economics foundation). (2009, October 19). The Great Transition. Retrieved December 31, 2009, from nef (the new economics foundation): http://www.neweconomics.org/publications/the-great-transition

CHAPTER 7

Systemic Thinking

- Cause and Effect
- Feedback Loops
- Linking Thinking
- Complexity

To understand how a business may operate in a responsible manner, it is necessary to first consider the nature and consequences of relationships. In a highly complex, fast changing, and interconnected world, it is no longer possible to view problems in the linear fashion of cause and effect. To operate responsibly, organisations need to be aware of how their operations are part of a larger system of interrelationships and processes of change.

Consider the case of Sainsbury's wishing to reduce the amount of plastic bags used in their stores, to reduce the environmental impacts of their production and disposal. The supermarket chain commissioned designer cotton bags to be produced, but came under fire from campaigners as the bags were produced in China, a country notorious for low labour standards. The store was also criticised as the cotton bags were not produced from fair trade cotton. Thinking in a linear way, the bags sold well, and so would have reduced the use of plastic bags, but Sainsbury's did not think of the contradictions or unintended consequences of producing the bags. It could be argued that Sainsbury's should not be criticised for trying to achieve an environmental objective, but it is becoming increasingly apparent that short-term solutions to individual problems often have a negative knock-on effect.

In order to progress sustainably, organisations need to understand the complexities of the system in which they operate. Systems thinking attempts to show how events are separated by distance and time and that small events can cause large changes in complex systems. Peter Senge writes extensively about systems thinking. He describes it as "a discipline for seeing the "structures" that underlie complex situations, and for discerning high from low leverage change"[1]. Senge believes that in order to change a system, it is first important to understand the interconnections within it, and where change can best be attempted from (the leverage point).

Cause and Effect ●●●

When considering a problem that has occurred, it is common to try to work out what the cause of the problem is. What caused the child to fall off its bike; the business deal to fall through; the deadline to be missed? Finding a single cause may not be easy; it is likely to be due to a number of factors. And trying to impose a solution to a problem, may in itself cause further problems, either directly with regard to the initial problem (see problem A in the diagram below), or in other areas (problem B).

Figure 1

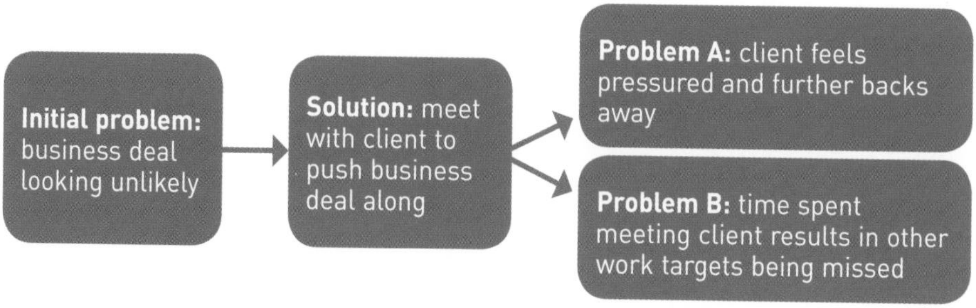
Initial problem: business deal looking unlikely
Solution: meet with client to push business deal along
Problem A: client feels pressured and further backs away
Problem B: time spent meeting client results in other work targets being missed

1 Senge, P. (1990). The Fifth Discipline. New York: Doubleday.

In some circumstances, a solution may itself escalate a problem, such as Problem A above. In this instance, spending time with the client makes them feel pressured to secure the deal, and further compounds the problem.

Feedback Loops ●●●

Feedback loops are used in systems thinking to illustrate how events are connected. There are two types of feedback loops: positive and negative.

Positive feedback loops are also called reinforcing, or amplifying feedback loops. A positive feedback loop is where the response to something happening makes it happen more. This is the case in the situation described above, where the client feels more pressured as the salesman tries to clinch the business deal.

Figure 2 - Positive feedback loop

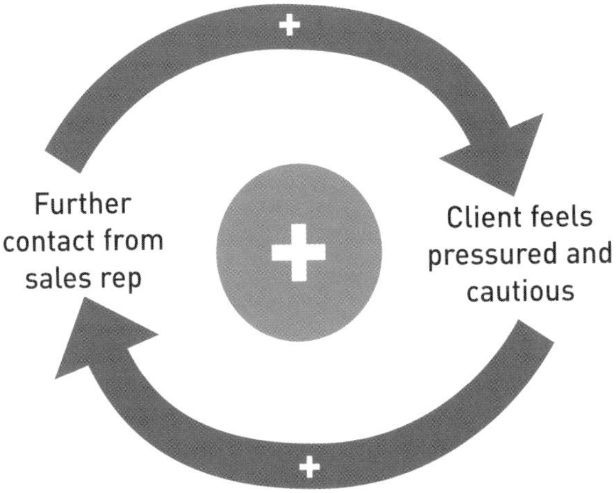

The positive feedback loop described above is drawn out in Figure 2. In this, the + symbols on the arrows shows a reinforcing action. So the client feels pressured and cautious, which attracts increased contact from the sales rep. This further increases the feeling of pressure and cautiousness from the client, and so the cycle continues. Were the client feeling low levels of pressure and caution it would attract lower contact from the sales rep, which would further reduce any feelings of pressure and caution. Hence the positive feedback loop reinforces the situation.

If Figure 2 were drawn as a graph, it would follow either of the two lines as follows:

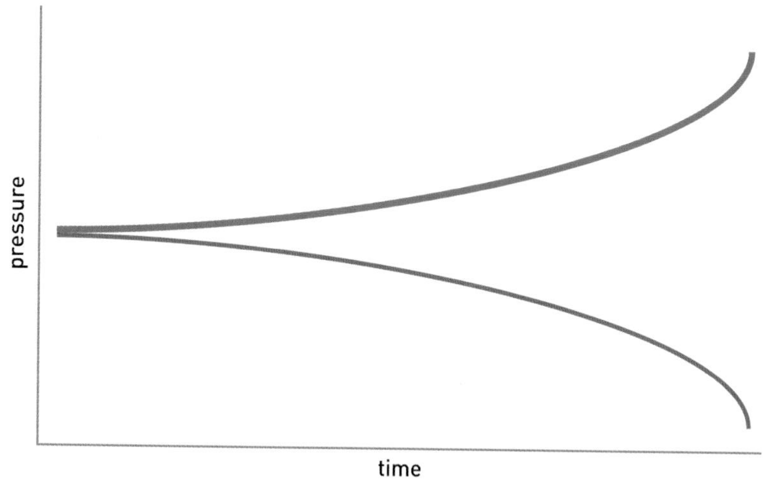

The upper curve shows an amplification of high pressure as the salesman increases contact. The lower curve shows the reaction from the client who does not feel pressure but reassurance from the salesman's contact. This shows that in a positive, or reinforcing, feedback loop, the outcome can follow two paths, which can accelerate to great extremes of pressure.

Negative feedback loops are also known as balancing, or stabilizing feedback loops. A negative feedback loop is where the response to something happening makes it happen less. An example (see Figure 3) would be that if someone is hungry they would eat food, which makes them less hungry. Notice the labelling of the arrows, with either "+" or "-". These show a balancing action. The hunger is met with increased food consumption, which in turn reduces the hunger. This causes lower food consumption, which then causes hunger to increase once again.

Figure 3 - Negative feedback loop

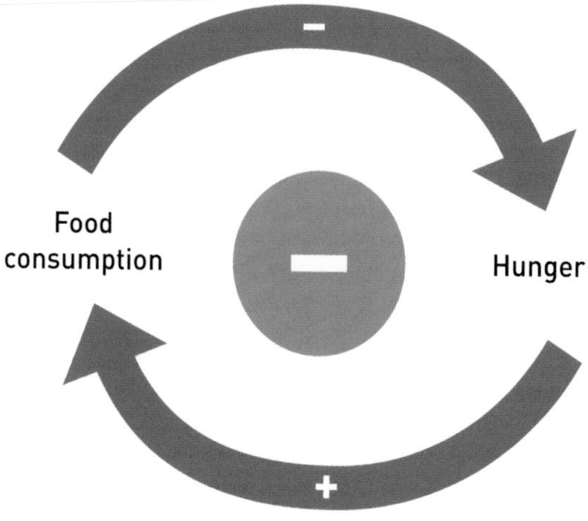

If Figure 3 were drawn as a graph, it would look as follows:

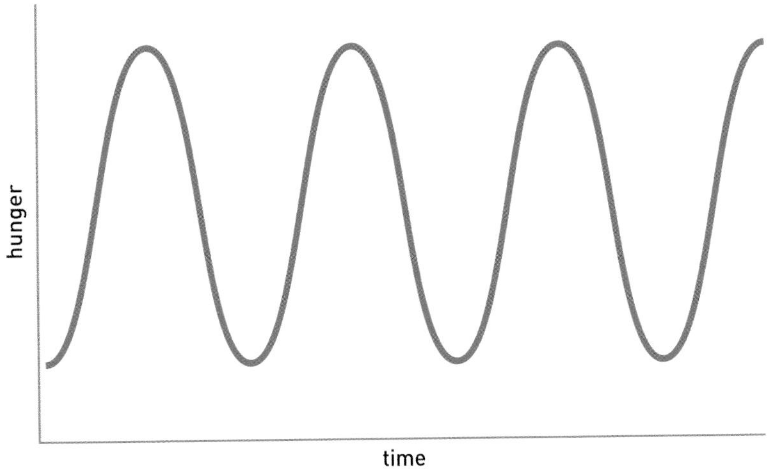

The curve shows hunger levels over time, as the person responds to their signals to continue or to stop eating. Over time, this feedback loop, or system, is attempting to create a balance.

Linking Thinking ●●●

Thinking systemically, and recognising feedback loops, are important elements to being able to manage businesses in responsible and sustainable ways. By gaining an understanding of how elements within a system interact, businesses can place themselves in a better position to have a positive influence on this system. Not being aware risks unwelcome consequences of action. Thinking systemically is also referred to as "linking thinking" and "holistic thinking"[2].

> *Without a holistic view, decisions may lead to unexpectedly nasty consequences further down the road.*
>
> **Forum for the Future**

Complexity ●●●

Just as scientists are continually striving to gain understanding of the complex world of the natural environment, so too are organisational theorists of business organisational dynamics. Complexity science is becoming increasingly developed

2 Forum for the Future (2008) Acting now for a positive 2018, preparing for radical change: the next decade of business and sustainability. December 2008. http://www.forumforthefuture.org/library/acting-now-for-a-positive-2018.

in this field. One strand of complexity science is *complex adaptive systems*. This is most relevant to understanding both the system in which organisations interconnect with the natural environment and to understanding organisational dynamics and the web of economic activity within these. Lewin and Regine define complex adaptive systems as:

> *. . . a diversity of agents that interact with each other, mutually affect each other, and in doing so generate novel behaviour for the system as a whole...but the pattern of behaviour we see in these systems is not constant, because when a system's environment changes, so does the behaviour of its agents, and, as a result, so does the behaviour of the system as a whole*[3].

Rather than try to complicate the idea of systems thinking, this illustrates that the key to understanding a system is to understand the relationships that play within a system, rather than the elements themselves. Just as in the above example, having a good understanding of the relationship between the client and salesman would help identify whether greater contact would either pressurise the client, or put them at ease. Without this understanding, the salesman does not know the best approach to take to reach a sale.

There are two types of complexity (Senge, 1990)[4]:

Detailed complexity	complexity in which there are many variables
Dynamic complexity	situations where cause and effect are subtle, and where the effects over time of interventions are not obvious

Conventional methods of forecasting and planning take into account detailed complexity, but are unable to consider dynamic complexity.

Chapter 1 referred to the realisation by businesses that raw materials are finite. In Chapter 1, the future situation was described as "endless consumption will not be possible. Where a business needs raw materials, they will need to be adaptable to cope with future shortages through planned replenishment, finding alternative sources of raw materials or adapting their business model to recover and reuse components. In addition resources are not only threatened by over-consumption, but also burning fossil fuels to power production is itself having a detrimental effect on the environment, with consequences such as flooding, drought and forest fires further reducing the availability of these scarce resources."

3 Lewins and Regine. (2001). Weaving Complexity and Business. New York: Texere LLC.

4 Senge, P. (1990). The Fifth Discipline. New York: Doubleday.

It is now possible to see this as a system of great complexity, with interconnections, relationships, and feedback loops operating.

Complexity is about many parts and the many and changing relationships and interconnections between these parts. In highly complex situations it is difficult or even impossible to predict the outcome of an action or intervention. The present state of the environment, and economy, is the largest and most unpredictable system that all businesses operate within. In a culture interested in predicting the futures, with targets, and assessments, the next generation of leaders needs to become more able to manage uncertainty and unpredictability.

CHAPTER 8

Leadership in a Changing World

- The Changing World
- Future Leaders
- Styles of Management
- A Crisis in Trust
- Boardroom Scepticism
- Business as Leaders

The Changing World

The world is changing. Many ways of making money today will not be profitable tomorrow. Basic services and resources that the natural world now provides cheaply will become more and more expensive. Business organisations are facing change at a fast rate, with technology speeding this along. Future changes may include a need to adapt to the availability of resources, as those that are presently taken for granted start to deplete. With the change comes unpredictability and uncertainty. Understanding the systems that these changes are part of will give organisations an upper hand in influencing the change, succeeding at the change, and finding opportunities within this. A number of businesses are realising this, and working to adapt their business strategies to ride this change. According to Forum for the Future[1], a profound strategic shift on sustainability is occurring, with leading businesses such as BT, Marks and Spencer and Unilever changing their approach to sustainability from one of looking at how sustainability should be included in the business, to building the business strategy based on sustainability issues [2]. For these business leaders, sustainability and the issues surrounding it really are carving the business agenda.

> *It is in business's self-interest to take a leadership role in reducing poverty, improving human well-being, and protecting the environment. Doing so will help secure stable and safe societies, preserve open and free markets, ensure access to critical resources, provide new product and business opportunities, avoid abrupt social and environmental changes, and, for the most astute and agile, carve out competitive advantage.*
>
> **Millenium Ecosystem Assessment[3]**

However, even those companies that are developing the business strategy around sustainability are not aware of what is ahead. The changes are largely unknown, and the challenges and opportunities that these changes will bring are yet to be discovered.

1 Forum for the Future: the UK's leading sustainable development NGO. www.forumforthefuture.org.

2 Bent and Draper (2007) Leader Business Strategies: profitable today, sustainable tomorrow. Forum for the Future. October 2007. http://www.forumforthefuture.org/library/leader-business-strategies.

3 Millennium Ecosystem Assessment. (2005). Ecosystems and Human Well-being: Opportunities and Challenges for Business and Industry. Washington, DC.: World Resources Institute.

> *No company in the world is currently prepared for the changes ahead... whatever happens next, business as usual is not an option.*

Forum for the Future[4]

Business success in the years ahead will depend on sound business strategy that not only builds a good business operation, but benefits society and the planet at the same time.

Future Leaders

Never has leadership been more challenging than it is now. Both public and private sector organisations are seeking to restructure and transform themselves to seize the opportunities of a globally, connected world where people, driven by values and equipped with knowledge, will collaborate and innovate. Leadership will play a pivotal role in making this happen. As organisations move out of the old systems and into the new, evolving systems of the unknown, leadership is breaking into new grounds. New ways of working require new ways of leadership, as leaders work to hold old systems together as new ones are created, and then transfer between the two.

To be best able to deal with the changes, future leaders will need to:

- be adaptable
- be effective at leading in uncertainty
- be prepared for the unexpected
- have technical and professional knowledge
- be able to manage their (and others') anxieties and emotions
- be willing to work in new ways (often outside of their "comfort zone")
- be able to inspire and empower people
- have self-knowledge of own strengths and weaknesses
- have integrity.

4 Forum for the Future (2008) Acting now for a positive 2018, preparing for radical change: the next decade of business and sustainability. December 2008. http://www.forumforthefuture.org/library/acting-now-for-a-positive-2018.

A report produced by the Work Foundation[5] in January 2010 entitled "Exceeding expectations: the principles of outstanding leadership" concludes that truly people-centred leadership leads to more effective performance. In their research the Work Foundation identified nine themes which they felt characterised outstanding leaders and of those nine they felt there were three key principles of outstanding leadership. The report indicates that outstanding leaders should:

- think and act systemically in that they will view things as a whole rather than compartmentalise. These leaders will connect the parts by a guiding sense of purpose and through reaction to their actions will instil loyalty and commitment, provide a springboard for motivation and creativity and show trust in their staff by enabling them to take personal risks and succeed
- see people as the route to performance because they are deeply people and relationship centred rather than just people-oriented
- be self-confident without being arrogant as self-awareness is one of their fundamental attributes. They are motivated to achieve excellence but realise they cannot create performance themselves so they will act as conduits to performance through their influence on others.

Executives themselves acknowledge there is a gap in the leadership behaviours needed for the future and current leadership practices in their organisations.

Opportunity Now 2009[6]

There is some way to go before the present leaders fit these requirements. There are large disparities between what leaders need to be, and what they are now.

Three key problem areas are:

- style of management
- a crisis in trust
- boardroom scepticism.

5 Work Foundation. (2010). Exceeding Expectation:the principles of outstanding leadership. http://www.theworkfoundation.com.

6 Opportunity Now (2009) From website: http://www.opportunitynow.org.uk/research/leadership_for_change/index.html accessed 31 December 2009

Style of management ●●●

There are many styles of leadership. To give a view of the spectrum, the three classic styles are:

- laissez-faire (or free reign)
- autocratic (or authoritarian)
- participative (or democratic).

Laissez-faire leadership is fairly hands-off, with minimal direction and contact from the manager. This works well if the leader is working with a good team of well-trained and motivated individuals.

Autocratic leadership is at the other end of the scale, where leaders make decisions without consultation. Autocratic leaders are relied on for direction. Although this can mean that motivation and involvement are low, this style of leadership can suit organisations where decisions need to be made quickly and decisively.

Participative leadership seeks to find a middle ground through the leader's making decisions with others in the organisation. This is not a sign of weakness in the leader, but more a recognition that the leader does not have all the knowledge, and so better decisions can be made as a team.

Whilst it is often said that good leaders would use all three styles of leadership according to the situation, in reality, one style tends to dominate. Traditional styles of management based on hierarchies of command and control and influencing based solely on the power of position, whilst still definitely alive and kicking, are fast becoming outdated. In the new era, leaders will need to work in a flatter structure, across an organisation, to inspire and motivate a shared vision. Many of the present day leaders are still in the hierarchical mindset, so new skills and behaviours will need to be developed in the leaders of the future.

Edelman's 2009 trust barometer shows that less than 40% of informed people aged 35-64 trust business to do what is right in North America, the UK, France and Germany.

Opportunity Now 2009[6]

A Crisis in Trust ●●●

Future leaders will need to overcome the crisis in trust that present leaders are facing. As touched on in Chapter 1, trust in business and government is at a low, but this trust is essential for the transformation of organisations. Without trust, employees will not engage with leaders. Engagement is essential for any change programme to be successful.

Research indicates that, globally, confidence in leaders has been steadily declining in the last eight years. This is an enormous issue, as the pace of development and need for responsibility increases. The future needs leaders that can be trusted, and whom people trust.

Boardroom Scepticism

In July 2009 the Chartered Management Institute published a report "Lean and Green: leadership for the low-carbon future"[7] with some startling findings. The key messages to come out of the report were that managers do actually recognise the importance of cutting carbon emissions, but too few are taking action. This is a significant realisation, and reveals that there are barriers to moving towards a low-carbon economy that need to be removed. The next finding in the report is that although a large number of managers understand the importance of environmental impacts to the business, there is resistance at the senior management level. The reports states that "boardroom scepticism risks squandering widespread management enthusiasm," and recognises that it is the younger and junior managers that have the greatest levels of interest in change in this area. As already discussed, there are business benefits to embracing sustainability as an organisation, and this needs to be not only recognised by senior management, but led by the senior management.

> *Chief executives need to show leadership by demonstrating commitment and communicating a clear sense of direction.*
>
> **Wehrmeyer et al, 2009**

The Chartered Management Institute has produced a number of reports, papers and guidance to encourage and assist managers to integrate sustainability into the business agenda. The Institute advises organisations to:

- ensure that senior management lead change by putting in structures to resource low-carbon projects, allocating board level responsibility for change, ensuring that all employees have an understanding of the environmental agenda
- build in measurement capacity, so that the organisation has an understanding of its environmental impact and can measures changes to this. By doing this, management can get an understanding of where carbon emission reductions can be best achieved
- create value from environmental projects through cost-saving, gaining competitive advantage, gaining new business, considering business opportunities in low-carbon innovation of new products and services.

7 Chartered Management Institute. (2009). Lean and Green: Leadership for a low-carbon future. London: Chartered Management Institute

Business as Leaders ●●●

As well as business leaders taking responsibility within their own organisations, these leaders need to ensure that their business is leading too. A Forum for the Future report, "Acting now for a positive 2018"[8], suggests a number of actions that businesses should be taking now to lead into a positive future. The report suggests:

- looking for opportunities – new business opportunities that not only have benefits now, but also have positive on-going social and environmental benefits
- creating alliance with others – working with all stakeholders (including competitors) to find the most sustainable outcomes, and finding ways of creating change
- supporting the right kind of globalisation – one that benefits all parties
- engaging with institutional shareholders on sustainability – the shareholders need to understand the issues to back the longer-term vision
- developing creative partnerships – with other companies, the government, etc to work together to find solutions to problems.

It is becoming increasingly recognised that modern leaders need to be authentic in everything they do and be proficient at engaging with employees and others. Taking the business that they lead with them in this is paramount to thriving in the changing world that the future brings. Those businesses that are embracing new ways of working, and exploring opportunities are not only building firm foundations for themselves, but will be ahead of the competition as and when governments start driving low-carbon targets.

8 Forum for the Future (2008) Acting now for a positive 2018, preparing for radical change: the next decade of business and sustainability. December 2008. http://www.forumforthefuture.org/library/acting-now-for-a-positive-2018.

SECTION 3

Workplace

- Diversity
- Health and Well-being
- What Makes a Great Place to Work
- Work-life Balance
- Skills, Talent and Training

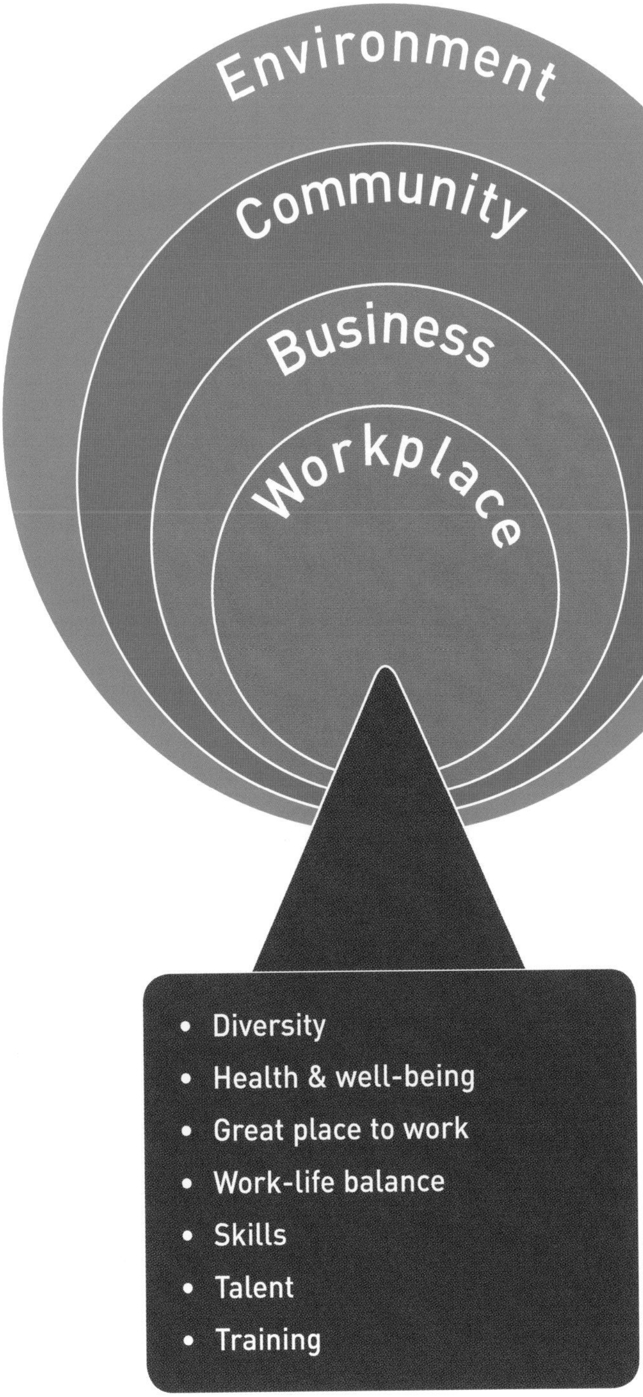
Environment
Community
Business
Workplace
• Diversity
• Health & well-being
• Great place to work
• Work-life balance
• Skills
• Talent
• Training

Workplace

Recognise and value difference

Enhanced terms and conditions

Skills and talent developed

Participation for all

Organisational change for good

Nice place to work

Strategies for inclusion

Integrity and trust

Business ethical practice

Leadership for the future

Employee engagement

CHAPTER 9

Diversity

- What is Diversity?
- How the Concept has Evolved
- The Case for Diversity
- Managing Diversity

What is Diversity?

Diversity is an acceptance of individuality and difference that is based on respect for these and an acknowledgment that they can enhance and enrich both people and organisations. It is recognised that combating discrimination, promoting equal opportunity and valuing the differences in individuals is morally, socially and economically advantageous. It adds value to an organisation - by making it more attractive to investors, would-be employees and customers - and improves output, both in quality and quantity. Diversity is for everyone with responsibility for directing, managing, supervising or influencing others within an organisation.

This recognition that everyone is different not only covers visible factors, such as colour of skin, but also invisible factors such as personal characteristics and background. These differences can be classified under three headings.

- **Social category diversity** - This relates to demographic differences such as age, race and gender.
- **Informational diversity** - These are organisational differences including educational background, length of service and function.
- **Value diversity** - This recognises psychological differences in personality and attitudes.

Many of these characteristics are protected under discrimination legislation in terms of race, disability, gender, religion and belief, sexual orientation and age. Responsible businesses will try to harness these differences to create a productive environment in which everyone feels valued, their talents are fully recognised and utilised and at the same time the goals of the organisation are being achieved. Diversity is valuing everyone as an individual and a business should extend that beyond employees to include customers, suppliers and other stakeholders.

The difficulty for any business is that in recognising and valuing difference it also becomes clear that there is no single method of dealing with employees as each one will have their own unique pattern of personal needs, values and beliefs. Responsible businesses are constantly striving for the notion of "best practice" but in the case of diversity it may only offer a theoretical solution rather than a truly practical one. It may be more appropriate to apply a "reasonable in this situation" approach, in other words, treat each case and individual separately recognising that the organisation's systems and procedures may have to be adapted.

How the Concept has Evolved

Legislation covering equal pay, sex and racial discrimination was enacted during the 1970's, a period of great change in terms of social and economic perspectives, and this was followed by laws relating to disability in the 1990's. Employment equality legislation affecting religion, religious belief and philosophical belief also came into force in 2003 followed by sexual orientation in 2004 and finally protection against age discrimination in 2006 and this has been partly driven by European legislation.

Case Study[1, 2 and 3]

Case studies

1. Age

One of the first cases brought under the age discrimination legislation happened in Northern Ireland in October 2008. The case involved a 58 year old man who had been turned down for a job as a salesman in a Belfast timber yard.

The tribunal concluded that, but for his age, he would "more probably than not" have been selected and also drew an inference of discrimination from the use of the phrase "youthful enthusiasm" in the original recruitment advertisement. The tribunal also made a link between the issue of age and the concept that had been referred to as "enthusiasm", "motivation" and "drive". There was also evidence that there had been age-related questions in the interview process. A spokesperson for the Equality Commission said that the decision of the tribunal highlighted the fact that discrimination on the grounds of age was unlawful.

Another tribunal held in April 2009 decided that a former NHS manager was discriminated against because of her age and as result was awarded £39,000 in damages. The lady was 56 years old at the time of the interview process and because of her years of service had previously indicated that she was planning to retire in 2010. The tribunal felt that she had been passed over for the position because she was nearing retirement and in their view that was age discrimination.

2. Religion/sexual orientation

A Christian registrar disciplined for refusing to conduct same-sex civil partnerships lost her appeal against this ruling. The registrar, employed by a London Council, said that she could not carry out same-sex ceremonies "as a matter of religious conscience" and as result her employer issued her with verbal and written warnings but did not suspend her.

In July 2008 an employment tribunal ruled that she had been harassed and discriminated against by the council because of her religious beliefs but in December 2008 the employment appeal tribunal ruled that the earlier tribunal had "erred in law" and there was no basis for concluding that

1 BBC News. (2008, October 1). Man wins age discrimination case. Retrieved November 21, 2009, from bbcnews.co.uk: http://www.news.bbc.co.uk/go/pr/fr/-/1/hi/northern_ireland/7180732.stm

2 BBC News. (2009, April 10). Payout in age discrimination case. Retrieved November 21, 2009, from bbcnews.co.uk: http://www.news.bbc.co.uk/1/hi/england/north_yorkshire/8002740.stm

3 BBC News. (2009, December 15). Registrar loses partnership case. Retrieved January 15, 2010, from bbcnews.co.uk: http://www.news.bbc.co.uk/go/pr/fr/-/1/hi/england/london/8413196.stm

discrimination had taken place. In December 2009 the Court of Appeal in London upheld the appeal tribunal's ruling and this was based on the legislation that requires a modern liberal democracy such as the UK to outlaw discrimination in the provision of goods or services on the grounds of sexual orientation.

A spokesperson for the Council said that the judgement confirmed that public sector employees must carry out their duties without discrimination and an Executive Director of the National Secular Society stated that "because a person has strong religious views it does not give them the right to discriminate against and to deny services to others of whom they disapprove".

3. Philosophical belief[4]

A man has been told that he can take his employer to tribunal on the grounds that he was unfairly dismissed because of his views on climate change. He had been made redundant from his post as head of sustainability but he felt that his beliefs had contributed to his dismissal and in March 2009 a judge ruled that he could use employment equality laws to make a claim for unfair dismissal. However the company he worked for appealed against this decision as it believed his views were political and that "green views" were not the same as religious or philosophical beliefs. The appeal court disagreed with this and found in favour of the employee. The solicitor representing the employee said, "Essentially what the judgement says is that a belief in man-made climate change and the alleged resulting moral imperative is capable of being a philosophical belief and is therefore protected by the 2003 religion or belief regulations."

4 BBC News. (2009, November 3). Eco-employee wins bid to appeal. Retrieved December 12, 2009, from bbcnews.co.uk: http://www.news.bbc.co.uk/go/pr/fr/-/1/hi/england/oxfordshire/8339652.stm

However, all these initiatives have been based on trying to create a level playing field for groups that have been seen to be disadvantaged in the past. They have attempted to end or reduce discrimination and thereby improve social justice which means they have been about equal opportunities but not really about diversity. All this legislation has been important and all businesses have to ensure that they comply but it is also true to say that there has often been limited success in achieving the goals that the legislators intended.

In the last few years it has been realised that there should be a shift from equal opportunities to diversity for two important reasons. Firstly, the equal opportunities approach is insufficiently holistic in its attempts to eliminate discrimination and many disadvantaged groups are still not covered by the legislation (and where they are they are dealt with as homogeneous groups rather than as individuals). The second reason refers to the growing evidence from research that shows that culturally diverse teams are often more creative and effective than homogeneous teams in meeting organisational goals. This indicates that there is a business case for diversity but the challenges facing a business wishing to make this shift are far greater than simply managing equal opportunities and complying with its legal obligations.

In October 2007 a new Equality and Human Rights Commission was established to add to the already existing Commissions for Equal Opportunities, Racial Equality and Disability Rights.

Responsible businesses cannot afford to ignore the fact that many individuals involved with their business operation suffer from some form of disability and the business may well be in breach of legislation if it fails to take action on making its premises accessible. Supermarkets, banks and public service providers have a greater obligation to provide fully accessible services.

Disability is defined under the Disability Discrimination Act (DDA) as, "A physical or mental impairment which has a substantial and long-term adverse effect on the person's ability to carry out normal day to day activities."

Disability Facts and Figures[5]**:**

- 9 million adult disabled people in the UK.
- 6.9 million disabled people are in employment – almost 20% of the UK workforce.
- 17% of disabled people are born with their disability meaning 83% acquire their disability during their working life.
- 70% of disabled people have difficulty accessing goods and services.
- 80% of city centres pose significant problems for disabled shoppers.
- 25% of high street businesses have been rated as having poor disability access.
- 20% of disabled people have difficulty accessing hospitals and clinics.
- 17% of disabled people have difficulty accessing Banks or Post Offices.
- 17% of organisations questioned had a spontaneous awareness of DDA.
- The majority of small businesses "file" or discard information on DDA.
- By the year 2020 50% of the population will be over 50.
- Current statistics prove that the majority of disabilities are acquired after the age of 50 which means that by 2020 32% of the population could well be disabled.
- A stroke is the most common cause of severe disability in the UK : every year strokes affect more than 150,000 individuals, of whom 10% are under retirement age.
- Approximately 9 million people have some kind of hearing impairment.
- There are 2 million visually impaired people.

The statistics relating to access to city centres and shopping will also affect the employees and therefore would appear to contravene the notion of inclusion and could also be perceived as indirect discrimination.

By 2024 the retirement age for both males and females will rise to 66 and by 2044 it will have risen to 68. This is due to the fact we are all living longer which is bringing about an increased burden on the state pension provision. As the majority of disabilities are acquired at, or after, the age of 50 there is a potential for employers to experience vastly increased numbers of disabled employees.

5 UK council for access and equality. (2009, December 20). Facts and figures. Retrieved December 20, 2009, from ukcae.co.uk: http://www.ukcae.co.uk/factsfigures.html

The Case for Diversity

The social justice or equality case – is based on the argument that everyone has a right to equal access to employment and when in employment should be entitled to equal pay and equal access to training and development. All employees should also be free of any direct or indirect discrimination and harassment and bullying.

- **Direct Discrimination** occurs when a person can prove they have been treated less favourably than another person on prohibited grounds.
- **Indirect Discrimination** occurs where there is a practice, provision or criterion, applied uniformly, which would put a specific group of people at a particular disadvantage and is not shown to be a proportionate means of achieving a legitimate aim. This covers formal requirements, conditions and provisions as well as informal practices.

This can best be described as the right to be treated fairly and current legislation sets out minimum standards.

Case Study[6]

One of the largest law firms in the city of London announced that from the middle of 2010 it would allow its top partners to work a four-day week or take additional leave in an effort to encourage more women into the role. Most city law firms already allow junior lawyers and support staff to work flexibly but the most senior lawyers have had to work full time.

In 2010 it is expected that 62% of the graduates recruited will be female but at the beginning of 2010 only 15% of its partners are women. The firm suggested that the lack of female partners was not due to sexism but rather because many young women found the prospect of becoming a partner unappealing and law firms in general had not been active enough at offering alternatives to improve retention. Many female staff leave in their early thirties, on the verge of becoming partners, deciding that starting a family is inconsistent with the demands of a top law firm. The firm found that its brightest young women lawyers were leaving at twice the rate of their male counterparts and so is introducing new ways to encourage its female staff to stay on.

6 Catalyst. (2007, October 1). Companies With More Women Board Directors Experience Higher Financial Performance, According to Latest Catalyst Bottom Line Report . Retrieved January 11, 2010, from catalyst.org: http://www.catalyst.org/press-release/73/companies-with-more-women-board-directors-experience-higher-financial-performance-according-to-latest-catalyst-bottom-line-report.

The business case - as already indicated, to provide real equality of opportunity a business needs to treat individuals differently in ways that are regarded as fair and ideally tailored to the needs of that individual. The social justice case and the business case for diversity are overlapping in that employees who feel that they are being treated unfairly will underperform as they will be much less committed to meeting the goals of the organisation and obviously the reverse is also true. Businesses that fully embrace diversity have experienced much better overall financial performance.

A study of Fortune 500 companies over a four year period correlated those with the highest representation of women directors to those with higher financial performances and found that companies with the highest percentage of women board directors considerably outperformed those with the lowest percentages by 53% on return on equity, 42% on return on sales and 66% on return on invested capital. The study, "The Bottom Line: Corporate Performance and Women's Representation on Boards"[7] also found the strongest results prevailed at companies with three or more women board directors.

The DTI published "Building Better Boards[8]" in December 2004, which was a product of extensive discussions with business and it concluded that there were real benefits to be had by more diverse boards. The key messages are as follows.

- Companies should be thinking more systematically about the effectiveness of their boards, their recruitment processes and the way in which they develop their own people.
- Boards which have the scope to consider a wider range of perspectives and generate richer, more informed discussion of the issues facing the company, are more likely to anticipate problems and produce high quality solutions.
- Board members with diverse experiences and backgrounds bring varied and complementary perspectives, contribute in the making of strong and dynamic boards and lead to companies that can compete successfully in the global economy.
- There are real business benefits which companies can derive from broadening the base of their boards and bringing in fresh minds with different skills and new perspectives to contribute to the growth and development of the business.
- Good corporate governance is ultimately about people. The key to building better boards is a commitment from the top down to the dynamic development of the board in the best interests of the company.
- This report can provide managers with an overview of the scope of development available for their talented executives, enabling them to make a positive contribution in a boardroom in the future.

7 Catalyst Inc. (2007, October). The Bottom Line: Corporate Performance and Women's Representation on Boards. Retrieved January 11, 2010, from catalyst.org: http:www.catalyst.org/publication/200/the-bottom-line-corporate-performance-and-womens-representation-on-boards

8 DTI. (2004). Building Better Boards. Retrieved January 11, 2010, from berr.gov.uk: http://www.berr,gov.uk/whatwedo/businesslaw/corp-governance/better-boards/page17362.html

- It can also provide an overview for aspiring executives as to the skills required to secure a position on the board of a UK company. It also includes a range of case studies demonstrating how individuals and businesses have pursued their own and their staff's development.

It is becoming more and more apparent that those businesses prepared to introduce diversity policies to their organisations which go well beyond the requirements of current legislation (thereby ensuring that diversity is embedded in the culture of their practices) are much better prepared to deal with the prospect of increasingly complex legal obligations in the future. There are also three broad areas of benefit to any business that incorporates diversity into all that they do relating to improvements in employee relations, marketing edge and the image and corporate reputation of the business.

With regard to employee relations it is true to say that people will aspire to work for businesses with good employment practices and they need to feel valued at their place of work. Businesses wishing to be competitive will want to gain the best possible contribution from the whole of their staff. Skill shortages and also difficulties in filling particular vacancies have caused many businesses to widen the pool from which they recruit, leading to a more diverse workforce, and in some cases they have also produced a range of alternative employment packages and working arrangements. This all leads to the creation of an open and inclusive workplace culture where the employees feel respected. Valuing diversity means activating and promoting the processes that that will achieve this inclusive environment: putting into place policies and procedures that welcome and include different perspectives and practices. Inclusion is the state where social and environmental barriers to equality of access and opportunity, contribution to and participation in the workplace are removed.

Such organisations will see a marked improvement in absence and retention rates because employers who offer good working conditions benefit from more positive and committed employees, who are less likely to leave and employees who are happier at work are less likely to suffer from stress or become sick, leading to fewer disruptions in production or service. These businesses will also find that they will attract a better quality of applicant when recruiting which in turn brings about a diverse workforce which tends to be more creative and innovative.

It is also important to realise that diversity not only involves how employees see themselves but also how they perceive others as these perceptions will affect how they interact with other individuals involved with the business. For a diverse group of employees to operate effectively as an organisation, HR managers need to ensure that there are systems in place to deal effectively with communications and the workforce's adaptability to change. Successful businesses will be those who invest the time and money now on the resources necessary to manage diversity in the workplace going forward.

The benefits to the business brought about by workplace diversity are as follows.

Increased adaptability

Often businesses with a diverse workforce can supply a greater variety of solutions to problems found within the business as their employees can bring individual talents and experiences to the fore when making suggestions or generating ideas that can bring about a much greater flexibility and adaptability within the business making it better able to cope with changing markets and customer expectations.

Broader service range

With an increased set of skills and experiences, as well as different languages and cultures to draw upon, many businesses find themselves in a position to provide goods or services to a much wider customer base, usually on a global level.

Variety of viewpoints

A diverse workforce with a larger pool of ideas and experiences can meet strategic targets more efficiently as well as meeting the needs and requirements of the customers more effectively. However this can only happen if there are channels of communication available for staff to put across their points of view and also, crucially, staff confidence to do so.

More effective execution

Employees can gain inspiration from being proud of their place of work and as a result will perform to the highest level of their ability which means that company-wide strategies can be executed leading to greater productivity, profit and better returns on investment.

Business in the Community's "Race for Opportunity" campaign is a network of over 160 private and public sector organisations working across the UK to promote the business case for race and diversity by:

- raising awareness of barriers to progress in the workplace
- communicating the need for the introduction of policies that better represent ethnic minorities
- highlighting the responsibilities of leaders in delivering race diversity
- making clear the business argument for investing in race diversity.

The campaign has identified four key areas of business activity which demonstrates the business case for working on race in the UK and in June 2009 the Benchmarking Report "Transparency at the heart of diversity" was published which looked at these areas. The report looks at:

- employment including attraction, recruitment, selection, development, progression and retention of talented ethnic minority people
- how organisations market goods and services to ethnic minorities as profitable consumers
- community involvement activities and initiatives that ensure the inclusion ethnic minority individuals and communities
- how organisations engage ethnic minority businesses in their supply chain and as business partners.

The Current UK Landscape[9]

Just over 60% of ethnic minorities in the UK are currently employed by comparison with just over 75% of the white population.

Ethnic minorities make up 11% of the working age population, 20% of the secondary school population and almost 25% of the primary school age group.

Employment by ethnicity at the end of 2008 showed 76.2% employment for white individuals with the smallest proportion of employment being amongst the Pakistani population at 48.3%.

Figure 1

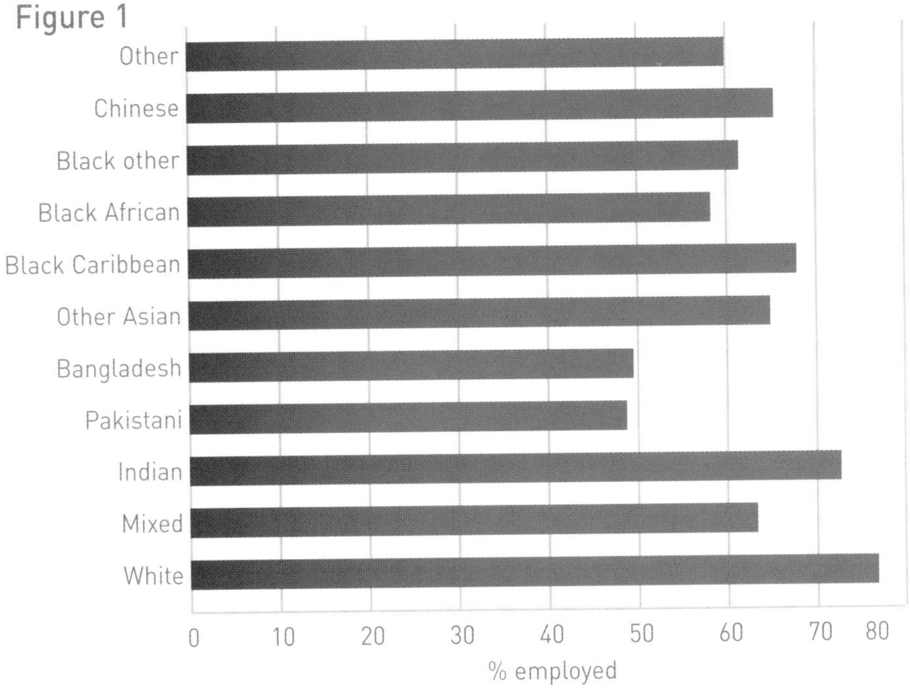

9 Business in the Community. (2009, June). Resources. Retrieved January 11, 2010, from bitc.org.uk: http://www.bitc.org.uk/resources

90% or more of the employers network monitored the ethnicity of job applicants, effectively communicated their policies and objectives on race, were committed to engaging with ethnic minority customers, ensured that their community involvement benefited ethnic minority people and communicated their commitment to race with existing and prospective suppliers.

Seventy nine organisations provided information on the total number of people they employed broken down by ethnic minority and by their position within the organisation and it showed that 4.3% of those were employed at board level, and that 5% of senior executives, 6.9% of managers and 9.8% of other employees were from ethnic minority groups.

The Benefits

Diversity policies within the organisation fit very well with quality assurance models of excellence such as Investors in People. These policies also create the type of environment where people from all backgrounds can work together free from stereotyping, harassment, prejudice and disrespectful behaviour and they are also likely to bring about cultural change.

The second broad area of benefit mentioned previously was marketing edge or market competitiveness and this relates to the fact that a diverse workforce can enhance the development of new product or service ideas as well as simply improving an existing product or service leading to a widening customer base. Examples might include financial services businesses offering packages aimed at ethnic minority businesses or supermarkets who are now offering a range of products to suit the preferences of a variety of nationalities.

The third broad area of benefit relates to image and corporate reputation as many major businesses have now realised. As a result they have expanded their reporting of corporate social responsibility (CSR) to include information concerning their policies and targets relating to diversity. These businesses have accepted the fact that their social responsibility goes beyond environmental issues as a healthy business needs to flourish within a healthy society (and, as seen in earlier chapters, the needs of people, communities and businesses are interrelated). An increasing number of businesses recognise that their overall image is very important in attracting and retaining both customers and employees. It could be argued that the CSR position of a business creates a form of contract between the business and the community or communities in which it operates.

The ethical behaviour of a business is also very important when it comes to corporate reputation so the setting of standards utilising value statements that the business ensures are adhered to will send out clear and positive messages to present and future customers', suppliers and employees.

This can also be achieved by the introduction of innovative "dignity at work" policies which attempt to eliminate all forms of intimidating behaviour by clearly stating that any such behaviour would be seen as contravening the values of the business and will be treated as serious disciplinary matters.

Case Study

A global soft drinks company has produced its own Workplace Rights Policy because, as they state themselves, they value the relationship they have with all their employees. They feel that the success of their business depends on every employee in their global enterprise.

The company's Workplace Rights Policy is guided by international human rights standards and applies to the whole company which also encourages their independent bottling partners to uphold these principles within their businesses.

The policy covers:

- freedom of association and collective bargaining
- forced labour
- child labour
- discrimination
- work hours and wages
- safe and Healthy Workplace
- workplace security
- community and stakeholder engagement.

The policy's key words are Respect, Communication, Rights, Trust, Dignity and Community. The employees of the company are also encouraged to highlight any conflict that they feel arises between the language of the policy and the laws, customs and practices of the place where they work.

Managing Diversity ●●●

Managing diversity is crucial if employees are to have the opportunity to maximise their potential and be encouraged to develop themselves to further enhance their contribution to the business. Employees with different backgrounds can offer new ideas and perceptions which can greatly improve the business's efficiency along with its products and services. To manage this diversity successfully a business must encourage and capture creativity and innovation in order to maximise the benefit of its capacity for growth and increased competitiveness.

As the economy becomes increasingly global, the workforce becomes increasingly diverse. Organizational success and competitiveness will depend on the ability to manage diversity in the workplace effectively.

As can be seen by the example of the Coca Cola Company, the lead needs to start at the top of the organisation so the board members will have to be fully committed or change will not occur. However there are often challenges for any management who wish to bring about a more open workplace and these can include the breaking down of cultural and language barriers as excellence in communications is central. People must be willing and able to talk to each other and listen to each other, and respect different views and ideas. Ineffective communication, on the other hand, can result in complexity, ambiguity, lack of teamwork, low morale and conflict. Management may also experience resistance to change from some of the workforce who would prefer things to stay the same. Another challenge will be for the organisation to produce appropriate diversity policies which will maximise the benefits to the business. A staff development programme will also have to be developed but training alone will not be sufficient. A strategy should be in place to ensure that diversity permeates through every department and function within the organisation.

To achieve success with regard to the introduction of diversity policies the following steps have proved to be useful. By involving every employee in formulating and implementing diversity initiatives the business is far more likely to remove the possibility of resistance to change. Encouraging employees to express themselves by giving their ideas and opinions enables an attitude of openness and equality to be created. Many organisations promote diversity in leadership positions which provides visibility for the policies and highlights the benefits of diversity in the workplace. Many businesses also carry out an annual employee satisfaction survey which provides comprehensive coverage of important issues including diversity. The results from these surveys will then be used to inform the management of how best to revise their diversity policies.

A number of responsible businesses have appointed a 'diversity champion'. This is someone within the business who agrees to take on the task of identifying and understanding the best practice in that particular industry and reporting back to a senior member of the organisation. Many organisations promoting diversity run membership schemes for businesses and are good places to find help and support.

Managing diversity can also lead to ensuring that employee well-being is considered as an essential element of employee engagement and motivation as well as of retention of talent. It is a continuing process, and is at least partly about managing conflict, complexity and ambiguity. Ultimately organisations should aim to make managing diversity a mainstream issue, owned by everyone so that it influences all employment policies and working practices.

CHAPTER 10

Health and Well-being

- Sickness and Absence
- Mental Well-being
- Management Standards for Work-related Stress
- NICE Guidance

Sickness and Absence ●●●

Absence from work cost the UK economy £13.2 billion in 2007 as the average employee took almost seven (6.7) days off sick, while the gulf between absence rates in the public sector and the private sector grew to a record level, as new research revealed in May 2008.

The CBI/AXA Absence Survey[1] showed that average absence levels across the public sector stood at 9 days, which is 55% higher than the 5.8 day average of the private sector. The private sector improved its absence levels over 2007, while the public sector stood still. The authors of the survey estimated that £1.4bn of taxpayers' money could be saved if public sector organisations matched the private sector average.

The survey also revealed that of the 172 million days lost to absence in 2007, more than one in ten (12%) are thought to be non-genuine. These 21 million "sickies" cost the economy £1.6bn and two-thirds (65%) of employers think that some staff are using them to extend weekends. 60% said that fake sickness was used to extend holiday, and a third of employers (34%) suspect that sickies are used for special events like birthdays and major football games. One solution to this problem may be to look at issues concerning employee engagement which will be explored in the next chapter.

Long-term absence (20 days or more) also continued to be a serious concern for firms. Although only 5% of absence spells became long-term, they accounted for a massive 40% of all time lost, costing £5.3bn. Long-term absence accounted for half (50%) of all time lost in the public sector, but under a third (31%) in the private sector. Those with long-term illnesses need time to recover so responsible businesses will look at cases, like those involving stress or back pain and offer phased returns to work. Businesses that keep in touch with employees and offer flexible working have been successful at reducing long-term absence levels.

A spokesperson for the CBI stated that a fresh, proactive approach to managing long-term absence was needed to help stem the flow onto incapacity benefit as this will help employers to retain skilled employees, many of whom will find that work can improve their health and outlook. They also questioned whether there was a medical explanation for the higher levels of long-term absence in the public sector or whether low morale, poor management and a culture of absence are at least partly to blame.

The NHS, which continues to struggle to deal with people suffering from these conditions, is partly to blame, but arguably the bigger culprit is ineffectual management that lets people drift rather than helping them to get better.

1 CBI. (2008, May 15). Absence and sickness survey. Retrieved January 11, 2010, from cbi.org.uk: http://www.cbi.org.uk/ndbs/press.nsf/0363c1f07c6ca12a8025671c00381cc7/90ab71d2f4d981da8025744200523b87?OpenDocument

Absence levels varied greatly across organisations, and there were 9.3 days of difference between the best and worst performers. The survey showed that, while a certain level of absence is both acceptable and inevitable, absence can be managed and reduced through a mixture of 'carrot and stick' policies, like offering medical insurance, health support or flexible working, whilst also having formal absence management processes, such as not paying sick pay for the first three days of absence. There were many individual examples of superb performance across different types of public sector organisations which suggests that the right policies can make a difference.

It was suggested that short-term absence shouldn't be an issue for employers who have a positive workplace culture where people are treated fairly and believe they have a future. Minor ailments, such as colds, were named as the most significant cause of short-term absence, while back pain came second.

Illness was easily the most common reason for absence, but over half of employers said staff taking time off to deal with home and family responsibilities was a cause of absence. A third of employers said staff took time off to wait for medical appointments, which highlights the need to make GP opening hours more flexible. Long-term absence – which is mainly due to stress, anxiety and depression and to back pain and other musculoskeletal disorders – is still a big problem, accounting for forty per cent of lost working time. Non-work-related stress, anxiety and depression was the most significant cause of long-term absence among non-manual staff. In 2007 the average direct cost of absence was £517 per employee - or 3.1% of payroll - which includes lost production and the expense of covering absence with temporary staff or overtime. The CBI also estimates that indirect costs, such as lower customer satisfaction, add another £263 per employee per year. When these indirect costs are added to the direct cost, the UK lost £19.9bn to absence in 2007.

When early intervention and treatment are so well established and readily to hand it is no accident that employers who provide access to this have lower absence rates than those who don't.

When asked what three steps the government could take to help employers reduce absence, 56% of respondents also asked for more flexible GP hours and 60% wanted a better partnership between GPs and occupational health professionals. More than two-thirds of employers want them to prioritise the introduction of capability-focused medical certificates. "Fit notes" would help an employer understand what duties an employee can perform, helping them to make arrangements where possible for an earlier or phased return to work.

More than two thirds of organisations (69%) said they have a well-being policy, which encourages staff to lead healthier, happier lives. 70% felt that 'praise for a job well done' is the most important factor in raising staff morale. However, while 68% of private employers believe morale is good or satisfactory in their organisations, only 54% of public employers agreed.

Another report published in 2008[2] suggested that as ill health costs the economy over £100bn per year a fundamental overhaul of the support given to workers who are off work through illness is needed. The report, commissioned by ministers, called for a new fit-note system as well as fit for work schemes to be embedded in the NHS to help people back to work.

The reforms could help cut the numbers on incapacity benefit which currently sees some 350,000 people a year move from long-term sick notes in to the system. This means that Britain has one of the highest proportions of people on benefit in Europe and numbers have more than trebled since the 1970s to 2.7m.

The author of the report believed that workers need help at an earlier stage to stop them slipping out of work and into a spiral of dependency because, as already indicated, some 172 million working days are lost each year, costing the economy £100bn in lost productivity, benefits and taxes. For most people their work is a key factor in their self-worth, family esteem and identity but it is so easy to fall out of work and move to a place where their confidence and well-being suffers. Businesses must do more to help people, because early intervention can stop the longer-term problems emerging.

The report proposed the creation of a new fit note which encourages GPs to spell out what the individual can do rather than cannot do. These notes could be given to the employer with the agreement of the employee in order for the employer to give appropriate support to enable a return to work.

The report also said businesses should do more to facilitate flexible working, such as shorter working weeks or a change of duties, to get staff back as quickly as possible.

Larger businesses should also establish their own occupational health and rehabilitation teams and promote healthy lifestyles through subsidised gym membership and encouraging staff to walk and cycle to work.

The key recommendations of the report were for:

- GPs to change the current sick note system to a fit-note one spelling out what a patient can do
- employers to offer more support to staff including healthy lifestyle promotion as well as access to occupational health teams
- the NHS to call for a pilot "fit for health scheme" which will work via GP referral. Case managers will be appointed to manage an individual's absence through access to physiotherapists, counselling and advice. Such a system would be essential to smaller companies which could not support their own occupational health teams.

2 BBC News. (2008, March). Illness costs UK £100bn. Retrieved January 11, 2010, from news.bbc.co.uk: http://news.bbc.co.uk/go/pr/fr/-/1/hi/health/7297174.stm

Mental Well-being ●●●

Mental well-being is a dynamic state in which the individual is able to develop their potential, work productively and creatively, build strong and positive relationships with others and contribute to their community. It is enhanced when an individual is able to fulfil their personal and social goals and achieve a sense of purpose in society[3].

The working environment, the work itself and the individual concerned all have a bearing on mental well-being at work.

Work can benefit mental well-being providing self-esteem, identity and, of course, an income, but it can also have an adverse effect.

Recent statistics confirm that work-related stress is widespread in the UK working population and is not confined to particular sectors or high risk jobs or industries. That is why a population-wide approach is necessary to tackle it.

Summary of statistics from the Health and Safety Executive[4].

- In 2008/09 an estimated 415 000 individuals in Britain, who worked in the last year, believed that they were experiencing work-related stress at a level that was making them ill.
- The 2009 Psychosocial Working Conditions (PWC) survey indicated that around 16.7% of all working individuals thought their job was very or extremely stressful.
- The annual incidence of work-related mental health problems in Britain in 2008 was approximately 5,126 new cases per year. However, this almost certainly underestimates the true incidence of these conditions in the British workforce.
- According to self-reports an estimated 230,000 people, who worked in the last 12 months, first became aware of work-related stress, depression or anxiety in 2008/09, giving an annual incidence rate of 760 cases per 100,000 workers.
- Estimates indicate that self-reported work-related stress, depression or anxiety accounted for an estimated 11.4 million lost working days in Britain in 2008/09

3 The Government Office for Science. London. Foresight Mental Capital and Wellbeing Project. (2008).

4 Health and Safety Executive. (2010, February 8). Statistics. Retrieved February 8, 2010, from hse.gov.uk: http://www.hse.gov.uk/statistics/causdis/stress/index.htm

- Data suggests the incidence rate of self-reported work-related stress, depression or anxiety has been broadly level over the years 2001/02 to 2008/09, with the exception of 2001/02 where the incidence rate was higher than the current level.
- Surveillance data from General Practitioners indicates that 30.9% of all diagnoses of work-related ill-health are cases of mental ill-health, with an average length of sickness absence per certified case of 26.8 working days.

The Health and Safety Executive (HSE) also estimates the costs to society of work-related stress to be around £4 billion each year with 13.5 million working days lost in 2007/8.

The Mental Health Foundation[5] mounted a survey to highlight this area of concern. A total of 577 respondents completed a questionnaire which sought information on the amount of time they devote to work, their reasons for it, their feelings about it and the impact it has on other aspects of their life. The key findings from this survey are outlined below.

- One third of respondents feel unhappy or very unhappy about the time they devote to work.
- More than 40% of employees are neglecting other aspects of their life because of work, which may increase their vulnerability to mental health problems.
- When working long hours more than a quarter of employees feel depressed (27%), one third feel anxious (34%), and more than half feel irritable (58%).
- The more hours you spend at work, the more hours outside of work you are likely to spend thinking or worrying about it.
- As a person's weekly hours increase, so do their feelings of unhappiness.
- Many more women report unhappiness than men (42% of women compared with 29% of men), which is probably a consequence of competing life roles and more pressure to 'juggle'.
- Nearly two thirds of employees have experienced a negative effect on their personal life, including lack of personal development, physical and mental health problems, and poor relationships and poor home life.

The HSE have designed the "Management Standards" approach to help employers manage the causes of work-related stress requiring management and staff to work together. The standards refer to six areas of work that can lead to stress if not properly managed. The HSE have felt it necessary to produce these standards for managers as bad management practice is a major contributor to stress in the workplace. Line managers play a vital role in identifying and managing stress within the business as they are likely to see the problems which cause stress first hand and are often the first point of contact. The HSE feel that it is essential that managers have the skills and behaviours to be able to manage these situations.

Unfortunately a survey published in November 2009 shows the impact that bad management has on staff as almost half of workers polled in the UK said that they

5 Mental Health Foundation. (2003, April 22). Whose life is it anyway? Retrieved January 15, 2010, from mhf.org.uk: http://www.mhf.org.uk/media/news-releases/news-releases-2003/22-april-2003/

had left a job because of bad management and that, given the option, they would rather take a pay cut than be managed by someone with poor skills. The survey, conducted for the Chartered Institute of Management, was part of the launch platform for a programme to improve management skills.

Part of the reason seems to be the number of people that end up with management responsibility without having sought it, and without being properly trained or prepared for it. 68% of respondents said that they had entered a management role by chance rather than by intent, with 40% suggesting they had not wanted the responsibility at all.

The Chartered Institute of Management has launched a manifesto[6] for a "Better Managed Britain" to address what it believes is a major problem, affecting the well–being of workers at all levels in businesses across the country.

What are the HSE Management Standards for Work-related Stress?[7] ●●●

The Management Standards define the characteristics, or culture, of an organisation where the risks from work-related stress are being effectively managed and controlled.

The Management Standards cover six key areas of work design that, if not properly managed, are associated with poor health and well-being, lower productivity and increased sickness absence. In other words, the six Management Standards cover the primary sources of stress at work. These are:

- **demands** – this includes issues such as workload, work patterns and the work environment
- **control** – how much say the person has in the way they do their work
- **support** – this includes the encouragement, sponsorship and resources provided by the organisation, line management and colleagues
- **relationships** – this includes promoting positive working to avoid conflict and dealing with unacceptable behaviour
- **pole** – whether people understand their role within the organisation and whether the organisation ensures that they do not have conflicting roles
- **change** – how organisational change (large or small) is managed and communicated in the organisation.

6 Management Manifesto pledge. (2010, February 8). Retrieved February 8, 2010, from managers.org.uk: http://www.managers.org.uk/practical-support/management-community/blogs/Are-you-ready-to-take-the-management-pledge-894

7 Health and Safety Executive. (2010, February 8). Management Standards for work related stress. Retrieved February 8, 2010, from hse.gov.uk: http://www.hse.gov.uk/stress/standards/index.htm

The Management Standards represent a set of conditions that, if present, reflect a high level of well-being and organisational performance.

The Management Standards:

- demonstrate good practice through a step by step risk assessment approach
- allow assessment of the current situation using surveys and other techniques
- promote active discussion and working in partnership with employees to help decide on practical improvements that can be made
- help simplify risk assessment for work related stress by:
  - identifying the main risk factors for work related stress
  - helping employers focus on the underlying causes and their prevention; and
  - providing a yardstick by which organisations can gauge their performance in tackling the key causes of stress.

NICE Guidance[8]

In 2009, the National Institute for Health and Clinical Excellence (NICE) said the cost of work related mental illness was £28bn. They also said that employers need to pay more attention to the levels of stress and anxiety in the workplace.

Their report, in line with the HSE, indicated that bad managers were the single biggest cause of problems but said simple steps such as giving positive feedback, allowing flexible working and giving extra days off as a reward could cut the impact by a third. As well as taking measures like these, NICE urged employers to invest in training for managers and mentoring for staff to help career development.

The report provided similar figures to the HSE quoting that 13 million working days a year are lost because of work related stress, anxiety and depression but provided a much larger estimate of the cost. Once the pay of staff, lost productivity and replacing ill employees are taken into account, the cost to employers hits £28.3bn a year.

To convince employers to act, NICE has designed a calculator to show the potential savings of supporting staff more. It suggests that for the average firm of 1,000 staff, £250,000 a year could be saved.

An expert in workplace psychology from Lancaster University who helped draw up the recommendations, said, "You cannot overestimate the importance of saying 'Well done,' to staff, but so often it does not happen. Managers will tell you when you are doing something wrong, but not when you are doing it right." He also went on to say that the problem was not just taking time off but that "presenteeism", where people come to work but add no value, is, if anything, more of a problem.

His remarks are supported by a recent survey by the Chartered Institute of Personnel

8 NICE. (2009, November 5). New guidance on mental wellbeing. Retrieved December 11, 2009, from nice.org.uk: http://www.nice.org.uk/newsroom/pressreleases/pressreleasearchive/PressReleases2009.jsp?domedia=1&mid=BFF2563A-19B9-E0B5-D4795A6FB7EA2096

and Development which revealed a quarter of UK workers describe their mental health as moderate or poor, yet nearly all continued to work regularly.

The NICE report said with the right environment work can even be a force for good as it can offer stability, purpose, friendship and distraction.

The main recommendations of the report were as follows.

Recommendations made for employers in organisations of all sizes include:

- promote a culture of participation, equality and fairness that is based on open communication and inclusion
- create an awareness and understanding of mental well-being and reduce the potential for discrimination and stigma related to mental health problems
- ensure systems are in place for assessing and monitoring the mental well-being of employees so that areas for improvement can be identified and risks caused by work and working conditions addressed. This could include using employee attitude surveys and information about absence rates, staff turnover and investment in training and development, and providing feedback and open communication
- if reasonably practical, provide employees with opportunities for flexible working according to their needs and aspirations in both their personal and working lives. Different options for flexible working include part-time working, home-working, job sharing and flexitime
- strengthen the role of line managers in promoting the mental well-being of employees through supportive leadership style and management practices.

Recommendations made for professionals working in occupational health services along with those involved in national initiatives and programmes from government and the Federation of Small Businesses include collaborating with micro, small and medium-sized businesses and offering advice and a range of support and services. This could include access to occupational health services (including counselling support and stress management training).

> *Mental health problems in UK workplaces are both widespread and largely invisible. Many employers ignore such issues, yet bear the consequences every day through reduced productivity and high absence from work. The NICE report highlights the preventative effect which well-managed workplaces and well-designed jobs can have on resilience. We need more UK workplaces to embrace these practices if the burden of mental health problems is to be reduced.*

Stephen Bevan, Managing Director of The Work Foundation [9]

The health and well-being of employees makes an essential contribution to business success and employees are at their most productive when they are in a responsible workplace that supports their health and well-being. Even a small on-going investment in the well-being of employees can pay big dividends for the business. This investment can improve the bottom line, reduce absenteeism, improve staff retention and also create a motivated and vibrant workplace. Creating healthy workplaces makes good business sense and hopefully leads to healthy profits.

Encouraging 'Wellness' to Improve Health

If employees are encouraged to protect their health this can enable them to deal more effectively with unavoidable stresses at work. Organisations can help by offering:

- individual development plans and regular appraisals to provide an opportunity to review work-life balance on a regular basis
- information and guidance on health issues
- health screening
- subsidised private healthcare
- on site exercise facilities or subsidised access to gyms
- healthy eating options.

9 The Work Foundation. (2009, November 5). Reaction to NICE guidance. Retrieved January 11, 2010, from theworkfoundation.com: http://www.theworkfoundation.com/pressmedia/news/newsarticle.aspx?oItemid=191

Case Study[10]

A London based company involved in the pharmaceutical industry had the objective of ensuring the personal well-being of its employees and found that it helped to maintain the innovation and creativity needed to remain competitive in a global environment. Its health and well-being initiatives included:

- health promotion activities
- home-work balance initiatives
- ergonomically designed working environments
- fitness opportunities
- healthy eating options in restaurants
- health assessments
- a counselling and life management programme
- fast-track healthcare insurance
- rehabilitation programmes
- integrated occupational health/HR interventions.

The benefits to the business were as follows.

Cost savings

- £500-£700,000 saved through improved productivity after counselling.
- £80,000 saved on health insurance costs for psychological illness.

Improved Health and Safety

- Global accident and occupational illness rates reduced by 61%.
- High employee awareness and rating for employee assistance programme.

Improved image

- 84% of employees proud to work for the company.
- 82% of employees think it a good place to work.
- 80% of employees felt they had flexibility to balance work and personal life.
- 88% of employees stated that the company had a commitment to their health and well-being.

Recognition

- The company was named Britain's Healthiest Large Employer in 2006.
- Recognised as top employer by Science magazine for four consecutive years.

10 Business in the Community. (2009). Healthy People = Healthy Profits. BITC.

CHAPTER 11

What Makes a Great Place to Work?

- What Does Make a Great Workplace?
- What is a 'Good Job'?
- Trust and the Psychological Contract
- Employee Engagement

What Does Make a Great Workplace?

According to the Great Place to Work® Institute[1], a global research and management consultancy with operations in 45 countries, every business can be a great place to work. The Institute provides a range of offerings including the assessment and evaluation of different aspects of workplaces, but they are best-known for their global Best Workplaces Programme, which is the largest of its kind with a total of 3,800 organisations representing 1.8 million employees.

The underlying concept behind the Best Workplaces Programme is that by congratulating and highlighting best practices, other organisations will recognise the benefits of becoming a great workplace, gain an understanding of how to work towards this goal and ultimately be encouraged to follow suit. This, which is aligned with their mission to improve society by creating better workplaces, will in turn benefit the daily lives of millions of employees in the countries where the Institute operates.

Their approach is based on the major findings of 25 years of research - that trust between managers and employees is the primary defining characteristic of the very best workplaces. At the heart of their definition of a great place to work - a place where employees "trust the people they work for, have pride in what they do, and enjoy the people they work with" - is the idea that a great workplace is measured by the quality of the three, interconnected relationships that exist there:

- the relationship between employees and management
- the relationship between employees and their jobs/company
- the relationship between employees and other employees.

How it Plays Out in the Workplace

Credibility

- Communications are open and accessible.
- Competence in coordinating human and material resources.
- Integrity in carrying out vision with consistency.

Respect

- Supporting professional development and showing appreciation.
- Collaboration with employees on relevant decisions.
- Caring for employees as individuals with personal lives.

Fairness

- Equity - balanced treatment for all in terms of rewards.
- Impartiality - absence of favouritism in hiring and promotions.
- Justice - lack of discrimination and process for appeals.

1 Great Place to Work Institute UK. (2010, January 11). What makes a great place to work? Retrieved January 11, 2010, from greatplacetowork.co.uk: http://www.greatplacetowork.co.uk/great/index.php

Pride

- In personal job, individual contributions.
- In work produced by one's team or work group.
- In the organization's products and standing in the community.

Camaraderie

- Ability to be oneself.
- Socially friendly and welcoming atmosphere.
- Sense of "family" or "team."

Similar to previous years, the Institute published in 2010 the UK's Best Workplaces covering an extensive range of organisations from different sectors and sizes, with turnovers of up to £27 billion. The following is a selection of some of the innovative ways in which these organisations endeavour to make their business a great place to work.

What is a 'Good Job'? ●●●

In November 2009 the Work Foundation published the results of a survey which was intended to answer this question in response to various government initiatives to affect the quality of the jobs available to the UK workforce[2]. In 2004 Gordon Brown, who was then Chancellor of the Exchequer, argued that the UK should aim for both 'full and fulfilling employment'. Implicit in this aspiration is the notion that just 'having a job' – regardless of its quality – is not sufficient. The objective must be to ensure that for as many people as possible work in the UK is a source of well-being, personal growth, fulfilment, autonomy and meaning. In other words the jobs available in today's labour market should offer 'Good Work'. The survey concluded that there is a significant weight of evidence to support the argument that job quality, employee health, and an employee's ability to perform productively at work are closely linked.

There appears to be a broad consensus among many experts about the characteristics which define 'Good Jobs'. The important factors can be summarised as follows:

- employment security
- whether the work is characterised by monotony and repetition
- whether employees have autonomy, control and task discretion
- the extent to which there is an appropriate balance between the efforts that workers make and the rewards that they receive
- whether workplace procedures are seen to be fair
- the strength of workplace relationships – or social capital.

The survey results also indicated that despite consensus over the important factors that constitute Good Jobs, and the evidence underpinning it, it was clear that a large number of jobs in the UK fail to conform to the core criteria of a Good Job. Indeed, it suggested that many organisations have either not been convinced by the case for Good Jobs and have difficulty turning its principles into practice, or do not feel the need to offer anything but 'bad jobs'.

2 The Work Foundation. (2009, November 23). Employers believe'good jobs' are linked to success. Retrieved December 11, 2009, from theworkfoundation.com: http://www.theworkfoundation.com/pressmedia/news/newsarticle.aspx?oItemId=199

A study on the role of work and low income families completed in 2005[3] highlighted what gets people from this group back to work and then keeps them there.

Re-entry Factors	Sustainability Factors
Financial gain	Financial gain
Better standard of living	Better standard of living
Psychological and emotional benefits	Psychological and emotional benefits
Strong motivation to work and escape benefits	Strong motivation to work and escape benefits
Childcare arrangements	Childcare arrangements
Support from family and friends	Support from family and friends
	Nature of the job and work activities
	Relationship with employer
	Relationship with colleagues

The Work Foundation survey found that employers believe 'good jobs' are linked to success and it also indicated that these employers support new government policies to spur creation of good jobs. However, although these employers are committed to improving the quality of jobs in the UK they feel that they lack guidance on how to achieve it.

Far from seeing decent quality jobs and commercial or organisational success as conflicting objectives, the study shows that growing numbers of employers see them as mutually supporting goals. Employers understood a 'good job' to involve being valued and appreciated, interest and fulfilment, job satisfaction, autonomy, decent working conditions, morale and teamwork, effective management, and staff development.

Not surprisingly, the study's results are consistent with the seven key determinants of good work mentioned earlier and although 78% of the employers did not mention pay, 22% cited it as an important feature.

Poor quality of jobs was seen as being part of an underlying explanation for many persistent workforce issues they faced including sickness absence, retention, poor motivation levels and difficulties hiring the right people.

3 Department of Work and Pensions. (2005). The role of work in low income families. DWP.

Employers understand that staff well-being can affect productivity, but often do not know how to improve matters. The Work Foundation[4] suggests that employers should be encouraged to share best practice through their networks and large organisations should promote good work through their supply chains as routes to higher productivity and more consistent performance.

The research involved a series of workshops with UK private and public sector employers and a survey of 600 organisations. The major findings include:

- organisations either agreed or strongly agreed that the following were problems for their organisations: sickness absence (49%); recruitment of key staff (50%); staff retention and under performance (33%); staff 'presenteeism' or de-motivated/uninterested/ineffective staff (25%)
- employers listed the major factors in organisational effectiveness as being fair pay (81%); fulfilling and interesting jobs (59%); investment in staff training (72%); a culture of trust (75%); flexible working (31%); employee engagement (51%); autonomy (58%) and keeping up with technology (54%)
- nearly half of employers surveyed (41%) saw a role for external agencies to help them with the 'good jobs' agenda
- significantly more – at least 5% – public sector organisations had well-being policies in place than private sector firms though respondents did not see the presence of personnel policies as equating to better job quality
- almost all respondents saw job quality as vital to maintaining customer satisfaction.

As there now appears to be strong link between 'good jobs' and successful businesses, employers are committed to improving the quality of jobs in the UK but still feel that they lack guidance about how to achieve it as indicated in the survey. As a result of this, the Work Foundation are holding an event in 2010 on the theme of "Creating Employee Engagement and Productivity through Good Jobs"[5]. Poor quality jobs are seen as part of the underlying explanation for persistent workforce issues and problems. The Work Foundation feel that by improving productivity through job quality and also by exploring where the good jobs agenda fits with employee engagement, a route to improved performance will become clear.

The research of both the Great Place to Work Institute and the Work Foundation into great workplaces or good jobs highlight two very key terms that appear regularly in their findings and these terms are "trust" and "employee engagement".

4 The Work Foundation. (2009, November 23). Employers believe' good jobs' are linked to success. Retrieved December 11, 2009, from theworkfoundation.com: http://www.theworkfoundation.com/pressmedia/news/newsarticle.aspx?oItemId=199

5 The Work Foundation. (2010, January 9). Creating employee engagement and productivity through good jobs. Retrieved January 9, 2010, from theworkfoundation.com: http://www.theworkfoundation.com/events/eventdetail.aspx?oItemId=99

Trust and the Psychological Contract ●●●

The Great Place to Work® Institute believes that trust underpins and affects the quality of every relationship, communication, project and effort with which a business is engaged. Trust is the essential pre-condition on which all real business success depends.

In a report published last year (2009)[6], the Institute states that contrary to what many people think, trust is a tangible asset that can be created. But it can also be damaged. It takes time to rebuild trust and, in order to achieve this, they suggest that organisations need to think and communicate differently. Greater trust offers greater savings in cost, time and quality, as well as improving relationships. In the business world, as well as the world at large, trust is becoming more important as a vehicle for economic and political success because there is so little of it around. The issue of trust must be addressed as it is the key to enhanced business performance and accelerated recovery.

What is the Psychological Contract?

The psychological contract has been described as representing the mutual beliefs, perceptions, and informal obligations between an employer and an employee. It sets the dynamics for the relationship and defines the detailed practicality of the work to be done. It is not the same as the formal written contract of employment which, for the most part, only identifies mutual duties and responsibilities in a generalized form.

During the recruitment process, the employer and interviewee will discuss what they each can offer in the prospective relationship. If agreement is reached, most employers will impose a standard form contract, leaving the detail of the employee's duties to be clarified "on the job". But some of the initial statements, no matter how informal and imprecise, may later be remembered as promises and give rise to expectations. Whether they are incorporated into the parallel psychological contract will depend on whether both parties believe that they should be treated as part of the relationship. The more responsible and better organised employers are careful to document offers to reduce the risk of raising false expectations followed by disappointment.

The reality of employment rights and duties emerges through the interpersonal relationships formed in the workplace. How employers, supervisors and managers behave on a day-to-day basis is not determined by the legal contract. Employees slowly negotiate what they must do to satisfy their side of the bargain, and what they can expect in return. Hence, the psychological contract determines what the parties will, or will not do and how it will be done. When the parties' expectations match each other, performance is likely to be good and satisfaction levels will be high. So long as the values and loyalty persist, trust and commitment will be maintained.

If managed effectively, the relationship will foster mutual trust between the parties, matching the objectives and commitments of the business to those of their

6 Great Place to Work Institute UK. (2009, August). Trust: The key to enhanced business performance and accelerated recovery. Retrieved January 11, 2010, from greatplacetowork.com: http://resources.greatplacetowork.com/article/pdf/trust_-_final.pdf

employees. But a negative psychological contract can result in employees becoming disenchanted, demotivated and resentful of perceived authoritarianism within the business. This will result in an increasingly inefficient workforce whose objectives no longer correspond to the business they work for.

Psychological contract breach may occur if employees perceive that their employer has failed to deliver on what they perceive was promised. This is particularly the case where managers themselves are responsible for breaches, for instance where employees do not receive promised training, or performance reviews are badly handled. Managers cannot always ensure that commitments are fulfilled - for example where employment prospects deteriorate or organisations are affected by mergers or restructuring – but they may still take some blame in the eyes of employees.

Employees are likely to respond negatively to any perceived breach and the response is likely to be in the form of reduced loyalty and commitment. The perception that the psychological contract has been breached may arise shortly after the employee joins the company or even after years of satisfactory service. The impact may be localized and contained, but if morale is more generally affected, the performance of the business may be diminished. Further, if the activities of the business are perceived as being unjust or immoral in relation to its employees, its public reputation and brand image may also be damaged.

Managers need to remember:

- employment relationships may deteriorate despite management's best efforts: nevertheless it is a managers' job to take responsibility for maintaining them.
- preventing breach in the first place is better than trying to repair the damage afterwards
- but where breach cannot be avoided it may be better to spend time negotiating or renegotiating the deal, rather than focusing too much on delivery.

. . . employees are increasingly recognised as the key business drivers. The ability of the business to add value rests on its front line employees, or "human capital."

Organisations that wish to succeed have to get the most out of this resource. In order to do this, employers have to know what employees expect from their work.

The psychological contract offers a framework for monitoring employee attitudes and priorities on those dimensions that can be shown to influence performance[7].

CIPD

7 CIPD. (2010, January 11). The Psychological Contract. Retrieved January 11, 2010, from cipd.co.uk: http://www.cipd.co.uk/subjects/empreltns/psycntrct/psycontr.htm

Employee Engagement ●●●

> *In good times, employee engagement is the difference between being good and being great, and in bad times, it's the difference between surviving and not. In good times and bad, low engagement reduces performance and profit.*

James K. Harter, Ph.D., Gallup's chief scientist of workplace management and well-being and co-author of 12: The Elements of Great Managing.

Employers want employees who will do their best work, or 'go the extra mile'. Employees want good work: jobs that are worthwhile and motivate them. More and more organisations are looking for a win-win solution that meets their needs and those of their employees. What they increasingly say they are looking for is an engaged workforce.

So what is employee engagement? It can be seen as a combination of commitment to the organisation and its values plus a willingness to help out colleagues (organisational citizenship). It goes beyond job satisfaction and is not simply motivation. Engagement is something the employee has to offer: it cannot be 'required' as part of the employment contract.

The Gallup organisation has discovered[8] that the world's top-performing organizations understand that employee engagement is a force that drives performance outcomes. In the best organizations, engagement is more than a human resources initiative - it is a strategic foundation for the way they do business.

Research by Gallup and others shows that engaged employees are more productive. They are more profitable, more customer-focused, safer, and more likely to withstand temptations to leave. Gallup claims that the best-performing companies know that an employee engagement improvement strategy linked to the achievement of corporate goals will help them win in the marketplace.

8 Gallup. (2010, February 8). Employee Engagement. Retrieved February 8, 2010, from gallup.com: http://www.gallup.com/consulting/52/Employee-Engagement.aspx

Gallup have devised a calculation of employee engagement known as the "engagement ratio" which is a macro-level indicator of an organisation's health that allows managers to track the proportion of engaged to actively disengaged employees. Through their research they find that:

- in average organizations, the ratio of engaged to actively disengaged employees is 1.5:1
- in "world-class" organisations, the ratio of engaged to actively disengaged employees is near 8:1.

Through their rigorous research they have identified two key discoveries as to what makes for a good workplace. Firstly, "there are no great companies but only great workgroups" and secondly, there are some core elements that link powerfully to key business outcomes and these best predict great employee and workgroup performance.

Employees should really know what is expected of them with all the right materials and equipment readily to hand. The work role allocated to them should match their skills and talents and there should also be a culture of praise and positive feedback indicating that management do care about their well-being and employees need to feel that their opinions count. There should also be ample opportunity for staff development and appropriate appraisal that enables the employee to learn and to grow. A positive workplace culture will engender excellent teamwork and mutual respect and trust between colleagues and also allow friendships to form. Another very important factor is that the objectives and philosophy of the business are in line with those of the employees and that each employee feels that their particular job is a crucial element in achieving those objectives. Quality and a sense of pride in their work are also keys to achieving employee engagement.

Case Study[9]

Employee Engagement at BT

BT is keen to create a climate where everyone can achieve their full potential, where people understand what they need to do to help the company be successful and are enthusiastic and able to play their part. BT believe that people who are engaged in their work are productive, motivated and are achieving their personal best.

How they Monitor Engagement at BT

BT monitors employee engagement through CARE, their employee survey, gathering feedback on a quarterly basis.

Their CARE survey explores five key dimensions of the BT employee experience. These are:

- how we feel about our day to day work
- what it's like to work in our team
- our relationship with our direct manager
- perspectives on senior leaders
- the way we feel about working for the company.

Managers receive a report based on their team's survey responses. BT encourages them to discuss this with their team to build on any strengths identified and address areas for improvement.

How they Build Engagement at BT

BT works with its leadership teams to design and deliver engagement activities aligned to the delivery priorities for each business.

For example, in the 2009 financial year, they held an event to gain feedback from employees and to engage them in their business strategy. The event opened with a Q&A session where business leaders answered questions raised by employees. Employees had the opportunity to hear directly about BT strategic objectives, to discuss their reactions to them and any issues they foresaw. The event also included an exercise on improving the customer experience and increasing people's awareness of the need to collaborate and be accountable.

9 BT. (2010, January 11). Responsible Business. Retrieved January 11, 2010, from btplc.com: http://www.btplc.com/Societyandenvironment/Ourapproach/Responsiblebusiness/Responsiblebusiness.htm

During the event they launched a number of initiatives designed to increase engagement, for example initiatives aimed at simplifying processes to fix problems, gaining funding for projects and improving recognition. One such example is Smooth Operators, a recognition scheme in BT Operate, which encourages line managers and colleagues to focus on improving performance by "catching people doing the right thing".

BT also runs engagement programmes across their businesses such as the "My Customer Programme". This has three main elements.

- Back to the Floor – where leaders spend valuable time with colleagues and look at the end-to-end process, identifying opportunities to improve the customers' experience of BT.
- The Challenge Cup – a tournament designed to encourage people to create improvements for the business and for customers.
- Customer Connected – a programme offering fun and engaging learning modules to help employees to understand the impact they have on customers' overall experience.

MacLeod Review

The Department for Business, Innovation and Skills (BIS) commissioned an in-depth study[10] into employee engagement and to report on its potential benefits for organisations and employees. The independent reviewers were encouraged to examine whether a wider take up of engagement approaches could impact positively on UK competitiveness and performance, and meet the challenges of increased global competition.

There was an unequivocal yes from the authors of the report when it was published in July 2009. Since Autumn 2008 they had seen many examples of companies and organisations where performance and profitability had been transformed by employee engagement. They had met many employees who were only too keen to explain how their working lives had been transformed. And they had read many studies which showed a clear correlation between engagement and performance – and most importantly between improving engagement and improving performance.

Engagement matters because people matter – they are your only competitive edge. It is people, not machines that will make the difference and drive the business.

10 Clarke, D. M. (2009). Engaging for success:enhancing performance through employee engagement. BIS.

The authors of the report argue that if employee engagement and the principles that lie behind it were more widely understood, if good practice was more widely shared, if the potential that resides in the country's workforce was more fully unleashed, the UK could see a step change in workplace performance and in employee well-being, for the considerable benefit of the economy and society.

The report argues that wider delivery of employee engagement could have a positive impact on UK competitiveness and performance both during the downturn and in powering through to recovery. It concludes that while there are some excellent examples of good employee engagement, there are barriers to uptake, particularly amongst smaller businesses, and that government can play a unique role in giving the subject profile and bringing together role models with those who have delivery mechanisms and levers to help galvanise the collective effort.

The report also concluded that leadership, line management, employee voice and integrity are key enablers of engagement and that 'the correlation between engagement, well-being and performance is repeated too often for it to be a coincidence'.

The report recommends:

- the government should work to raise awareness of employee engagement benefits and techniques
- a senior sponsor group bringing together business, the public sector, not-for-profit organisations and unions, should be set up to boost understanding of this vital topic
- the government and its agencies should work together to ensure that support is tailored to the needs of organisations in different sectors
- a range of more practical support for organisations should be made available by March 2010.

Employee engagement is when the business values the employee and the employee values the business[10].

Both the research from Gallup and the approach taken by BT emphasise the importance of group or team in how an individual feels about their workplace.

The CBI suggests that those businesses that succeed in the twenty-first century will be those that will take the opportunity to adapt to a low-carbon future. Engaging employees through embedding sustainability into core operations will allow them to take full advantage of this shift.

The CBI argues that engaging their employees in a sustainability programme makes real business sense. A successful programme can deliver improved staff productivity, a stronger corporate identity, a reduced environmental impact and a more committed workforce.

They have produced a document called "Getting involved: a guide to switching your employees on to sustainability"[11]. The guide is for businesses looking to set-up employee engagement programmes focused on sustainability.

Employers who do this will see organisational improvements and an environment where all staff work better together.

The CBI states that in many organisations, teams and departments often work in groups that can be hard to integrate. Employee engagement programmes focused on sustainability can bring together employees with a common interest in environmental issues to develop a team spirit, breaking down barriers and increasing levels of communication between staff.

The CBI suggests that getting this right can make a difference: so much of what provides a competitive edge in today's economy is intangible and can only be developed through collaboration and co-operation between employees.

Some of the benefits of bringing their employees together through an engagement programme on sustainability include:

- stronger organisational group identity
- increased sharing of ideas between employees
- better understanding of different teams' capabilities
- clearer understanding of client requirements
- new opportunities for cross-selling a product or service.

This viewpoint adopted by the CBI concerning sustainability as a trigger for improved employee engagement was confirmed by research carried out by the Carbon Trust which showed that UK employees are more than ready to help cut costs around the workplace. In fact it seems that the employees are keen for their employers and colleagues to do more and they see reducing energy use as an easy win.

Employees are increasingly accepting responsibility for helping to save money around the workplace according to this research , with the majority (87%) saying it is important for them to help their employer cut costs in the current climate, and 78% willing to be more energy efficient to save money. Almost half (46%) of UK employees say they are now more likely to try to help their employer save money than before the recent recession.

11 CBI. (2009, August). Getting involved a guide to switching your employees on to sustainability. Retrieved January 11, 2010, from cbi.org.uk: http://climatechange.cbi.org.uk/uploaded/Getting%20involved%20a%20guide%20to%20switching%20your%20employees%20on%20to%20sustainability.pdf

The research was commissioned by the Carbon Trust[12] as part of its campaign to help businesses save at least £1million a day by saving energy. It reveals that whilst individual employees are happy to shoulder some responsibility, they also want their colleagues to do their bit, with over two-thirds (67%) believing that their colleagues should do more to help save money around the workplace.

The need for collective action is underlined by the fact that 82% of employees say they regularly or occasionally see colleagues wasting energy – and therefore money – around the workplace. Yet the research also reveals that employers are failing to galvanise their employees' enthusiasm - almost half of employees (48%) said they would be more willing to help their employer save costs around the workplace if they knew what they could do, whilst 42% would be motivated into action if their employers simply asked for their help.

In the light of this enthusiasm many businesses have appointed 'Carbon Champions' or 'Carbon Teams' as part of their employee engagement initiatives. Not only will this approach raise awareness with teams and champions but also the businesses benefit from appointing a company Business or Carbon Champion to co-ordinate and facilitate their resource efficiency programme. To maximise the impact of the programme, the Champion must have the support and commitment of senior management. Secondary to this is the support required from the project team(s) in delivering the programme.

The key role of the Business/Carbon Champion is to co-ordinate and facilitate the resource efficiency programme. However they are not required to complete all the tasks by themselves but they should act as the key focal point for communications, resources, action, programmes and training to create conditions for success. They should also be able to identify and appoint supporting team members.

Only by ensuring that employees from all areas are involved can a company successfully integrate resource efficiency into its culture. Ideally, teams should be cross-functional - people with different roles and experiences will bring different skills and ideas and will ensure a wider buy-in to the programme. Team working will also lead to the identification of ongoing opportunities for cost savings.

It would appear that UK workers want to participate in creating a better, fairer and more sustainable world and they do expect their employer's brand to encompass this aim. There was evidence of this in Chapter 2 where hotel staff were so keen to be involved in sustainability that it became part of a regional and then national staff development programme and also in Chapter 3 where 69% of BT employees say they are proud to work for that company because of the company's reputation for social responsibility. Research carried out by Ipsos Mori[13] in 2006 found that 86% of employees surveyed believed that it is important that their employer is responsible in society and the environment and 47% of employees were more likely to join or stay with an employer that addresses social issues.

12 Carbon Trust. (2009, March). UK employees ready to help cut costs around the workplace. Retrieved January 11, 2010, from carbontrust.co.uk: http://www.carbontrust.co.uk/news/news/press-centre/2009/Pages/employee_resources.aspx

13 Ipsos Mori. (2006). Engaging Employees through Corporate Responsibility. Ipsos Mori.

So it can be seen that a great place to work must incorporate diversity and inclusion and health and well-being as seen in the previous two responsible workplace chapters. Added to this are a host of concepts including employee engagement and trust which will be greatly affected by the employer's perceived brand image. Health and well-being and employee engagement will also be greatly influenced by work-life balance policies and also how much an employer recognises and utilises the talents of their workforce. These are looked at more fully in the next two chapters.

CHAPTER 12

Work-life Balance

- Definition
- What is Flexible Working?
- The Benefit to Employees
- The Business Case

Definition ●●●

Work-life balance is about people having a measure of control over when, where and how they work. It is achieved when an individual's right to a fulfilled life inside and outside paid work is accepted and respected as the norm, to the mutual benefit of the individual, business and society.

Organisations are under constant pressure to produce goods and services of the right quality and the right price as and when customers want them. This pressure can often mean that new ways of working have to be found to make the best use of staff and resources.

Striking a balance between the needs of the individual employee, involves customer and organisation involves the following.

- **For Employees** - Different individuals will have different expectations and needs at different times in their life cycle and they will want to achieve a better balance between work and home life.
- **For Customers** - Organisations need to respond to the demands of their customers if they are to continue to be successful.
- **For Organisations** - Organisations need to be able to manage costs, maintain profitability and ensure that teams work effectively together so matching business needs with the way their employees work.

It is important that each employee is fully aware of the different demands on their time and energy and that through negotiation with their employer they have the ability to make choices in the allocation of that time and energy. They must also be clear about the values to apply to the choices available in order to reach an appropriate working arrangement. Work-life balance is about adopting working arrangements so that everyone - regardless of age, race, or gender - can find a balance that enables them more easily to combine work with their other responsibilities or aspirations.

A survey carried out by the CIPD[1] on employee attitudes established that two of the biggest concerns for these employees were working long hours and the intensity of that work. The survey also showed that 75% of those questioned felt that they were working very hard and many of those also felt that they could not work any harder. Twenty per cent, including many managerial and professional workers stated that they took work home every day and technology has meant that many are continuously accessible. One third of partners of people who work more than 48 hours per week felt that it had a negative impact on their personal relationships. Despite all these factors which create overlap between home and work only 33% of those workers questioned indicated that their employer had family-friendly practices or personal support services in place.

There is no 'one perfect solution', and tough choices will often still have to be made. The aim of work-life balance is to offer a wider range of options so that people can

1 CIPD. (2009, May). Employee outlook Spring 2009. Retrieved January 21, 2010, from cipd.co.uk: http://www.cipd.co.uk/subjects/empreltns/general/_employee_outlook_spring_09.htm. Ben Willmott and Claire McCartney.

have more control and have the freedom to choose what they believe is best for them within the constraints of the needs of the business.

It is also important for the employer to recognise that the majority of their employees will have family and caring responsibilities.

More and more people do jobs – they work and they look after children or elderly relatives. The majority of families (68%) with dependent children have two working parents. With these families there is as much focus on the role of the working father as the working mother. There are over 1.9 million families with dependent children headed by a lone parent and 53% of these parents are working. In the last census it was estimated that there were 5.2 million carers in England and Wales many of whom do paid work as well. Approximately 11% of those individuals in full time work are also providing some form of unpaid care[2].

Other people may also be unable or unwilling to work normal full-time hours but potentially could be valuable employees. These might include:

- people combining work with continuing education
- those with duties or interests outside work
- employees needing time off for religious observance
- people who have retired from full-time work but are available on a part-time or temporary basis.

Work-life balance is not just for women. Many men stand to benefit in their roles as fathers, partners or dependants. Society also benefits as the general consensus is that stronger and more stable families provide good adult role models, fewer broken relationships and a reduction in crime and other anti-social behaviour. So everybody in the general community stands to benefit from policies to improve employees' work-life balance.

Employees who work flexibly often have a greater sense of responsibility, ownership and control of their working life. If a manager helps an employee to balance their work and home life this can be rewarded by increased loyalty and commitment. An employee may feel more able to focus on their work and to develop their career.

Flexible patterns of work can help a business to address issues relating to achieving the right balance by maximising the available labour and improving customer service. Flexible working can also help the business to reduce absenteeism and at the same time increase productivity, employee commitment and loyalty. CIPD research into employee engagement shows that flexible workers are more likely to be motivated to achieve results for their employers[3].

2 ACAS. (2010, January 21). Flexible working and Work-Life Balance. Retrieved January 21, 2010, from acas.org.uk: http://www.acas.org.uk/CHttpHandler.ashx?id=661&p=0

3 CIPD. (2005, February 23). Flexible working brings significant challenges. Retrieved January 21, 2010, from cipd.co.uk: http://www.cipd.co.uk/pressoffice/_articles/23022005094500.htm?IsSrchRes=1

What is Flexible Working?

The term flexible working covers flexibility in terms of time, for example part-time work or shift work and also location, for example, home working, hot desking, flexi-time, time off in lieu, annual hours, shift swapping, staggered hours, job sharing, compressed working hours, self rostering, zero-hours contracts, sabbaticals and career breaks, term-time working, mobile working and V-time working are all examples of flexible working practices.

Flexible arrangements should comply with the current legislation on working time.

The Working Times Regulations cover:

- holiday entitlement
- the maximum average working week
- the right to rest breaks during the working day
- the right to rest periods between working days
- hours when working at night.

In general, workers aged 18 and over are entitled to:

- 5.6 weeks' holiday a year (previously 4.8 weeks' holiday a year)
- work no more than six days out of every seven, or 12 out of every 14
- take a 20-minute break if their shift lasts for more than six hours
- work a maximum 48-hour average week.

Workers aged 16 and 17 are entitled to:

- take at least 30 minutes' break if their shift lasts more than four and a half hours
- work no more than eight hours a day and 40 hours a week
- have 12 hours' rest between working days and two days off every week
- 5.6 weeks' holiday a year (previously 4.8 weeks).

Working at Night

There are special rules regarding employees working at night (usually between 23.00 and 06.00, although this can vary by mutual agreement).

A night worker is someone who regularly works for at least three hours during this period. They must be offered a free health assessment before they start working nights and on a regular basis after that.

In general, workers under 18 are not permitted to work at night.

Mobile workers are excluded from the night-time-working limits. Instead, they are entitled to 'adequate rest'.

Other legal provisions governing work-life balance, much of them driven by EU directives include the following.

- **Parental leave** - There is a right to 13 weeks' unpaid parental leave for men and women at any time up to the child's fifth birthday. This must be taken in blocks of time, or in multiples of one week, with 21 days' notice given to the employer.
- **Time off for dependent care** - The right to take unpaid time off to deal with family emergencies, for example, concerning an elderly parent, partner, child or other person living as part of the family.
- **Maternity leave** - All women are entitled to 26 weeks maternity leave, plus an extra 26 weeks additional maternity leave, making 52 weeks in total.
- **Paternity leave** - Fathers are entitled to 2 weeks paid paternity leave, which can be taken as a single block of one or two weeks within the 56 days following the child's birth.
- **Adoption leave** - Employees adopting a child are entitled to 26 weeks' ordinary adoption leave and 26 weeks' additional adoption leave. Only one parent may take adoption leave: if they qualify, the other parent may take paternity leave.
- **Right to request flexible working** - Employees with children under the age of 17 (under age 18 if disabled) and those with caring responsibilities for adults including those with elderly or disabled relatives can request a change to their working arrangements, for example, in their hours, time or place of work. The employer can refuse such a request on specified business grounds but must follow a detailed procedure.
- **Part-time work** - Part-timers are entitled to the same hourly rate of pay and the same entitlements to annual leave and maternity/parental leave as full-timers but on a pro rata basis. Part-timers must also have the same entitlement to contractual sick pay and no less favourable treatment in access to training.
- **Detriment** - An employer cannot subject an employee to a detriment because they attempted to exercise their rights to work flexibly or take maternity, paternity, adoption or parental leave. Employees who suffer unfair treatment at work for these reasons may make a separate complaint to an employment tribunal as well as any discrimination or constructive unfair dismissal claim.

The Benefit to Employees

The main benefit of working flexibly for employees is that it gives them the chance to fit other commitments and activities around work and make better use of their free time.

Obviously flexible working is particularly helpful for employees who have young or disabled children or who care for an adult.

However, while such employees have the statutory right to request flexible working, those without the right may find flexible working helpful too. For example:

- working from home may allow them to feel more in control of their workload
- staggered working hours may help them avoid the stress of commuting at peak times
- to volunteer for community projects or pursue other interests

The Business Case

The DTI suggests the following reasons for organisations to consider work-life balance.

1. As a recruitment tool to attract the best talent/ become an "employer of choice".
2. To retain employees.
3. To improve customer service.
4. To increase return on training investment.
5. To create a more diverse workforce, to reflect the customer base.
6. To reduce absenteeism, sickness and stress.
7. To improve productivity and performance.
8. To increase morale, commitment, engagement and loyalty.
9. To improve organisational flexibility and change competency.

Other things can be added:

10. To improve knowledge management.
11. Visible evidence of corporate social responsibility.
12. Wanting to meet legal requirements.

Business Impact of Flexible Working

Introducing a flexible working policy can greatly benefit a business as well as its employees and many employers believe that promoting flexible working makes good business sense and can bring the following improvements.

- Greater cost-effectiveness and efficiency, such as savings on overheads when employees work from home or less downtime for machinery when 24-hour shifts are worked.
- The chance to have extended operating hours, for example later closing times for retailers.
- The ability to attract a higher level of skills because the business is able to attract and retain a skilled and more diverse workforce. Also, recruitment costs can be reduced.
- More job satisfaction and better staff morale.
- Reduced levels of sickness absence.
- Greater continuity as staff, who might otherwise have left, are offered hours they can manage. Many employers find that a better work-life balance has a positive impact on staff retention, and on employee relations, motivation and commitment. High rates of retention means that you keep experienced staff who can often offer a better overall service.
- Increased customer satisfaction and loyalty as a result of the above.
- Improved competitiveness, such as being able to react to changing market conditions more effectively.

Employers may initially incur additional costs in adopting policies to support work-life balance including increased managerial workloads. Such costs are however generally outweighed by the gains in achieving strategic objectives. The biggest obstacle to implementing good practice is in many cases the difficulty of persuading individual line managers to accept more flexible working arrangements.

In the CIPD survey "Flexible working and paternity leave"[4], part-time working was the most common option of flexible working offered by organisations. For the female employees questioned as many as 71% were working part-time as compared to 38% of the males in the survey. The most popular option for males was variable working hours with 49% indicating that they could vary their start and finish times. This option was also adopted by 52% of the females in the survey. In third place for both was the option of job sharing (34% of the females and 23% of the males). Approximately 20% of both sexes worked from home as the fourth most popular option. It was also noted that there was a gap between employers offering a range of flexible working options and the take-up by the employees.

4 CIPD. (2004, October). Flexible working and paternity leave. Retrieved January 21, 2010, from cipd.co.uk: http://www.cipd.co.uk/subjects/hrpract/flexibleworkingpractices/paternityflexwork.htm. Duncan Brown, Rebecca Clake, Gerwyn Davies, Sue Nickson.

The work-life balance survey conducted by BERR[5] (now the Department of Business Innovation and Skills) shows that more men than ever are keen to work flexibly, making up 43% of employees who requested a change to working patterns in the past two or three years. The survey also reported that 49% of employers have seen an increase in productivity following the implementation of work-life balance options.

Other practical measures taken by many responsible employers are offering extended leave and other time off options such as career breaks for carers, sabbaticals, study leave and secondments which may sometimes involve community support activities.

Also many workplaces are providing increased levels of support as well as flexible working practices through such things as employee assistance programmes, subsidised insurance or loans, childcare loans or allowances and crèche facilities.

But an effective work-life balance strategy is not simply about complying with the law. It is about finding out about employees' needs and priorities and considering how they can be met in ways that are consistent with the needs of the business. Employers are increasingly concerned to protect their reputation and 'employer brand'. Work-life balance policies are an important way for employers to identify their commitment to quality of life and social responsibility.

> *The new spirit of cooperation between employers and workers will be a real fillip for UK competitiveness as we return to growth, delivering more flexible working and a welcome improvement in the work-life balance.*

Albert Ellis, Chief Executive Officer of Harvey Nash

Research by the CBI[6] and recruitment experts Harvey Nash between April and September 2009 revealed that as a result of the perceived easing of the recession employers have shifted their view on the need to change their working patterns such as cutting shifts or agency staff from 62% down to 36%. However the use of flexible working has risen with half of employers reporting that they had encouraged more flexibility in the recession. In particular, teleworking, or working from home, has soared in popularity, with two thirds (66%) of firms making use of it, 20% higher than the 46% recorded in 2008. The rate of change is emphasised by the fact that only 11% of employers made use of this flexibility in 2004.

5 BERR. (2007, December). The Third Work-Life Balance Employer survey: main findings. Retrieved January 21, 2010, from berr.gov.uk: http://www.berr.gov.uk/files/file42645.pdf

6 CBI. (2009, November 16). News release Tough pay restraint ahead,but hiring freezes start to thaw. Retrieved January 21, 2010, from cbi.org.uk: http://www.cbi.org.uk/ndbs/press.nsf/0363c1f07c6ca12a8025671c00381cc7/e820ef4f16ede4bc802576630045d98e?OpenDocument

The statutory right for individuals to request flexible working continues to work well. Nearly all requests by parents (93%) and carers (94%) are being granted.

Over two thirds (70%) of employers think the new Agency Workers Directive, due to be implemented in December 2011, will lead to a decline in the use of temporary staff, which will damage the job prospects of many school leavers, graduates and unemployed people. The Agency Workers Directive must come into force in the UK by 5 December 2011, the European Union (EU) has announced. The EU set the implementation date as it published the official wording of the directive - which will give temporary staff in the UK equal rights with permanent staff after 12 weeks with an employer.

The UK secured this 12-week qualifying period due to a deal previously struck by the CBI and the TUC. All other member states have to give equal rights to temps from their first day – unless they reach such an agreement domestically.

Having work-life balance policies in place and ensuring that they are being fully utilised enables a business structure to promote "agility" as well as flexibility. Agility is about having the opportunity to gain access to new skills, the ability to flex over time providing greater freedom to scale up or down as the business or business cycle requires. This greater agility allows businesses to better organise their operations nationally or globally and to build networks. This will require the business to maximise the potential of information technology with its physical resources and human resources through collaborative strategic management.

Case Study[7]

A long-hours and "jacket on the chair" culture in City law firms is draining talent from the legal profession, according to research published in October 2008. The study of 13 top City law firms showed that law firms are still suspicious of home-working and of employees who want a healthy "work-life balance".

Despite some reforms in recent years that allow a degree of flexible working, the economic climate prevailing at the time was threatening to "turn the clock back". It gave a warning that law firms would tighten their belts and be even less willing to see employees and partners working partly from home or part-time - damaging the recruitment and retention of women lawyers in particular.

The study identified several working practices that present barriers to flexible working including the long-hours culture and need to be seen in the office with annual targets for lawyers of 1800 billable hours and higher in many law firms. A working week of 50-60 hours is typical.

There is also suspicion that working from home is seen as a "soft option"; a belief that working flexi-time means shorter hours - when the opposite is often the case - and a mistaken belief that clients want their lawyer on hand around the clock.

Clients often work for organisations that are trying to improve work-life balance and often favour law firms who had a culture of flexibility, the study finds. That is especially marked among younger clients, who put more importance on this.

The study calls for more team working, rather than things being built around a partner; communication with clients to ensure that deadlines are realistic; less emphasis on being present in the office; and the measurement of "output not input".

7 Addleshaw Goddard. (2008, October 14). Working Families publishes new research this week on work-life culture and practice in the legal sector. . Retrieved January 21, 2010, from addleshawgoddard.com: http://www.addleshawgoddard.com/view.asp?content_id=3986&parent_id=968/press release

CHAPTER 13

Skills, Talent and Training

- The Widening Skills Gaps
- Marketable Skills and Employee Engagement
- Talent Management
- Managing Hidden Talent

The Widening Skills Gaps ●●●

Talents are those patterns that one cannot turn on and off at will. Great managers realize that, while talents are the differentiating factor in excellent performance, they are also neither created nor altered. In contrast, one's skill sets and knowledge can be impacted and altered through education and training.

In the last part of the twentieth century industrial economies evolved into knowledge based ones across the developed world. High technology manufacturing and knowledge based services such as financial, business, communication and computer consultancies now employ almost half of the UK workforce[1]. Recruiting and retaining employees with the right skills and talents is a key priority for senior managers worldwide. In the longer term demographic changes across an ever developing world will cause the workforce to shrink and demand will outstrip the supply of knowledge workers. As the rate at which knowledge and information is growing exponentially it has been predicted that the top ten "in demand" jobs in 2010 would not have existed in 2004[2]. By 2020 40% of all jobs will need a graduate level qualification (Level 5). However 70% of the 2020 workforce is already in employment and 50% of the current workforce is only qualified to Level 2[3].

So it can be seen that these labour shortages will be heightened further because large sections of the potential labour force will not have the required level of skills or education necessary to be able to participate effectively in a knowledge based economy. Skills gaps such as this will greatly impede the future competitiveness of any knowledge based business. It is important to resolve this as knowledge based businesses in the UK contribute over 41% of "gross added value" and according to balance of payments data knowledge based services account for 70% of service sector exports[4].

Many of today's businesses have created complex organisations and value systems across borders where globalisation is the norm. Talent as well as suppliers can all be sourced globally for cost effectiveness and risk avoidance and to a large extent the recognition of diversity does help to address talent shortages. Employers can only benefit from creating inclusive workplaces and sourcing talent globally across many diversity strands. By 2011 the working age population in Europe will begin to decline and by 2030 there is a predicted shortfall of 20 million workers so many businesses

1 Lee, B. a. (2006). The Knowledge Economy in Europe. London: The Work Foundation.

2 McCleod, K. F. (2009). 2020 vision. Retrieved January 9, 2010, from shifthappens.wikispaces.com: http://www.shifthappens.wikispaces.com

3 Leitch Review of Skills. (2006). Prosperity for all in the Global Economy. HMSO.

4 Office of National Statistics. (2008). UK Balance of Payments:The Pink Book. London: ONS.

are already attempting to mitigate this by encouraging women to return to work after career breaks and also by encouraging older workers to stay in the workplace longer[5].

In February 2010 a report on research carried out by Future Foundation for Friends Provident, the pensions and insurance group, entitled "Vision for Britain 2020" was published stating that by 2020 elite workers will be able to demand more in salary and benefits and experience a higher degree of personal and professional fulfilment than ever before. By contrast, those excluded from this are predicted to be complacent and unwilling to change. Almost 60% of the respondents expected a salary increase every year and more than two-thirds feel their job is safe despite an uncertain economic climate.

The negative effect of this is the rapidly widening gap between skilled and unskilled employees which will result in the country's workforce being split into the "elite and the excluded" over the next 10 years.

The report also predicted that by 2020 the elite workers in technical, professional and managerial posts will occupy a more powerful role, pressuring employers to radically rethink how they attract and retain their specialist skills. On the other side of the jobs scale almost a million workers, typically unskilled men with poor prospects and limited expectations, will fall into the "excluded" bracket.

The report painted a "worrying portrait" of the British workplace and that this polarisation trend would lead to a growing band of excluded workers. At the same time, a new breed of elite worker is also beginning to emerge who, by 2020, will carry more power than ever before. The statements "our people are our greatest asset" will take on a new meaning for employers by 2020.

The report also went on to say that new measures of assessing employee productivity will be critical in the 2020 "knowledge economy" and suggests that while outsourcing work overseas will continue the number of foreign workers in Britain will fall[6].

As the older employees retire they take knowledge and experience with them so it is not surprising that a study by Accenture[7] covering 850 top executives in Europe, Asia and North America found that two thirds were deeply worried about the threat of not being able to recruit and retain the best talent. These executives put talent management second only to competition as the main threat to their businesses.

5 EU Green Paper. (2005). Confronting Demographic Change:A new solidarity between the generations. Commission of the European Communities.

6 Friends Provident. (2010, February 16). 2020 vision reveals a British workforce divided into the 'powerful' elite and the excluded. Retrieved April 23, 2010, from friendsprovident.co.uk: http://www.friendsprovident.co.uk/common/layouts/subSectionLayout.jhtml?pageId=fpcouk/SitePageHTML%3APress+Release+Display+Page+Rebranded+Media&repositoryItemId=fpcouk/pressreleases%3Afppr160210workforcedivided&pageNum=1

7 Accenture. (2008, January 22). Top executives cite competition, global economy and attracting and retaining talent as top threat. Retrieved January 11, 2010, from accenture.com: http://newsroom.accenture.com/article_display.cfm?article_id=4637

It could be argued that talented workers are the most important business asset in a knowledge based economy so a failure to retain this talent could have an adverse affect on a business's ability to survive and remain competitive in the future. During periods of recession many businesses make the mistake of cutting back on staff training and development but sustained investment is essential if skills gaps are to be avoided.

The Chartered Institute of Personnel and Development's (CIPD) "Recruitment, Retention and Turnover survey"[8] 2009 shows that despite increased labour supply the key resourcing challenge remained a lack of necessary specialist skills (73%). A majority of organisations (56%) are preferring to focus on retaining rather than recruiting talent in response. The survey finds 'additional training to allow internal staff to fill posts' has been the most effective recruitment initiative (75%). Similarly, 'offering increased learning and development opportunities' (47%) is the most favoured action to address retention. This environment offers real opportunities for ambitious and motivated employees to secure learning and career progression opportunities that might have been more difficult to come by when firms were recruiting more regularly.

Research carried out by the CIPD as long ago as 2005[9] showed that many UK employers are tackling skills shortages by creating a culture where managers work with staff to provide learning opportunities that support both the needs of the organisation and employees. All employers will need to embrace this approach if they are to avoid facing skills shortages and compete successfully for talent.

Moving from training to learning enables employers to support, accelerate and direct the learning process and, in doing so, they will deliver business benefits. The report carried out over a 4 year period highlighted the shift from training to learning and also showed that the learning is a progressive movement from the delivery of content to the development of learning capabilities in the employee. Learning places far more emphasis on the individual but it is a worthwhile process as each person gains new skills and knowledge. It is a self-directed, work-based process, leading to an increase in the flexibility of both the organisation and the employee.

However learning will only happen if individuals actually want to learn, and what or how they will learn depends on the organisation and individual themselves. Employers should encourage individuals to take responsibility for their own learning and make sure the relevant support is provided to ensure learning ties in with the business objectives.

Successful and responsible organisations are those that can persuade and encourage their employees to learn. Combining business requirements with the learning strategy will ensure employees make use of their skills within the organisation and gain support from managers.

The learning and development function is vital to maintain business success or to aid economic recovery and to ensure that organisations are well placed for growth. The

8 CIPD. (2009, June 17). Recruitment dries up but training and career opportunities open up as employers focus on retention. Retrieved January 11, 2010, from cipd.co.uk: http://www.cipd.co.uk/pressoffice/_articles/170609randrrelease.htm

9 CIPD. (2005). Training to Learning. CIPD.

economy also needs effective learning and development to increase skills utilisation within the workplace and drive any productivity benefits[10].

> *Now is precisely the time to keep investing in the skills and talents of our people. It is the people we employ who will get us through. When markets are shrinking and order books falling, it is their commitment, productivity and ability to add value that will keep us competitive. Investing now in building new skills will put us in the strongest position as the economy recovers.*

Open letter in national newspapers October 2008.

Companies that do not train are 2.5 times more likely to go bankrupt, and they are less likely to retain vital talent. Organisations in the UK spent £38.5 billion on training in 2008. More recently this spending has come under pressure in tough times and Learning and Development (L&D) and HR professionals need to ensure that spending is efficiently allocated and that L&D policies fit with business objectives[11].

Marketable Skills and Employee Engagement

Through research carried out by the CIPD in September 2009[12] the key marketable skills for job seekers were established by combining an online poll of over 100 HR professionals with the views of over 3,000 employees.

Both groups identified transferable/flexible skills as the key attribute applicants should be demonstrating in the current climate but the employees also had to fit with culture and values of the organisation as equal first with 'interpersonal skills' in third place. Twenty per cent of those HR professionals questioned indicated that business acumen was also a key attribute in making job applicants stand out from the rest.

It would now seem to be the case that a "flexible mindset" and skills are considered by many employers to be more important than more traditional measures such as qualifications and technical or professional knowledge. In addition to this, interpersonal skills and customer service skills are also very important in helping candidates stand out from the crowd. Demonstrating the right attitude and fit with the culture of the organisation will increase the chances of a successful application.

10 CIPD. (2005, April 5). Employers must engage with staff to solve skill shortages. Retrieved January 9, 2010, from cipd.co.uk: http://www.cipd.co.uk/pressoffice/_articles/11042005124000.htm

11 CIPD. (2008, November). Retaining talent in a recession. Retrieved January 11, 2010, from cipd.co.uk: http://www.cipd.co.uk/research/_lenaring_development_in_recession.htm?IsSrchRes=1

12 CIPD. (2009, September 2). Develop flexible skills and a flexible mindset to stand out from the crowd in a difficult jobs market, recommends CIPD survey. Retrieved January 11, 2010, from cipd.co.uk: http://www.cipd.co.uk/pressoffice/_articles/020909MarketableSkillsTopicalResearch.htm?IsSrchRes=1

The perceived culture of an organisation or the "employer brand" is an important aspect of recruiting and retaining talent and, as already quoted in Chapter 11, 86% of employees surveyed by Ipsos Mori in 2006 believe that it is important that their employer is responsible in society and the environment and 47% of those employees questioned were more likely to join or stay with an employer that addresses social issues.

As well as proving to be the right fit for the organisation it is also important that these employees are put into roles which best fit who they are. Research carried out by another Ipsos Mori found that the best measure of the degree to which employees feel that their talents are being used in their jobs is their level of agreement with the notion that they are in jobs which best suit them. Having the opportunity to do "what they do best" every day is very closely tied to the integration of a person's talents. Employers need people who will give the best of their talents, their creativity and their initiative but in order to achieve this, employers need to engage with their staff. Responsible workplaces do their utmost to gain this engagement as employee engagement is an emotional and intellectual commitment to the business and its success. Employees who are genuinely engaged experience a purpose and meaning in their work which makes them fully committed to advancing their organisation's aims and objectives.

The Gallup study "Engaged Employees Inspire Company Innovation[13]" showed that a business' most engaged employees are the ones most likely to be the business's best source of new ideas. These same employees are much more likely to react positively to creative ideas offered by colleagues and will be more inclined to involve customers in the innovation and improvement process. It is obvious that a business wanting to maximise the potential talents of its workforce must first engage it as training alone will not be sufficient. The concept of psychological contract, described in Chapter11, also helps to underpin employee engagement as it engenders trust between employee and employer.

The best managers realise that specific talents are needed for every role and that every job, however easy it might be, will require talent. For example, the best receptionists will have a talent for winning others over and they easily establish a trust relationship with their visitors within seconds of an interaction.

Growing your own talent is a very effective way for businesses to obtain the skills needed whilst at the same time saving money as recruitment costs generally outweigh training costs. Businesses indicate that they have saved money by improving the skills of their internal staff and have also experienced improved employee retention and improved employee motivation. The most successful businesses are those that use formal rather than ad-hoc training

13 Gallup. (2006). Engaged employees inspire company innovation. Gallup Management Journal .

Talent Management ●●●

Talent consists of those individuals who can make a difference to organisational performance, either through their immediate contribution or in the longer-term by demonstrating the highest levels of potential.

Talent management is the planning of and putting into place systems that will identify, attract, develop, engage, retain and fully utilise those employees who will be of particular value to a business. This will either be through their future potential or because they currently have a crucial role in meeting the objectives of the business operation.

This concept has evolved into a common and essential management practice and is no longer just a part of the recruitment process. Talent management is much more than this as it now covers areas such as organisational capability, employee development, performance enhancement and succession and continuity planning.

There is a strong business case for adopting a strategic approach to talent management as indicated in the Accenture study where top executives globally see talent management as one of their key priorities. The increasing interest in talent is as a direct result of internal and external factors putting pressure on businesses to implement a talent management strategy. Internal factors will be such things as the business wanting competitive advantage, a flexible workforce and the elimination of any skills gaps, whilst at the same time taking into account their overall business strategy. External factors will include, for example, competitive global markets, government policies, developing technology, workforce diversity and demographic trends.

Case Study[14]

Developing and engaging their people

BT seeks to provide opportunities for personal growth and professional development. They believe that talented people increasingly want to work in companies that commit to and invest in the long-term development of their employees.

Their approach to developing and engaging people includes:

- learning and development principles and commitment
- career planning and development
- talent management
- employee engagement
- employee communications
- employee networks.

Building on a long tradition of volunteering at BT, they are developing a volunteering programme that is jointly inspired by the organisation and its people. The programme will support those BT people who wish to make a contribution in their local communities by working with charities and community organisations of their choice.

They define volunteering as, "An activity that involves spending time, doing something that aims to benefit the environment, communities, individuals or groups and which involves the development or transfer of skills and enhances the motivation and commitment of BT people."

BT is recognised as an Investor in People (IiP). IiP is a business improvement framework that incorporates good practice for training and development and which challenges businesses to improve working practices. This framework was devised by leading UK business and employee organisations. BT is the second largest privately owned company to achieve the IiP accreditation.

BT's talent management programme focuses on attracting, identifying and engaging, developing, deploying and retaining the people they need to deliver their business strategy. The diagram below shows the five key stages of their talent programme. The uncertain economic outlook makes effective talent management particularly important. BT continue to invest in their graduate, modern apprentice and Fast Track recruitment programmes to ensure they have the talent they need to succeed in the long term. They also focus on developing the existing workforce.

14 BT. (2010, January 11). Developing and engaging our people. Retrieved January 11, 2010, from btplc.com: http://www.btplc.com/Careercentre/Aboutus/BToverview/BToverview.htm

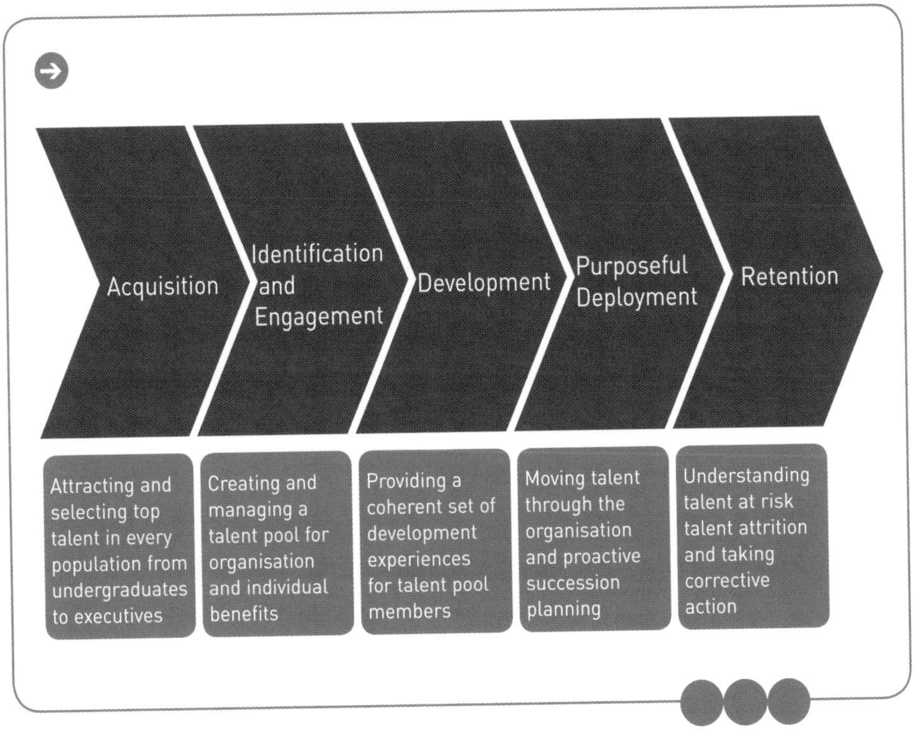

The Chartered Management Institute commissioned an All-Party Parliamentary Group on Management to discuss the question, "Can UK plc win the war for talent?"[15].

The group defined talent management as "the additional management processes and opportunities that are made available to people in the organisation who are considered to be 'talent'."

Themes and questions emerging from the meeting were:

- talent management has a key role to play in supporting the UK's competitiveness in the face of global competition, especially from India and China.
- the UK will experience a sharp decline in the number of unskilled jobs in the coming years and there will be a growing need for high-level skills.
- employers continue to face difficulties in identifying potential. By relying on performance measures as a proxy, they risk overlooking talented individuals.
- line managers play a pivotal role in the implementation of talent management. They need to be supported and trained to fulfil this role effectively.

The group felt that it was crucial for any business to ensure that their talent management policies were fully in line with the organisation's business objectives as many businesses fail to make the links explicit and have adopted a fragmented

15 Chartered Management Institute. (2007, November). Can UK plc win the war for talent? Retrieved January 21, 2010, from managers.org.uk: http://www.managers.org.uk/listing_1.aspx?doc=10:4439&id=10:286&id=10:108&id=10:9

approach to staff development and to their performance and reward policies. Talent management needs to be aligned with business strategy as only then will the right talent be identified and nurtured and so match the long-term growth plans of the business.

There are difficulties in being able to identify talent as there is a difference between current performance and achievement and future potential and capabilities. It would a mistake for managers to assume that performance is synonymous with potential as it could mean that talented employees are overlooked. Standard measures used to indicate potential are flawed and can again lead to a failure to spot talented individuals.

Any talent management policy should ensure that it is completely transparent as highlighting individuals as "talented" could lead to resentment amongst colleagues. Line managers also play a crucial role in this whole process as many employees, having been identified as talent, feel that their line managers have too much influence on their career. The identification of talent often relies on line managers so it very important for a responsible business to educate and train its line managers in the management and nurturing of talent. It would be very short sighted of any manager to operate on the basis that there is a finite pool of talent available as it is the responsibility of every manager to grow the people within their sphere of influence. Encouraging the use of coaching may also help to improve a manager's ability to recognise potential.

Other methods for developing talent include the notion that management and staff development should be thought of as a continuous process across an extended period of time with the opportunity for regular reflection, improved self-awareness and the consolidation of learning. This emphasises the importance of gaining experience in a range of situations with sufficient time to grow into each role but this can only be achieved if it is built into an individual's development plan. It should also be realised that it can only be over a period of time before an individual's potential can truly be established. The mix of work roles might include a period of time overseas if relevant to that particular company.

A responsible workplace would view under-performance as placing someone in the wrong situation for their abilities rather than labelling them as a "failure". Alternative roles should then be sought with the emphasis that learning has been gained from the experience.

It can be seen that there is no single approach to talent management that suits all organisations, instead each business should realise that there are a number of different elements and perspectives that it could use to support the achievement of its business objectives.

Employers squandering the talents of workers

The Work Foundation report "Knowledge Workers and Knowledge Work"[16] found that too many employers were poorly equipped to weather the recent recession because they used workers' skills and talents poorly, tied them up in rules and procedures, and gave them little say over how they did their work. This major new survey found that:

- 40 per cent of employees have more skills than their jobs require
- 65 per cent of workers said the primary characteristic of the organisations they worked for was 'rule and policy bound' – though just five per cent said this was their preference
- 40 per cent said they had little or no flexibility over the hours they worked
- 20 per cent of graduates are in 'low knowledge content' jobs.

A co-author of the report said: 'So far in this recession employers have been reluctant to lose the skills, talents and experience of their workforces. Yet at the same time they seem to be failing to make the most of them. Many people could be doing more, but are denied the chance to do so.

'To keep job losses to a minimum, organisations should be taking full advantage of widespread opportunities to give people more responsibility, move away from rules and procedure-based workplace cultures, and re-organise work and use new technologies to give individuals more flexibility over hours. More autonomy for people and less intensive management should be the order of the day. Trapping so many workers in roles in which their skills and abilities are poorly matched with their jobs is a waste both of economic potential and human possibility.'

One of the main findings of the report indicated that the UK has a '30-30-40' shaped workforce: 30 per cent of jobs have a high knowledge content (requiring greater cognitive complexity), 30 per cent have some knowledge content, and 40 per cent have less knowledge content.

Managing Hidden Talent ●●●

Through experience and research the Work Foundation[17] has identified six key principles to manage hidden talent which is based on a concept that assumes that most organisations have large amounts of talent that they never discover or exploit, whilst still thinking they lack talent. To tackle this problem they have developed the "Good Work Principles of Talent Management" which they use to help organisations address their talent management issues holistically.

16 The Work Foundation. (2009, March). Knowledge Workers and Knowledge Work. Retrieved January 21, 2010, from theworkfoundation.com: http://www.theworkfoundation.com/research/publications/publicationdetail.aspx?oItemid=213

17 The Work Foundation. (2010, January 21). Managing hidden talent. Retrieved January 21, 2010, from theworkfoundation.com: http://www.theworkfoundation.com/research/leadershipres/articles.aspx

The principles are as follows.

1. Talent management should be owned by business leaders and line managers as part of normal activity and no longer should it be a case of relying on HR or external consultants to be wholly responsible for talent identification. Those closest to the talent are the managers and they should be practising continuous evaluation of their staff.

2. Talent management must comprise consistent and transparent approaches to promotion and succession planning as a major negative impact on the psychological contract is inconsistency and a lack of transparency. An employee's response is often to withdraw goodwill and effort and therefore keep their talent to themselves or even worse they could offer their skills to another employer.

3. Employees should play an active role in the management of their own talent and a responsible employer should encourage each employee to explore their potential and recognise how this can then best be used to the mutual benefit of the employee and the organisation.

4. A clear distinction should be made between assessment and development as individuals should be allowed to take risks and this may involve temporary failure but we do all learn from our mistakes. It would be both unfair and unethical to assess an employee's performance in the context of a learning experience.

5. The content of "talent pools" should be regularly reviewed – no employee should be "written off" and decisions ear-marking individuals as talented should be revisited on a regular basis as an individual's performance and motivation can change. If those currently not in the talent pool feel they have been ignored and written off the organisation will lose the potential and motivation they might have offered.

6. Organisations should maintain an open mind about sources of talent to encourage diversity by looking for talent in less obvious places as so much potential can be hidden through personality, prejudice and lack of opportunity.

The majority of businesses now realise that talented workers are their most important asset and a failure to retain this talent could adversely affect the ability of the business to compete effectively in the future. The responsible workplace will maintain staff training and development and ensure the health and well-being of their employees through flexible working and true employee engagement.

A new right for employees to request time to train from employers in England, Scotland and Wales with 250 or more employees was effective from April 2010. Employees can request any training they think will improve both their and the business's performance and employers have to consider formal requests for time away from work for training. The training can be accredited or unaccredited and can be in the workplace, at home or abroad. There is no limit on the amount of time employees can request. The employer does not have to pay for the training or for the time given to it.

Employers must:

- accept the request and inform the employee of their decision in writing
- meet the employee to discuss their request - and within 14 days of that meeting, inform the employee of their decision in writing

within 28 days of receiving a request.

If needed, the employer can ask for more information. The employer can agree with the request but make alternative suggestions as to where the training might take place, for example, or what the training should be.

An employer may only refuse a request for time to train for certain pre-set business reasons.

The right to request training will be extended to all employees from 6 April 2011.

SECTION 4

Business

- Consumers
- Suppliers
- Borrowing, Banking and Investment
- Integrity and Reputation
- Products and Services
- Shareholders and other Stakeholders

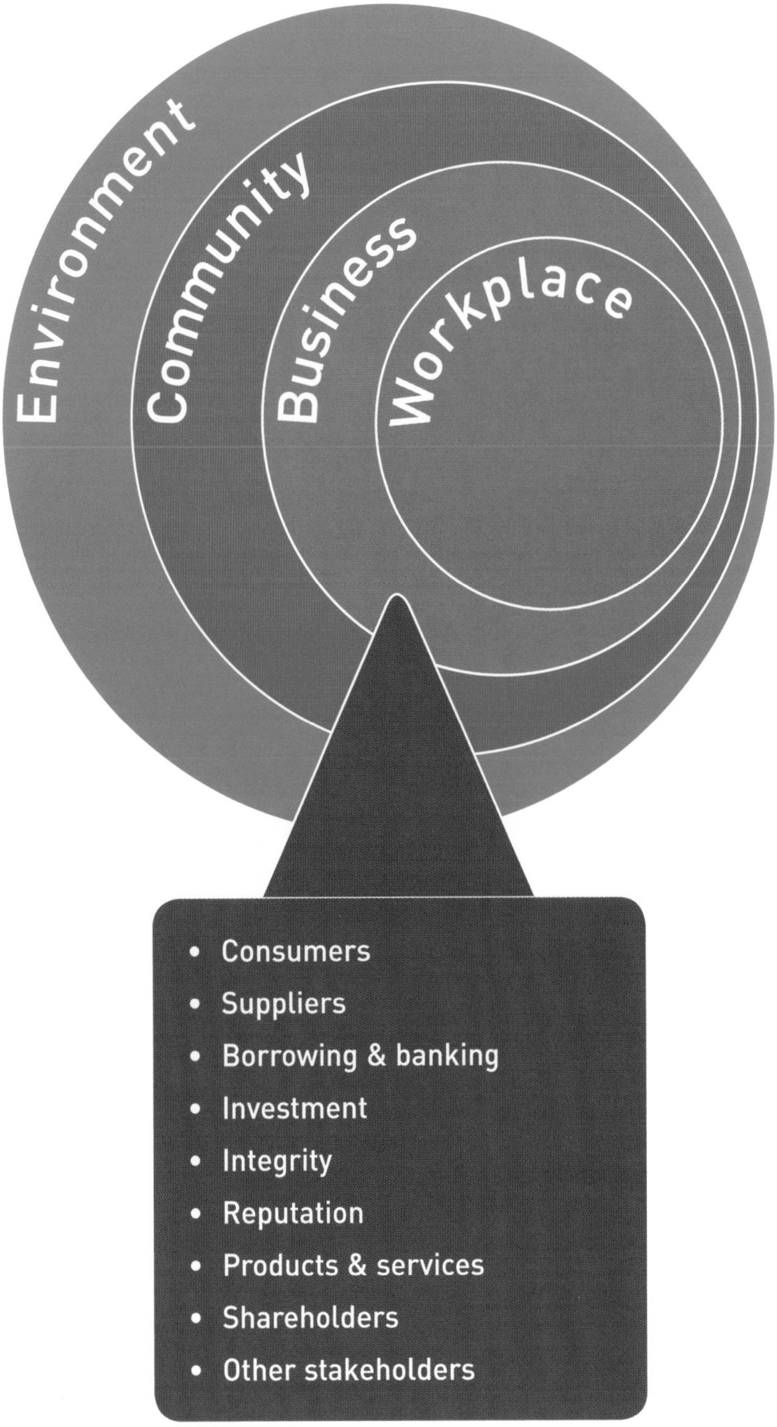

- Consumers
- Suppliers
- Borrowing & banking
- Investment
- Integrity
- Reputation
- Products & services
- Shareholders
- Other stakeholders

Business

Reputation and image is good
Ethical products or services
Stakeholders are heard
Pricing is fair
Open to scrutiny
New opportunities identified
Sustainable supply chain
Influencing legislation
Brand image positive
Linking thinking
Environmentally aware

CHAPTER 14

Consumers

- Consumers and Carbon
- Carbon Reduction Labelling
- Genuine Claims and no Greenwash!
- Sustainable Marketing

Consumers and Carbon ●●●

The report "Consumers, Business and Climate Change", prepared by the Sustainable Consumption Institute at The University of Manchester in October 2009[1], highlights the fact that, as consumers, our lives are based on goods, services and activities that depend on the production of greenhouse gas emissions. Taking UK emissions alone, a conservative estimate is that 75% of emissions are influenced directly or indirectly by consumers. At the same time, much hope is being invested in international negotiations, often led by individual countries, as a way of tackling climate change. But with emissions rising exponentially the report states that solutions are needed more quickly than governments can achieve on their own.

Consumption transcends national boundaries. Businesses serve consumers, operate globally and can work quickly. So the report suggests that the opportunity is there for consumers, helped by businesses, to lead a "green revolution".

The report highlights the fact that the rise in emissions is due to growing consumption combined with an expanding global population.

- **Consumption** is directly linked to greenhouse gas emissions through fossil fuel power generation, industrial processing and agriculture.
- **Global population** is set to increase from close to 7 billion in 2009 to 9.2 billion by 2050. Although producing much lower emissions per person than developed countries, developing countries are seeking rising living and consumption standards, which will raise greenhouse gas emissions still further.

The authors of the report realise that it is neither desirable socially nor possible in reality to deny countries the opportunity to develop and raise living standards, so the aim must be to find routes to low-carbon improvements in living standards in both developed and developing countries.

Attempts to reduce consumer emissions often involve trying to impose measures on people to limit their activities but more often than not they fail to achieve the reductions required. Nevertheless the authors of the report feel that consumers can play a crucial and powerful role in the fight against climate change. With help and support to change their behaviour voluntarily, and to seek low-carbon products and services, it is suggested they can:

- reduce emissions in the least expensive way
- have an immediate impact
- have an impact which can be sustained
- stimulate competition for low-carbon innovation by businesses
- empower governments to enact low-carbon policies.

Consumer action can achieve both improved living standards and a rapid reduction in carbon emissions – more rapid than can be achieved by governments alone.

1 Sustainable Consumption Institute. (2009). Consumers,Business and Climate Change. Manchester: Sustainable Consumption Institute.

Surveys around the world show that consumers are willing to tackle climate change. But they face some common barriers – the availability and price of low-carbon products, lack of information, and a sense of hopelessness in the face of a huge problem. The challenge for decision-makers is therefore to overcome these barriers and to unleash consumer and business against climate change.

The first step in empowering consumers is to remove the individual barriers they face when trying to make low-carbon choices and this can be done by providing cheaper options and incentives, more information on the impact of consumer choices on the environment and giving out clear messages that "ethical" consumers are not acting alone.

However, individual strategies are not by themselves enough. The choices made by consumers are affected not just by the products they find in a store, but also by the cultural context in which they live. The report recommends that low-carbon choices, products and actions must become the social norm by:

- using taste-makers, early adopters and consumer champions to make low-carbon fashionable
- instilling low-carbon habits at work and explaining how these can be applied at home
- promoting carbon numeracy in schools and among the young so they can influence their households and be the low-carbon generations of the future
- encouraging low-carbon advocates and adopters to communicate with and support each other via virtual and real low-carbon clubs and communities
- developing community-wide strategies to reduce carbon.

Another key recommendation in the report is that low-carbon choices must also be integrated into everyday life. It is not enough simply to substitute a high-carbon product with a low-carbon one instead both business and consumer should recognise that goods and infrastructure are interconnected and need to evolve consistently. Developing low-carbon products in conjunction with appropriate changes to the infrastructure will put consumers at the heart of the fight against climate change.

The slowness of change brought about by government alone was more than confirmed in March 2010 when it was reported in the financial press that the global green economic stimulus of 2009 had achieved little, with only a fraction of the money for environmental projects spent, according to a study from HSBC. The "green stimulus" came about in the wake of the financial crisis, as governments sought to spend money and create jobs as quickly as possible.

About $82bn of public sector stimulus funds were spent during 2009, or 16 per cent of the total pledged to schemes such as high-speed rail, renewable energy and electricity grid upgrades which are exactly the changes to infrastructure required to complement changes to consumer choices. However, HSBC predicted that most of the remaining funds would be spent in 2010, forecasting that $248bn would go on green projects in 2010, followed by $146bn in 2011 and $28bn in 2012.

However other aspects of the recommendations coming from the Sustainable Consumption Institute seem to have been more than matched.

Carbon Reduction Labelling

At the end of Chapter 1 it was suggested that Accountants should stop counting beans and count carbon instead and it now seems that carbon counting is as important as calorie counting to Britain's shoppers.

The full extent of their carbon consciousness was revealed in February 2010 in the results of a survey carried out by the Carbon Trust[2]. This showed that carbon counting now stands shoulder to shoulder with calorie counting when it comes to the weekly shop.

The Carbon Trust states that the research is a clear call to action for British businesses to show their carbon commitment and therefore sign up to the Carbon Reduction Label in order to satisfy the UK consumer's appetite for green shopping. The research revealed that:

- 86% of consumers want their favourite brands to help combat the threat of climate change by reducing their carbon footprint
- almost half (43%) are actively seeking information about the carbon impact of the products they buy and more than half (52%) would be more loyal to a brand if they could see at a glance they were taking steps to reduce their footprint
- it seems that they are more ready than ever to stand by their carbon principles, with almost a quarter (22%) of respondents willing to stop buying their favourite brands if they didn't commit to bearing the Carbon Reduction Label
- cars, electrical goods and food were the products they most wanted to see making the carbon commitment.

Since 2007 the Carbon Trust has worked with more than 65 brands and 4,000 individual product lines to measure and reduce the carbon footprint of many everyday household items.

Companies that display the Carbon Trust's Carbon Reduction Label are making a commitment to reduce the carbon footprint of their product or service. The carbon footprint of a product or service is the total carbon dioxide (CO2) and other greenhouse gases emitted during its life, from production to final disposal. The

2 Carbon Trust. (2010, February 17). Does my carbon footprint look big in this. Retrieved February 18, 2010, from carbontrust.co.uk: http://www.carbontrust.co.uk/news/news/press-centre2010/2010/Pages/does-my-carbon-footprint-look-big-in-this.aspx

Carbon Reduction Label currently appears on products worth £2.7 billion in annual sales.

Morphy Richards irons carry the Carbon Reduction Label as do other staples such as Kingsmill bread, Walkers crisps, Tate & Lyle sugar and Tesco milk, orange juice, light bulbs, and washing detergent.

A spokesperson for the Carbon Trust claimed that British consumers are increasingly looking for simple ways to reduce their carbon footprint, without sacrificing on price, taste or convenience. They want to protect the environment, but are often confused about how they can make a difference. They don't want to hear about big numbers and global targets as this is beyond their scope to control so they want to see at a glance which companies and brands are doing their bit to tackle climate change. These sentiments more than echo the Sustainable Consumption Institute's report findings.

More positive news was reported at the end of 2009 when it was revealed that green spending in the UK had increased by 5 per cent compared with the previous year. It was suggested that British consumers are taking their own steps towards a sustainable future with each UK household now spending on average £251 on items such as energy efficient light bulbs, appliances, carbon offsetting and even "green" mortgages. Data from the Co-operative Bank shows spending in the UK on environmentally friendly products amounts to more than £6.4bn, but this is still a fraction of total household expenditure.

A spokesperson for the bank stated that many people in the UK are working hard to adopt a greener lifestyle. But, while ethical consumers play a vital role in the early adoption and development of products and services the amount being spent still only accounts for less than 1 per cent of total household expenditure. He went on to say that for the UK to reduce carbon emissions by 30 per cent by 2020 there will need to be a change in take-up of low-carbon technologies and this will need a contract between business, government and the consumer.

More research featured the media at the end of 2009 revealed that British consumers are the most ethical in Europe. According to IGD, a market research company, shoppers in the UK are more likely to buy goods based on environmental, animal welfare or fair trade claims than their counterparts in Europe. About 41 per cent of British consumers have bought ethical products, compared with 34 per cent in Germany, 31 per cent in France and 12 per cent in Spain.

The research provided evidence that British consumers were retaining their ethical and environmental concerns despite the economic pressures of the recent recession.

However shoppers also felt less able to make a difference through shopping decisions. Only 23 per cent of those asked in 2009 believed that they could make a difference to the environment in this way which is down from 44 per cent in 2007. After the recent financial crisis consumers have had the chance to take stock and the research would suggest that they feel that they don't have enough empowerment as they also feel that they have no control over the big issues. This increases the need for responsible retailers to be more transparent about the sourcing of products[3].

An on-line survey conducted by "Which?"[4] magazine in May 2009 asked members which product would they be more likely to buy if they had green claims. The results of the survey were as follows:

Household appliances	67%
Gardening products	53%
Cleaning products	47%
Cars	46%
Electrical goods	45%
Food and drink	44%
Toiletries and cosmetics	31%
Utilities	18%
Clothing and textiles	15%
Financial products	6%

This survey also found that consumers said that there are now so many green claims they don't know which ones to take seriously, but despite the fact that only 21% think green claims are always true 56% of those asked are still likely to buy a product with a green claim.

3 IGD. (2009, October 13). Shoppers will continue to be careful after recession. Retrieved April 10, 2010, from igd.com: http://www.igd.com/index.asp?id=1&fid=6&sid=25&cid=1209

4 Which? (2009, May). 'Eco' ads under fire. Which? , p. 7.

Genuine Claims and No Greenwash

In 2009 MP's on the Environmental Audit Committee (EAC) reported that the 'meaningless' environmental claims' to promote products was a growing problem. The Advertising Standards Authority (ASA) received 369 complaints about green claims in 264 adverts in 2008 and it upheld 21.

The EAC wants ministers to bring in a green labelling scheme to prevent the problem of "greenwash".

Companies must ensure claims are clear and meaningful and hopefully any new code introduced will mean that consumers can trust the claims that are made.

More research carried out by the Carbon Trust[5] in the same period identified that consumers increasingly scrutinise business actions on climate change, they want to see clearer, more credible information on what companies are doing to reduce their environmental impact. The research showed that 70% of consumers do not feel confident that they can clearly identify which companies are environmentally responsible. Six in ten consumers (59%) are sceptical about the environmental claims companies make, and 44% of consumers would like more information on what companies are actually doing to be environmentally responsible.

The research showed that consumers look to a range of indicators to understand whether or not a company is environmentally responsible, but the most important criteria they rely on are what they read in the media (38%) and third party endorsement or accreditation (34%). The least popular factor consumers use to judge whether a company is behaving in an environmentally responsible manner is what advertising tells them (6%).

It also revealed that people expect to see evidence of action from public sector organisations as well as business – 81% feel it is important that public sector organisations tackle climate change and cut carbon, compared to 62% who believe it is important for all businesses.

The ethical and environmental reputations of leading DIY, furniture and garden retailers fell across the board in 2009 despite a veritable blitz of green initiatives. According to a variety of press and television reports, every home or gardens retailer featured in the poll suffered a fall in how ethically aware consumers rated their behaviour.

These findings came at the same time as concern was being expressed by the EAC and the Carbon Trust research outlined above was published amid the same fears of a "greenwash" in companies' marketing of their environmental credentials. It had previously been reported that the Advertising Standards Authority, the advertising watchdog, was cracking down on spurious green claims regarding, for example, carbon neutrality.

5 Carbon Trust. (2009, March 12). Green expectations:consumers still want to buy green but expect evidence of action. Retrieved February 11, 2010, from carbontrust.co.uk: http://www.carbontrust.co.uk/news/news/press-centre/2009/Pages/green-expectations.aspx

It was suggested by many pundits that the decline in ratings by concerned consumers of the retailers' environmental conduct was a symptom of the economic climate at the time. Consumers appeared more nervous and less trusting of companies and they were withholding their belief until they had sorted out what is or isn't "greenwash".

There is a possibility that in their desperation to be on-message on environmental and social concerns, such as the use of child labour, retailers were saying what "sounded right", even if it was some way from the truth. However, this is only likely to create mistrust which obscures even the activities of well-meaning companies. As customers become more suspicious, companies need to be more careful about how they talk about their environmental or social standards. Various reports suggested that nearly 80 per cent of concerned consumers do not believe that they have sufficient information on the environmental and social impacts of goods to make an informed choice.

Consumers' knowledge and understanding of the environmental impact of products or services is changing rapidly and four months after the Times article and the Carbon Trust's previous research there was a more positive shift in thinking. Fresh research from the Carbon Trust published at the end of June 2009[6] revealed that almost two thirds of consumers (63%) were more likely to buy a product if they knew action was being taken to reduce its carbon footprint. At the same time 70% of consumers wanted businesses to do more to help them make more informed environmental choices about the products they buy.

This fresh research found that green credentials do carry consumer weight. A commitment to reduce a product's carbon footprint has a positive impact on the brand's reputation, as 58% of the consumers questioned said that they value companies that are taking action to reduce their carbon emissions.

The research also concluded that environmentally responsible brands must provide a much clearer picture of their actions as only 12% of consumers think that companies are doing enough to cut carbon emissions and tackle climate change. This is linked to their call for help on making better choices, and a demand from just under half (47%) for information on how to reduce the footprint of a product when using it.

The research showed that consumer understanding of sustainability continued to grow as 60% of consumers understood that a product such as a chocolate bar or loaf of bread has a carbon footprint. More than two thirds of the UK's carbon footprint comes from products and services.

However giving consumers the kind of information they need to help reduce carbon footprints may not be completely straightforward.

6 Carbon Trust. (2009, June 29). High Street failing on Footprinting. Retrieved February 11, 2010, from carbontrust.co.uk: http://www.carbontrust.co.uk/news/news/press-centre/2009/Pages/carbon-footprint-research.aspx

In Chapter 5 reference was made to the fact that the "myth of food miles" was misleading to consumers in that the carbon emissions produced by foods transported from other parts of the world may well be lower than food stuffs produced in the UK as the production processes and storage might be more costly to the environment. The same reasoning could also be applied to "product miles". Some doubt could also be cast on carbon labelling as a more appropriate alternative as there is a danger that the calculation of carbon emissions for a particular product might stop at the "factory gate". In other words no account is taken of the transportation implications or the far more complicated task of trying to establish how much carbon is being emitted by the consumer when cooking or using a particular product.

A good example of that might be chickpeas. Chickpeas are sold in supermarkets in two versions: dried or cooked. The carbon footprint of the latter is far higher than the former. The only processing involved in drying chickpeas is to lay them out in the sun to drive off moisture. By contrast, heat is needed to cook chickpeas before they are tinned. Hence the carbon gram total for tins of cooked chickpeas would be far greater than those on packets of the dried variety. Also the weight of a tin is likely to exceed that of the dried version and this will have a big impact on fuel usage in the transportation phase and therefore carbon emission plus there will be different options for recycling the packaging.

This may seem straightforward but the customer can't eat dried chickpeas. They will have to cook them and when they take them home they may find that the carbon emitted when cooking those chickpeas exceeds the figure for the tinned variety - because cooking small portions at home is inefficient compared with that of large industrial kitchens. But did the consumer use gas or electricity? Gas is more efficient and less prone to carbon emissions.

Consumers want to see businesses taking action on environmental issues and also want to be better informed as to the likely impact of their buying choices so any carbon labelling of products must be able to give the consumer the full picture. The Sustainable Consumption Institute have identified that there is a need to look at the whole life-cycle of a product from raw material to disposal or recycling. This will be covered more fully in Chapter 18 where some examples will be given.

The Carbon Reduction Label devised and promoted by the Carbon Trust does take account of the whole life-cycle of the product but they admit that it will be relatively easy to calculate the carbon emissions on some products and far more complicated for others so may well involve some best estimates.

Consumers do want this information and may well also be a little frustrated by the fact that only a relatively small number of products will have this information on the packaging. Tesco have selected 30 products as part of a pilot programme but how many thousands of products do Tesco sell? Walkers crisps have displayed a carbon footprint for some time but none of the other snack foods made by the company have the same information as yet. Consumers will be made aware by this labelling that these companies are tackling and reducing their carbon footprint but on a day to day basis it may be some time before consumers can make fully informed decisions on everything they buy or choose not to buy.

Business leaders are only too aware of the need for change in their behaviours because of consumer pressure as was reflected in the "Lean and Green: Leadership for the low-carbon future" study carried out by the Chartered Management Institute and published In July 2009. Survey respondents were asked to consider a range of possible external drivers of green activity. Three factors emerged as significantly more important than the others: energy costs, ranked as important or very important by 77 per cent, and regulation and government (both 74 per cent). Pressures from customers (potential customers or existing customers) also emerged strongly[7].

The main problem for business will be to successfully persuade potential or existing customers that their efforts to reduce carbon emissions are genuine and not simply greenwash, but, as has already been shown in the Carbon Trust research, only 6% of consumers questioned would necessarily believe an advertising campaign in which a business made CR claims about itself. A new initiative from Business in the Community (BITC) will try to address this situation.

Sustainable Marketing ●●●

In February 2010 BITC launched a new publication targeted at marketing professionals to help them to build sustainability into, rather than onto, their brands as they believe that marketers have a crucial role to play in creating positive societal change on sustainability. The publication entitled 'How Can Marketers Build Sustainable Success?'[8] uses case studies from leading companies and the experiences of marketing directors to enable the profession to play a more central role in the debate around sustainability. The participants in the study unanimously agreed that corporate responsibility is increasingly being led by marketing and sales teams as much as by the corporate centre and that marketers are in a position to have a much greater role in taking the sustainability debate out to consumers.

Actively managing your responsibilities to customers, and being open and honest in your communications. It is about influencing customer behaviour to create both profit and positive societal change.

7 Chartered Management Institute. (2009). Lean and Green:Leadership for the low-carbon future. London: Chartered Management Institute.

8 BITC. (2010, February 1). What is Sustainable Marketing. Retrieved February 20, 2010, from bitc.org.uk: http://www.bitc.org.uk/marketplace/customers/sustainable_marketin.html

One participant saw the business case for embedding sustainability into the marketing of products as having a positive impact across six areas:

1. fuelling innovation
2. helping to win with customers
3. helping to win in developing and emerging markets
4. addressing the needs of consumers as "citizens"
5. generating cost savings
6. differentiating and building brands.

Another member of the group suggested that businesses about to embark on sustainable marketing programmes should remember that it is about:

- the renaissance of brand trust and affinity
- doing it first, telling people second (ensuring it is evidence-based)
- understanding (product) footprint and spotting the right issues
- ensuring that 'doing good is good for business'
- remembering that the desire to shout about it is much greater than most consumers' capacity to listen.

Sustainable marketing is about brands which are environmentally, socially and financially sustainable but if businesses really want to build a relationship of trust with their customers then they must be seen to be taking genuine and meaningful actions to improve society and the environment.

Case Study[9]

Marks & Spencer (M&S) announced at the beginning of March 2010 that it will expand its Plan A programme to cover all of its 2.7 billion individual M&S food, clothing and home items, in a bid to be the world's most sustainable retailer by 2015.

By expanding its Plan A commitments to incorporate wider stakeholder groups, such as supply chains and customers, as well as its employees, M&S is taking its responsibilities to people and planet seriously.

The eight-year extension of the retailer's eco and ethical programme will see each of the products in its 36,000 product lines carry at least one sustainable or ethical quality and will fully embed sustainability into the way they do business.

Marks & Spencer launched Plan A in January 2007 with ambitious goals to

- make M&S carbon neutral
- send no waste to landfill
- extend sustainable sourcing
- be a fair partner, set new standards in ethical trading and help customers and employees live healthier lifestyles.

By extending the original 100 Plan A commitments to 180, M&S hopes it will enable its 2,000 suppliers to adopt Plan A best practice and encourage M&S customers and employees to live 'greener' lifestyles.

The new Plan A commitments are divided into seven areas and include the following.

1. **Customers and Plan A** - to help customers to live more sustainable lives
2. **Make Plan A part of how we do business** - to accelerate their moves to make Plan A 'how we do business'.
3. **Tackling climate change** - make operations in UK and Republic of Ireland carbon neutral.
4. **Packaging and waste** - stop sending waste to landfill from stores, offices and warehouses, reduce use of packaging and carrier bags, and find new ways to recycle and reuse the materials used.
5. **Being a fair partner** - improve the lives of hundreds of thousands of people in the supply chain and local communities.
6. **Natural resources** - to ensure that key raw materials come from the most sustainable source possible, in order to protect the environment and the world's natural resources.
7. **Health and well-being** - helping thousands of customers and employees choose a healthier lifestyle.

9 BITC. (2010, March 1). M & S launch campaign to be most sustainable retailer by 2015. Retrieved March 3, 2010, from bitc.org.uk: http://www.bitc.org.uk/media_centre/news/plan_a_expansion.html

A key message throughout this book is that responsible and sustainable business practice is not just about climate change and environmental issues but should encompass every aspect of the business and its stakeholders. So far this chapter has largely concentrated on environmental issues because the UK's consumers will base many of their buying decisions in the future on how they see or perceive businesses conducting themselves on environmental matters.

However, the British consumer will also be concerned that they are treated fairly and honestly by any seller of goods or services. Obviously there is a whole raft of consumer protection legislation which already exists and which may well be extended to include more specifics on green claims in the future.

In order to address the wider issues of consumer protection and fairness BITC introduced their "Marketplace Responsibility Principles" in December 2006[10] and subsequently amended them in early 2010. The principles that are particularly relevant to consumers are as follows.

Respect your customers

Treat customers honestly and with integrity. Give full information about your product or service and honour your promises. Avoid false statements or other irresponsible marketing. Respond to complaints. See customers as having a legitimate interest in your business over issues and concerns beyond the direct commercial relationship.

Support vulnerable customers

Understand which of your customers may be unusually adversely affected by the product or service, or by interruption of supply. Take steps to mitigate these effects.

Seek potential customers within excluded groups

If appropriate, identify whether your product or service would provide real benefit for people that are currently excluded from it, whether through poverty, geography or disability.

10 BITC. (2010, February 10). What are the Marketplace Responsibility Principles? Retrieved February 20, 2010, from bitc.org.uk: http://www.bitc.org.uk/cr_academy/view_all_resources/marketplace_resources/responsible_supply_chain_management/general_supply_chain_resources/networks_events_publications_and_other_resources/business_in_the.html

CHAPTER 15

Suppliers

- Business Risks
- Business Opportunities
- Social, Economic and Environmental Issues
- Steps Needed (to create a responsible and sustainable supply chain)

> *Sustainable Procurement is a process whereby organisations meet their needs for goods, services, works and utilities in a way that achieves value for money on a whole life basis in terms of generating benefits not only to the organisation, but also to society and the economy, whilst minimising damage to the environment.*

Procuring the Future, Recommendations from the Sustainable Procurement Task Force, Defra 2006

Business risks

Managing a supply chain responsibly integrates management of economic, environmental and social issues arising in supply chains and utilising purchasing power to affect positive change while all the time retaining a respectful and fair approach to relationships with suppliers by treating them as partners.

Responsible supply chain management isn't simply a question of doing "the right thing" as it also makes good business sense. Through ensuring responsible management of its supply chain a business will be able to minimise risks and seize business opportunities. It will help build better and more sustainable long-term relationships with suppliers, in turn ensuring quality and security of supply.

Sustainable procurement matters to a responsible business because it will help to reduce the effect of certain business risks.

- **Reputational risks** - The exposure of irresponsible practice in the supply chain – perhaps due to the use of child labour by a sub-contractor or contaminated products – can result in severe damage to business reputation and customer trust, which can translate into tangible losses. Alternatively some companies have sought to realise reputational gains through becoming associated with positive supply chain initiatives such as Fair Trade.

Case Study

Retailer drops firms using child labour

In 2008 a leading cut-price fashion chain admitted that it had been buying clothes from suppliers who use child labour. The company said that it would be dropping three Indian companies that make thousands of clothes for its stores after discovering they had sub-contracted work out to companies that, in some cases, used children for embroidery work.

The chief executive said, "We are appalled, we feel let down and we are taking all the action we can to prevent this happening again."

The retail company insisted that at no time was it aware that children were being used to finish the products, ranging from T-shirts to skirts. It said that garments supplied by the companies involved accounted for only 0.04 per cent of the total amount brought in from around the world. The items made by the Indian companies were removed from the shops.

Case Study[1]

Cadbury's Dairy Milk became Fairtrade certified in late summer 2009 despite the global economic crisis at the time. The company realised that it was important that businesses keep making progress on core business issues and this decision by Cadbury clearly demonstrated that responsible business was still at the forefront of their agenda.

Cadbury is an excellent example of a company demonstrating leadership in responsible business and building on its 100 years as a value led organisation and it also demonstrated its commitment to its supply chains by improving the social and economic environment of its farmers as well as providing opportunities for thousands of more farmers to benefit from the system. Given that 15% of the chocolate bought in Britain was Dairy Milk, this step would help mainstream fair trade chocolate in the UK market.

This move also demonstrated how the integration of responsible business strategies can improve the capacity of key suppliers through responsible supply chain management and increase trust with key stakeholders.

The CEO of Cadbury also led the "Marketplace Programme" a Business in the Community initiative which aims to put responsible business practice at the heart of commercial operations. The programme works with companies to anticipate and address issues in the areas of customer and supplier relationships, product impact and innovation and business ethics.

1 BITC. (2009, March 4). Joanna Daniels backs Cadbury and its fair trade Dairy Milk. Retrieved February 9, 2010, from bitc.org.uk: http://www.bitc.org.uk/media_centre/comment/cadbury_fair_trade.html

- **Legal risks** - Faulty or dangerous products due to poor practice in the supply chain can result in considerable legal and compensatory costs. If a product is not fit for purpose or safe a product recall is a likely possibility. Press reports have highlighted that UK product recalls have more than doubled since 2004 and there has been much in the news about Toyota in the early part of 2010. It has also been found through online polls that following a recall for health and safety reasons 55 per cent of customers would "temporarily purchase another brand and then purchase the recalled brand once it was safe", 15 per cent would "purchase another brand and never purchase the recalled brand again" and 21 per cent would "avoid using any brand made by the manufacturer of the recalled products". Responsible management of supply chain risks as well as working with suppliers to increase their standards can minimise such business costs and foster customer trust.

Taking early action on issues within the supply chain such as environmental or safety standards may actually mean a business is compliant with new legislation and regulation such as WEEE & REACH prior to its coming into force giving the business an advantage over competitors who scramble to take action retrospectively.

Case Study[2]

Microsoft's Supply Chain Management - used with permission from Microsoft

Suppliers are a vital part of the business success of Microsoft, and an extension of their corporate footprint. They have a comprehensive Vendor Code of Conduct that sets tough standards based on social and environmental metrics for their approximately 35,000 contractors, suppliers, and vendors around the world. They seek to ensure conformance to these standards through direct engagement and training of their contracted direct material suppliers. They conduct informal and formal risk-based third-party monitoring based on the Electronics Industry Citizenship Coalition (EICC) Code of Conduct, laws, and regulations. This performance and capability assessment lets them identify performance gaps and improve processes to reduce risk and ensure a robust and sustainable supply chain.

Microsoft view their supply chain as an extension of the Microsoft business, so supplier conduct, conditions, and welfare are important to the sustainability of their business.

- They perform a greenhouse gas emissions assessment of hardware suppliers, which represents over 90 per cent of direct spending on materials from contract manufacturers.
- They conduct a Supplier Satisfaction Survey with 2,300 vendors, representing 75 per cent of Microsoft's total supply chain spending.

- They audited 84 factories and related facilities of their contracted manufacturing suppliers, and performed 113 follow-up site audits in 2008, in accordance with the Electronics Industry Citizenship Coalition (EICC) guidelines.
- Microsoft are monitoring the sub-tier suppliers of their contract manufacturing suppliers, completing 62 initial site evaluations in 2008. This is part of their effort to delve deeper into their supply chain.
- They help extend the life of over 500,000 PCs each year through their Digital Pipeline and Microsoft Authorized Refurbisher programme.

2 Microsoft. (2010, February 18). Corporate Citizenship. Retrieved February 18, 2010, from microsoft.com: http://www.microsoft.com/about/corporatecitizenship/en-us/our-focus/operating-responsibly/employees-and-suppliers.aspx

Operational risks - Working collaboratively with suppliers can help secure continuity of supply. All businesses are currently looking for ways to cut costs but when suppliers cannot finance their operations through bank credit, imposing unfair extended payment terms on suppliers could have unintended consequences. British businesses in 2009 were bearing the late payment burden of £30 billion as a million plus small and medium sized British businesses were hit by late payments – and collectively, were owed a staggering £30.4 billion, according to Bacs Payment Schemes Limited (Bacs), the organisation behind Direct Debit and Bacs Direct Credit.

That's a rise of more than £11 billion over two years in the amount outstanding to the country's SMEs (figures stood at £18.6 billion in 2007). While the average owed to individual SMEs at any one time had fallen from £38,000 in 2008 to £28,000 in 2009, the number of SMEs reporting that they were experiencing payment delays rose by just over 65%, up from 684,000 in 2008 to 1,085,000 in 2009.[3]

A fair approach to relations with suppliers can help secure the sustainability of a business.

3 Bacs. (2009, September). British businesses bear late payment burden of £30 billion. Retrieved February 11, 2010, from bacs.co.uk: http://www.bacs.co.uk/bacs/press/pressreleases/2009/pages/britishbusinessesbearlatepaymentburdenof£30billion.aspx

Case Study[4]

Supermarkets face supplier rules

A new code of practice has come into force which is intended to help farmers and food companies when they do business with the main supermarkets. Practices such as big chains altering supply terms retrospectively or asking suppliers to fund promotions such as two-for-one deals will be outlawed. Supermarkets will have to keep written records of negotiations with suppliers.

The National Farmers Union welcomed the code but said an ombudsman is needed to help enforce the rules. The government began a 12-week consultation in early 2010 to decide how the new ombudsman would work.

For years, suppliers and farmers have been complaining of unfair dealings and unreasonable demands from the big supermarket chains. The new Groceries Supply Code of Practice will give them access to independent arbitration and protect them from practices such as being asked to cover the cost of theft. Regulated by the Office of Fair Trading, it also requires retailers to train staff to use the code and appoint compliance officers.

It covers the 10 biggest grocery retailers - those with annual sales of over £1bn - whereas previously codes only covered the four largest chains.

An investigation in 2008 concluded that a stronger code of practice was needed. The Competition Commission found that large grocery retailers were passing on excessive risks and unexpected costs to their suppliers. In August 2009 it recommended that the government take steps to set up, as soon as practicable, an ombudsman to levy penalties on large grocery retailers for non-compliance.

4 BBC News. (2010, February 4). Supermarkets face supplier rules. Retrieved February 4, 2010, from news.bbc.co.uk: http://news.bbc.co.uk/1/hi/business/8497417.stm

Business Opportunities ●●●

As well as reducing business risks sustainable procurement also has the advantage of increasing business opportunities.

- **Increase supplier loyalty** - A supplier that comes to a business first with their innovations will provide that business with a significant competitive advantage. When suppliers develop new products or services they will be incentivised to come to a particular business before anyone else if there is a history of positive relations. Treating suppliers as partners, helping them improve their performance and be "fit for the future" will foster this type of loyalty and also help to increase security of supply.
- **Increased market share/new market** - Ethical consumerism is growing. The 2008 Cooperative Consumerism report found that the ethical market in the UK was up 15 per cent on the previous12 months and was now worth £35.5 billion. Developing more ethical and sustainable products to meet consumer demand can only be done through collaboration in the supply chain. Improving the standards of the business's products and services as well as the ethical reputation of the product can increase the market share of the business.
- **Access to investment** - A responsible approach to managing the risks in supply chains demonstrates good quality management making your business more attractive to potential investors. Investors, and particularly institutional investors, are increasingly factoring performance on environmental, social and governance issues into mainstream investment decisions. At a time when bank finance is increasingly difficult to secure, a business that displays good quality supply chain management could be viewed as more favourable by potential investors and over the longer term investment decisions will be increasingly affected by CR performance.
- **Winning new business** - When a business tenders for a project its supply chain may also be scrutinised. Increasingly businesses are facing the prospect of losing sales due to poor supply chain or CR performance generally. The ability to demonstrate excellent management processes, supplier diversity, good labour standards and carbon reduction in the supply chain will help a business gain a competitive advantage and may even be a prerequisite for awarding contracts, particularly with the public sector.
- **Cost savings** - Cutting carbon also results in direct cost savings for businesses. One of the easiest ways to economise in difficult economic times is to look for ways to reduce use of energy, waste and transportation.
- **Attract & retain talent** - Employees increasingly want to work for responsible businesses. Responsible supply chain management can bolster CR credentials and help businesses recruit and retain experienced staff and new talent in the procurement function and beyond.

The Legal Sector Alliance[5] identified the business benefits of sustainable procurement for their members because clients are increasingly asking their legal advisers to demonstrate their green credentials. Being ahead of the game can give firms competitive advantage, but equally, as more firms build environmental considerations into the procurement process, it will drive suppliers to develop more, better and cheaper low-carbon products and services. So it really is a win-win situation.

Business case	Example
Reduced exposure to reputation risk	Strengthened brand, enhanced community relationships, etc
Competitive advantage	Both public and private sector clients assess law firms on environmental credentials
Cost savings	Lower consumption of energy and other resources
Attract and retain talent	Employees are increasingly concerned with firms' environmental credentials
Anticipating legal obligation	Being ahead of the game on legislative requirements to reduce carbon consumption

The type of issues a business might face will differ depending on the industry, the type of products it is sourcing, the type of suppliers they are dealing with and the location of the supply chain. It is vital that a business analyses the risks through the lens of the particular business, its priorities and drivers. Responsible supply chain management should not be approached as a tick box exercise but should seek to ascertain the root causes of the risks. The types of supply chain issues can broadly be split into three categories: social, economic and environmental. In approaching all of these issues a business should remember that treating suppliers fairly and maintaining a collaborative approach will foster greater cooperation and transparency making it easier to achieve its aims.

5 Legal Sector Alliance. (2010, February 11). The benefits. Retrieved February 11, 2010, from legalsectoralliance.com: http://www.legalsectoralliance.com/node/161

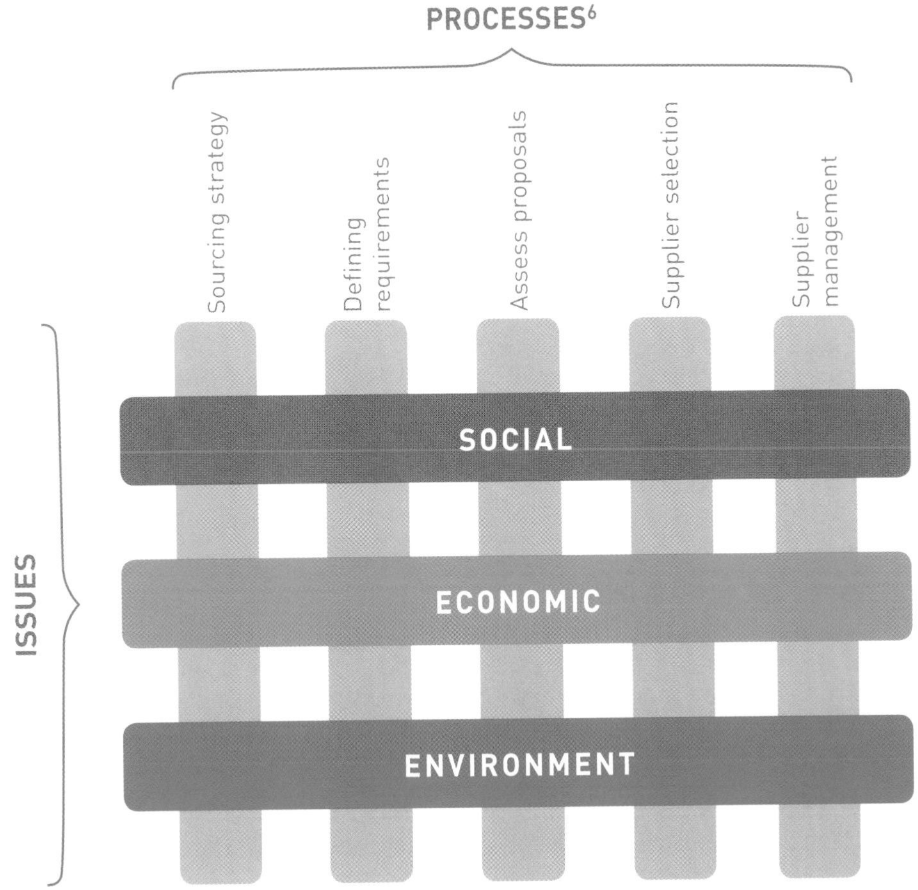

Social, Economic and Environmental issues ●●●

Social issues

Key social issues in the supply chain include those rights protected under the International Labour Organisation Declaration on Fundamental Principles and Rights at Work:

- freedom of association and collective bargaining
- forced and compulsory labour
- child labour
- discrimination in the workplace.

6 Legal Sector Alliance. (2010, February 11). Working with suppliers. Retrieved February 11, 2010, from legalsectoralliance.com: http://www.legalsectoralliance.com/impact/working_with_suppliers

Core human and labour rights abuses associated with employment as well as adverse community impacts can often cause company reputational damage, these include:

- living wage – are suppliers paying workers enough for an adequate standard of living?
- working hours
- working conditions including health and safety
- personal security
- adverse community impacts including:
  - displacement
  - damage to livelihood and interference with way of life
  - health impacts due to pollution.

Case Study[7]

Tesco aims to provide excellent value for their customers, which means sourcing the best products from around the world – at the best prices. Their intention is to help families stretch their budgets further, bring more products within the reach of ordinary people and help to drive economic growth.

As a founder member of the Ethical Trading Initiative (ETI), Tesco expect that all of their suppliers meet the standards set out under the ETI Base Code and guarantee their workers' rights within it namely:

- employment is freely chosen
- freedom of association and the right to collective bargaining are respected
- working conditions are safe and hygienic
- child labour shall not be used
- living wages are paid
- working hours are not excessive
- no discrimination is practised
- regular employment is provided
- no harsh or inhumane treatment is allowed.

7 Tesco PLC. (2010, February 11). Ethical Trading. Retrieved February 11, 2010, from tescoplc.com: http://www.tescoplc.com/plc/corporate_responsibility_09/suppliers_ethical_trading/ethical_trading/

To deliver this, Tesco source from many countries around the world. They believe that international trade helps people in developed and developing countries improve their quality of life, creating jobs and raising standards.

At the same time they recognise that regulation and levels of enforcement of labour standards vary in different countries. Tesco's ethical trading policy and programme applies to every country from which they source, including the UK, identifying risks and helping their suppliers to address them.

Tesco's approach to ethical trading has five stages: setting and communicating standards, monitoring supplier performance, addressing problems where they arise, building capacity to prevent problems and working with others to tackle the more complex and systemic problems they cannot address alone. Tesco's direct supply chain provides jobs for 1.8 million people around the world and their buyers receive more than 2,400 hours of training on ethical trading.

Economic issues

Possible economic issues within your supply chain include:

- supplier vulnerability – what is the financial health of your supply base?
- supplier dependence – what percentage of your suppliers overall business does your contract account for?
- supplier reliability – can you trust your supplier on quality and time?
- unfair or unreasonable payment terms
- supplier diversity and local sourcing
- bribery and corruption.

One positive piece of news at the end of 2009 was a report that public sector prompt payment policy is making a real difference to business cash flow. But the Minister for Trade, Investment and Small Business challenged both big business and suppliers to play their role to ensure prompt payment. Better invoicing, customer relationship management and prompt payment build confidence throughout supply chains.

By November 2009 nineteen out of twenty central government invoices were being paid within ten days, an improvement of 24% since November 2008. £73 billion has been paid to business within ten days by central government since June 2009. The wider public sector has also seen improvements in payment performance. The Forum of Private Business reported this month that the average payment time for local authorities in England is now eighteen days, with 42% of all invoices paid within ten days.

However, the Minister challenged the private sector to make stronger efforts to support small businesses in the current economic climate by ensuring swift payment. Twenty-two of the FTSE 100 have so far signed up to the Government's Prompt Payment Code, launched in December 2008. They are joined by over 640 other signatories, all committed to ensuring they pay suppliers within agreed terms.

> *Late payment creates uncertainty in the supply chain and carries a significant cost to UK business. In 2009 it is anticipated that UK business will pay £180 million in interest on overdue payments. That's £180 million of potential investment lost. Being a code signatory sends a very simple but very powerful message - we pay on time.*
>
> **Lord Davies**

Analysis of supplier invoices held by Experian indicates that suppliers can help improve speed of payment themselves by invoicing correctly and on time. All too often the basics of good business are missed and perfectly profitable companies fail[8].

8 BIS. (2009, November 25). Small Business Minister Calls on Business to Follow Government Lead and pay on time. Retrieved February 11, 2010, from nds.coi.gov.uk: http://nds.coi.gov.uk/clientmicrosite/content/Detail.aspx?ReleaseID=408948&NewsAreaID=2&ClientID=431

Case Study[9]

One of Tesco's core values is to treat people how they would like to be treated, and they aim to demonstrate this in their relationships with suppliers of all sizes and types. They listen to suppliers to make sure they understand their views, and share customer views with them so they fully understand the market for their products.

In 2008, over 2,300 suppliers covering all their markets responded to the first Group-wide anonymous supplier survey – Supplier Viewpoint. The survey confirmed that Tesco generally live up to their values and standards.

- 91% said they treat them with respect
- 93% said they are professional
- 92% said that Tesco are clear in their dealings with them
- 90% said they are reliable at paying on time
- 92% said they are committed to meeting customer requirements; and
- 92% said they maintain high quality standards.

Participating suppliers also provided suggestions for improving relationships. Specifically, they thought Tesco could better communicate their business plans, and work across functions within Tesco to solve problems. In the UK Tesco have run the Supplier Viewpoint survey since 2005. Over 90% of UK suppliers said they were trustworthy, consistent, clear, helpful, respectful and committed to meeting customer requirements.

9 Tesco PLC. (2010, February 11). Supplier relations. Retrieved February 11, 2010, from tescoplc.com: http://www.tescoplc.com/plc/corporate_responsibility_09/suppliers_ethical_trading/supplier_relations/

Environmental issues

Possible environmental impacts within the supply chain include:

- carbon and other greenhouse gas emissions
- accidental pollution
- damage to biodiversity
- water and other resource usage
- energy efficiency
- scarcity
- waste.

Case Study[10]

BT and environmental issues

BT is one of the largest purchasers in the UK, with an environmental influence that extends well beyond that of its own people and workplaces. They seek to influence the environmental performance of their suppliers and contractors through their purchasing policy. Their programme has three strands:

- assess their suppliers' environmental policies and procedures
- manage the environmental impacts of electrical or electronic equipment (EEE)
- audit waste management suppliers.

In the 2009 financial year BT surveyed a number of suppliers to assess their level of engagement on climate change. They also participated in the Carbon Disclosure Project Corporate Supply Chain Programme. Through the programme, they nominated 98 of their top suppliers to receive a questionnaire on climate change, looking at issues related to carbon risks and opportunities, emissions reporting, reductions targets and plans, governance, supplier engagement and product lifecycles.

Of the 47 suppliers that completed responses:

- 43% have developed emissions reduction targets
- 13% have developed emissions intensity targets
- 62% have an emissions reduction plan in place.

In BT's own survey of suppliers on their engagement on climate change it showed that:

- 54% of suppliers responding said they had a policy on climate change, compared with 35% in the 2008 financial year
- 43% monitor their CO2 emissions, compared with 25% in the 2008 financial year
- 45% have climate change targets in place, compared with 27% in the 2008 financial year.

10 BT Sustainability Report. (2009). Responsible Business. Retrieved February 9, 2010, from btplc: http://www.btplc.com/Responsiblebusiness/Ourstory/Sustainabilityreport/section/index.aspx?sectionid=fa1fc78c-15fb-4231-83d8-3dad1aa9c655

Steps Needed ●●●

Looking at the steps necessary in creating a responsible and sustainable supply chain management system the following sequence is recommended by the Legal Sector Alliance[11].

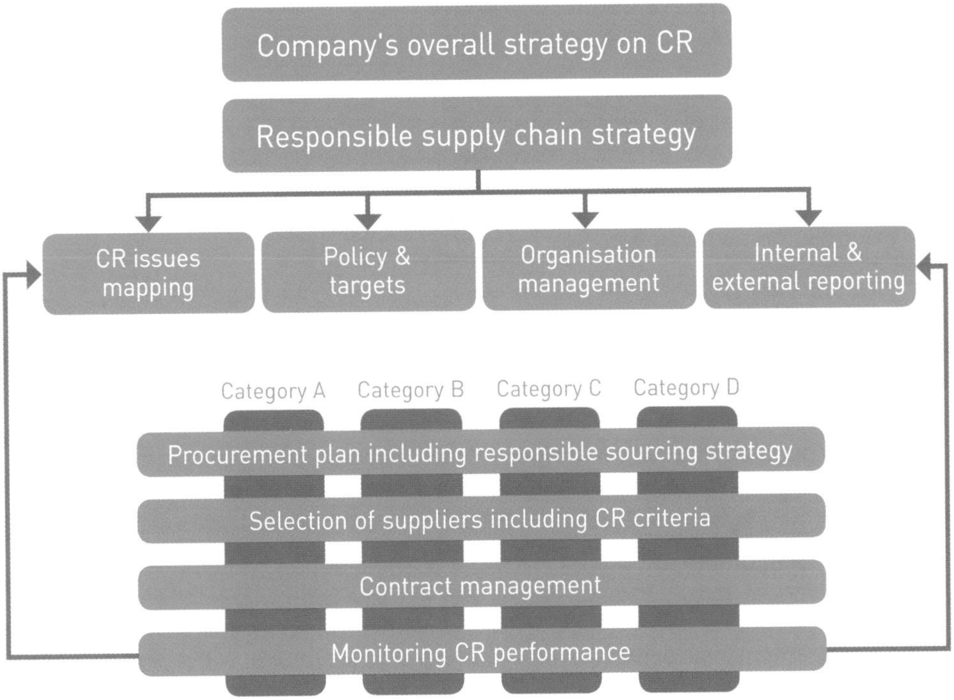

1 **Understand your business drivers**

The business needs to identify why responsible supply chain management is important to their business and let this guide the approach adopted, for example, cost savings, regulation reputation or competitive advantage. The supply chain programme must make sense for the business and its priorities.

2 **Carry out initial review and risk assessment**

In order to know its baseline a business needs to know its supply chain and have an understanding of any CR related activity taking place already. First they should carry out a full analysis of the supply chain looking at what they are spending in each category of purchase and with each supplier. The business may find analysing the flow of materials and information currently required to bring a product or service to a market a useful exercise and this can be aided by

11 Legal Sector Alliance. (2010, February 11). Working with suppliers. Retrieved February 11, 2010, from legalsectoralliance.com: http://www.legalsectoralliance.com/impact/working_with_suppliers

speaking to relevant staff to discover any learning from previous initiatives.

To ensure that the business takes action on the most important or high risk issues they need to carry out a risk and opportunity assessment of their current supply chain. Some leading businesses are also speaking to other stakeholders such as local communities and NGO's, to understand the potential issues. This could be particularly important where their supply chain has an international dimension, as these stakeholders will have a better appreciation of the impacts on the ground.

The business should map supply chain risks taking into account their business drivers. For example, if reputation has been identified as a key driver then the business could map items of purchase identified as having high reputational risks, alongside the importance of the item to their business.

3 Prioritise areas for action

When prioritising areas for action it is worth considering the following.

- **The level of risk.** The business could prioritise those suppliers or sectors which have high carbon emissions and/or present a particular reputational risk to the business.
- **The business's ability to influence their actions.** The business should prioritise key suppliers they deal with directly and those where they may have influence because of the size of contract.
- **The level of impact.** A business might consider targeting the top 10 suppliers by turnover. This often is the easiest way to make large cuts in total supply chain emissions. However, companies should remember to look at it from an environmental, economic and social perspective as well as the products/ services with the highest impacts may not be in the top spend, yet are where the biggest difference could be made.
- **Potential opportunities.** Businesses should prioritise suppliers or parts of the supply chain where innovation could occur or business opportunities can be realised.

4 Gather information from suppliers on identified risks

To establish the current baseline companies often ask questions on:

- positions - for example what are the supplier's policies on equality and diversity, environment, health and safety?
- processes - the business could look at the suppliers' environmental management systems, recruitment and whether they carry out due diligence or impact assessments
- performance - for example, the business could look at the supplier's carbon footprint, record of accidents, diversity of workforce, % of income generated under contract and wage levels.

5 **Develop policy**

A good and responsible supply chain policy should:

- have a clear purpose or statement of intent
- set out clearly the minimum expected standards
- reference internationally recognised human rights instruments such as the Universal Declaration on Human Rights and core ILO conventions
- have accompanying guidance notes so that those responsible for communicating it can give meaningful guidance to suppliers
- detail how the supply chain will be managed and monitored and how performance on issues such as labour rights or economic standards will feed into appraisals and renewal of contracts.

It is very important to ensure that the policy is communicated effectively both internally and externally.

6 **Set targets for improvement**

Companies should agree targets and assess performance, perhaps as part of supplier relationship management meetings. A responsible business should support suppliers to make the improvements they are asking for, as some may lack the expertise. Collaborating on joint projects can reduce the burden. Targets should be reviewed regularly as continual improvement in performance is aimed for but the business must realise that setting targets without building their capacity may lead to poor supplier relations and little or no improvement.

7 **Build the capacity of the staff**

Procurement staff can be given training on the various economic, environmental and social issues inherent in supply chains. The training should emphasise the business implications if the issues are not tackled and the need to consider them in procurement decisions. Specific training could cover how to use supplier questionnaires and the audit process to improve supplier performance and selection. Staff could be incentivised to consider supplier performance by working it into the bonus and appraisal structures.

8 **Integrate throughout the procurement process**

Before opening a tendering process the business should identify the social and environmental impact of their product or service and then establish if there are alternative methods of realising the business need that will have less negative impacts. The business should also consider the whole life costing of items in their procurement decisions. It may be that what they are buying now is not the most efficient way to fulfil the business need in the long term.

The selection of new suppliers gives businesses the opportunity to improve standards in their supply chain from the start. They should consider the use of a pre-contract supplier questionnaire to establish supplier performance on relevant issues by asking questions on labour and environmental standards.

It is also important for the business to follow-up on supplier performance after selection to ensure that supplier improvements are sustained over time. Businesses should monitor and assess supplier performance and where performance is not in line with targets or minimum standards, enter into a dialogue with the suppliers to try to identify the reasons for this and what support may be required to improve. Where there are incidents of non compliance with minimum standards as outlined in the business's policy, their response will depend on the seriousness of the breach.

9 **Report externally and internally**

Reporting internally will help a business to share good practice across the business and reporting externally will improve its relations with all stakeholders as it will improve understanding of what actions the business is taking and what progress is being made. A responsible business should make its supply chain policy publicly available possibly on their business website. The information provided should include their approach, targets and KPIs together with the results of their monitoring, the steps they have taken to overcome problems encountered, and their targets for the future. It should also include information about targets that have not been met and explanations about why and what action is being taken in response. Reporting the problems as well as the successes will enhance the trust stakeholders have in any reporting as well as increasing transparency and accountability.

Throughout the whole process good communication is essential and the business should always tell suppliers:

- why they are asking them about their CR performance
- about the business case for CR
- which suppliers the business has selected to engage with, and why
- what they will do with the information the suppliers provide
- what the business does and doesn't expect from them, including timescales for compliance
- the likely implications of good or poor performance.

CHAPTER 16

Borrowing, Banking and Investment

- Changing Finance and Capital Conditions
- Filling the Funding Gap for SME's
- Responsible and Sustainable Investment
- Consumers Switching to "Ethical Banks"

The recent recession in the UK has become the catalyst for business change as new trends are emerging in supply chains, corporate finance and workforce dynamics which were highlighted in a report published by the CBI in late 2009[1]. The report, entitled "The Shape of Business - The Next 10 Years", finds that the recession has raised concerns about commercial models, supply chains and finance that will reshape business behaviour well into the next decade.

The report flagged four key areas of UK business where fresh approaches will be developed because of the previous economic downturn and one of these areas relates to how businesses will finance growth in the next ten years or more. The Director General of the CBI suggested that it was the start of a new era for businesses, in which attitudes to finance and to corporate leadership are changed for a generation by the shock of the past two years of recession and what was now needed was a more balanced, less risky pathway to growth – one in which the short-term returns may be lower, but the long-term rewards for management success will be a lot more sustainable and secure.

Changing finance and capital conditions

The report suggests that the legacy of the recession is expected to have significant implications for the cost and availability of bank finance for a considerable period for a number of reasons.

- There will be increased scrutiny and regulation of the financial services industry. Such regulation is likely to constrain banks' ability to take as much risk in their lending practices as they did prior to the recession, which will impact businesses' ability to access credit.
- The capacity of the banking sector has reduced considerably as foreign banks have withdrawn from the UK corporate lending market. During 2007, they accounted for around 60% of the growth in lending to UK businesses. These lenders are not expected to return in such significant numbers, so the aggregate supply of credit available to businesses will remain constrained. While foreign banks were more frequently used by large businesses compared to small and medium size enterprises (SMEs) (85% of which use one of the big four banks), the impact of reduced capacity in the banking sector is likely to affect all businesses seeking finance as lending to large businesses by UK banks will displace some lending to SMEs[2].
- Bank lending will also be constrained during the lengthy process of balance sheet repair, with capital diverted for some time.

1 CBI. (2009, November 23). The shape of business:the next 10 years. Retrieved February 11, 2010, from cbi.org.uk: http://www.cbi.org.uk/pdf/20091123-cbi-shape-of-business.pdf

2 Bank of England. (2009, December). Monetary Trends December 2009. Retrieved March 2, 2010, from bankofengland.co.uk: http://www.bankofengland.co.uk/publications/other/monetary/TrendsDecember09.pdf

- Finally, the mistakes made in the pricing of risk which characterised the period leading up to the recession has already been reversed, and is unlikely to be repeated by the next generation of market participants who were witness to these mistakes. Tighter due diligence requirements and higher borrowing costs for businesses will be the result.

Given these trends, the report suggests that the coming decade will see companies operating in a climate in which the availability, cost and degree of freedom to use capital is more constraining than in the recent past. This is expected to have an impact on companies' finance strategies and may lead them to seek alternative sources and types of capital.

The report indicates that businesses will reduce gearing and their reliance on debt, the attractiveness of which has declined and that wider sources of capital, such as supply chain finance and sovereign wealth funds will become more important and CEOs will be more cautious in their use of capital for investment and innovation.

The report goes on to suggest that debt will be a less attractive source of finance for business over the next five to ten years and that businesses will reduce current debt levels and will seek a wider range of sources and types of finance. Outstanding corporate debt at the end of 2009 was £484bn, a fall from its summer 2008 peak, but still twice the level it was in 2002.The report notes that there has already been a marked positive shift in the perceived attractiveness of equity as a source of corporate finance while the attractiveness of bank borrowing has collapsed. In the first seven months of 2009, UK businesses repaid bank loans of nearly £32bn and raised £25bn in equity, representing a complete turnaround from previous years.

The report notes that small businesses see debt as a less dependable source of finance and their trust in banks as lenders has declined. It notes that these businesses will take steps to ensure they are not exposed to unexpected changes to credit lines in future – business growth and investment will need to be financed in other ways. Therefore, businesses of all sizes will seek to reduce levels of gearing, which will be done by increased retention of earnings and paying out smaller dividends to shareholders.

This report also notes that sovereign wealth funds in particular are likely to be a much more important source of large business finance over the next ten years. These funds are government or state run and are usually created by profits from natural resources such as oil, gas or minerals. They can be highly secretive and their assets grew dramatically when oil prices rose to record levels. Some of the largest Sovereign Wealth Funds can be found in the oil-rich Middle East. Projections are for sovereign wealth funds to double from their current level to around $8tr in 2015 according to the report.

Another alternative is supply chain finance (SCF) which is expected to develop as a much more important part of future strategies. Supply chain finance allows a supplier to sell its invoices to a bank at a discount as soon as they are approved by the buyer. That allows the buyer to pay later and the supplier to secure its money earlier. Instead of relying on the creditworthiness of the supplier, the bank deals with the buyer which is usually a less risky prospect. Larger companies will be prepared to finance their suppliers, and smaller firms will look upstream for funds. In particular, this will become commonplace where businesses have built up mutual trust and developed collaborative relationships. This can be part of the responsible and sustainable supply chain system outlined in Chapter 15.

This source of finance is seen by many supply chain experts and managers as the great hope for easing problems with suppliers and is also perceived by many businesses as less risky than bank lending because as customers, large businesses will have a very good understanding of suppliers' peaks and troughs in demand, and they will also be willing to work with them to ensure their survival.

At its most basic it allows both the buying business and the supplier to improve their working capital. Companies such as J Sainsbury, Nestle and Volvo have all used it improving their working capital by holding on to their money for longer.

However not every business is so happy with this source of finance as some suppliers reacting to a new Bank of England supply chain finance initiative warned it could slash their margins and encourage companies to increase payment times.

The Bank launched the supply chain finance facility as part of its £125bn effort to boost the economy in 2009.

At the time the Procurement Intelligence Unit suggested that by using supply chain finance and extending payment times, companies could cut their working capital by up to 7.5%. But the savings come at a cost to suppliers, who face charges of 2% to 3% of an invoice's face value if they take advantage of the credit. The customer then pays the invoice directly to the lending bank.

Big companies cut their working capital through supply chain finance by extending payment times. Suppliers who would struggle to survive with the longer payment time can choose to be paid early, reducing the risk of disrupting supply chains as payment times extend.

The Intelligence Unit's analysis found that those organisations embracing SCF have shored up their supply chains, ensuring increased availability of working capital for themselves and their suppliers and they also stated that if only a proportion of the UK's largest organisations implemented it, billions of pounds of working capital could be freed up.

But suppliers warned that if their customers extended payment times and offered SCF, it could be hugely damaging to their businesses as having to pay a charge of 2% or 3% to get paid on time may make the contract unviable.

Many of the CBI report's findings were supported by another survey conducted by Ipsos MORI in October and November 2009 and sponsored by the CBI and business advisory firm Deloitte. The survey of business leaders, mostly CEOs and chairmen, representing a UK workforce of almost 1m and a global turnover of around £1 trillion, revealed a shift in attitudes towards financing and supply chains.

Over half (55%) said that they will now only tolerate a lower level of risk from gearing and, within that group, 70% said an economic recovery would not reverse their position. Two thirds (68%) expect no improvement in credit availability in 2010 and are reshaping their business financing. 50% said they would use less bank debt, 44% said they would rely more on equity finance and 26% said they would make more use of bond issuance.

A bond is essentially a tradable IOU which companies will issue to raise money and, in doing so, will have an obligation to repay the bondholder according to specific terms. Once issued, bonds - including the right to receive the issuer's repayments - can be traded on established markets. In most cases, a bond is redeemable at face value on a particular date, and has a fixed rate of interest that is paid at regular intervals through to maturity.

And when asked about supply chain fragility during the recovery, only 24% said that they were not concerned. Businesses were most worried about a unique, specialist supplier going bust, that the supplier's own supply chain would collapse, and that the supplier would be unable to obtain working capital.

Because of these ongoing threats, 68% of firms said they would be strengthening the level of partnerships with suppliers in the coming years. One in three (30%) said they would be increasing their number of suppliers. And around one in five said they would be offering finance to key suppliers, reducing dependency on 'just in time' processes, and shrinking geographic distances to suppliers. It was suggested that businesses will be looking to reduce risk by seeking more collaborative ways of working through partnerships and joint ventures and perhaps create a flourishing system of supply chain finance where the largest businesses with the most solid balance sheets will help finance their smaller suppliers or customers.

The survey "Recession as a Catalyst for Change"[3] also showed that higher credit costs are hitting business investment plans but that investment for a low-carbon economy seems to have escaped the squeeze. 88% said they would invest as much as planned before the recession and 27% said they were planning to spend more than planned. Government policy on green issues is vital however, with two thirds (65%) citing it as an important influence on investment decisions.

Filling the Funding Gap for SME's ●●●

As indicated in the CBI report SME's will find it very difficult to obtain finance through bank borrowing even if their trust in the banks returns and there are warnings that any small business owner hoping for an easier time getting a loan or credit line in 2010 should watch out for two words: negative trends.

Bankers will be looking at a business's past two years of financial statements when evaluating credit applicants. The average business owner walking in with financial records from 2008 and 2009 will not appear to be a good credit risk and this problem

3 CBI. (2009, November 23). The recession a catalyst for business change. Retrieved February 11, 2010, from cbi.org.uk: http://www.cbi.org.uk/ndbs/Press.nsf/38e2a44440c22db6802567300067301b/89b9e675ce37cc56802576730036a50d?OpenDocument

will not begin to ease until the beginning of 2011 when hopefully borrowers can claim to have hit bottom and are now starting to recover.

The CEO of the National Association of Government Guaranteed Lenders said that the typical small business shows a 25% to 35% decline in revenue in records for 2008 and 2009 but not every business has negative trends. Some regions and industries are healthier than others. Some companies managed to sustain their earlier level of sales, profits, or even growth despite the recession. But 2008 and 2009 were bad and worse years for many businesses and until they have a better one it may be difficult to persuade a bank to make the loan.

Another suggestion raised in the CBI/Deloitte report as to how businesses could finance growth and investment in the future was for the government to close the funding hole created by the restriction of bank lending. The report recommended the creation of a new-style Industrial and Commercial Finance Corporation (ICFC), the body that was originally set up in 1945 to deliver finance to businesses. It was transformed into 3i, the private equity group, in 1983. It was proposed that it could be made easier for businesses if money could be raised locally perhaps through a new regional banking and investment institution. It was also recommended that policymakers cut the cost of raising equity for smaller firms by allowing them to offset that cost against tax.

The report highlighted that some sectors had been hit particularly hard by a downturn in the availability of credit, with official figures showing that the share of bank lending to UK factories fell from 29% to only 5% between 1986 and 2008 whilst over the same period, lending to property companies more than trebled from 11% to 36%[4].

These proposals came at the same time as the "Rowlands Review" was being prepared for submission to government ministers prior to a Pre-Budget Report. The review was set up to look into possible government help for small and medium-sized enterprises to access funding.

The former 3i executive and chairman of the Rowlands Review concluded in autumn 2009 that annually some 3,000 growth-focused SMEs, which he described as the engine room of the UK economy, were unable to access growth capital from high street banks and the private equity community – the latter he said has been lured in recent years by higher returns offered by private equity backed buy-out deals. It was also stated that the fund had to be commercially driven and not just another "shiny initiative" heaped on other shiny initiatives.

Plans for a £1bn capital growth fund to back expansion-focused SME's could be the catalyst for institutional investors to finance SME's on a regional basis and the fund could have a first close at around £500m, with a final close at around £1bn. The review concluded that the gap in the market was not recession related, but represented market failure.

The review also emphasised that small and medium sized enterprises play a vital role in the economy. They employ 13.7 million people, about 59% of the total private

4 CBI. (2009, November 23). The recession a catalyst for business change. Retrieved February 11, 2010, from cbi.org.uk: http://www.cbi.org.uk/ndbs/Press.nsf/38e2a44440c22db680256730006 7301b/89b9e675ce37cc56802576730036a50d?OpenDocument

sector workforce. SMEs also contribute as much as large businesses to UK output. The SME sector has seen strong growth recently with over a million more businesses at the start of 2008 than in 2000 and employment growth of 13% over the same period.

In addition it claimed that a vibrant SME sector is an important driver of economic growth. Through the process of economic churn, new businesses enter the market and displace less efficient established businesses. SMEs also bring forward innovation in products and business processes.

SMEs are likely to be critical to driving and sustaining the return to economic growth across the economy. As economic conditions stabilise SMEs will have opportunities to expand and grow to meet higher demand, to address new export opportunities and to serve new customers. It is also likely that vibrant SMEs will look to take on business from competitors that did not emerge from the recession as successfully. Whilst this growth will require additional levels of working capital, some of which may be financed through appropriate short term debt, it is likely that finance will be needed to support long term development and structural growth. It is important that the UK's SMEs are supported with the investment to grow and optimise their performance and help drive the economic recovery.

The review set out three options, including the creation of a new private sector institution with a network of probably three or four regional offices. The review also argued that whatever option the government chose it needed to be overseen by a single "central" fund manager with access to expert investors on the ground outside the South East and with a specific investment mandate.

The review stated that the equity gap would be best tackled with a mezzanine product, a term used for lending that is subordinate to bank debt, but which ranks ahead of equity as it is a type of financing that combines debt and equity characteristics. For example, a loan that also confers some profit participation to the lender. This product "would help address demand side aversion to pure equity, and provide a return above regular bank lending to reward investors" the review stated.

The review also recommended that the existing landscape of government intervention would benefit from simplification. Any new intervention should not add to, but be a part of a solution to resolve these problems, as well as providing a credible source of follow-on funding for growing SME's[5].

Responsible and Sustainable Investment ●●●

At the end of 2009 the UK government was being urged to use its new-found power over the banks to pursue environmental goals and create a "green bank" to finance the building of infrastructure for a low-carbon economy by environmental campaigners and companies. A green infrastructure bank could leverage £100bn of private finance for low-carbon investment in projects such as wind farms and energy efficiency improvements in homes, supporters argued.

5 BIS. (2010, February 11). Going for Growth. Retrieved February 11, 2010, from bis.gov.uk: http://www.bis.gov.uk/growth

To raise the money the bank would issue so-called "green bonds". The borrowing would be specifically for low-carbon investment and the bonds would be guaranteed by the government – making them a sound bet for investors.

Supporters said a state or privately run green bank, backed by green bonds, would tackle chronic underfunding of low-carbon projects such as wind farms. Wind power firms said creating an offshore grid would require between £10bn and £15bn of new investment. The UK government pledged just £525m for offshore wind power in its 2009 budget.

On a smaller scale the Carbon Trust already offers interest free loans of between £3,000 and £500,000 to help organisations finance and invest in energy saving projects. The Carbon Trust says that the 0% loan makes business sense because the anticipated energy savings offset the loan repayments. So any new equipment would pay for itself fairly quickly and then the business will continue to make savings year on year. The loans are government funded and unsecured and offer a straightforward and fast application process with no arrangement fees. Applicants receive a conditional offer within 24 hours of their application being processed and the loan can be repaid over a period of up to 4 years.

To be eligible for the scheme businesses must be private sector organisations that have been trading for at least 12 months and the project sites are based in England, Wales or Scotland. The businesses that are expected to apply should be SME's which have fewer than 250 full time or equivalent employees, a turnover not exceeding £43m and/or assets not exceeding £37m. Also there should be no controlling interest of more than 25% by a non-SME. Larger businesses can apply if they do not qualify for the CRC Energy Efficiency Scheme. For project sites in Northern Ireland any sized enterprise can apply.

The size of the loan offered and its repayment period is based on the projected CO2 savings of a project, which will be assessed by the Carbon Trust. Farmers in England can apply for a loan of between £3,000 and £20,000.

The Carbon Trust can give £1,000 of loan for every 1.5 tCO2 saved per annum from a project. Each project will be assessed on its potential to deliver real energy savings and examples could include such things as air conditioning, boilers and heating, refrigeration, building insulation, lighting and solar systems[6].

One example already earning its keep is at a convenience store in West Sussex, where a refrigeration system which uses cold air from outside to reduce the cost of chilling stock was installed. There is no water or refrigerant inside the store, and on colder days the system provides cooling for next to nothing. The owner obtained an £85,000 Carbon Trust loan to fund the installation, and has experienced an estimated 50% cut in energy use.

Earlier in the Chapter it was highlighted that 85% of SME's bank with the "big four" and this will also apply to the vast majority of larger businesses. This means that these businesses have not followed a growing trend which has seen a sharp rise

6 Carbon Trust. (2010, February 20). business loans eligibility. Retrieved February 20, 2010, from carbontrust.co.uk: http://www.carbontrust.co.uk/cut-carbon-reduce-costs/products-services/business-loans/pages/loans-eligibility.aspx

in the number of individual consumers switching to "ethical banking" alternatives. It would seem that it is far more important to be judged on how the business makes and uses its money rather than where it chooses to deposit it. In terms of putting the money to use the responsible and sustainable business is now likely to be making investments in green initiatives that will enhance its competitive edge but at the same time be seen to be acting in an ethical manner.

An article published in 2009[7] highlighted the fact that UK manufacturers were still persevering with environmental initiatives even in the midst of a recession and despite the lack of early returns on these investments. Independent research commissioned by a software specialist company reported that over half (56%) of UK directors in the manufacturing sector would not postpone their green investments due to the current economic climate.

Although 57% of UK manufacturers reported no measurable return on investment from their green strategies in the previous 12 months, over 40% of manufacturers still felt that green initiatives were key to cost reduction strategies in the next trading year. 56% of UK manufacturers also planned to increase their investment in green technologies in 2010.

The article indicated that pursuing a green strategy is a business imperative for manufacturers as they face up to increasing international legislative requirements in the coming years and that this time-table shows no sign of slowing down, regardless of the economy, and that is why organisations should continue to invest in green, even in the absence of a hard return.

Looking forward, the research showed that manufacturers do understand the cost saving potential of their green programs. However, in the current climate, all investments will be scrutinised for returns over the next 18 months. The article also suggested that green strategies will enter a pragmatic, business-oriented era reducing the possibility of 'greenwash'.

7 Infor. (2009, February 17). Green still fashionable despite the recession. Retrieved February 20, 2010, from infor.co.uk: http://www.infor.co.uk/company/news/pressroom/pressreleases/greenstillfashion/?source=PressR eleaseRSS

Case Study[8]

Google's investment in clean energy

Google has become one of the biggest corporate investors in clean energy as the company is a major energy user. Reducing its energy consumption is good for its profit margins and at the same time by eliminating its carbon footprint it is greatly enhancing its public image.

Google has supported and even proposed a policy to reduce America's dependence on fossil fuels. Likewise, the company has investments in several renewable energy sectors. The company hopes to generate one gigawatt of electricity within a few years.

Google's clean technology investments include the following.

- **RE<C** - Google has invested over US$45 million in its RE<C program to make renewable energy cheaper than coal.
- **Solar Thermal Power** - Google has invested US$10 million in two solar thermal start-ups: eSolar and BrightSource.
- **High Altitude Wind** - Google has invested US$15 million in Makani Power's unique technology which captures high altitude winds.
- **Enhanced Geothermal Systems** - Google has invested US$10.25 million in Potter Drilling and AltaRock Energy.
- **RechargeIT** - Google has developed this project to reduce America's transportation sector's greenhouse gas emissions by implementing plug-in vehicles. RechargeIT launched the GFleet, a free car sharing program for Google employees. The cars include regular and plug-in hybrid Toyota Priuses.
- **Plug-in Vehicles** - Google has invested US$2.75 million in Aptera Motors and US$2.75 million in Acta Cell.
- **Photovoltaic Solar Power** - Google has constructed a 1.6 megawatt rooftop solar system at its headquarters.
- **Google Ventures** - Last year Google launched this US$100 million venture capital fund for innovative start-ups. Google Ventures is set to invest in all sectors of clean energy; the fund's first clean technology investment went to Silver Spring Networks for its smart grid technology.
- **Google Energy, LLC** - Recently, Google applied to the US Federal Energy Regulatory Commission to be allowed to buy and sell bulk electricity like any utility company. If approved, Google will have greater access to renewable energy and will be able to purchase electricity at wholesale prices.

8 Energyboom. (2010, February 9). Google Inc:The who's who of corporate investment in clean energy. Retrieved February 20, 2010, from energyboom.com: http://www.energyboom.com/emerging/google-whos-who-corporate-investment-clean-energy

Further examples of responsible and sustainable investments made by business will be highlighted in Chapter 20 which considers the impact that businesses are having on their communities whether locally, nationally or globally.

Consumers Switching to "Ethical Banks" ●●●

Many judge that the actions of banks and bankers have been identified as the main cause of the recent recession and as a result their standing in terms of corporate image is at an all time low but as already indicated the vast majority of businesses in the UK have stayed with the big four banks. For most businesses it is simply about proximity, accessibility and convenience. The UK public on the other hand are starting to take a different view.

Ethical banks have been reporting that UK consumers have been flocking to ethical alternatives in the banking sector throughout 2008 and 2009, including the old mutual building societies. Triodos Bank saw its number of customers grow by a quarter in 2008, and the Ecology Building Society has seen a vast increase in savings deposited since the start of the recession, building on a 10% increase in 2007. Britannia Building Society, when merging with the Co-op Group to form a "super-mutual", noted that 140,000 new savings accounts had been opened in the quarter to February 2009.

The Cooperative Bank is probably the best known option in this sector. On its website, Ethical Consumer Magazine awards the bank's current account with a score of 9/20 on their rating system which ranks companies on 22 criteria including climate change performance, worker rights and environmental reporting. The best of the big four comes in with a score of 3.5/20 and the worst only scores 0.5/20.

44% of the British public are interested in finding out about the ethical credentials of the next financial product or service that they buy, according to a national online consumer survey, conducted by Ipsos MORI on behalf of non-profit research organisation EIRIS in November 2009[9]. The research explored post credit-crunch attitudes towards ethical finance. The EIRIS survey found that three-quarters of those interested in finding out more about the ethical credentials of a financial product or service said they were likely to take this into consideration when next buying a financial product or service.

Respondents surveyed felt that banks and financial institutions should prioritise current ethical concerns such as protecting human rights, tackling climate change, protecting the environment and investing in fair trade in their lending and investing activities, more so than avoiding 'sin' issues relating to the manufacturing of alcohol, tobacco and gambling which have traditionally been the focus of ethical investors.

9 EIRIS. (2009, November 18). Ethical Finance: Does Britain Care? Retrieved February 20, 2010, from eiris.org: http://www.eiris.org/media.html#eirisopinionpoll

Respondents were presented with a list of issues and asked 'to what extent do you think banks and financial institutions should prioritise the following issues when deciding who they will or will not lend money to or invest in on a scale of 1-10' (with 1 being low priority and 10 high priority). Issues emerging as the highest priority were protecting human rights (67% scoring 7 - 10), investing in fair trade (66%), protecting the environment (62%), avoiding arms manufacturers (61%) and tackling climate change (59%). A smaller proportion prioritised the avoidance of companies involved in the manufacturing of alcohol (22% scoring 7 - 10), tobacco (37%) and gambling (38%).

Every business currently operating in the UK is a potential investment but some are more reliant on a continuous flow of new capital than others. Therefore with the current trends mentioned above every business that is partially or wholly reliant on external investors should be concerned about their image and reputation in terms of how ethical or responsible they are seen to be. Banks may be more constrained in the future to only lend money to "better causes" and investors in shares or company bonds may wish to avoid businesses that have a poor track record on social and environmental issues, and at the moment that would appear to include many of the banks themselves.

What is or is not an "ethical investment" and the effect of corporate image and reputation will be explored more fully in later chapters in the Business section.

CHAPTER 17

Integrity and Reputation

- Business Ethics and Integrity
- What is Reputation?
- Reputation Risk
- The Cost of Reputation Loss

Business Ethics and Integrity ●●●

Business ethics is the application of values – such as honesty, integrity and fairness – to business behaviour. It is about how a business conducts itself rather than the nature of that business. It applies to any or all aspects of business conduct, from boardroom strategies to sales and marketing techniques; accounting practices to treatment of suppliers and customers. Standards of business ethics are usually set out in an organisational code of ethics or conduct. This can cover such diverse elements as treatment of suppliers, anti-competitive practices, bribery and corruption, environmental pollution, product safety and impact on local communities.

A commitment to high standards of business ethics involves the management of all aspects of performance. This can encompass corporate social responsibility (CSR), corporate responsibility (CR) or corporate citizenship. They all have in common that they are about organisations taking responsibility for the way they conduct their business and the impact of their operations, beyond a concern for the financial bottom line.

According to the Institute of Business Ethics, companies are increasingly trying to demonstrate that they do business responsibly[1]. More and more, they say, are adopting codes of ethics (or similar documents), and a growing number report publicly on their corporate responsibility. An Institute of Business Ethics (IBE) survey in 2007 showed that at that time 71% of companies with an ethics policy were providing training on its application, while other IBE research indicated very importantly that those who seek to embed their codes in this way financially outperform those that do not. A loss of trust between a business and any of its stakeholders (such as employees, customers, investors, suppliers or civil society) impacts negatively on business performance, says the IBE.

It notes that, conversely, in a time of reduced economic activity, a reputation for integrity may help maintain the loyalty of staff and customers and that although the importance of an ethical culture and a responsible reputation is being recognised, we still hear in the media of organisations being criticized because of ethical failings. Whether it is accusations of high-risk trading strategies by banks, extractive companies accused of environmental degradation or allegations of slave labour in the factories supplying Western supermarkets with clothes and toys, almost every sector has been touched by ethical scandal, notes the IBE.

The Institute of Business Ethics also published a briefing paper in February 2010 which provided an analysis of the major ethical concerns and lapses involving UK companies or multi-nationals with a UK presence as reported in the media in 2009[2]. The sectors which attracted the most media attention in 2009 were the financial services industry, extractive industries covering oil and metal mining companies, supermarkets and retailers, in that order.

1 IBE. (2007, July). Does Business Ethics Pay? - Revisited. Retrieved February 20, 2010, from ibe.org.uk: http://www.ibe.org.uk/publications/DBEP%20Revisited.pdf

2 IBE. (2010, February 15). Concerns & Ethical Lapses 2009. Retrieved February 20, 2010, from ibe.org.uk: http://www.ibe.org.uk/publications/Briefing%20_15.pdf

The briefing paper indicates that there were over 170 ethical lapses reported on by the media during 2009 and the frequency and types of issues reported were as follows.

Executive remuneration	21%
Treatment of staff	14%
Environmental issues	10%
Treatment of customers	7%
Competition	7%
Discrimination	7%
Unethical advertising	7%
Data protection or privacy	7%
Product safety	6%
Human rights	5%
Bribery and corruption	4%
Tax	3%
Supply chain/ethics	2%
	100%

The briefing paper notes that it is hardly surprising that financial services and executive remuneration head the lists as problems with the banking sector and staff bonuses continued to play a prominent role in the headlines throughout the year.

The true impact of the banking crisis on public trust in business in general was revealed at the end of 2009 when the IBE and Centrica published the annual "Perceptions of Business Transparency" report[3]. The report found that half of British adults believe that the conduct of banks linked to the financial crisis has damaged their trust in all businesses.

The report also highlighted the fact that businesses are facing a particular crisis in

3 IBE. (2009). IBE Publications. Retrieved February 20, 2010, from ibe.org.uk: http://ibe.rits-ds1.co.uk/2009/publications/publications.html

trust among 16-34 year olds. The research, conducted by Ipsos MORI, revealed that the proportion of 16-34 year olds who believe that companies generally behave ethically has plummeted by 13 percentage points from 64 per cent in 2008 to 51 per cent in 2009.

The authors of the report suggest that In the face of this decline in trust, businesses should be charged with rebuilding confidence by improving transparency - almost two-thirds of the British public (60 per cent) are calling for businesses to explain how they make and spend their money to the public – not just investors. However, the survey reveals that the British public believe that businesses have not yet grasped the nettle on this issue, with the majority saying that they do not explain the way they conduct their business clearly enough (62 per cent).

More than half of those surveyed (59 per cent) claim that they have not seen any changes in corporate openness and honesty in the last year, while a quarter (24 per cent) believe that openness and honesty has decreased in the same period. Around three-quarters (76 per cent) are sceptical that this will change, believing that that most large companies won't be open and honest about their behaviour unless forced.

Some of the figures from this research can also be found in another IBE briefing paper on the attitudes of the British public to business ethics published in December 2009 where overall 52% thought that UK business behaved very or fairly ethically, which was a small increase of 1% on 2008. The large drop in percentage came in the 16-34 year olds grouping as already mentioned but the 55+ age group were the least likely to believe that UK business acts in an ethical manner.

The survey also asked the respondents their view on which two or three issues most needed addressing and the top five were:

- executive pay 42%
- sweatshop labour 25%
- environmental responsibility 24%
- employees able to speak out about company wrongdoing 23%
- discrimination in the treatment of people 22%.

Environmental responsibility had decreased in importance by 8% compared with the same survey in 2008 but it was still the third most important issue for businesses to address as far as the British public was concerned[4]. It is interesting to note that the top three more or less mirror the top three most reported issues in the media during 2009 and that seems to confirm the findings of the Carbon Trust survey mentioned in Chapter 14 which found that consumers rely mostly on the media when forming their opinions as to how responsible a business really is.

4 IBE. (2009, December 13). Attitudes of the British Public to Business Ethics. Retrieved February 20, 2010, from ibe.org.uk: http://www.ibe.org.uk/publications/Briefing_13.pdf

On an international level an opinion poll carried out by the World Economic Forum (WEF) at the beginning of 2010[5] claimed to highlight a 'crisis of ethics' when it found that two thirds of people believe the current economic crisis is also a crisis of ethics and values.

The survey, based on 130,000 Facebook members from ten G20 economies, also found that only 25% of people believe that large, multi-national companies have a "values-driven" approach to their sectors. This proportion rose to 40% for small and medium-sized businesses. Half of respondents - in France, Germany, India, Indonesia, Israel, Mexico, Saudi Arabia, South Africa, Turkey and the US - believed that universal values exist.

When asked to identify which values were most important for the global political and economic system, almost 40% chose honesty, integrity and transparency, 24% chose others' rights, dignity and views, 20% chose the impact of actions on the well-being of others and 17% chose the preservation of the environment.

Almost two-thirds of respondents felt that people do not apply the same values in their professional lives as they do in their private lives. When asked whether businesses should be primarily responsible to their shareholders, their employees, their clients and customers, or all three equally, almost half of the respondents chose "all three equally".

What is Reputation?

The reputation of a business is very important to most if not all stakeholders involved but in particular those whose decisions do affect the continued success of the enterprise. There is a general consensus that reputation will affect:

- employees who will be much more loyal to a company with a good reputation. It will also help the business to recruit talent
- potential investors or partners who are more likely to take a risk with a business based on its reputation. Research has indicated that 90% think about reputation in investment decisions to a greater or lesser extent
- lawmakers and regulators. Reputation can help lessen the legal burden on a business
- the public at large where it is important to preserve a "social licence" to operate
- customers and suppliers who are also more likely to remain loyal to a business with a good reputation
- competition in that it may provide a barrier to entry for other businesses who cannot match that reputation.

5 World Economic Forum. (2010, January 10). Financial crisis is also a crisis of values – World Economic Forum poll . Retrieved February 20, 2010, from weforum.org: http://www.weforum.org/en/media/Latest%20News%20Releases/PR_faithvalues

A corporate reputation is a collective representation of a firm's past actions and results that describe the firms' ability to deliver outcomes to multiple stakeholders. It gauges a firms' relative standing both internally and externally.

Developing a good reputation is about the business, by its actions and conduct, creating trust as experienced by the different stakeholders, and it will often provide a reservoir of goodwill in times of crisis. Reputation should not be confused with image which is based on belief and personal evaluation of a business and is tied to the business directly not to the actions of that business. If the image is positive then the reputation will improve, however, reputation evolves more slowly than image because it is tied to actions.

A comparison between brand and reputation would show that a brand is what differentiates one business from its competition and it relates to the marketing of the company including advertising and publicity. Brand refers to the logos and names of the businesses. Reputation cannot be enhanced by name changes as it is a much larger concept including several elements and it is often referred to as "emotional capital" and like any kind of business capital it is subject to risk.

Corporate Reputation: Value drivers

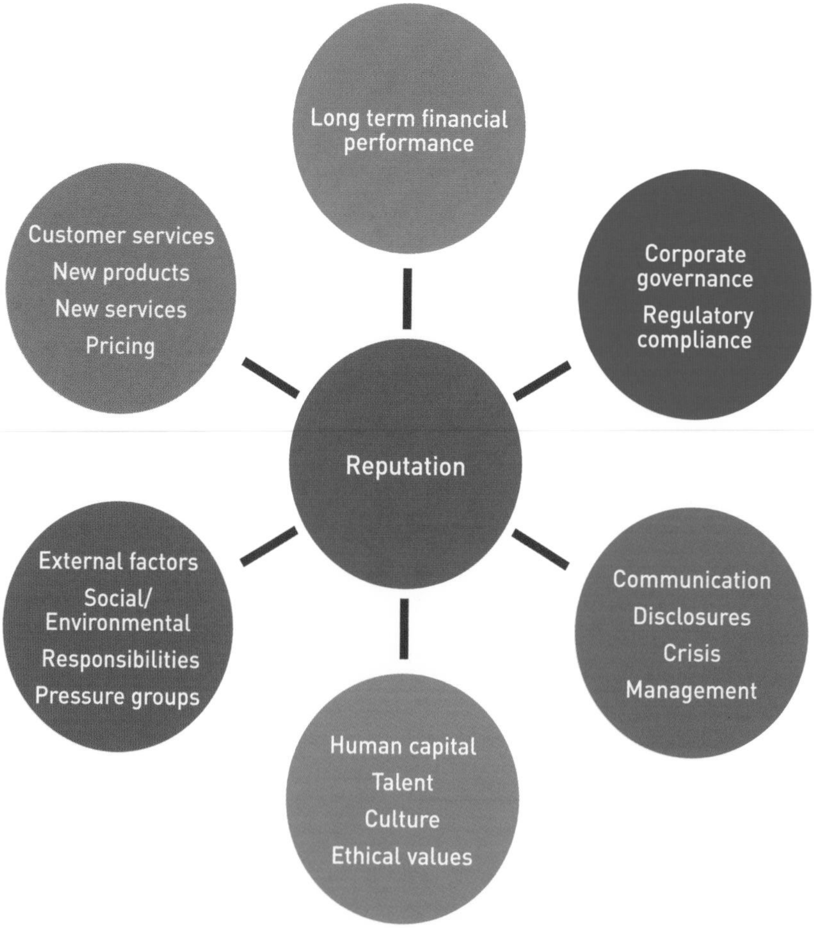

These same reputation drivers could potentially create value in the business because:

- a good reputation encourages consumers to buy products and services
- suppliers are willing to do business thus expanding opportunities
- talented employees want to join and stay with the business thus enhancing its innovation capabilities and value
- a favourable outlook from regulators and ratings agencies will decrease financing cost and again increase value
- investors will want to buy shares pushing up share price and therefore value
- positive feedback from the media and from pressure groups will increase value
- in times of crisis investors will give the company the benefit of the doubt which will ease any short term decrease in value.

Reputation Risk ●●●

Unfortunately, in the same way that a good reputation will have a positive effect on the value of a business, the opposite is also true. A loss of reputation or trust will result in a reverse of the above positive effects on value. As indicated earlier there is always a risk that a business will lose its valuable reputation and the majority of businesses regard "reputation risk" as a very important risk in its own right and therefore safeguards should be put in place to prevent it from happening.

Reputation risk is when there is a possibility that a business may be exposed to negative publicity and, as a result, may experience a loss of trust in its business practices, internal controls and its actions. This could have an impact on the liquidity or capital of the firm or cause a change in its credit rating which ultimately will affect its stakeholders.

Protecting a firm's reputation is the most important and difficult task facing senior risk managers, according to a report by the Economist Intelligence Unit[6]. In a survey of senior executives responsible for managing risk, reputational risk emerged as the most significant threat to business out of a choice of 13 categories of risk. 84% of respondents felt that risks to their company's reputation had increased significantly over the previous five years. The key conclusions of the Intelligence Unit's survey were as follows.

- **Reputation is a prized, and highly vulnerable, corporate asset** - Reputation is one of the most important corporate assets, and also one of the most difficult to protect, according to executives in the survey. .
- **Companies struggle to categorise reputational risk** - The survey found that 52% considered reputation risk as a risk by itself, whilst 48% considered it as a consequence of other risks such as operational, compliance or finance risks.

6 EIU. (2005, December 8). Four out of five companies say threats to corporate reputation are rising . Retrieved February 20, 2010, from eiuresources.com: http://www.eiuresources.com/mediadir/default.asp?PR=850001885.

- **Compliance failures are the biggest source of reputational risk** - The biggest threat to reputation is seen to be a failure to comply with regulatory or legal obligations, followed closely by failure to deliver minimum standards of service and product and, the risk that unethical practices will be exposed.
- **Smaller companies were lagging behind on reputational risk** - The survey showed that 80% of the largest companies had implemented processes for crisis management only 50% of smaller companies had done so.
- **The CEO is the principal guardian of corporate reputation** - The CEO was regarded having responsibility for managing reputational risk by most organisations in the survey.
- **Good communication is vital to protecting against and repairing reputational damage** - Most companies in the survey regularly monitored the perceptions of their customers, but communication with the other stakeholders was patchy. As a result the report suggested that these companies may be slow to address issues that may sully their corporate image. The report went on to say that good communications becomes even more important once a crisis breaks as a quick response often protects reputation.

In relation to the finding that the CEO is seen as the principal guardian of corporate reputation, a recent report in the Economist seems to back this up in a perverse kind of way. It describes a public-relations firm that has recently launched a service that claims to quantify how a company's media coverage affects its share price. One of its initial findings was that a bank's shares tend to fall whenever its boss makes a statement[7].

Interestingly the risk to reputation caused by environmental issues was considered insignificant at the time of the report but nearly five years later in February 2010 another report from the Economist Intelligence Unit entitled "Managing for Sustainability"[8] found that fully 86% of respondents agree that operating sustainable environmental and employment practices is important in terms of managerial and financial resources currently committed. Forty-seven per cent even say that sustainability is "very important" for their firms.

Among the three geographic focus areas of this survey, respondents in Asia-Pacific are most likely to state that operating sustainable environmental and employment practices is a very important goal (50%). In North America, the figure is 46%, and in Western Europe it is 39%.

According to these executives, the most important reason for promoting sustainability policies is that this is the right thing to do ethically (56%). Complying with laws and regulations (45%) and improving the company's image (43%) also feature. The report also found that motivations varied by industry. Respondents from the energy and

7 The Economist. (2010, March 15). Topping up the trust fund. Retrieved March 15, 2010, from economist.com: http://www.economist.com/business-finance/business-education/displaystory.cfm?story_id=15692379

8 EIU. (2010, February 8). The link between sustainability and profits remains unclear to businesses in short term, according to new research. Retrieved March 15, 2010, from eiuresources.com: http://www.eiuresources.com/mediadir/default.asp?PR=2010020801

natural resources sectors are more likely to say that their motivation is to comply with laws and regulations. Among consumer-facing industries such as retailing and consumer goods, doing the right thing ethically scored higher than the overall average, at 64%.

Case Study[9]

Mars: corporate reputation is seen as more important than ever

Mars, owner of the Mars, Snickers and M&M sweet brands, has announced that it is to spend millions of dollars annually certifying that the cocoa used in the $10bn (£6.8bn) of chocolate products it sells every year is sustainably sourced by 2020. The move by the company, which claims to be the largest end-user buyer of cocoa globally, came amid testing times for chocolate companies brought on by rising cocoa prices and falling supply.

The managing director of Mars UK, clearly recognises the need to secure long-term cocoa sourcing, saying that consumers and employees expected Mars to "do the right thing" because "nobody has to buy confectionery". She also said that consumers would be unforgiving if they cut their quality at a time when they were under economic pressure.

Spending millions of dollars ensuring its cocoa supplies meet "sustainable" criteria sends out a clear signal that Mars sees its corporate reputation as more important than ever.

Mars has committed to conditions such as paying farmers a minimum wage, conserving water and running ecological pest management programmes. At a time when cocoa prices have hit a 24-year high, and with analysts forecasting total global production in 2008-2009 to be down 66,000 tonnes on last year, this is no mean feat.

Business in the Community have looked at how more and more food manufacturers are striving to up their green credentials in spite of the recession and a spokesperson for BITC said that it would be understandable if food companies tried to dodge their ethical obligations but it has been found that they are "falling over themselves" to prove their social and environmental credentials.

9 BITC. (2009, April 9). Mars: corporate reputation is seen as more important than ever . Retrieved February 11, 2010, from bitc.org.uk: http://www.bitc.org.uk/media_centre/news/mars_sustainable.html

The Cost of Reputation Loss ●●●

Whether organisations are altogether comfortable with modern definitions of reputational risk, there is little doubt about the potential costs of failure to get to grips with it. In the Economist Intelligence Unit's report of 2005[10] it was established that companies found reputational problems to be the most costly in financial terms, relative to a series of other risks. Among those who had faced reputational problems, 28% described the financial toll as major. Loss of key skills and talent, the next most severe problem, caused a major financial hit for only 18% of those affected (although it is worth noting that 52% identified this as a source of minor losses, making it the leading cause of financial losses among the sample overall).

The likely actions which might provide a risk to reputation could include the following. Examples that might have led to loss of reputations are provided for illustrative purposes.

- **Non-compliance with regulation/legal obligations**

  Companies which employed illegal immigrants were named and shamed during 2008 in a further attempt by the UK government to crack down on people smuggling[11]. The move by the Home Office came four months after officials launched a concerted effort to identify and prosecute companies breaking the law. More than 200 companies have already been fined for hiring illegal labour.

  The UK Borders Agency published how many illegal immigrants each company was employing and how much it was fined. At that point some 35 firms were named on its website, alongside 37 directors. They were fined a total of almost £303,000 for employing 56 illegal workers. The vast majority were restaurants or take-aways.

- **Exposure of unethical practices**

  Some of Britain's brightest women students are turning their backs on careers in the City, with the Square Mile seen as unethical and rife with discrimination[12]. Banking in particular is seen as an unattractive job, whose high rewards are outweighed by poor promotion prospects for women. Most view banking as "demonstrably unethical".

  The findings, from a survey of 450 Oxford University undergraduates published in March 2010, prompted calls for financial services companies to enhance their appeal to women. The research was conducted by the university after approaches from a bank and management consultancy asking why only a third of Oxford applicants for graduate posts were women.

....

10 EIU. (2005, December 8). Four out of five companies say threats to corporate reputation are rising . Retrieved March 15, 2010, from http://www.eiuresources.com/mediadir/default.asp?PR=850001885.

11 BBC News. (2008, June 19). Illegal firms named and shamed. Retrieved February 20, 2010, from news,bbc.co.uk: http://news.bbc.co.uk/go/pr/fr/-/1/hi/uk/7462373.stm

12 University of Oxford. (2010). News releases. Retrieved March 15, 2010, from ox.ac.uk: http://www.ox.ac.uk/media/news_releases_for_journalists/index.html

It found that many students thought banking, accounting and consulting were unethical. 75 per cent believed the financial services industry was not supportive of society. Of eight sectors, women students viewed banking as the occupation in which they were most likely to find discrimination - 85 per cent thought "people like me" would face discrimination in financial services, compared with only half of men.

Almost 70 per cent of women thought that they would have poorer prospects for promotion, half thought they would face discrimination in workplace culture and pay, 35 per cent in day-to-day treatment, and just under 30 per cent in the flexibility of working hours.

- **Security breaches (examples: sensitive data leaks, hacking of customer financial data)**

  It was widely reported that one of Europe's biggest banks, HSBC, was fined during 2009 after three of its units lost the details of thousands of customers in the post. Britain's financial regulator imposed the fine of £3.2m as it had put its customers at risk of identity fraud.

  The Financial Services Authority said HSBC Life, HSBC Actuaries and HSBC Insurance Brokers had failed to put in place adequate systems and controls to protect customer confidential details from being lost or stolen. The units were fined £1.61m, £875,000 and £700,000 respectively.

  The Financial Services Authority (FSA) found that HSBC Life lost an unencrypted CD with the details of 180,000 policy holders, while HSBC Actuaries lost a disc with data on almost 2,000 pension scheme members.

  The FSA's enforcement director said that all three firms had failed their customers by being careless with personal details which could have ended up in the hands of criminals.

- **Safety breaches (example: fire caused by poor safety standards)**

  At least 21 workers died and 50 were hurt when a fire swept through a Bangladeshi factory making clothes for a budget retailer and other firms as they worked at night to fulfil orders. The blaze followed repeated concerns by a British charity about fire safety at factories making garments for Western shops.

  The fire started at about 9pm at the factory in early March 2010 trapping dozens of workers who were knitting jumpers. Eleven fire engines fought for more than two hours to bring the blaze under control. Thirteen of the dead were women, according to doctors.

  Clothing factories in Bangladesh are prone to fires as a result of poor safety standards. War on Want found poor safety at six factories supplying budget clothes lines for a number of retailers in a report in 2006, which alleged that the factories were missing fire extinguishers, emergency exits and fire alarms and did not practise fire drills.

- **Failure to deliver minimum standards of service and product quality to customers**

  In early 2010 a campaign organiser and students from schools across London gave a giant mock up 'bad school report' to Asda showing its failure to sell Fairtrade cotton uniforms[13]. The students demanded that Asda should start to sell Fairtrade cotton school uniforms as part of charity People & Planet's new 'Wear Fair' campaign which aims to get all UK schools to adopt Fairtrade cotton uniforms by 2015.

  The campaign is targeting Asda which lags behind other major supermarkets, the students say, because of its failure to offer Fairtrade cotton uniforms despite saying that they are 'passionate about Fairtrade'. They also handed in photos of 2000 students, who each wrote personal messages asking that Asda switches its uniforms to Fairtrade cotton.

- **Product recall**

  Toyota now need to reassure the world that, while it has made mistakes, its cars are safe and it can reclaim its place as one of the world's most admired companies. Toyota was forced to recall 8.5m vehicles around the world, including 1.7m in Europe and 180,000 in the UK at the end of 2009. The recall was prompted by safety fears about sticking accelerator pedals and failing brakes on a collection of Toyota's leading models.

  From a public relations point of view the recall has been a disaster as the fears about not being able to stop had even caused the US authorities to warn the public not to drive their cars and the president of Toyota was brought before Congress in Washington to explain the situation. Figures from the UK reported widely in the press and trade journals in early March 2010 showed Toyota's sales were down 5% so far for that year and its market share had declined from 6.81% to 5.01%.

  There are warnings from experts of lasting damage to the Toyota name, which has been built around safety and reliability. Credit rating agencies have threatened to downgrade the car maker over fears of a permanent loss of sales. However, after coming under fierce criticism, Toyota appears to have realised that it has little to lose anymore from speaking frankly about the errors it has made.

- **Poor crisis management**

  Eurostar came in for tough criticism over its handling of the crisis that severely disrupted its services in the run up to Christmas 2009[14]. An independent review said that contingency plans for helping stranded passengers were "insufficient". It also raised concerns over the poor conditions for passengers stuck on the trains in the Channel Tunnel.

13 People & Planet. (2010, March 3). Students give Asda a 'fail' over school uniforms. Retrieved March 15, 2010, from peopleandplanet.org: http://peopleandplanet.org/asda-action-story

14 BBC News. (2010, February 12). Eurostar snow delays criticised. Retrieved March 19, 2010, from news.bbc.co.uk: http://www.news.bbc.co.uk/1/hi/business/8511857.stm

Carriages lost air conditioning and lighting as a result of the power failure, while sanitary conditions also quickly became unpleasant, with passengers forced to designate one carriage as an "open toilet area" after toilets became blocked.

The report also said that the trains "had not undergone sufficient weather preparations" to withstand "extremely severe" weather conditions.

- **Failure to hit financial performance targets**

  Handheld computer maker Palm said its income for the year will be far below expectations because of lukewarm sales of its smart phones[15]. Figures for the third quarter of 2009 show it shipped almost one million sets, but just over 400,000 actually ended up in customers' hands. The company had expected to shift 600,000 models.

  Palm shares fell 14% after the results were released.

- **Risk by association with suppliers, partners, alliances, etc with poor reputations**

  Leading UK brands, including a national chain of chemists, a manufacturer of recycled toilet paper and a major mobile phone company are all owned by companies profiting from the environmentally devastating exploitation of the Canadian tar sands for oil. Three of the "big four" banks are also all playing a significant role in financing tar sands mining. It is claimed that tar sands exploitation produces carbon emissions between 2.5 to 8 times higher than conventional oil extraction.

- **Failure to address issues of public concern pro-actively (example: climate change)**

  An energy company has been criticised for sending out millions of low energy light bulbs to meet its target under a household energy cutting scheme. The Green Party accused Npower of taking inexcusable shortcuts instead of investing in more effective measures such as loft insulation. Npower said the bulbs were "part of a mix of energy-efficient measures". The regulator Ofgem said it had expressed concern with Npower about the practice of unsolicited mail-shots. The UK government ordered energy companies to help pay for measures to cut household energy consumption - such as cavity wall or loft insulation, or by issuing low energy light bulbs - two years ago. Low energy light bulbs were scrapped as an option in June 2009 - and the ban came into force at the start of 2010[16].

15 BBC News. (2010, March 19). Palm hit by slow smartphone sales. Retrieved March 19, 2010, from news.bbc.co.uk: http://news.bbc.co.uk/go/pr/fr/-/1/hi/business/8575903.stm

16 BBC News. (2010, January 2). Npower criticised over low energy light bulb handout . Retrieved February 23, 2010, from news.bbc.co.uk: http://news.bbc.co.uk/1/hi/uk/8437778.stm

- **Environmental breaches**

  In March 2010 orang-utan protestors from Greenpeace descended on the London headquarters of a confectionary giant after the company was revealed to be using palm oil, which is destroying the Indonesian rainforest home of the last remaining orang-utans, to make its products.

  Greenpeace released a report detailing the company's use of palm oil, which is a vegetable oil, and how this is destroying the last rainforest habitat of the endangered orang-utan. The report details how palm oil used in the confectionery products has come from the biggest and most destructive palm oil producer. This company, shows the report, is illegally destroying the Indonesian rainforest and, by doing so, causing more climate changing emissions. Other large companies have now cancelled contracts with this supplier.

- **Labour unrest**

  A strike by British Airways cabin crew went ahead after talks between the airline and the Unite union collapsed. The three-day walkout began at midnight on 20 March 2010.

  The BA chief executive said the strike was "deeply regrettable" but that the airline hoped that 65% of passengers would reach their destination during the action. A union spokesperson stated that BA "ultimately wants to go to war with this union". A total of 1,100 BA flights out of the 1,950 scheduled to operate during the first three-day strike were reported to be cancelled.[17]

- **Labour exploitation**

  A BBC investigation in early 2009 reported that a leading low-cost fashion chain was being supplied by workers in Manchester who were being paid little more than half the minimum wage. Here, the BBC said, was a sweatshop in the UK, with workers allegedly working 12-hour days, seven days a week for less than the legal minimum

In the examples of reputational risk given there were some specific and immediately identifiable costs involved such as the £3.2 million fine that HSBC paid or the £303,000 worth of fines for employing illegal workers. What is more difficult to quantify is the overall cost to a particular business caused by the loss of reputation created by one of these lapses. In the case of Toyota where sales for the first part of 2010 were down by 5% and it had lost 1.8% of its market share overall it may be possible to estimate the cost. Based on the fact that a 4% loss in sales during 2008/9 lead to the announcement of a £1.1bn loss in its most recent trading year Toyota might be expecting a loss of £1.4bn in its next trading period. So is the £300m extra loss due to a loss of reputation?

Responsible and sustainable businesses will be prepared for all eventualities and have mitigated all risks and therefore should maintain and enhance their good reputation in the marketplace and in society.

17 BBC News. (2010, March 19). BA cabin crew strike to go ahead as talks collapse . Retrieved March 19, 2010, from news.bbc.co.uk: http://news.bbc.co.uk/1/hi/business/8576727.stm

CHAPTER 18

Products and Services

- Responsible or Unethical Practices?
- Ethical Consumerism
- Sustainable Products
- The Carbon Footprint of Products and Services

Responsible or Unethical Practices?

The impact of products and services offered by a business can have a positive or negative effect on customers and the society at large. Managing the impact of products means taking into account the social and environmental impacts of the product and addressing them during the design process, through product modification, or through the development of new products. Actively discouraging product misuse by product design or through influencing customers is fundamental to minimising the potential harm of a product.

The Business in the Community's "Marketplace Responsibility Principles" referred to in Chapter 14 also covers the products or services offered by a business. The two principles most relevant to products and services are as follows[1].

Manage the impact of product or service - The responsible business should take account of social and environmental impacts as part of the product development process. It should also aim to identify unintended impacts of product or service as used. It should seek opportunities for new products to address social and environmental problems and also address the impact of the product when it reaches its end of life.

Actively discourage product misuse - A responsible business will identify the potential for harm created by misuse of its products and also aim to prevent or reduce misuse through product design or by influencing its customers. The business should understand and encourage improvement in the business processes operated by suppliers and identify and prioritise areas of risk, poor performance and factors outside the company's control that may affect its operations.

If a business were foolish or unethical enough to want to ignore these principles it may well attempt unethical practices relating to products, examples of which might include:

- selling goods abroad which are banned in its home market
- omitting to provide information on the possible side effects
- manufacturing or distributing unsafe products
- the product has built in obsolescence
- wasteful and unnecessary packaging
- deception on size and content
- inaccurate and incomplete testing of products
- treatment of animals in product testing.

1 BITC. (2008, March). The Marketplace Responsibility Principles. Retrieved January 21, 2010, from bitc.org.uk: http://www.bitc.org.uk/cr_academy/view_all_resources/marketplace_resources/responsible_supply_chain_management/general_supply_chain_resources/networks_events_publications_and_other_resources/business_in_the.html

Case Study

Some recent stories in the news

Retailers stop selling wasteful TV's[2]

Eight leading electrical retailers – which between them account for more than 50 per cent of television sales in the UK – have joined a new scheme to remove the least energy efficient TVs from their shelves. The companies involved in the initiative – Best Buy UK, Comet, Co-operative Electrical, DSGi (Currys and PC World), John Lewis Partnership, Home Retail Group (Argos), Marks & Spencer, and Sainsbury's – have also undertaken to educate their customers about the benefits of buying an energy efficient TV.

The retailers' initiative has been launched by Defra and the Energy Saving Trust ahead of this summer's football World Cup, when television sales are expected to receive a considerable boost.

A sizable 7.5 per cent of the average domestic electricity bill is spent on powering televisions. According to figures from Defra and the Energy Saving Trust, the worst performing 42 inch televisions on sale today can cost around £75 a year to run, whereas an equivalent sized energy efficient TV – one carrying the 'Energy Saving Recommended' logo – would cost only £33 a year to run.

KFC cuts down on packaging in 2009[3]

KFC, the world's largest chicken fast food chain cut 14,000 tonnes of its meal packaging in the UK and Ireland in 2009. KFC switched its Fillet and Zinger burgers from cardboard 'clamshells' to paper wrappers in early 2009. It has also moved its classic chicken meals from cardboard boxes to paper bags. A little later in the year it replaced foil wrappers for its Mini Fillet Burgers to paper wrappers.

KFC, which has 720 stores across the UK and 30 stores in Ireland, said the move was part of a wider drive by the business to improve its environmental performance.

2 energy saving trust. (2010, March). Retailers TV pledge. Retrieved April 15, 2010, from energysavingtrust.org.uk: http://www.energysavingtrust.org.uk/Media/Corporate-Media/Press-release-folder/Retailers-TV-pledge

3 KFC. (2010). News and PR. Retrieved April 15, 2010, from kfc.co.uk: http://www.kfc.co.uk/about-kfc/news-and-pr/

Christmas crackdown on hundreds of dangerous and fake goods[4]

Hundreds of potentially dangerous and fake goods were seized by trading standards officers in Newham at the end of 2009. They were confiscated from shops in the borough as part of a crackdown on counterfeit goods in the run-up to Christmas. Many of the goods did not have the CE mark which certifies a product has met EU consumer safety, health or environmental requirements. The dangerous haul included:

- toy helicopters and spaceships with sharp parts which could come loose and get stuck in a child's throat and with sweets attached which could breach food safety standards
- fake toys using the 'Disney' and 'Spiderman' trademarks which easily fall apart into small pieces
- fake stationery sets using the 'Hannah Montana' trademark
- illegal cosmetics which do not conform to health and safety standards and could cause an aggressive allergic reaction as the ingredients label is inadequate.

4 Newham London. (2009, December 7). Christmas crackdown on hundreds of dangerous and fake goods. Retrieved March 15, 2010, from newham.gov.uk: http://www.newham.gov.uk/News/2009/December/Christmascrackdownonhundredsofdangerousandfakegoods.htm

There is a whole raft of consumer protection legislation that exists to eliminate as much of these unethical practices as possible and the Office of Fair Trading (OFT) plays a major role in this. Its own mission statement is to make "markets work well for consumers". They achieve this by promoting and protecting consumer interests throughout the UK, while ensuring that businesses are "fair and competitive". Another important organisation is the Advertising Standards Authority (ASA) which is the UK's independent regulator of advertising across all media, including TV, internet, sales promotions and direct marketing. Their role is to ensure ads are legal, decent, honest and truthful by applying the Advertising Codes. Both the ASA and the OFT will be involved if any selling or marketing carried out by a business is considered to be in breach of current consumer legislation but they will also take a view on practices that might be considered unethical but not necessarily "illegal".

Examples of unethical marketing practices:

- lack of clarity in pricing
- dumping – selling at a loss to increase market share and destroy competition in order to subsequently raise prices
- price fixing cartels
- encouraging people to claim prizes when they phone premium rate numbers
- "bait and switch" selling – attracting customers and subjecting them to high pressure selling techniques to switch to a more expensive alternative
- high pressure selling- especially in relation to groups such as the elderly
- counterfeit goods and piracy
- copying the style of packaging in an attempt to mislead consumers
- deceptive advertising
- irresponsible issue of credit cards and the irresponsible raising of credit limits
- unethical practices in market research and competitor intelligence.

Case Study

Some recent stories in the news

'British classics' made with meat from the other side of the world

Campaigners say products on supermarket shelves are misleading customers and supermarket brands have been identified as selling products labelled "British" or "traditional" which contain meat from thousands of miles away.

A shepherd's pie sold by one supermarket as part of its British Classics range with a Union Jack on the packaging is made with lamb from New Zealand, 11,000 miles away, but at least it does list the meat's country of origin unlike another food manufacturer's chicken dinner meal from its "British Traditional" range. This product carries a picture representing the English countryside, but it is made in a factory in the Republic of Ireland and contains intensively produced chicken from Thailand, 6,000 miles away.

A spokesperson for the Honest Food Labelling Campaign stated that the Food Standards Agency (FSA) say that a business cannot portray a product using words or images that misrepresent the food, so if they are using a scene of rolling countryside then that should imply those ingredients are from that scene. He also went on to say that the FSA defines 'traditional' as something made in its original form so a "roast chicken dinner" would imply small-scale production and not mass production by a business.

Hard pressed shoppers being "duped" by similar packaging[5]

A study commissioned by the British Brands Group in 2009 revealed compelling evidence that shoppers are being tricked into buying products whose packaging closely resembles that of leading brands. According to the survey one in three shoppers interviewed admitted to having accidentally bought the wrong product because its packaging was similar to that of a well known brand.

There was also evidence that similar packaging brings to mind the original product, with 65% of consumers agreeing that it can be confusing or misleading when the packaging of two grocery products looks similar. Similar packaging imitates key elements of the presentation of familiar and trusted brands. The use of these distinctive features clearly misleads consumers into believing that the copy actually is the brand or is connected with the brand manufacturer.

The survey also found that shoppers are keen to see clear packaging with 64% of those interviewed believing that similar packaging suggests a connection that did not exist with a leading brand. The top three reasons given by shoppers for why they perceive packaging to be similar were colour (79%), overall design (60%) and shape (54%).

One person in the survey suggested that as branded products owe as much to their packaging design as to their brand names and as their owners invest vast amounts to differentiate themselves, build consumer goodwill and brand value, copying unfairly expropriates that goodwill and steals value so it is tantamount to theft.

The research suggests that packaging products to resemble closely familiar brands may breach new consumer protection regulations. As a result the British Brands Group was calling on the OFT and Trading Standards to investigate and take action where breaches occur. In other European countries, companies are better able to take action themselves.

5 British Brands Group. (2009, May 6). British public duped by similar packaging. Retrieved March 15, 2010, from britishbrandsgroup.org.uk: http://www.britishbrandsgroup.org.uk/upload/File/Parasitic%20copying%2049.pdf

Defra to clamp down on 'greenwash' and misleading labels[6]

The Department of Environment, Food and rural Affairs (Defra) launched two initiatives in March 2010 aimed at tackling so-called 'greenwash' in marketing and clamping down on misleading environmental claims in the labelling of energy-using products.

The consultation on greenwash aims to update the government's Green Claims Guidance, first published in 2003. Working on this issue with industry in 2009, Defra said it found there was a lack of awareness amongst marketers that such guidance existed, and that much of the advice it gives is behind the times in terms of the environmental issues it focuses on.

Defra believes it is important to tackle this issue because, although consumers are increasingly interested in more environmentally responsible products, most still find it difficult to identify genuinely green goods. Such confusion, Defra contends, is inhibiting the development of goods and services that are genuinely environmentally responsible.

Defra aims to update its guidance so that it improves the quality of environmental claims by businesses, and reduces the number of claims that may be misleading – so that genuine environmental claims can be seen as more than greenwash, at the same time protecting consumers and businesses from unfair marketing. As is the case now, compliance with the Green Claims Guidance will be purely voluntary and will not be regulated or enforced by the government.

The second consultation launched by Defra – aimed at ensuring that energy-using products meet minimum performance standards and are accurately labelled – will be enforceable. Defra is proposing to introduce civil sanctions such as fines to reflect the environmental damage caused for manufacturers and importers that fail to comply with energy efficiency standards or give inaccurate information on their energy labels.

Research by the Carbon Trust published in February 2010 found that consumers are increasingly looking to labelling to provide energy efficiency information – with 43 per cent saying they are actively seeking information about the carbon impact of the products they buy and 52 per cent claiming they would be more loyal to a brand if they could see at a glance they were taking steps to reduce their carbon footprint.

Sustainable Marketing is about creating brands and companies that are fit for the future both commercially and for society.

6 Defra. (2010, March 23). Consultation on the introduction of civil sanctions. Retrieved April 23, 2010, from defra.gov.uk: http://www.defra.gov.uk/corporate/consult/eup-labelling2010/index.htm

Responsibility in core business operations can help a business increase market share, create and take advantage of new markets, and win new contracts for business. Bringing products and services to market in a responsible way can also improve product quality helping to attract new customers looking to purchase high quality goods and services that have been brought to market in a more responsible way.

Ethical Consumerism ●●●

Consumers are now more aware than ever of how goods and services are produced and their impact. The Co-operative Bank's Ethical Consumerism Report 2008[7] found that this driver in consumer behaviour was leading to the emergence of a diverse ethical market which included ethical food and drink, green home, eco-travel and transport, ethical personal products and ethical finance. The report found the UK's ethical market alone was worth £35.5 billion, up 15% on the previous year.

The overall increase in ethical spending between 1999 and 2008 was over £22.5bn with the following contributions made from each ethical consumerism category towards that amount:

Ethical food and drink	18%
Green home	25%
Eco travel	7%
Community	4%
Ethical personal products	5%
Ethical Finance	41%
	100%

7 Co-operative Bank. (2009). Ten years of Ethical Consumerism:1999-2008. Manchester: Co-operative Bank.

The above table shows that the biggest contributor to the increase was in the Ethical Finance category followed by buying green products and appliances for the home. When comparing the Ethical spending by the average household per year over this period the survey showed that the overall spend increased from £242 to £735 per year broken down as follows:

	1999	2008	% increase
Sustainable home products	43	89	107%
Green mortgages	0	18	1,800%
Renewable energy	0	13	1,300%
Clothing	21	49	133%
Cosmetics	7	20	185%
Local shops	67	82	22%
Food and Drink	81	244	201%
Transport	7	65	829%
Energy efficiency	16	155	869%
Total	£242	£735	204%

As can be seen from this table over half of the ethical spending per household is on food and drink and energy efficiency but some of the most dramatic percentage increases have happened in products that were not available in 1999. Of those that were the biggest change has occurred within the areas of transport and energy efficiency.

The Co-op's survey revealed that by the end of 2009 one in every two UK adults claim to have purchased a product primarily for ethical reasons compared to only one in four in 1999.

For the purposes of the survey 'energy efficiency' included energy efficient electrical appliances, energy efficient boilers & rechargeable batteries, 'transport' included all eco-travel & transport, 'renewable energy' included micro generation & green energy tariffs, 'food & drink' included all ethical food and drink, sustainable home products' included sustainable timber, buying for re-use (household products) & energy efficient light bulbs, 'clothing' included ethical clothing, charity shops, buying for re-use (clothing), clothing boycotts and real nappies.

For business to business transactions it is increasingly becoming a requirement for companies bidding for contracts to demonstrate their Corporate Responsibility (CR) credentials across core business. Having a poor record on CR issues, for example an environmental prosecution, could damage an important tender for business. Being able to prove and illustrate responsible business practice on a range of marketplace issues such as supplier diversity and environmental performance is not only a key indicator of management processes but also now a specific key element to winning many new contracts.

As was seen in the previous chapter the quality of goods distributed should always maintain a high standard. If a product is not fit for purpose or safe a product recall is a likely possibility. Not only is this an extremely costly process but also, as in the case of Toyota, is likely to result in severe reputational damage leading to sales depression and lost profit. Responsible management of supply chain risks as well as working with suppliers to increase their standards can eliminate such business costs and foster customer trust. Security and continuity of supply is also essential as losing a strategic supplier could have serious knock-on consequences for the business. One piece of research showed that after a product recall for health and safety reasons 15% of customers questioned would buy another brand and never buy the recalled brand again and 21% would avoid using any brand made by the manufacturer of the recalled product.

In this age of global supply chains, consumers often know little about the "life story" of the products that businesses make and sell which they buy – where they come from, who has made them and how or where they go after they have finished with them. Yet most of the environmental issues and some social issues faced by the UK can be traced back to everyday products.

Sustainable Products ●●●

There is rapidly growing recognition that product sustainability is the way forward. Researchers and designers are looking to develop new types of products with reduced environmental and social impacts. Manufacturers are seeking to reduce waste and minimise carbon emissions. More retailers are marketing "green" or "ethical" products. And household spending on ethical products and services has grown rapidly as shown in the Co-operative Bank's report.

The UK sustainable development strategy "Securing the Future"[8] highlighted the interdependence of economic, social and environmental goals. It notes that products are fundamental to all three aspects of sustainable development as they are the currency of production, trade and innovation underpinning jobs and development. They help the UK to meet its basic needs an enhance the quality of life. But most environmental and some social impacts arise from the manufacture, distribution, use and disposal of products.

8 DEFRA. (2005). Securing the Future- UK Governmnet strategy for sustainable development. Retrieved March 15, 2010, from defra.gov.uk: http://www.defra.gov.uk/sustainable/government/publications/uk-strategy/

An EU study on the Environmental Impact of Products (EU EIPRO) identified those products consumed in the EU that have the greatest environmental impact throughout their lifecycle[9]. The study looked at both private and public expenditure and volume consumed and its findings in the following key consumption areas were:

- housing: Buildings and appliances (20-35%)
- passenger transport (15-20%)
- food and drink (20-30%)
- clothing (5-10%)
- other (including tourism and leisure) (c5%).

Food and drink, private transport and housing (including buildings and appliances) were consistently the most important areas across the different studies and the different environmental impact categories compared. Together they account for 70–80% of the environmental impact of private consumption and approximately 60% of total consumption expenditure.

Products can also be the focus of social and ethical issues at home and abroad such as the labour conditions of production workers, the fairness of trading relationships or the treatment of animals

A report by Defra in 2008[10] on sustainable products and materials identified the following three main steps to their approach to improving product sustainability.

- Develop the overall vision of what is meant by sustainable which means understanding environmental, social and economic impacts and trends, how they interact, how far and how fast the UK needs to tackle them and the products' overall contribution to these impacts.
- Assess the impacts which means looking at both the scale of impact associated with the product in question and the criticality of that impact in environmental or social terms.
- Put in place the improvement strategy to tackle the impacts and deliver greater sustainability. .

9 European Commission. (2006, May). Environmental Impacts of Products. Retrieved March 15, 2010, from ec.europa.eu: http://ec.europa.eu/environment/ipp/pdf/eipro_report.pdf

10 http://www.defra.gov.uk/environment/business/products/documents/prod-materials-report0708.pdf

This approach applies to 'products' in a wide sense, including services. In some cases, making a "product" more sustainable could mean delivering what it is that the consumer needs or wants in a significantly different way, through a different type of product or service. Defra's sustainable products approach sits within their overall vision for a sustainable future, based on the principles of:

- living within environmental limits
- ensuring a strong, healthy and just society
- achieving a sustainable economy
- using sound science responsibly and
- promoting good governance.

The report included an attempt to describe what the future might be like with regard to sustainable products and services. The intention was to stimulate debate and action to help turn the possibilities into realities. It envisioned a future where:

- all products are "sustainable products". Sustainability is a normal and expected part of product and service design, manufacture, distribution and marketing
- businesses compete to drive up standards of sustainability across the range of products on the market. They recognise the economic benefits of resource efficiency and understand the importance of a healthy natural environment in underpinning their long term survival
- businesses at different stages of the chain routinely work together to minimise overall negative impacts and
- consumers routinely take into account environmental and social considerations when buying, using and disposing of products.

To achieve this, the Defra report indicated a need for action to:

- drive the development of new products that are more sustainable than all of the current options
- move the market average towards the most sustainable of what is available and
- cut out the least sustainable products.

The report concluded that a range of actions will need to be taken by government, business and consumers to drive changes across product lifecycles. The report recognised that, while products help to meet basic needs and enhance quality of life, there is a clear link between today's environmental pressures and the food we eat, homes we live in, appliances we use, cars we drive and clothes we wear.

Defra's intention is that all businesses are clear on what action they need to take to minimise the environmental and social impacts associated with their products, and on the relative priorities attached to tackling different impacts.

Defra's vision for each stage of Product Lifecycle[11]

Research and design - Product design is sustainable design. Whole lifecycle environmental performance is a normal consideration for researchers, innovators and materials scientists and the UK is a leader and an influence internationally.

UK innovators and designers lead the way on new mainstream products and services. These differ from products available today. They use fewer newly extracted raw materials and more recycled materials. Some products are replaced with technology or other types of services. Products are designed so that they are modular, multi functional, repairable and upgradeable. They are more efficient and have fewer environmental impacts in use. Products have improved longevity and can be more easily reused or recycled when they do come to the end of their life.

Raw material acquisition - The UK has a strong and thriving economy which is based on sustainable sources and takes into account the full range of impacts in the way that it harnesses and harvests resources. For those renewable resources which require replenishment the UK will harvest them at the rate necessary to ensure an enduring supply. Where non-renewable materials are essential the UK will re-use, remanufacture or recycle existing stocks.

Manufacture - Sustainability should be a key criteria in product specifications both to meet normal business models and because it provides consumer appeal and is communicated along the supply chain. Manufacturers will ensure that their materials are responsibly sourced and their products will be designed so as to minimise impacts throughout their lifecycle. Where products for the UK market are manufactured abroad, UK retailers and consumers drive improved environmental and social standards. There are high levels of remanufacturing. Manufacturers communicate relevant and clear information about products to retailers and distributors.

Distribution and Retail - Retailers will demand sustainability as a pre-requisite when sourcing products and services. They will ensure that their products are sold with appropriate and useful information about their lifecycle including information about how to use and dispose of products to minimise impacts.

Use and maintenance – Consumers will have confidence that all the products and services available on sale are sustainable. They will expect lifecycle assurance when they buy a product with clear information on where the product has come from, how it was made, how to maintain and use it, and what to do when they no longer want or need it.

11 DEFRA. (2008). Progress Report on Sustainable Products and Materials. London: DEFRA.

Both government and businesses will have sustainability requirements as a normal part of their procurement contracts and through these they drive competition amongst designers, manufacturers and retailers to achieve further sustainability improvements.

Business and individual consumers will use the products they buy in ways which minimise environmental impacts. Changes in product design and product information will have made this normal and easy to do.

End of life - Improvements in product design, manufacture and use will mean that less waste is generated and what is generated can be more easily reused or recovered. All businesses and households will re-use their wastes where possible and routinely separate their waste into different types for recycling and recovery.

The Sustainable Development Commission has also published an advisory booklet on product road mapping to tackle climate change, resource depletion and poverty[12]. The guidance claims to show how a sustainable approach to products makes sense for people, planet and business.

The booklet contains a 12-point sustainability health-check for businesses, covering product development, manufacture, transport, product use and disposal, as well as the well-being of people involved in supply chains.

It notes that focusing on the lifecycles of individual products and services using a road mapping approach a business can help to promote positive decision-making to resolve conflicting priorities, and identify solutions in areas such as reducing waste and carbon, or improving labour conditions. It also notes that this makes good business sense as a responsible approach to products and services can save money, attract customers and drive innovation to keep pace with a fast changing world.

The Carbon Footprint of Products and Services ●●●

Importance of product carbon foot printing

In line with Defra's desire for sustainable products the Carbon Trust scheme for product carbon foot printing offers a unique view of greenhouse gas (GHG) emissions, taking a single product from raw materials through manufacturing, distribution, use and disposal/recycling, and calculating the emissions created as a result of all related activities and materials[13]. It can also be applied to the delivery of a service.

12 Sustainable Development Commission. (2007). You are what you sell Product road mapping:driving sustainability. London: Sustainable Development Commission.

13 Carbon Trust. (2008, October). Product carbon footprinting:the new business opportunity. Retrieved March 8, 2010, from carbon-label.com: http://www.carbon-label.com/casestudies/Opportunity.pdf

Overview by the Carbon Trust

Product carbon footprinting addresses businesses' need to better understand how their products and supply chains impact carbon emissions, and to respond to growing consumer demand for carbon information and low-carbon products.

PAS 2050, the first standard method for calculating life cycle greenhouse gas (GHG) emissions of products, was published in October 2008 by BSI British Standards, co-sponsored by the Carbon Trust and Defra. This standard integrates product life cycle assessment with GHG emission accounting which is necessary in order to reliably and consistently calculate product-level emissions.

To support consistent communications of product carbon footprints, the Carbon Trust simultaneously sponsored the Code of Good Practice on Product GHG Emissions and Reduction Claims and developed the Carbon Reduction Label to provide companies with a certified, consistent and comparable way to display their products' footprints, along with a commitment to reduce those footprints over time.

Over 20 leading companies applied the method across a wide range of products during the development process, leading to a standard that is both robust and practical for businesses to implement and the experience of these companies has already revealed the value of measuring product-level GHG emissions. These companies have:

- uncovered the true drivers of carbon emissions across a product's life cycle
- identified high-impact emission reduction – and cost savings – opportunities
- strengthened supplier relationships
- developed better business and management practices in general.

Product labelling provides further benefits, as seen by the companies who have communicated their products' carbon footprints using the Carbon Trust Carbon Reduction Label. They have already:

- realised additional emission and cost savings, driven by the Carbon Reduction Label's required commitment to ongoing reductions
- differentiated their products to customers
- improved their corporate brand and reputation.

Product carbon footprinting and labelling is still in its early stages but is growing rapidly. Companies who act now can seize an advantage by:

- participating in the growing internationalisation of the standard and Carbon Reduction Label
- building a reputation for excellence in the growing product carbon footprinting 'industry' of consultants, certifiers, software providers and database developers
- responding to accelerating consumer demand for product carbon information and lower carbon products, and gaining from the cost savings that result from reducing emissions.

The Carbon Reduction Label as Explained by the Carbon Trust[14]

The Carbon Reduction Label shows the total greenhouse gas emissions from every stage of the product's lifecycle, including production, transportation, preparation, use and disposal and in the case of a Business to Business (B2B) product the carbon footprint measurement is up to the factory gates. While it is essential that the footprint calculations take every greenhouse gas into account, the figure is given as their total CO2 equivalent as is consistent with other recognised GHG reporting.

The Carbon Trust explains that while most people assume that carbon labelling refers to on-pack labelling, there are many other effective channels that providers of products and services can exploit, including:

1. point of sale material
2. websites belonging to the product manufacturer or service provider
3. online reseller product catalogues (products) and online directories (services)
4. advertising, mail-packs, product brochures, catalogues, business cards, local directories and other sales materials
5. product manuals where carbon-reducing usage advice can be explained.

The Carbon Reduction Label is underpinned by the PAS 2050 and is receiving input from stakeholders around the world. By then applying its own set of proprietary data and comparability rules, the Carbon Trust Footprinting Company can ensure that measurement is comparable across different products within any particular category, enabling manufacturers and consumers to make quick and valid comparisons.

The Label includes a reduction element whereby the company is committed to further reduce the carbon footprint over the following two years. If the commitment is not met, the company will no longer be able to use the label.

Recent research studies carried out for the Carbon Trust and other organisations concluded that companies believe that climate change is one of the factors most likely to affect their corporate reputation. The Carbon Trust also has evidence to show that the Carbon Reduction Label could be a deciding factor in customer choice. Carbon Labelling is thus a valuable way for companies to demonstrate their carbon commitments to their consumers.

The use of the label is empowering consumers and it offers businesses a way to display their products' carbon footprint information consistently, credibly and with a commitment to reduce the footprint over time.

14 Carbon Trust. (2010, March 15). Carbon Reduction Label explained. Retrieved March 15, 2010, from carbon-label.com: http://www.carbon-label.com/business/label.htm

Looking at the whole "life of the product through its phases" the following questions will be raised:

- what materials are used and where did they come from? Where are they going?
- which phases of the cycle require energy (fuel, electricity)?
- what could cause direct emissions?

Tesco are one of the companies working with the Carbon Trust and they have started the labelling process with a small selection of products including the following:

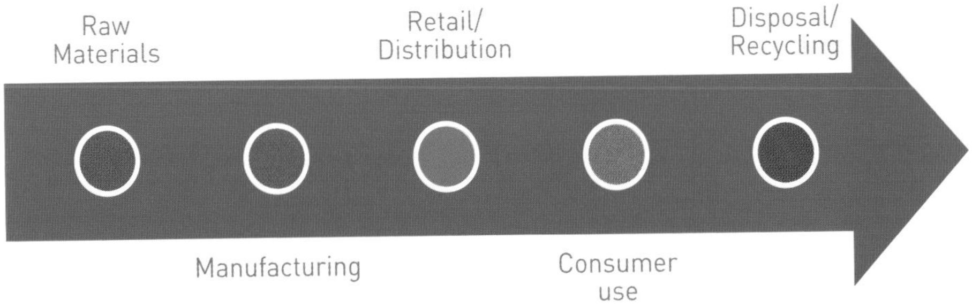

Product	Grams CO2 per unit	Production	Distribution	Store	Use	End of life waste
Orange juice	240g per 250ml	93%	1%	4%	1%	1%
60w pearl light bulb	34kg per 1000 hours use	1%	0.1%	0.1%	99%	0.1%
King Edward 2.5 kg	160g per 250g serving	33%	1%	3%	56%	7%
Organic new 1.5kg	160g per 250g serving	40%	1%	4%	51%	4%

It can be seen that in the case of certain products such as orange juice the production phase is where the vast majority of emissions take place whereas an ordinary 60w light bulb emits 99% of its carbon during consumer usage. However with the two types of potato although there are differences in the various phases of the product life cycle they both ultimately generate 160g of carbon per 250g serving which begs the question what use can be made of the extra information?

The Carbon Trust worked with HBOS to calculate the carbon footprint of a service which proved more difficult. The footprint calculation included activities and materials involved in both the opening and subsequent operation of the Halifax Web Saver account. In this case, 'per year of account operation' was chosen as it allowed HBOS to calculate a single standard number to use across all its Web Saver customers, regardless of how much they saved or how old their account was. So users of the account will be told that:

> *The carbon footprint of this account is 200g per year and we have committed to reduce it.*
>
> *This is the total carbon dioxide (CO2) and other greenhouse gases emitted in providing the account, including setup, ongoing use and closure.*

As already indicated, the labelling scheme is in its infancy so there may be some initial frustration on the part of consumers wanting to make fully informed choices and if only some products and services carry the label that may not be possible. However the label in itself is a sign that the business is committed to reducing its carbon footprint whereas an alternative product without a label provides no such clue. Other factors will also come into play. For example, a similar account to the HBOS saver account that might be offered by the Co-operative Bank may still be preferred if the bank itself is considered far more ethical in its dealings.

Case Study[15]

Leading Haymarket titles become the first magazines in the UK to carry the Carbon Reduction Label. The respected environmental title "ENDS" and leading marketing business magazine "Marketing" will display the Carbon Trust's Carbon Reduction Label from the end of September 2009, after having undergone a rigorous and detailed carbon foot printing process. The label will display each magazine's commitment to reduce their overall carbon footprint, and in the case of ENDS also show the total grams of carbon emitted per copy produced as certified by the Carbon Trust.

The footprinting study by the Carbon Trust looked at every stage of the magazines' life cycle, from paper mill to printing press and from editorial activities to reader behaviour. Some of the things the magazines learned included that the type of paper used and the power source at the paper mill will have a significant impact on a magazine's overall carbon footprint. Office emissions make up a larger part of the footprint of niche business magazines such as ENDS.

A Director of Haymarket said that the company has been working hard to reduce carbon emissions through recycling, wastage reduction and other initiatives, but until this point it had been difficult to measure the impact of the supply chain on their product emissions. The PAS 2050 labelling process had not only provided a benchmark for them but it had also identified how they can continue to reduce their carbon footprint through improvements in the way they source paper and printing and they are committed to reduce their carbon emissions in the next two years.

15 Carbon Trust. (2009, September 30). Leading Haymarket titles become the first magazines to carry the Carbon Reduction Label. Retrieved March 15, 2010, from carbontrust.co.uk: http://www.carbontrust.co.uk/news/news/press-centre/2009/Pages/haymarket-carry-carbon-reduction-label.aspx

CHAPTER 19

Shareholders and other Stakeholders

- Ethical Investment
- Principles for Responsible Investment
- Share Ownership and Ethical Choices
- Investor Engagement

Ethical investment ●●●

Ethical investment can be defined as an investment philosophy which attempts to balance the regard for the morality of a business and its activities and regard for return on investment. Ethical investors will be seeking to invest in businesses which make a positive contribution to the quality of the environment and society. These concerned investors will choose businesses that operate ethically, provide social benefits and are sensitive to the environment. Ethical investment has also been referred to as "socially conscious investing".

A spokesperson for UKSIF[1], the sustainable investment and finance association stated that increasing numbers of investors want to make money and make a difference. As the UK gradually moves out of recession, they see it as vital that people carefully consider the impact of their investments to help build a sustainable economic recovery. They suggested that one simple way to make a difference would be to consider green and ethical funds as part of an ISA.

A survey conducted in 2009 as part of "National Ethical Investment Week" found that 49% of people would like to make money and make a difference. The desire to make a positive impact was highest among older investors. According to the Investment Management Association (IMA), there was more than £5.6 billion invested in green and ethical funds in the UK in 2009 up from £2.5 billion in 1999.

More and more people are taking an interest in green and ethical issues covering subjects as diverse as human rights, climate change and genetically modified foods. It is possible to actively support or avoid these causes through everyday buying decisions and there are also increasing opportunities to make ethical choices in terms of finance. There is a growing awareness that, alongside simply choosing to buy or not to buy their products, those who invest their spare money can also influence businesses towards better social and environmental behaviour.

If an investor has any concerns that the business in which they have invested might be exploiting third world countries or damaging the environment or simply is carrying out activities they do not approve of they may prefer to switch to an ethical investments which is also referred to as Socially Responsible Investment (SRI).

Socially Responsible Investment - Definition

- Socially responsible investment (SRI) - actively screen out investment in businesses and sectors considered "unethical".
- Social Impact Investment (SII) - target investment in the building of schools and hospitals for example.
- Social Enterprise Investment (SEI) - organisations that pursue a combination of social and economic objectives.

These are collectively known as ethical investments and they follow a strategy of focusing on the positive social and/or ecological impact of a company in addition to its financial return.

1 UKSIF. (2010, February 11). Ethical Investments on the rise:ISA opportunity. Retrieved March 15, 2010, from uksif.org: http://www.uksif.org/about/Latest_News

In the UK the main SRI market is represented by the FTSE4Good index. This index measures the performance of companies on globally recognised corporate responsibility standards which cover the following categories:

- environment – working towards environmental sustainability
- social and stakeholder – developing positive relationships with stakeholders
- human rights – up-holding and supporting universal human rights
- supply chain labour – ensuring good supply chain labour standards
- countering bribery.

FTSE4Good have a number of methods to monitor company performance on the above criteria including annual reports and web-sites and responses to written questionnaires.

Principles for Responsible Investment[2]

There is also a growing awareness amongst investment managers of the demand for social responsibility in investments. This has seen many in the UK and overseas sign-up to the six principles of the UN 'Principles for Responsible Investment'.

Launched in 2006 the Principles for Responsible Investment were developed by an international group of institutional investors reflecting the increasing relevance of environmental, social and corporate governance issues to investment practices. The process was convened by the United Nations Secretary-General.

In signing the Principles, these investors publicly commit to adopt and implement them, where consistent with their fiduciary responsibilities. They also commit to evaluate the effectiveness and improve the content of the Principles over time. They believe this will improve their ability to meet commitments to beneficiaries as well as better align their investment activities with the broader interests of society.

The benefits to signing the PRI include:

- a common framework for integrating environmental, social and corporate governance (ESG) issues
- access to examples of good practice from a global network of peers including many of the world's largest institutional investors
- opportunities to collaborate and network with other signatories, reducing research and implementation costs
- reputational benefits from publicly demonstrating top-level commitment to integrating ESG issues
- participation in the annual PRI signatory event
- access to a standard reporting and assessment tool.

2 UNEP Finance Initiative. (2010, March 15). Principles for Responsible Investment. Retrieved March 15, 2010, from unpri.org: http://www.unpri.org/files/pri.pdf

There are three main categories of signatory.

Asset owner - Examples include pension funds, government reserve funds, foundations, endowments, insurance and reinsurance companies and depository organizations.

Investment manager - Investment management companies that serve an institutional and/or retail market and manage assets as a third-party provider.

Professional service partner - Organizations that offer products or services to asset owners and/or investment managers.

There is a suggested, voluntary fee of $10,000 to help the work of the secretariat in supporting signatories and promoting the Principles. From 2011 an annual mandatory fee is proposed.

Looking at the Share Ownership Survey 2008[3] published by the Office of National Statistics in early 2010 provides a breakdown of the ownership of ordinary shares in quoted companies in the UK. The results of the survey show how the value of UK quoted shares was distributed between sector of beneficial owner at 31 December 2008. At the end of 2008 the UK Stock Market was valued at £1,158.4 billion, a decrease of £699.8 billion (37.7%) since the end of 2006. The following table compares the years 2006 and 2008:

Beneficial ownership of UK shares 2006 and 2008

	£bn 2006	£bn 2008	% 2006	% 2008
Rest of world	742.4	481.1	40.0	41.5
Insurance Companies	272.8	154.9	14.7	13.4
Pension Funds	235.8	148.8	12.7	12.8
Individuals	238.5	117.8	12.8	10.2
Unit Trusts	30.0	21.3	1.6	1.8
Investment Trusts	45.1	22.1	2.4	1.9
Other financial institutions	179.1	115.3	9.6	10.0
Charities	16.1	8.7	0.9	0.8
Private non-financial companies	33.5	34.7	1.8	3.0
Public sector	2.0	13.0	0.1	1.1
Banks	63.0	40.6	3.4	3.5
Total	1,858.3	1,158.3	100.0	100.0

3 Office of National Statistics. (2010). Share Ownership Survey 2008. London: Office of National Statistics.

The survey showed that FTSE 100 companies continued to dominate the UK stock market. The proportion of funds invested in these companies varied between 64.9 % for individuals and 96.5% by private non-financial companies. Overall, 84.6% of equity investment in quoted companies was in FTSE 100 companies. Those sectors which are likely to come under increasing pressure due to their commitment to the Responsible Investment Principles such as Pension Funds, Unit Trusts, Public Sector and Insurance Companies will, however, when added to the number of individual investors who are looking to invest more ethically, ultimately account for up to 52% (£602.4bn) of the total ownership of ordinary shares in the UK based on 2008 figures.

The UK Sustainable Investment and Finance (UKSIF) survey "Responsible Business: Sustainable Pension 2009"[4] was the second survey of the pension funds of the UK's corporate responsibility leaders and it found clear evidence of progress in addressing Responsible Investment. The report said that it is encouraging that in the second survey there were clear signs of progress in the adoption of Responsible Investment policies. More funds now have a Responsible Investment policy and more significantly of those funds that completed both surveys more than half have achieved a higher ranking in 2009. Also, for those funds that did not achieve a higher ranking, half were assessed as having made progress over the two years.

Key results include:

- four fifths of funds now have a Responsible Investment (RI) policy, compared with only two thirds in 2007
- almost all the trustees of larger funds now believe that ESG factors can have a material impact on the fund's investments in the long term, increasing from three quarters in 2007. Overall, trustees of three quarters of participating funds agree, up from two thirds
- a third of funds give "great" significance to alignment with the plan sponsor's CSR/ Sustainability policy, up from a fifth; the total for "great" and "some" significance was unchanged at two thirds
- nine tenths of funds with a RI policy exercise their shareholder voting rights, compared with only three quarters in 2007.
- four fifths of funds monitored whether their RI policy was being carried out, an increase from three quarters in 2007
- detailed communication to members and other stakeholders about the RI policy and its implementation remains relatively low. A tenth of funds communicate annual voting records. Less than a tenth disclose the fund's engagement strategy or about participation in collaborative investor initiatives.

Share Ownership and Ethical Choices ●●●

Different individuals will have different principles and ethical investments reflect this in that they don't all have the same objectives. The first step for an investor towards positive investing is to identify what social, environmental and other ethical issues are

4 UKSIF. (2009, June). Sustainable Pensions Report 2009. Retrieved March 15, 2010, from uksif.org: http://www.uksif.org/cmsfiles/281411/Sustainable_Pensions_Report_2009.pdf

most important to them. Areas of concern can be wide ranging, from animal testing to gambling, from human rights to nuclear power, from environmental enhancement to community involvement. Surveys by EIRIS have shown that the most prominent areas of concern were operations in oppressive regimes, breaking environmental regulations and testing products on animals. The companies that respondents most liked their pension fund to favour over others when making investments were those with good records on environmental issues and employment conditions. Identifying these areas will reflect the type of companies ethical investors will want to invest in or to avoid. Some possible reasons for choice are given in the following table:

Negative criteria: investments to avoid	**Positive criteria: investments to select**
Animal testing takes place	Community involvement
Genetic engineering is being utilised	Good corporate governance
Health & Safety breaches have occurred	Disclosure/quality information provided
High environmental impact	Good environmental initiatives
Human rights issues	A good equal opportunities record
Intensive farming operations	Positive/sustainable products and services
Military use/weapons	Responsible supply chain management
Nuclear power	A good employer
Pesticides manufacture/distribution	
Pollution convictions	
Pornography/adult entertainment	
Non-sustainable timber/deforestation	
Third world concerns	
Traditional – alcohol, tobacco & gambling	
Water pollution	

It is important, however, to remember that there is no such thing as a perfect company. All are involved in activities that someone somewhere will object to and none go far enough in terms of positive social and environmental contribution to satisfy all of the people all of the time. Ethical investment is about compromising and prioritising.

Looking at ethical shares the question is often asked about where should funds draw the "green line"? Arms suppliers are easy targets but then what about mining and supermarkets? Opinion is split over the inclusion of supermarket groups in ethical portfolios as traditional concerns such as tobacco, alcohol and forms of gambling can all be purchased in store and as already indicated no ethical fund would invest in the shares of companies engaged in tobacco, arms or pornography. But they are possibly the easy ones to screen out of an investment portfolio. The more difficult question to answer is what about other businesses such as oil companies, airlines and supermarket groups? Are they suitable for inclusion in an ethical investment portfolio?

One of the UK's biggest ethical funds lists in its top 10 investments companies such as those involved in gas exploration and production, exploring for oil and a leading supermarket. Yet it goes to great lengths to ensure the fund's holdings meet the expectations of investors.

In 2008 a large Insurance company said that it would exclude airlines from ethical funds. That followed feedback from its annual ethical investor survey, in which 30% of respondents stated they would prefer airline stocks to be excluded. Oil, gas and mining stocks are also contentious, as are companies engaged in operating nuclear power stations. Should investors screen out fossil-fuel companies on environmental grounds, or include the ones that are making strides to develop alternative energy sources?

In Britain, some ethical funds hold shares in Tesco but others screen them out. Some argue that they should invest in Tesco to put pressure on it to improve. Tesco itself has pointed out that it is in the ethical FTSE4Good index and says that it maintains high ethical standards. Tesco states that sustainability is at the core of its strategy, it is increasing local-sourcing of products, reducing packaging and aiming to halve distribution emissions by 2012.

When deciding what is or is not ethical there are many questions and contradictions. For example with regard to pornography is a hotel chain unethical for allowing guests to watch "adult films" and is every telecommunications company that allows "adult chat or entertainment" via its phone lines or internet service also being unethical?

Another very important aspect of shareholding is that once the company has issued the shares the transfer of ownership subsequently is outside the control of that company. Can an ethical company's reputation be tarnished by its own shareholders?

A very recent example may well be that of the Innocent Smoothie company which denies a sell-out after 58% of its shares were bought by Coca-Cola in April 2010 who, as a result, now have a majority stake. The founders of the company insisted that they would keep operational control of their small and ethically-minded British business and the existing directors would continue to run the business and the injection of additional cash will only help to enhance their goal of bringing healthy drinks to a global market. They claimed it was not a sell-out but more a continuation of their work with no change in their commitment to natural healthy food, to sustainability and to giving 10% of their profits to charity.

As well as being another example of a UK business falling into foreign ownership it is also another example of a business set up with high-minded goals that has been taken over by a very large and conservatively-run business.

Once an investor has decided their individual criteria, there is a diverse range of ethical funds available and different funds suit different investors. Some funds select a set of criteria which they believe will appeal to the widest range of investors. Others take a precisely focused approach, designed to appeal to a particular market. It is therefore very important to look behind the 'green' or 'ethical' label to what the fund is actually investing in before deciding to invest.

An investor should ask:

- how the fund researches the activities of the companies in which it invests?
- is there an ethical committee or advisory board that is independent of the investment process, to make sure the fund adheres to its published ethical policy?
- how good is the fund's communication with investors, for example, does it have mechanisms in place to allow investors to voice their concerns?
- how active is the fund in engaging or communicating with companies? Does it encourage companies to improve their social and environmental performance?

Ethical investing works in two ways:

- by using power as a shareholder to influence corporate behaviour
- by choosing to invest only in companies who behave in a socially responsible manner.

Ethical investment is not confined to shares traded in stock exchanges. Many investors prefer to back individual projects or causes. Such directed investment is known by a variety of terms including, alternative investment, mission-based investment and socially directed investment. Examples of cause-based investment might include regeneration projects in inner cities or the support of projects in developing countries. The cause-based investment sector is currently dominated by financial institutions such as Triodos Bank and the Ecology Building Society.

There are three main strategies that funds can adopt to implement their ethical investment policies.

- **Engagement**

  No companies are excluded but areas are identified in which companies can improve their environmental, social and ethical performance. The fund managers then 'engage' with the companies to encourage them to make such improvements.

- **Preference or integration**

  The funds will adopt social, environmental or other ethical guidelines which they prefer companies to meet. These guidelines are applied where all other things are equal (e.g. financial performance).

- **Screening**

  An 'acceptable list' of companies is created based on chosen positive and/or negative criteria. Funds are invested only in those companies on the list.

At the end of 2007 the amount of money allocated to Socially Responsible Investments (SRI) as part of Assets under Management (AuM) amounted to just under a quarter of all assets managed by the Investment Management Association. In terms of the three main strategies the proportion of the total for each was simple Screening 5%, Integration 41% and Engagement 54%.

Case Study[5]

In June 2005 the Co-operative became the world's first insurance company to launch a customer-led Ethical Engagement Policy and this also included their investment business.

Customers of The Co-operative Insurance and Investments asked that the company used its position as a major investor, to engage companies on a commercial level. In this way, they could challenge major businesses from the inside, to improve their performance in relation to issues of concern to their customers, such as climate change and human rights, in a way that other organisations could not. They actively vote at AGMs and meet with the companies in which they invest to encourage them to be better, fairer businesses.

The decision to adopt a customer-led Ethical Engagement Policy was a major step for the company as it meant going into uncharted waters because they were the first insurer in the world to do it. Since they recognise that people's concerns change over time, they are committed to regularly re-appraising their customers' views and updating their policy accordingly.

The Co-operative's Responsible Shareholding team implements their Ethical Engagement Policy across all the companies in which they invest. Company performance on corporate governance and social, ethical and environmental management is analysed to identify where good or bad management of an issue may impact upon share price, and to identify where a company's practices may conflict with their customers' ethical concerns. The Co-operative Asset Management is a signatory to the UN Principles for Responsible Investment.

5 Co-operative Financial Services. (2010, March 15). Ethical Insurance and investments. Retrieved March 15, 2010, from goodwithmoney.co.uk: http://www.goodwithmoney.co.uk/ethical-insurance-and-investments/

Their Ethical Engagement Policy does not mean that they refuse to invest in certain business activities but rather it means that they will invest in most companies, but seek to use their influence as a shareholder to try to improve the ethical performance of these businesses in line with their customers' views.

Through their Ethical Engagement policy they aim to protect their customers' investments, champion their customers' expectations of corporate behaviour and challenge those companies not promoting customers' financial interests and values to change.

Their approach to the engagement process is by:

- identifying areas of improvement for individual companies and groups of companies affected by similar issues and this involves in-house research, external consultation and written requests to companies for information
- making recommendations for changes in policy and/or behaviour – such as defining models of best practice
- supporting management to implement change – for example, facilitating contact between management and relevant external organisations
- monitoring performance against best practice and policy commitments – a key aspect of this stage is encouraging full public disclosure of material information
- attending company AGMs to raise questions and gain direct access to senior management and non-executive directors
- using its vote at AGMs to signal support or concern on a specific issue – each time they do not support the board, they write to the company to explain their position
- through collaboration with like-minded investors – behaving that where possible institutional investors should work together from a position of collective strength.

According to Co-operative Insurance an estimated 70% of the market value of the UK's largest companies relates to 'intangible assets' or 'goodwill'. Some of the major risks to goodwill that businesses face relate to their management of corporate governance and social, ethical and environmental (SEE) issues.

A 2008 Harvard Business School[6] study "doing well by doing good" decided that while doing good did not appear to destroy shareholder value the authors found only a very small correlation between corporate behaviour and good financial results apart from public misdeeds, which had a discernible negative impact. They also felt that the minor correlation that did exist could well be explained by deep pockets – a history of strong financial performance may simply give a company the wherewithal to contribute to society. Indeed, of the various forms social responsibility can take, cash contributions to charities have shown a stronger correlation with success than have socially responsible corporate policies or community projects.

The study suggested that:

- corporate misdeeds are costly to companies – if the public finds out. There have been examples of the serious consequences of corporate scandal but they first need to be exposed
- companies doing good is unlikely to cost shareholders. Only 2% of the companies surveyed imposed a direct cost to their shareholders
- profitability should not be the primary rationale for corporate social responsibility as companies should not necessarily expect to be rewarded for engaging in socially responsible activities.

The researchers interpreted the weak link between corporate social performance and corporate financial performance by deciding that it pays to be good, but not too good. They suggested that it may be that companies do best when they find a middle ground: doing enough to satisfy regulators and activists, but not doing so much that they risk the disapproval of analysts and investors.

However another study by the Carbon Trust in 2008 "Climate change – a business revolution?"[7] looked into how tackling climate change could create or destroy company value. One of its key conclusions was that tackling climate change could create opportunities for a company to increase its value by up to 80% if it is well positioned and proactive. Conversely, it could threaten up to 65% of value if the company is poorly positioned or a "laggard". The scale of the opportunities and threats analysed by the Carbon Trust are therefore very significant for investors and business managers.

The Carbon Trust report suggested that the opportunities and risks are driven by shifts in consumer behaviour, technology innovation and regulation. Regulation is usually the key initiator of change although the cost of carbon is not the decisive factor in many sectors which means that the impact of tackling climate change will vary by sector.

The Carbon Trust identified four ways in which value could be created or destroyed: sector transformation, upward demand shift, downward demand shift and increased volatility. In response the Carbon Trust report recommends that strategic

6 Harvard Business Review. (2008, January). Doing well by doing good? Don't count on it. Retrieved March 15, 2010, from hbbr.org: http://hbr.org/2008/01/do-well-by-doing-good-dont-count-on-it/ar/1

7 Carbon Trust. (2008, September). Climate Change - a business revolution? Retrieved March 15, 2010, from carbontrust.com: http://www.carbontrust.com/publications/CTC740_business_rev%20v5.pdf

investors should discriminate between sectors and companies on the basis of their opportunities and risks. Businesses should incorporate climate change in their core strategy and investment decisions. Policy makers should work with business and investors to create a policy framework which rewards early action and an efficient transition to a low-carbon economy.

The Carbon Trust framework identified four interrelated drivers of value.

- in some sectors specific regulations are being introduced to incentivise or mandate change, for example, introducing maximum product emissions standards. These will expose competitive differences of capability to respond
- changes in consumer preferences will affect demand for different products. This will also be affected by the availability of lower carbon substitute products
- technology breakthroughs will be critical in certain industries. Winning companies will be those that are able to access the best technologies at lowest cost
- policy makers have already begun to introduce a 'cost of carbon' which applies to the CO2 emissions of some businesses. This will expose competitive differences between operations.
- These drivers influence not only costs, but more importantly, relative costs and competitive advantage as well as shifts in demand for product types. Together this determines value creation opportunities and value-at-risk.

The Carbon Trust believes that company preparation for the move to a low-carbon economy is essential to creating and preserving value. However, the faster the pace of change required, the more difficult it will be for companies to prepare and avoid incurring costs that place value at risk. This places a considerable responsibility on companies to anticipate and prepare in advance. The Trust also recommends that investors including asset managers and advisers include tackling climate change as a key driver of investment strategy.

This final sentiment is echoed by another study carried out by Experts in Responsible Investment Solutions (EIRIS) in 2009[8] which identified that engagement on the part of investors is key as many large companies face significant climate change risks and opportunities. The report states that investors must understand the impact these issues will have on their portfolios and integrate climate change into their engagement strategies or alternatively when they are exercising their voting rights. The authors, as with the Carbon Trust report, concluded that climate change has the potential to seriously impact shareholder value, especially in the medium to long term. Investors they say, need to understand the risks to their investments and also the role they should play in the wider policy debate. The report stated that for companies and their investors, climate change presents a number of risks and opportunities as follows:

- opportunities might arise from the decisions made at the UN Climate Change Conference in Copenhagen at the end of 2009 as they may create significant opportunities linked to the development of green stimulus packages or a clearer regulatory framework

8 EIRIS. (2009, August). http://www.eiris.org/news/archived_pr.html#press-release9 Retrieved March 15, 2010.

- regulatory challenges in terms of national and international policy frameworks for reducing GHG emissions are providing an imperative to reduce operational emissions and any new national or international legislation that creates further directives and acts should be fully taken into account by Investors when determining risks and opportunities regarding investing in companies with exposure to climate change. The report also recommends that environmental taxes and compliance costs need to be factored into a companies' operational costs
- changing market dynamics brought about by higher and fluctuating energy costs present a significant impact, in particular for energy-intensive industries. However, changing consumer attitudes and demand patterns will open up opportunities for new technology, products and markets
- changing weather patterns will provide the physical risks of climate change including damage to assets as a result of flooding and extreme weather events.
- reputational risk is an important factor as seen in Chapter 17 where it was highlighted that customer, employee, investor and societal perceptions are having an increasing impact on brand value.

The EIRIS study indentified the following key challenges for investors.

- There is a high level of unmitigated risk in terms of Climate Change found amongst the global top 300 companies and as a result asset owners should demand that their asset managers integrate climate change in their investment process and should monitor their performance in this regard.
- High risk companies are improving but there is still a long way to go and this gives an opportunity for investors to exercise their voting rights and to engage companies to minimise risk.
- The quality of quantitative disclosure remains a challenge for investors and they should demand greater transparency to evaluate the exposure and performance to climate change of their portfolios.

EIRIS identified the following steps for investors to take in order to protect or enhance their investments.

- **Identify portfolio risks** - An understanding by the investor of the carbon profile or footprint of their portfolio is an important first step but for a complete picture of a company's risk profile investors should also look beyond emissions intensity to how the company is responding to the challenges of climate change.
- **Factor in carbon** - This involves fully understanding carbon risks and opportunities both within the portfolio and also the wider economic picture. This isn't just about divesting from high impact companies. Investors should factor in carbon when pricing very high and high impact companies and they should also identify those companies actively managing their risks or seeking out opportunities. A focus on investing in climate change solutions companies, such as renewable energy or energy efficiency, is another way to factor in carbon.

- **Engage** - This includes using investor influence to engage with companies and the wider policy debate. Company engagement includes focusing on specific issues and sectors or by encouraging improved disclosure from all companies on how they are responding to climate change.

Investor Engagement

Recent financial press coverage of various business leaders and politicians has highlighted the need for shareholders to be urged to play their part in governance. Good corporate governance, it was suggested, is like any relationship where there is a two-way street. After years of focus on company behaviour, the recent credit crisis has led regulators to turn the spotlight back to investors as stewards of the companies in which they invest.

Some prominent ministers have been outspoken on the subject of "ownerless corporations", criticising shareholders for behaving like gamblers and "absentee landlords", while the review of UK banks' corporate governance which was published in November 2009, laid a share of the blame for the collapse of the banking system on their shareholders for not holding them to account.

It has also been suggested that a disproportionate amount of corporate governance reform has focused on companies rather than investors but there is now a definite trend towards "joined-up thinking" between corporate governance and investment decisions which is thought to be long overdue.

The comply-or-explain policy has been criticised for allowing investors to opt out of engagement. This means that, to an extent, those that invest time and resources in engaging will carry those who will not engage. However if engagement improves the market overall will benefit. Most companies spend time and money engaging with their shareholders. Yet many shareholders argue that they have too many investments to engage with them all.

Case Study[9]

A coalition of global investors from 13 countries, managing over US$2.1 trillion of assets added its voice to the increasing calls for better corporate reporting on environmental, social and corporate governance (ESG) activities.

The international investor coalition wrote to 86 major companies in early 2010 urging them to honour the reporting requirements of the United Nations Global Compact, the world's biggest voluntary corporate responsibility initiative. Each of the 86 "laggard" companies has previously joined the UN initiative but failed to produce the mandatory annual report on how it puts the initiative's ten principles into action.

This is the third year that investors have engaged with UN Global Compact participant companies on the issue of transparency. In 2008, the engagement resulted in 33% of "laggard" companies subsequently submitting their reports, in 2009 positive responses increased to 47.6% (50 out of 105 companies), including from firms such as BHP Billiton, Severn Trent, The Gap and LVMH. The investor coalition also praised 44 companies, including Bayer, Nikon and Inditex, for producing high quality sustainability reports deemed useful for investors.

9 UNPRI. (2010, February 15). Investors step up pressure on corporate responsibility reporting. Retrieved March 15, 2010, from unpri.org: http://www.unpri.org/files/lal10_final.pdf

ESG issues are now a vital part of corporate reporting. A company's ability to manage and mitigate exposure to ESG issues is an important factor for many mainstream investors, and if companies do not report then investors cannot make sound investment decisions.

A note of caution was raised in April 2010 when it was indicated by several leading businessmen that companies will have to make a judgment call when answering the question of how can a company can focus on both customer and shareholder? The chief executive of one major company came out against shareholder value as the main driver of a company's business model. The debate is over whether companies should be using short-term goals to fuel profits or should now be adopting strategies which are against the traditional City benchmark of "shareholder value". The CEO said that he was more concerned about customers than shareholders.

Can it be possible for a business to reconcile the needs of shareholders looking for a return and customers looking for good value? And has the recession given companies the opportunity to rethink their business models to reflect this dynamic? It was suggested that the pursuit of long-term shareowner value is totally consistent with focusing on the customer. Doing good is totally consistent with good business. Building greener buildings, for example, not only results in a greener planet but a more efficient, lower-cost business.

The key phrase should be "long term". Consumers and employees value brands, companies, products and services more highly if they embrace social issues. It should all be a question of long-term focus rather than short-termism.

In theory the pursuit of shareholder value and a focus on customers should be neatly aligned, but in reality it can be much more complex. The factors that drive share value are not just the performance and objectives of a business but they also driven by sentiment and emotional responses, analysts' assessments and financial gearing.

In times of crisis, businesses should focus on getting their model right, rather than expect to be guided by the investment community. Turbulence generates opportunities, and effective leaders should see how they can thrive on the shifting business landscape to reshape their sector to their advantage.

Customer focus should lead to enhanced shareholder value through higher profits. The more the business focuses on customers the better the business will understand its value drivers, which in turn should facilitate higher sales and higher margins. Unless they are looking for a very quick sale, investing time and resources in customer focus will add shareholder value.

It must not be forgotten that although the stakeholders of a company do include consumers and shareholders, there are also suppliers, employees, the financial community, government, and the media to take into account. Companies must properly manage the relationships between stakeholder groups and they must consider the interests of each stakeholder group carefully. Therefore, it becomes essential to integrate public relations into corporate governance to manage the relationships between these stakeholders which will enhance the organization's reputation. Corporations or institutions which behave ethically and are governed in a good manner build a "reputational capital" which, as was shown in Chapter 17, provides competitive advantage.

SECTION 5

Community

- Local, National and Global
- Philanthropy
- Volunteering
- Employability

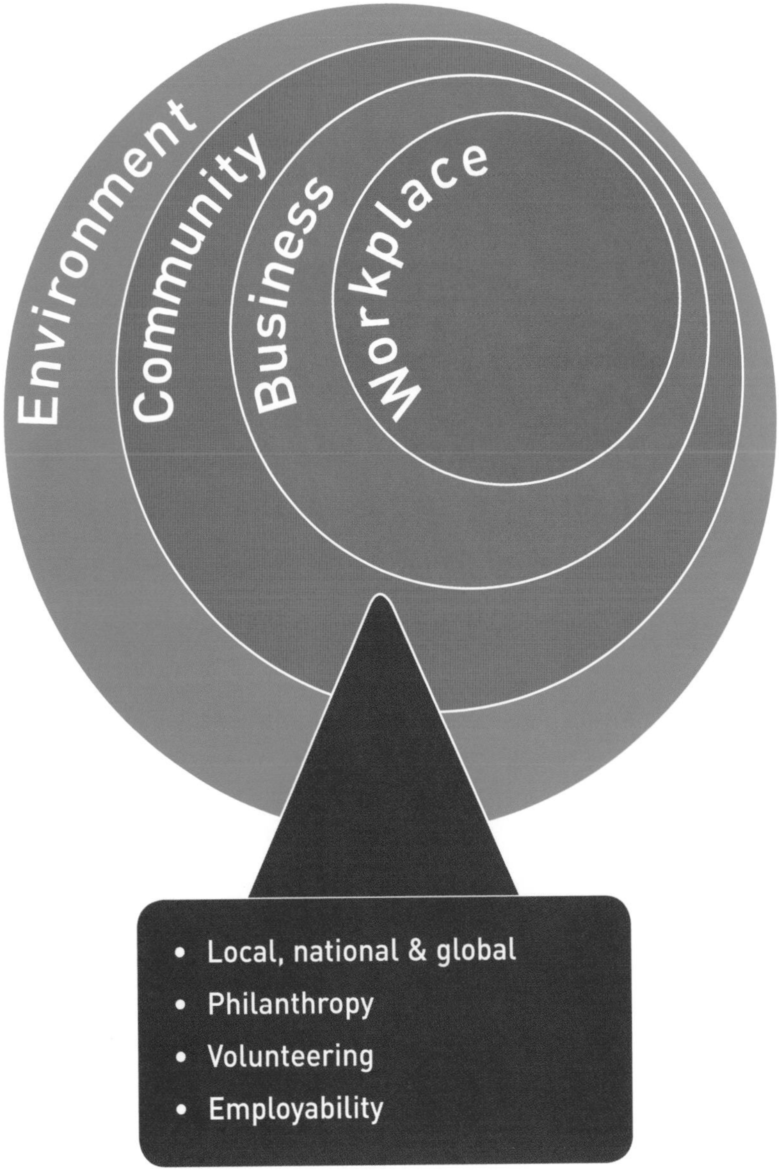
Environment
Community
Business
Workplace
• Local, national & global
• Philanthropy
• Volunteering
• Employability

Community

Responsive to public feeling

Employee volunteering

Sponsorship and charitable donations

Partnership with local groups

Open door policy

Neighbours

Sustainable community

Improving society

Benefit community projects

Local schools supported

Employment opportunities

CHAPTER 20

Local, National and Global

- Community Involvement and Awards
- Case study- Local
- Case study - National
- Case studies – Local, National and International

Community involvement and awards ●●●

Different businesses use the term "community involvement program" or Corporate Community Involvement (CCI) in different ways. Some use it to describe their whole orientation towards community issues, while some use it more specifically to cover their support and encouragement for their staff who volunteer for duties in community organisations. Others still use the term to refer to their efforts at community consultation on such issues as environmental impact or social policy. All these different programs can be solid bases for a community business partnership, and all of them can offer benefits for participating businesses.

It must also be clarified that in the case of a multi-national company operating on a global scale its "community" is wherever it operates and therefore it will need to see community involvement as local, national and international. It is highly likely that the most benefit will be gained by communities in the developing world rather than the company's own "backyard", but there should be room for both types of project.

Businesses benefit from formalising their social responsibility in the form of a fully articulated community involvement program or as Business in the Community (BITC) refer to it a "corporate community policy" that is integrated into their wider development strategy. These involvement programs can see a business or community group state a formal policy or program that details a commitment to helping or working in their local community. A community investment policy enables the business to identify its priorities and ways of operating in terms of how it invests in or contributes to the community.

A policy is a company's statement of intent regarding its performance on a specific aspect of responsible business. Policies enable a company to translate its values into commitments and responsibilities, and provide the basis on which a company can set objectives and targets. It enables the company to be more strategic and more consistent in the ways in which it operates.

Many companies make their policies freely available to the public, for example, in their corporate reports or on their website. A partnership based around a community involvement program is not only a very open and public way for a business or community group to state their intent to work with a partner in the community, but is also a way to gain input from a number of community groups.
Companies are increasingly recognising that they have a significant impact on the communities in which they work and that they have a responsibility to recognise their impact and make a positive contribution to local communities. When integrated into the business, taking community issues seriously can provide real benefits like:

- improved recruitment, retention, and motivation of staff
- increase in positive reputational benefits
- improved relationships with local communities
- increased potential for innovation as result of partnerships.

Establishing a strong community policy helps to provide a framework for a business to communicate how it will act responsibly within the community.

A business could also decide to work with a community group or groups to consult on issues it wishes to address in its own operations. Community involvement programs can provide opportunities for a business to gain feedback and to make a public show of its commitment to operating in a certain way or addressing a particular issue.

It is not enough to simply write a community policy. In order to get real value from working with the community and build this idea into the business, there must be management systems and processes in place throughout the business to ensure that the commitments outlined it the policy are valued and taken seriously.

Strategic community investment should set out how a company will maximise its positive impacts prioritising those that are most relevant to its core business products, services, employees and customers both in the short and long term. Community Impact refers to the immediate and longer term effect both, positive and negative, of a business's operation on a specific community which result directly from the corporate policies, core products and services and individual initiatives of the business.

There are a number of recognised components that comprise community investment, including working in partnership with charitable organisations, employee engagement, payroll giving, donating in-kind goods to charities, as well as using cause-related marketing to raise funds and awareness about charities and good causes.

Engaging employees in community programmes develops a wide range of skills and competences including communication, project management, leadership and team working. Engaging with consumers offers businesses the opportunity to demonstrate publicly their brand values, and use products, sales and marketing to support charities, key social issues and mobilise consumers behind good causes.

For a community group, this sort of partnership can help get its message across to business, or can further its endeavours to achieve social outcomes and benefits.

Community investment focuses on how companies manage their activities in the community and create a positive impact for both the community and the business. Methods of community involvement programs in a community business partnership include:

- formalised social responsibility policies or programs
- employee volunteering support programs
- consultation programs with a group or groups.

Business in the Community (BITC) campaigns for business action that builds healthy, wealthy, inclusive local economies and tackles pressing social issues[1]. They aim to maximise the value of investment, enterprise and employment opportunities for local communities to increase social equity and cohesion. They award the "CommunityMark" to companies who have demonstrated excellence across each of five principles in their approach to community investment. The five principles are that companies have:

- identified the social issues that are most relevant to their business and are most pressing to the communities that they work with
- worked in partnership with their communities leveraging their combined expertise for mutual benefit
- planned and managed their community investment using the most appropriate resources to deliver against their targets
- inspired and engaged their employees, customers and suppliers to support their community programmes
- measured and evaluated the difference that their investment had made in the community and on their business and they also strive for continual improvement.

1 BITC. (2010, March 21). CommunityMark. Retrieved March 21, 2010, from bitc.org.uk: http://www.bitc.org.uk/community/communitymark/index.html

Case Study[2]

Local

The John Lewis Partnership Newcastle branch through their expansion programme saw attracting and developing Partners as vital in helping them to achieve succession targets and organisational goals. The 'Fit for Our Future' programme aims to achieve these goals through an integrated approach to 'attracting and developing' their talent, producing Partners who are passionate about retailing and developing leaders of the future.

John Lewis Newcastle have dedicated resources and their programme to both attract new talent and develop the talent within their existing partners. Attending careers fairs, providing NVQ and BTEC placements and supporting their partners as mentors in local schools and colleges are just some of the ways they have managed to engage partners both future and present.

Impact

- Since 2006, 52 placements have secured permanent or temporary employment, eight graduates have been employed and thirty eight Partners have gained promotion.
- 30% of vacancies were classed as 'hard-to-fill' by North East Employers in 2008, John Lewis found recruiting specialised roles such as Chef vacancies particularly hard but through partnerships in 2008 they placed 2 Chefs, 1 Goods Handling and 1 Kitchen Porter.
- John Lewis Newcastle currently have 312 Non-Management Partners qualified to NVQ level 2 in a vocational qualification relating to their current role, which makes them well on target to achieve their aim of 400 by 2010.

2 BITC. (2009). John Lewis Newcastle, Attract and Develop Talent. Retrieved March 18, 2010, from bitc.org.uk: http://www.bitc.org.uk/resources/case_studies/afe2154.html

Case Study[3]

National

O_2 sets aside £5m for community projects

Mobile phone operator O_2 announced in March 2010 a £5 million project offering cash-in-hand grants to young people who plan to make a difference in their local communities. The three year programme, "Think Big", will allow 13-25 year olds to apply for a £300 grant to fund projects designed to address local problems as identified by young people. Successful projects will be eligible for an extra £2,500 funding.

The O_2 chief executive stated that young people are good citizens and are passionate about being part of the solution to community issues and not the cause of the problem. He also went on to say that O_2 were creating an opportunity for young people to reconnect with communities and societies, and use their passion and enthusiasm to benefit those communities.

O_2 plans to work with 1,000 young people across 500 projects each year. Around 5,000 O_2 staff members will also get involved as trained mentors and role models for young people.

The chief executive of the National Youth Agency, which is helping O_2 with the project, said: "Every day I meet incredibly inspiring young people who are prepared to stand up and work and do something, and who have overcome enormous challenges.

"We're incredibly proud to be part of this programme. A major international company is saying 'we believe in young people'."

3 O2. (2010, March 10). O2 drives social action with ground-breaking £5m investment in young people. Retrieved April 23, 2010, from mediacentre.o2.co.uk: http://mediacentre.o2.co.uk/Press-Releases/O2-drives-social-action-with-ground-breaking-5m-investment-in-young-people-279.aspx

Case Study[4]

International - with permission from Microsoft

Microsoft provides support to communities in three ways: technology skills training, strengthening non-governmental organisations through technology and engaging their employees in their communities. With their thousands of partners around the world they are committed to creating sustainable technology solutions that make a lasting difference in peoples' lives.

Microsoft state that technology fosters economic opportunity and creates jobs in all types of societies across the world. Microsoft partners with governments, businesses and citizens to nurture an environment where opportunity and growth can flourish.

The company sees Information Technology as a means of addressing societal challenges by advancing national priorities, sustainable economic growth and social advancement in key areas such as:

- improving healthcare through the use of health IT systems will help providers to adopt a "patient-centric" approach that allows them to control costs while also improving quality. Microsoft suggests that health IT will extend healthcare beyond the hospital or surgery into the home and to populations that have limited access to quality healthcare
- reforming education by investing in IT innovation to improve education quality, particularly in maths and sciences, is critical in making students more employable when they complete their education. By promoting lifelong skills training, governments and businesses can contribute to growth and enhance competitiveness of their overall economy
- IT holds tremendous promise to improve energy efficiency and reliability across a range of sectors and technologies. Supportive government policies include providing direct funding for basic research on renewable and sustainable low-carbon energy sources, promoting market-based incentives for private investment in low-carbon energy sources and technologies and enacting regulations that reduce barriers to technology adoption
- Microsoft suggest that IT is helping to make government activities more transparent, improving the public's ability to interact with their government and also allowing government agencies to better coordinate their efforts to serve their citizens.

4 Microsoft. (2010, March 21). Corporate citizenship our focus on strengthening economies. Retrieved March 21, 2010, from microsoft.com: http://www.microsoft.com/about/corporatecitizenship/en-us/our-focus/strengthening-economies/

Some examples of Microsoft's Investments in Education

Microsoft Unlimited Potential is where their business and corporate citizenship efforts meet. Unlimited Potential aims to bring the benefits of information and communications technology to underserved communities around the world. Their work focuses on transforming education, fostering local innovation, and enabling jobs and opportunities.

Microsoft Elevate America is part of our overall effort to provide up to 2 million people over the next three years with the technology training they need to succeed in the 21st century economy. Toward that goal, they are providing 1 million vouchers for Microsoft E-Learning courses and Microsoft Certification exams.

Microsoft Partners in Learning is a global initiative that aims to increase access to technology and improve its use in learning and has benefited more than 90 million students, teachers and education policymakers in 101 countries since 2003.

The Microsoft Community Technology Skills Program has partnered with governments and non-governmental organizations to train millions of people each year in the basics of digital literacy at more than 17,500 centres in over 100 countries and regions.

Case Study[5]

Local, National and International

In the 2009 financial year, BT gave £25 million - in time, cash and in-kind contributions - to activities which support society. More than 3,000 BT employees volunteered for schools, charities and other community organisations. The time, expertise and money that they give supports their CR strategy to work with their community partners to increase communication and ICT skills. It also motivates BT employees and enhances the company's reputation.

BT aims to continue investing at least 1% (in cash, time and in-kind support), of underlying pre-tax profits in community and environmental programmes. Their strategy is to enable more BT people to get involved in helping the communities where they operate. This will increase the proportion of their community investment given in time (compared to cash and in-kind).

BT's current projects include the BT "Better World Campaign" which gives disadvantaged young people in the UK and around the world the skills they need to succeed in life and to improve their world. The Campaign supports a key part of their CR strategy, to work with their community partners to increase communication and ICT skills.

BT's vision is of a world in which:

- young people most in need are always listened to, helped, and have their needs and opinions acted upon
- parents, teachers, government and those in business work together to achieve lasting improvements in the communication skills of young people
- young people use communication skills to collaborate and effect real social change on the issues that matter to them.

BT aim to realise this vision through three key objectives:

- to help young people with a communication need
- to help improve their communication and collaboration skills
- to help them use those new found skills to improve their communities.

Employee engagement is achieved by encouraging their people to get involved in volunteering schemes and other initiatives.

5 BT Sustainability Report. (2009). Society and environment:Our approach. Retrieved March 20, 2010, from btplc.com: http://www.btplc.com/Societyandenvironment/Ourapproach/Sustainabilityreport/section/index.aspx?name=our%20communities

BT promote community ICT and skills and thereby increase social inclusion through communications technology.

BT will respond to disasters and help by maintaining critical communications infrastructure and by supporting the Red Cross

BT are supporting the sustainability of the next Olympic Games to be held in London in 2012.

They also aid fundraising through their telecommunications systems which is helping charities to raise millions of pounds.

Preserving BT's communications heritage and making art more accessible through technology.

The quality of their community investment programme is independently evaluated. They achieved a score of 91% in 2009, against their target of 82% due to improved programme management, and better alignment with their CR goals.

BT's community partners

BT'S strategic charity partner in the UK is ChildLine, an organisation that provides support for children and young people, including a 24 hour helpline. They support ChildLine through strategic and technical support, fundraising, and by donating, money, equipment and expertise. BT employees also volunteer as ChildLine counsellors.

BT Global Services works with UNICEF to support education, technology and communications skills for disadvantaged children in South Africa, Brazil and China. In the 2009 financial year, the second year of the programme, BT supported a community project in Brazil which aimed to strengthen young people's life and communication skills through education and the use of ICT.

BT also works with the disability charity Scope, on two key projects which demonstrate how ICT can help disabled people to achieve a better quality of life. The Wheeltop project provides customised communication devices for students with profound communication needs. The No Voice, No Choice campaign aims to influence government to increase support for people with communications impairments.

BT partners with specialist charities to provide resources for young people with communication difficulties. For example, Openreach has worked with child communication needs charity I CAN to develop Ready Steady Talk, a teaching resource for pre-school children. In the 2010 financial year, BT Betterworld Campaign will develop its Communication Cookbook resource into a literacy programme for volunteers.

In partnership with the UK Youth Parliament, BT runs the Seen and Heard Awards which recognise young people around the globe who have changed their lives and communities for the better. This gives them the opportunity to ask questions and have their views heard among key influencers.

BT has supported the EverybodyOnline project since 2002. Run by the charity Citizens Online, this programme is designed to help disadvantaged communities and individuals across the UK use digital technology. Project officers in local communities work full-time to promote digital inclusion. They develop a network of local access points, learning programmes, partner organisations and volunteers.

In the 2009 financial year, two new projects were launched in Bristol and Caithness (Highlands), whilst BT's projects in Dorset and Cornwall came to an end.

The projects:

- enabled over 17,000 people to attend sessions to try out new technology in locations where they feel comfortable
- helped over 5,000 of these people to significantly improve their skills
- developed local networks, bringing in over 120 new volunteers
- helped over 40 people into employment, saving an estimated £ 360,000 in state benefits
- developed projects in art, music and multimedia to engage people in ICT using the things that matter to them.

In July 2008 BT was awarded the CommunityMark by Business in the Community. It is awarded after a rigorous assessment of a company's community investment programmes and consultation with its partners and employees. The CommunityMark lasts for three years.

Case Study[6]

Tesco's community involvement

In every country in which they operate Tesco work with local communities to provide jobs and services and support local causes. They are committed to being a good neighbour.

Their stores are at the heart of thousands of communities around the world Tesco always aim to make a positive contribution to these communities, both in the way that they do business and also by supporting local causes.

Tesco say that their success depends on listening and responding to customers and to changes in society. They respond to customers' expectations by offering "quality products at affordable prices". They also provide good jobs and careers for 470,000 people, growing the local economies where they live. Small, regional producers supply a growing number of locally sourced products.

They invest in many disadvantaged communities, opening stores which help to regenerate areas, and offering opportunities to the people who live there. In the UK alone, they have now created over 4,000 jobs for long-term unemployed people through their jobs guarantee programme.

They fund education programmes around the world, helping children learn about health and the environment, and donate equipment to schools.

More than 260 Tesco Community Champions in six countries are working in their stores specifically to support local charities and organisations. The 266 Community Champions in China, the Czech Republic, Malaysia, Slovakia, South Korea and the UK dedicate their time to supporting local initiatives, organisations and charities as well as national initiatives.

Tesco considers itself to be a "good neighbour" and the biggest way that it contributes to any community is through its new stores. In 2008 in the UK they opened 187 new stores, providing almost 12,000 new jobs. Building new stores also creates jobs for the construction industry.

By opening stores Tesco is regenerating communities by revitalising disadvantaged areas through working in partnership with local agencies. Since 2000, when they opened their first Regeneration Partnership store in Seacroft, Leeds, they have created jobs for the long-term unemployed in 20 stores. In 2008 they opened Regeneration Partnership stores in Aston (Birmingham), Gorton and Cheetham Hill (Manchester), providing almost 900 jobs, nearly 500 of which were for long-term unemployed people.

6 Tesco Corporate Responsibility Report. (2009). Community involvement. Retrieved March 20, 2010, from tescoplc.com: http://www.tescoplc.com/plc/corporate_responsibility_09/community/

Tesco are also making a difference by giving at least 1% of pre-tax profits to charity and in 2008 they gave £57 million or 1.9%. As part of this commitment they have set up a number of ways to help and support charities in the UK and overseas whether through substantial campaigns or through one-off grants.

Tesco aim to choose a charity which is close to the hearts of their staff and customers, works locally in the communities they serve and is focused on delivering practical benefits. The Charity of the Year becomes the main focus for staff fundraising and this receives a 20% top-up from the Tesco Charity Trust.

They give schools the chance to get free equipment and they run the UK's longest running schools voucher programme which over the last 17 years has donated approximately three million items of equipment worth around £150 million to over 35,000 schools and clubs in the UK.

Other targets for Tesco are to:

- Raise £5 million across all our markets through staff and customer fund-raising
- Grow Culture Centre members in South Korea to 962,400
- Organise at least 750 community activities in stores or offices in China
- Hold 150 community events in Poland
- Extend educational project on global warming to 7,000 students in Turkey
- Plant 950,000 more trees in Thailand.

These case studies provide an insight into the community involvement policies of several large businesses and in all cases monitoring, measuring and full reporting takes place. There are many more innovative and inspirational examples that could have been included in this chapter as community involvement is now seen as an essential part of responsible and sustainable business practice.

CHAPTER 21

Philanthropy

- Integrating Philanthropy
- Which Charity or Good Cause
- Venture Philanthropy
- Philanthrocapitalism

Integrating philanthropy with business is now seen as an essential aspect of running a responsible and sustainable business. Social, environmental and economic responsibility practices are constantly changing, and even small to mid-sized businesses realise that they need to adapt to what is increasingly becoming a new management standard in all sizes of business.

The marketplace dynamics have changed with respect to discussions about "doing good in society," more commonly referred to as corporate social responsibility. What used to be a simple matter of donating money has now become a critical component of reputation management and cultivating a competitive business edge. Businesses now have to better integrate their philanthropic contributions into their business functions, and make it a core part of their strategic marketing and communications planning.

Small to mid-size companies may in fact have an advantage over larger businesses engaging in this, as they are able to adapt to these challenges more quickly.

Businesses seeking to introduce or expand their involvement in philanthropic endeavours should start by asking several key questions:

- when looking at the cause selected, how will the business properly contribute to the community to advance public interest?
- what impact will this activity have on their reputation, their brand, their stakeholders and also on their performance?
- how will the business demonstrate the effectiveness of what they are doing over the long-term? They should not focus only on the short-term bottom line because, as already established earlier in this book, sustainable development is a long-term process.
- how can the business be more accountable? Stakeholders will want to know what progress the business is making so there needs to be transparency in all its actions.

Corporate philanthropy efforts must adopt an integrated approach up front. Not only should an organization's philanthropy reflect the consensus of all its stakeholders, it should be part of a company's vision and culture. It is advisable to make the business's philanthropy part of its human resources process. Asking employees to donate some of their time to the effort, will empower staff across all departments and divisions.

There are effectively three ways that a business could contribute to a charity or good cause and they are cash donations, gifts in kind and employee involvement. As referred to in Chapter 19 the Harvard study 'doing well by doing good' found the strongest correlation between cash donations and subsequent success but views on this are changing as more and more it is being realised that employee participation in good causes brings a host of other benefits. The benefits of employee volunteering are fully explored in the next chapter.

A company is able to claim Corporation Tax relief on gifts to charity. If gifts of money are made to a charity by a company it should be paid gross - before tax is deducted. These donations are deductible from the total profits of the business when calculating Corporation Tax. The charity doesn't need to make a Gift Aid tax repayment claim because no tax has been paid. The charity can claim exemption from tax on company donations.

The company can claim relief as long as the donation is a payment of money that is not a distribution of profit such as a dividend. Companies can also claim Corporation Tax relief on other gifts to charity such as gifts to charity of land, buildings or shares by companies and gifts to charity of company equipment.

The following do not count as qualifying donations:

- gifts that come with a condition about repayment
- gifts where your company or a person 'connected' to your company has received a benefit over a certain value in return
- gifts that come with a condition or arrangement that the charity will purchase property (other than as a gift) from your company or a connected person.

Which Charity or Good Cause●●●

It is advisable for any business to carry out research to ensure that any cause taken up will mean the most to that business and its stakeholders. It would be a mistake if the business skipped corners with its research. Customers and stakeholders will want to be asked which causes they would want to be associated with. A business's philanthropy should not steer too far away from its core products or services and corporate social responsibility can be integral to product development.

Businesses looking to make decisions about which charities or causes to get involved with may well seek help from the Centre of Charitable Giving and Philanthropy. This is the UK's first independent, multidisciplinary and academically-based centre which was created by the Office of the Third Sector in partnership with Carnegie UK Trust, the Economic and Social Research Council and the Scottish Executive. The aim of the centre is to support high-quality research to develop the necessary evidence base to improve understanding of charitable giving and philanthropy. It will address vital questions such as:

- what impact do economic conditions have on donations to charity?
- what motivates people, including the super-rich, to give to charity?
- how can good causes use these donations most effectively?

The Centre will have three 'spokes', which will lead on particular programmes of research:

- individual and business giving
- charitable giving and social distribution
- institutionalised giving structures.

The Centre will support research to improve understanding of how and why people give to charity. This will provide an evidence base to help third sector organisations, the government and businesses to encourage charitable giving.[1]

Ideally the business will want to make an impact that speaks to their specific community. For smaller businesses, there are many opportunities to get engaged with not-so-well known non-profit making organisations that represent a diverse range of causes. It might be an idea for the business to select a smaller group working on the issue that it wishes to impact that may well have existed for some time but has been overlooked. It may be better to avoid the same few non-profit organisations that all the big corporations already support.

The most recent figures obtainable show that by early 2010 there were 161,916 'main' (i.e. not a subsidiary of another organisation) charities listed on the Charity Commission register. The total annual income of these main registered charities stood at £52.65 billion.

In 2010 over 45% of registered charities are very small with an annual income of £10,000 or less and nearly 77% have incomes under £100,000, and this number receive less than 2% of the annual charitable income. Around 8% of charities in England and Wales receive 90% of the total annual income reported to the Commission. In 2007 the largest 651 charities (0.39% of those on the register at that time) attracted over 49% of the total income. There are many opportunities therefore for a business to get involved with a smaller charity as can be seen by these figures[2].

A study by Policy Exchange carried out in late 2008 established that City philanthropists were then focusing on the advantages of a "charity begins near home" approach. The study suggested that at that time bank chiefs, private equity bosses and asset managers had become increasingly conscious of the benefits of giving within their local communities rather than to large national or overseas charities as a way of making their money go further. It noted that, if a business has less to give as a donation or contribution then giving to a smaller, more local cause will have a bigger impact. Which can be very important from the point of view of business-minded philanthropists who have a results-based interest in philanthropy.

1 CGAP. (2008, October 1). CGAP Launch. Retrieved April 23, 2010, from cgap.org.uk: http://www.cgap.org.uk/news/3/61/CGAP-Launch.html

2 Charity Commission. (2010, April 9). About Charities - Facts and Figures. Retrieved April 9, 2010, from charitycommission: 'http://www.charitycommission.gov.uk/About_us/About_charities/factfigures.aspx

The report argued that City high-flyers are seeing clear benefits to a model of giving that allows financiers to monitor their donations closely and see the effects for themselves. Businesses may only have smaller sums to donate so they target them to people and organisations doing good in their local community as they may well feel the benefits themselves as part of that community. This could be described as a kind of "enlightened self-interest"[3].

A business may make the mistake of not properly marketing their philanthropy to key stakeholders as it is one thing to announce publicly what they are going to do, but they also have to make sure that their programmes are properly communicated to their employees, suppliers, shareholders and distributors.

Corporate social responsibility reports and regular updates are the vehicle for sharing the impact of the business's philanthropy hopefully by showing how it relates to the brand, product and company values, how it has increased employee productivity and how it has become a source of innovation and growth for both the cause they are funding and the company itself. A lot of businesses fail to collaborate effectively with the cause/project they fund or work with.

One way to avoid this would be to form a "charity partnership", as recommended by Business in the Community (BITC)[4], which should focus on the joint objectives of both the charity and the business. When managed well, this can bring together many of the components of a community investment programme and can also introduce new ways of working.

As with any business decision, a charity partnership needs to have realistic ambitions and a well-defined structure; many charities will want to have an equal share in terms of managing the relationship.

Just as charities will not always want to be seen as 'worthy' beneficiaries, companies should see that partnerships with charities can bring benefits beyond the positive impact on the local community, such as skills development training for their employees and an enhanced reputation.

Venture Philanthropy ●●●

The link between charities and business has created benefits and new links with private equity and there is now an emerging model, known as venture philanthropy (VP) which aims to boost the productivity of the third sector, using venture capital techniques of due diligence, ongoing engagement and rigorous performance measurement.

3 Policy Exchange. (2008, November). Community can play a crucial role in enabling UK philanthropy to weather the storm. Retrieved April 23, 2010, from policyexchange.org.uk: http://www.policyexchange.org.uk/assets/Building_Bridges.pdf

4 BITC. (2010, April 9). Charity Partnerships. Retrieved April 9, 2010, from bitc.org.uk: http://www.bitc.org.uk/community/community_investment/strategy/charity_partnerships.html

Yet whilst VP remains limited in size, its influence continues to grow as larger, 'traditional' grant-makers adopt some of its key principles. According to the European Venture Philanthropy Association, the key characteristics of European venture philanthropy are:

- high engagement
- tailored financing
- multi-year support
- non-financial support
- organisational capacity-building
- performance measurement.

Venture philanthropy is a way of supporting organisations through the provision of management and technical support in addition to financial resources. VP takes the principles of venture capitalism and applies them to philanthropy. Just as venture capitalists take an active approach to funding businesses (investing management time as well as money) so venture philanthropists invest time and skills (perhaps taking a position on the board of trustees) alongside cash to support voluntary and community organisations.

Venture Philanthropy's financial input is sometimes described as "Patient Capital". This is because the Venture Philanthropist is willing to fund organisational as well as project costs for longer time periods than traditional trusts and foundations in order to see the organisation as a whole develop. Venture Philanthropy can also be compared to the well established principle of "engaged funding" where the involvement of the grant making trusts and foundations goes beyond hard cash[5].

At the end of 2009 economists were being urged by one of Britain's top civil servants to offer free help to charities, in an initiative that would allow practitioners of the "dismal science" to atone for any errors they made during the financial crash.

Although some charities might wonder whether economists have done enough damage already the argument is that the voluntary sector can gain from having access to their analytical skills and it was also suggested that economists will gain from working with charities through gaining more experience of the real world and being able to apply their skills to problems on the ground.

"Pro Bono Economics" was launched at the Treasury in September 2009 to encourage members of the 1,100-strong government economics service to take part.

Lawyers and accountants are already used to giving pro bono help to the voluntary sector but until this initiative economists were probably not so aware that their skills might be useful. A pilot project was running at that time in which a Bank of England economist was advising Barnardo's on the benefits of a programme to prevent the sexual exploitation of girls. The Treasury argued that civil servants would benefit from

5 NCVO. (2010, April 9). Venture Philanthropy. Retrieved April 9, 2010, from ncvo-vol.org.uk: http://www.ncvo-vol.org.uk/advice-support/funding-finance/income-sources/venture-philanthropy

getting out of Whitehall as not only does it allow charities to bolster their economic expertise but it also offers fantastic experience to economists in real-life scenarios.

To reflect the desire for businesses to work more closely with charities, a report published in 2009 urged more link-ups between businesses and charities and suggested a new pact between the government, business and charities to help local communities through the recession. Charities, voluntary groups, and social enterprises – the third sector – were urged to take the lead in working out a programme to channel requests for help to business rather than bombarding them with pleas for aid.

The report was produced by a task force commissioned by the Cabinet Office and headed by the vice-president of Business in the Community[6] to identify innovative schemes to support local communities "at particular risk of fracture" during the recession. It was set up following the UK government's decision to allocate £42.5m to charities and other third sector organisations to help them cope with the pressure placed on them by recession. Money was made available for a wide variety of projects, including help for 40,000 unemployed people to undertake charitable volunteer work.

The report placed heavy emphasis on the need for closer links between the business community and charities at a local level and suggested that the government should try to improve existing models of cross-sector collaboration. Business complaints that charities have historically looked at companies as a "big chequebook" during recessions are echoed in the report but the task force points out that third sector organisations now recognise them as "a partner with more to offer than money".

Philanthrocapitalism

This new kind of philanthropy is about harnessing giving and the ingenuity of the business world, often in partnership with government, to solve society's thorniest problems. Although the best known philanthrocapitalists are Americans, philanthrocapitalism is also catching on in Britain. The recent economic crisis provides an opportunity to take it to the next level.

That is why in early 2010, after consultation with some of Britain's most innovative philanthropists and social entrepreneurs the "Philanthrocapitalist Manifesto" was launched which challenged all the party leaders to adopt this programme. The manifesto has three main themes.

- First, government, business and charity need to join together in a high-profile national campaign to increase giving and volunteering.
- Second, government needs to work with the City to turn Britain into the world leader in social investing – the idea that business can make a profit and do good at the same time.

6 BITC. (2009, July). Building Stronger Communities, Business and the third sector: Innovation in tough times. Retrieved April 23, 2010, from bitc.org.uk: http://www.bitc.org.uk/resources/publications/building_stronger_co.html

- Third, each pound given needs to work harder. While there are pockets of excellence in the charity sector, too much is fragmented and inefficient.

The biggest opportunity, however, lies in creating better partnerships between philanthropy and government. Barack Obama's new White House Office of Social Innovation could be a model for other governments.

In early 2010 there were further calls for the UK to follow Obama's lead with the government committing to an equivalent of the US's $50m social innovation fund. It was argued that if the government were to establish its own £50 - £100 million fund it would boost venture philanthropists' work combating social problems. These comments were in response to the launch of the Philanthrocapitalist Manifesto which it was felt was 'a bold start at generating ideas for encouraging an environment of more giving, more social investment and better philanthropy'.

It was also suggested that the fund, if created, should be channelled through philanthropic organisations which will match the funding and pass it on to 'high impact, result oriented non-profit making organisations' which have a good track record in tackling social problems. With a constraint on public spending the suggestion was that it is going to be all about delivering more for less. There is a need to experiment with new models that combine the best of public sector, third sector and private sector.

The first female director of Oxfam is on a mission to persuade business to assist in the charity's goal of improving the lives of the poor and she asserts that easing poverty can be good for business. She believes that the private sector's ultimate object of making money is aligned with improving the lives of people in poverty, and she says that there is a "major opportunity" for wealth creation. Poor people are in trade and not in employment in big services so they are selling their own produce. Once business understands that they should start seeing how the private sector can engage with poor people. She also feels that for too long, non-governmental organisations (NGOs) did not talk to business but now, the charity is making an effort to speak the language of business and she has learnt the meaning of "patient capital". She also feels that there has been a big change in corporate social responsibility and now businesses are addressing how to carry out their core business in emerging markets. The director is an ardent campaigner and has been involved in promoting the Robin Hood tax levy on financial transactions.

Despite the challenges she is convinced that business will shape the future of developing countries as the consumer industries of the West are pretty saturated and will therefore be looking to developing countries. It is in a company's interest to be seen as treating people right she argues and also that the ultimate goal is to grow countries' trade to replace aid but it will not happen for a long time. "The rules on trade, "she suggests," are just not fair to the poorest countries"[7].

7 Oxfam. (2010, January 11). Oxfam announces fund to fight poverty on its doorstep. Retrieved April 23, 2010, from oxfam.org.uk: http://www.oxfam.org.uk/applications/blogs/pressoffice/?p=9831

Another campaign launched in 2010 saw the Welsh secretary become the first cabinet minister to back the campaign which would raise money through a levy on financial transactions and he applauded the "Robin Hood tax" as being an 'innovative financing arrangement'. This tax would see money raised from a levy on financial transactions used to fund international aid, combat climate change and boost public services.

The campaign calls on G20 leaders to place a 0.05% tax across the full range of banks' financial transactions. Campaigners believe it could generate £255bn a year. The former UK Prime Minister Gordon Brown has spoken out in the past about the need for a similar kind of transaction tax – the Tobin Tax, a tax on currency transactions named after the American economist who devised it in 1972 but was later thought to be moving into line with US President Barack Obama, who is proposing a tax on individual banks.

The cabinet secretary suggested that issues such as global warming, global poverty and the prospect of cuts to public services cannot on their own be solved by public spending so part of the alternative is the application of innovative financing arrangements such as a financial transactions tax and this is what the Robin Hood Tax represents. Given the simplicity of the proposed solution, added to the popular feeling that speculation in the finance sector caused the crisis, it is perhaps not surprising how wide-ranging the Robin Hood Tax campaign is.

The TUC, Oxfam, Greenpeace, the Salvation Army and the RSPB all suggested that this is a policy with huge and broad popular support. Global poverty, climate change and public services need urgent attention. So Robin Hood might be about to do one final service to global social justice.

An analysis of the value of charitable trusts in August 2009 showed a fall of 10 per cent due to the recession. The survey, the "Charity Market Monitor 2009", carried out by the Centre for Charitable Giving and Philanthropy found that the impact of the recession on charity fundraising showed 41% of the top 300 charitable trusts saw a fall in the value of their grant-making in 2008 and, overall, their net asset value fell by 10 per cent. This was to have a negative effect on grant-making during 2009[8].

However by April 2010 the news was much more positive as philanthropic activity was on the rise according to figures from the Charities Aid Foundation (CAF) which showed a 250% rise in the value of donations to Charitable Trust Accounts compared to 2009.

In the first quarter of 2010 CAF, one of the UK's biggest providers of charitable trusts, opened 51 new Charitable Trust Accounts with a total of £70m in donations. In the same period in 2009 donors put £20m into new CAF Trust Accounts. The charity is now opening as many accounts each month as it was in early 2008 before the recession began.

In March 2010 payments to charities from CAF Charitable Trust Accounts totalled more than £18m, over three times the amount distributed in March 2009.

A spokesperson for CAF indicated that during the recession committed donors did not stop giving but many had fewer funds to put into trusts. They had been waiting until their personal finances had improved, or were now more certain, and it looks as if like those people are now making the major commitments to philanthropy that they have been planning for some time[9].

As already stated, donations made by business can also be surplus goods that otherwise might end up in landfill, on market stalls or simply piled up in the storage area of the business, but donating gifts in kind, whether it is old furniture, laptops, pallets of washing up liquid or mobile phones, is a great and easy way to support a charity or community group.

Channelling surplus products, furniture and even portacabins to a school, community centre or charity ensures that your company can avoid the environmentally unfriendly alternative of disposing of them as waste. It is a great way to either support an existing charity partnership or to begin developing one[10].

8 CGAP. (2010, January). Charity Market Monitor 2009. Retrieved April 3, 2010, from cgap.org.uk: http://www.cgap.org.uk/news/24/76/Charity-Market-Monitor-2009.html

9 CAF. (2010, April 19). Site search. Retrieved April 23, 2010, from cafonline.org: http://www.cafonline.org/default.aspx?page=29&terms=first%20quarter%20hike%20in%20donations%20to%20charitable%20trusts&Button1=&

10 BITC. (2010, April 9). Gifts in Kind. Retrieved April 9, 2010, from bitc.org.uk: http://www.bitc.org.uk/community/community_investment/strategy/gifts_in_kind.html

Case Study[11]

Sainsbury's Donates 5,000 PCs and Monitors to IT Charity for Use in Developing Countries.

Supermarket giant Sainsbury's has provided 4,390 PCs and 4,572 monitors to IT charity Computer Aid International, boosting access to IT in developing countries. The equipment, donated between July and October 2009, is being professionally refurbished at Computer Aid's London headquarters for use in agriculture, healthcare and education projects across Africa and South America. 256 PCs and monitors have already been sent to the APPBG, an Association of Small Banana Producers in Ecuador, to improve the day to day running of the fair trade banana enterprise and its trade unions.

Sainsbury's is using Computer Aid's PC decommissioning service, which guarantees complete data destruction and compliance with all UK legislation, including the WEEE directive, Data Protection Act and Environment Act. All viable PCs and laptops are professionally refurbished to extend their life by another three to four years, with any unusable equipment fully recycled in an environmentally friendly way.

Computer Aid's asset tracking service is also enabling Sainsbury's to identify the exact projects that are benefiting from its out-of-use PCs and monitors. Many will be distributed through the charity's not-for-profit partner organisations, such as the British Council, Eritrea, which equips public libraries with PCs, and the African Medical and Research Foundation, Kenya, which provides PCs to rural hospitals to enable remote diagnosis by specialist doctors in city locations.

Sainsbury's substantial donation will make a significant contribution in enabling disadvantaged communities to actively participate in the global digital economy. Every PC refurbished by Computer Aid will go on to provide at least 6,000 hours of computer access, which is enough time to train 60 children to a vocational level of IT literacy.

11 Computer Aid International. (2009, November 16). Sainsbury's unwanted PCs are sent to help Fair Trade banana producers in Ecuador . Retrieved April 23, 2010, from computeraid.org: http://www.computeraid.org/news-detail.asp?ID=24

In Kind Direct re-distributes new goods donated by some of Britain's best-known manufacturers and retailers to thousands of voluntary organisations working at home and abroad. Founded in 1996, In Kind Direct has since gone on to assist 7000 charities, working with more than 800 donor businesses and funders. In Kind Direct is proud to be one of The Prince's Charities.

More charities benefited from the service provided by In Kind Direct during 2009 than ever before as In Kind Direct's network of charities increased by 35% to over 4,000. In Kind Direct significantly increases the flow of goods to UK charities, through effective, efficient redistribution of surplus goods sourced from manufacturers and retailers. By providing a service to a network of partners, In Kind Direct enables charities, voluntary groups and social enterprises to help people in need both at home and abroad, whilst inspiring growth in corporate giving, promoting responsible business practices and diverting usable goods from landfill.

Their redistribution model demonstrates the highly practical way in which product donations can free up scarce cash resources to allow charities to do significantly more for the people they help. In Kind Direct increased the value of goods distributed to £16.1 million an increase of £5 million on 2008[12].

Many businesses enable their employees to donate to charity through a payroll giving scheme and that may well be the same charity that the business is itself aligned with as part of its CSR strategy. Payroll giving allows tax relief at source for individuals who give to charity by deducting donations directly from their pay or occupational pension. The scheme was revised in April 2000 when minimum donations were abolished. In some schemes, employers agree to match their employees' donations.

There are also many examples of businesses allowing or encouraging their employees to collect for charities during working hours, often as a major event. For example, all staff in a supermarket wearing costumes for a charity such as "Children in Need". The charity obviously benefits but so does the business through enhanced reputation, customer satisfaction and employee engagement.

The other growing area of business contribution to good causes is the rising number of employee volunteering schemes which will be looked at in Chapter 22. However, when a company quotes a specific amount of contributions made it will often include the cost of the volunteering scheme either through some estimate of time taken or in some cases the business has a paid volunteering scheme.

12 InKind Direct. (2010, February 25). InKind charity network increases in 2009 by 35%. Retrieved April 3, 2010, from inkinddirect.org: http://www.inkinddirect.org/news/charity_network_increases_in_2009.asp

Case Study

Cost-benefit analysis of a volunteer

Scenario: A manager on £30,000 per year with limited knowledge or experience of project management was paid for two weeks to manage a project in the local community with three unemployed volunteers. The two weeks provided the manager with invaluable insight into project management skills and left him/her feeling fully confident that they could tackle similar projects within the business itself without further training. The manager was also able to oversee three potential employees who were also developing skills needed not only for the community project but also for the business. At the end of the period the manager was very confident that two of the three would make excellent employees of the business and would, as a result of their recent experience, need a far shorter induction period on joining the business.

Cost to business: 2 weeks pay plus employer's contributions approximately £750.

Benefits: A manager "trained" in project management skills-average cost of training course £1,000 which provides knowledge but not experience. Two new employees without recruitment costs which the CIPD estimated to be £6,125 per employee in 2009[13]. The business may also have avoided the need to recruit another manager with project management experience where the recruitment cost rises to £9,000.There is also the saving on induction training.

So the business spends £750 but in doing so saves at least £13,250 if not more. Obviously this is fictional example but the benefits are clear to see.

13 CIPD. (2010, April 9). Employment, Turnover and Retention. Retrieved April 9, 2010, from cipd.co.uk: http://www.cipd.co.uk/subjects/hrpract/turnover/empturnretent.htm

At the end of 2006 total expenditure on corporate responsibility from all the FTSE 100 companies was £985.76m, up 3.9% on 2005 and showing a huge rise in money terms since 2002 of 59%. The growth in interest in corporate responsibility had come from consumer pressure and campaigns, coupled with a push from institutional investors such as pension funds, concerned about the ethics - and therefore the reputations - of companies in which they hold shares.

By 2009 the commitment to charitable giving alone had risen to a record £1.4 billion a year. However, in relative terms, corporate giving remains very low despite a decade of persuasion to give more. According to the ESRC Research Centre for Charitable Giving and Philanthropy at Cass Business School, it accounts for only 1%-3% of all charity-sector income. In 2009 ESRC pointed out that while corporate charitable giving accounts for a minuscule amount of the overall charity-sector income it is vital to particular charities that depend on business support.

In 2006 the top 15 companies in a Guardian survey devoted 1% or more of pre-tax profits to social, environmental, and community issues, 22 gave between a 0.5%-1%, and 19 of the FTSE 100 companies allocated less than 0.01% of their pre-tax profits. In 2009 ESRC ranked the supermarket chain Tesco fifth in their top 300 corporate-givers' listing as the table's fastest-moving big corporate donor. Tesco has promised to maintain its CSR budget at 1% or more of pre-tax profits. In 2009 the £57 million quoted by Tesco equated to 1.95% of their pre-tax profits.

However laudable the examples of corporate giving provided in this chapter are, the relatively low percentage donated by business becomes even more insignificant when announcements are made such as the one in April 2010 which stated that city bankers were paying themselves £6.8 billion in bonuses. This is an average of £70,000 per person and is nearly 5 times the total amount given by all businesses to charity in 2009. It would appear to be completely insensitive in the current climate and perhaps makes a mockery of any claims these businesses are making regarding CSR. It would also appear to provide another strong argument for the Robin Hood tax levy.

The issue of taxation also leads to another area of potential controversy as there are a significant number of large businesses who in recent years have moved their centre of operation to another location in order to gain savings in their tax liability. Nowadays it is rare for big business to see the payment of taxes as an explicit social duty and this is despite the fact that these public companies are also claiming to practise corporate social responsibility and will be highlighting their charitable and green activities in their annual reports.

Would Tesco even have to give vouchers to customers so that their local schools can have new equipment, or would businesses have to get involved with local community projects due to lack of public funding if every £1 of profit made in the UK was taxed in the UK?

There is now a feeling that things may be beginning to change. Research also shows that nearly 60% of financial directors in the UK do now regard tax as an ethical issue and there are a significant minority of companies who agree that paying tax is a key part of corporate responsibility, if not the core corporate responsibility to society. Tax is probably where CSR should begin.

CHAPTER 22

Volunteering

- What is Employer-Supported Volunteering?
- Benefits for Employees
- Benefits for the Business
- Benefits for Third Sector Organisations

What is Employer-Supported Volunteering? ●●●

This is a policy adopted by employers who believe that by allowing their employees to spend some of their time in working for voluntary sector organisations or community projects both the business and the individual will benefit. The time spent may be during normal working hours or even in the employee's own time but, in either case, the volunteering is recognised and supported by the employer and it may well have been suggested, or encouraged, by the employer in the first instance. Often the volunteering process is monitored through a formal programme or scheme.

In 2007, 36% of employees had an employer supported volunteering scheme available to them. This has jumped since 2005, when 24% of employees in England and Wales worked for employers with schemes. It is reported that approximately 70% of FTSE 100 companies have some kind of employer supported volunteering programme. This is in marked contrast to SMES, with 20% of employees of medium sized businesses and 14% of employees of small businesses having an employer supported volunteering scheme[1].

One reason for the much smaller figures for SMES is due to the private sector's unrealistic expectations of staff volunteering schemes. In May 2009 research revealed that some businesses expected voluntary organisations to pay them to send volunteers to projects. As a result 85% of businesses that make enquiries about employee volunteering schemes back off when they realise they have to pay for them. These businesses need to realise that the management of volunteering programmes is time-intensive and does cost the voluntary sector[2].

Obviously the amount of time an employee spends on any volunteering scheme will vary from business to business and project to project.

Employer-supported volunteering programmes will help to develop and maintain relationships which will be beneficial to employers, voluntary organisations and local communities. They give employers the opportunity to help tackle local issues in areas such as:

- education
- employment
- support for disadvantaged people
- regeneration
- community cohesion.

1 Volunteering England. (2010, February 20). What is employer supported volunteering? Retrieved February 20, 2010, from volunteering.org.uk: http://www.volunteering.org.uk/WhatWeDo/Projects+and+initiatives/Employer+Supported+Volunteering/About+Employer+Supported+Volunteering

2 Red Foundation. (2009, May). Red launches new ESV survey. Retrieved April 24, 2010, from redfoundation.org: http://www.redfoundation.org/news/36

The voluntary sector where businesses and their employees can be involved is also referred to as the "Third Sector". The UK government defines the third sector as non-governmental organisations that are value driven and which principally reinvest their surpluses to further social, environmental or cultural objectives. It includes voluntary and community organisations, charities, social enterprises, cooperatives and mutuals. They also include housing associations within the third sector.

Getting involved

Businesses are becoming more active and involved in helping their employees to take part in volunteering. Many businesses have already set up programmes to support their employees' volunteering activities, as they recognise the importance of investing in their community. As already seen in previous chapters employees do want their employer to be socially and environmentally responsible and to have the opportunity to have an active role themselves will only add to their engagement and sense of pride. In many cases the volunteering schemes will require new partnerships to be formed and the adoption of creative and innovative approaches that engage the private, public and voluntary sectors.

By supporting their employees' volunteering efforts an employer can make a worthwhile contribution towards their social responsibilities and it can also be included in their annual reporting as part of the corporate social responsibility process.

An employer-supported volunteering scheme can complement and enhance other investment programmes, which might include:

- charitable and community donations
- a payroll giving scheme for employees
- a 'charity of the year' partnership
- office equipment recycling
- other ways of giving employees' time, such as secondments.

The benefits of employer-supported volunteering

Employee volunteering has many potential benefits for everyone involved with it. By setting up an employer-supported volunteering programme the business can benefit:

- their staff - employees feel valued and usually enjoy volunteering when it reflects their interests and skills. This can make a real difference to how employees feel about themselves and their employer
- their business - a motivated workforce is often more productive when meeting business priorities. A programme that is in line with these priorities can bring tangible benefits to the company and will enjoy continuing support
- the volunteer organisations they work with, who get to benefit from the business's human resources in addressing community needs. Employers can play an important part in helping to solve community problems.

Benefits for employees ●●●

Encouraging employees' voluntary activities helps a business to demonstrate that it values its staff. Employees may already be involved with some form of volunteering based on their own time and initiative. By setting up an employee volunteering scheme the business is showing that it recognises the importance of their volunteering work. If the business allows its employees to do some of their volunteering during normal working hours then it can help them find time for things like family activities and therefore have no detrimental effect on their work-life balance.

There are other ways in which an employer-supported volunteering scheme can benefit your staff.

Providing individuals with opportunities to develop their professional and personal skills

Nowadays people want to make a difference and training through employee volunteering is a win-win option for employers, workers and communities. In addition to engaging employers and building corporate reputation, employee volunteering can build skills across a wide spectrum such as communication, project management, leadership and team working. The Deloitte Volunteer Impact Survey 2008[3] of Human Resources Executives in the US found that 91% of survey respondents agree that

3 Deloitte. (2008). Volunteer Impact Study 2008. Retrieved February 9, 2010, from deloitte.com: http://www.deloitte.com/dtt/cda/doc/content/us_comm_VolunteerIMPACT080425.pdf

skills-based volunteering would add value to training and development programmes, particularly as it relates to fostering business and leadership skills.

According to the 2010 Deloitte Volunteer IMPACT Survey[4], more than eight in 10 companies (84 per cent) believe that volunteerism can help nonprofits accomplish long-term social goals, and are increasingly offering skills-based volunteer opportunities to employees. In fact, corporate managers report that the top priorities when determining workplace volunteer activities include the potential to alleviate a social issue (36 per cent), help the nonprofit function more effectively (31 per cent) and serve more clients (31 per cent). Conversely, while volunteerism is often widely cited for its benefits related to employee recruitment and retention, criteria related to business interests ranked lower.

Top criteria when determining volunteer activities, as identified by the survey respondents:

- has high potential to help alleviate a societal issue (36%)
- helps non-profit making organisations function more effectively (31%)
- helps the non-profit making organisation to serve more clients/beneficiaries (31%)
- helps build the business's brand (15%)
- enhances employee morale (23%).

In a 2007 survey of 18 –26 year olds, Deloitte found that the future leaders from this age group are keen to be involved in community activities that have a meaningful impact on their communities. Sixty two per cent said that they preferred to work for an organisation that gave them opportunities to apply their skills to non profit organisations and 70% said companies should use volunteering as a professional development tool[5].

In addition to staff training and development, getting staff involved in community projects often also brings staff together from different parts of the business thereby fostering collaboration for the business.

4 Deloitte. (2010, May 3). Deloitte survey finds businesses believe volunteerism has power to make real difference. Retrieved May 8, 2010, from deloitte.com: http://www.deloitte.com/view/en_US/us/About/Community-Involvement/89e8d24a1aa48210VgnVCM200000bb42f00aRCRD.htm

5 Deloitte. (2007). Volunteer Impact Survey 2007. Retrieved February 9, 2010, from deloitte.com: http://www.deloitte.com/dtt/cda/doc/content/us_comm_volunteerimpact_survey_results2007

Case Study[6]

Impacts on Barclays

The social aspect of team-building meant I just knew a lot more people, and that meant when you've got a business issue, I just knew who to go and speak to, for example.

Barclays Volunteer

Employee volunteering has had a number of positive impacts on Barclays, including increasing employees' pride in the company, increasing staff job satisfaction, improving team working and raising Barclays' profile in local communities. These can have knock on effects in terms of recruitment and retention.

- Sixty-eight per cent of volunteers felt that their understanding of colleagues had increased as a result of employee volunteering, while 61% reported that their team-work skills had grown.
- Fifty-eight per cent of managers reported that their staff worked better together after volunteering. Nearly half (49%) of managers saw employee volunteering as 'very effective as a team building exercise', while a further 39% rated it as 'quite effective'.
- However managers saw employee volunteering as less appropriate for delivering formal training. Only 9% rated employee volunteering as a very effective method of training and 36% of them judged it to be 'not very effective'.
- Taking part in regular volunteering increases job satisfaction: the more times an employee has volunteered through Barclays the more likely it is that his or her job satisfaction has increased.
- More volunteers than non-volunteers would recommend Barclays as an employer (67% of volunteers compared with 58% of non-volunteers).
- Pride in Barclays increased with the number of times staff had volunteered: those who had volunteered four or more times were more likely to agree that they talked to family and friends about Barclays' support for the community than those who had volunteered only once (78% compared with 64%).

6 Barclays. (2004, October 20). More Community Work Equals a Happier Workforce . Retrieved April 23, 2010, from barclays.com: http://www.newsroom.barclays.com/Press-releases/More-Community-Work-Equals-a-Happier-Workforce-140.aspx

Although I get head hunted a lot... for me, [employee volunteering is] one of the main reasons I have stayed with Barclays.

Volunteer

Employee volunteering at Barclays allows volunteers to experience many personal benefits and to make a significant contribution to the work of a wide range of organisations. The research showed that Barclays is well on its way to meeting its objective of bringing long lasting tangible benefits to local communities.

Given a desire to harness the potential of volunteering to enhance staff development and internal collaboration many businesses will give the responsibility for voluntary activities to the human resources department. Businesses also frequently use the HR intranet to offer volunteering as one of the training options available to staff looking to brush up on certain skills and acquire knowledge.

Enabling employees to explore and cope with new situations and challenges

As part of a science in schools programme a partnership was formed between Derby North East Education Action Zone in the Midlands and employees from an engineering company who spent time in 10 primary schools around Derby to help improve the science classes being taught there.

The programme has helped the pupils to perform well above the national average. For the company, however, projects such as these are about more than philanthropy.

The company uses community initiatives as part of its trainee programmes. Rather than calling it "volunteering" they prefer to use the term 'employee development through community involvement' and as the description suggests, the company sees these projects as an opportunity to develop staff skills, in particular, communications, team working and project management.

A London-based law firm, has also found volunteering to be a useful way to develop its junior staff, giving them opportunities to learn skills that would be impossible to acquire on the job at such an early stage in their careers. It can be very difficult for young lawyers to get "client-facing" work as the client will usually expect a partner to do the work. So the firm finds that volunteering will help them to develop management and leadership skills that would not be available to them in their normal day to day work.

Enhancing the way staff members feel about themselves through a sense of personal achievement

A recent study carried out in Germany and published in various journals in February 2010 highlights the benefits of volunteering to the employees. The study of how people with full-time jobs were affected by volunteering indicated that volunteering has many psychological benefits and may improve people's enjoyment of work. The research found that the more time people spent volunteering, the more likely they were to switch off from work and have a better day the next day. The voluntary work provided the employees with the opportunity to detach themselves from their paid work and at the same time fulfil important psychological needs such as the need to connect with others, autonomy and competence.

The study used a sample of 105 people, who worked an average of five days and volunteered for an average of 6.7 hours a week. They volunteered with a range of organisations, from the fire service to church groups. They answered questions about whether they felt their needs were satisfied, how detached they felt from work, how much they felt they had learned and their well-being. The results were compared to see how after-work activities affected their moods.

The study showed that volunteering can bring many positive experiences such as the satisfaction of needs that aren't met through work, mastering new skills and relating to people socially and it also helps people to thoroughly disengage from their work[7].

Benefits for the Business ●●●

The business will benefit from a well-motivated workforce. Motivated employees typically have higher morale, achieve better results, and are more likely to stay with the business.

Other potential benefits include:

- an enhanced reputation and profile
- better relations with the local community and media
- improved access to networks, alliances and local strategic partnerships
- easier recruitment
- enhanced investor relations
- team building among staff.

Benefits for Third Sector Organisations ●●●

Of course, the main purpose of employee volunteering is to benefit the organisations the business works with. These organisations can benefit by:

- gaining access to volunteers with varied skills who can plan and carry out important tasks
- improving their understanding of working with the public and private sectors.

What can employer-supported volunteers do?

There are several ways that employees are able to volunteer with many employers already helping their staff to participate in volunteering activities, which include:

- individual volunteering
- team challenges – for example, refurbishing community buildings, clearing green spaces or organising Christmas parties for children
- fundraising - allowing staff to use work time and business resources for fundraising, for example Children in Need or Sport Relief
- one-to-one support
- skills transfer – using professional or practical skills as needed by the voluntary organisation, community project or charity.

7 British Psychological Society. (2010, February 15). Benefits of volunteering. Retrieved February 17, 2010, from bpsoc.com: bpsoc.publisher.ingentaconnect.com/content/bpsoc/joop/pre-prints/joop1086.

Case Study[8]

'Give Me Five' employee volunteering

A water services and infrastructure management group employing 11,000 staff started a volunteering scheme called 'Give Me Five'. This enabled the company to make a sustained contribution to the community by investing the time, skills and expertise of its employees in community projects, in a way that through employee personal development the business also benefits.

Employee engagement in volunteering programmes enables the company's community investment programme to meet its objectives of supporting youth education, combating social exclusion and improving the environment. The scheme is designed and managed to focus on a range of local community activities in areas in which the company has a presence.

The Give Me Five programme allows employees to take 30 hours of 'work time' per year to volunteer which they match with their own time. Some activities involve weekly volunteering by individuals over a period of years; others are made by groups of employees undertaking specific one-off projects. The total cost of the scheme, including staff time, materials, cash support, gifts in kind and management, is approximately £160,000 per annum (2003/4 figures)

Over 50 senior managers also demonstrate their commitment, and enhance their own development, by volunteering through the Give Me Five programme. More widely, the success and sustainability of Give Me Five relies very heavily on the commitment and support of all managers throughout the company who may take part and/or sanction the participation of individuals who report to them.

Impact

- 'Give Me Five' offers organisations like EBLOs (education business link organisations), Prince's Trust, Young Enterprise, Special Constables, Age Concern, WaterAid - just to name a few - an opportunity to tap into the skills and expertise of the company's employees free of charge.
- Since its inception in 2000, the scheme has accumulated 750 participants and completed more than 20 one-off projects.
- Generated circa 17, 000 hours of activity in the community in 2005.

8 Business in the Community. (2010, February 9). 'Give me five' employee volunteering. Retrieved February 9, 2010, from bitc.org.uk: http://www.bitc.org.uk/resources/case_studies/hc_ee_afe_374.html

Volunteering England, which promotes improvements in the quality, quantity, impact and accessibility of volunteering are very keen for more and more employers to take part in volunteering schemes. According to the organisation, six out of 10 volunteers say that the activities give them an opportunity to learn new skills. Volunteering England offers a range of resources - from information and research, to advice and contacts - for companies wanting to introduce a volunteering scheme. .

Business in the Community (BITC) offers a range of guidance and alternative schemes to help businesses to become involved. Those that may be of most interest are detailed below.

Cares

Cares is a network of more than 350 partner companies that address social issues in communities by volunteering their employees' skills and time during business hours. The programme operates throughout the year and welcomes new partners to support city-based and regional Cares partnerships in 35 locations in England, Wales and Northern Ireland.

Cares offers well-established expertise in employee engagement that delivers benefits for companies, employees and communities. In addition to providing a brokerage service for high-quality volunteering opportunities, Cares also campaigns nationally to increase the impact of employee volunteering in communities of greatest need and addresses social issues including education, employability and economic renewal.

ProHelp

ProHelp is a national network of over 600 professional firms committed to making a difference in their local community by providing free advice and professional support for community investment initiatives. It is made up of socially responsible professional firms that provide pro bono support to communities in need of their support. There is a network of 27 groups in city, urban and rural locations that enables these professional firms to support local communities. They try to maintain a quality service and members benefit from enhanced in-house skills and corporate reputation, and business development links through the national network. In 2009 ProHelp supported over 2,200 community groups, including schools, voluntary organisations and community groups, with £1.4m of free professional advice.

Benefit to the firms involved

Being a member of ProHelp gives their business the opportunity to make a difference in the local community and develop the skills of their employees through a managed pro bono programme. It can help by:

- providing employees with opportunities to use their professional skills outside their day-to-day environment
- linking pro bono work to their Continuing Professional Development (CPD) programme
- develop their understanding of key social issues in their local community
- managing the administration of their pro bono programme
- building new business contacts locally and regionally
- working collaboratively with other firms that need a range of professional skills and expertise
- communicating their achievements in order to build their reputation to internal and external audiences.

Volunteering Plus

Volunteering Plus is a BITC service that recognises and accredits the work of employee volunteers. It provides a framework that captures the learning and development gained from volunteering, which in turn is accredited by City & Guilds. It also helps companies to identify increases in their own skills base. To realise the potential of employee volunteering as a means for personal professional development, it must be formally accredited.

Accreditation offers tangible benefits to all those involved. For the employee there is formal recognition of the key skills and professional development gained through volunteering. For employers it is a means to providing flexible training and development opportunities in new environments and at the same time it is expanding the business's skills base and motivating employees. For community partners it offers quality assurance, focused and motivated volunteers and the fact that both the volunteer and the community partner benefit from the activity[9].

There has been a proposal for a "European Year of Volunteering 2011" (EVY) as a result of a civil society initiative led by European volunteering organisation networks. The aim of the networks' drive for EYV 2011 is to recognise over 100 million European volunteers and their contribution to society. Proposals for the EYV 2011 include initiatives to reward and recognise voluntary activities, empowering organisations in the voluntary sector and to raise the profile of volunteering and its value in society[10].

9 Business in the Community. (2010, February 9). Employee volunteering. Retrieved February 9, 2010, from bitc.org.uk: http://www.bitc.org.uk/community/employee_volunteering/index.html

10 EYV 2011. (2010, February 11). The European Year of Volunteering 2011. Retrieved February 11, 2010, from eyv2011.eu: http://www.eyv2011.eu/PublicImageVoting.asp

CHAPTER 23

Employability

- Enterprise and Employability
- Developing Employability
- Jobs for the Future
- Case Studies

Employability skills have never been more important. If the UK is to succeed in an increasingly competitive marketplace, we have a responsibility to build vibrant, economically active communities and help individuals take the steps to build better working lives.

Stephen Howard Chief Executive, Business in the Community

Enterprise and Employability

The International Business Leaders Forum (IBLF) warns that as companies consider their triple bottom line, many understand and act upon their environmental and social impacts but few appreciate the economic impact they have on society. Often confused with the financial bottom line – revenue, profit and loss – very little attention is given to other economic aspects such as jobs created directly or through the company's value chain, income generated, wages paid, human capital invested, goods bought and sold, taxes contributed and community investment. At a time when economic growth is under threat due to the financial crisis, it is appropriate to examine this aspect of a company's contribution to society in more detail by looking at how companies can retain human capital and broaden the experiences of their employees, develop employability skills in society at large and create more job opportunities through supporting entrepreneurs and small businesses.

In the UK alone there are over 4 million businesses and at the start of 2010 unemployment figures totalled 2.45 million people. Although an over simplistic notion it would seem to be the case that through initiatives like the one proposed by the IBLF and other regeneration schemes, if one in two businesses created an extra job unemployment could be eliminated and the "holy grail" of full employment might be achieved! Unfortunately it is too simplistic as there is an ever widening skills gap and the majority of the current unemployed do not have the level of qualifications needed. It will not be sufficient for businesses to create new jobs as they will also need to ensure that people in the communities in which they recruit have the necessary skills and qualifications to be employable.

IBLF believes supporting enterprise and employability to create jobs and increase income for communities is the most direct and effective way in which business can contribute to sustainable development and the eradication of poverty. IBLF works with businesses to help them accelerate the economic development of local communities, particularly through creating jobs, developing skills and improving linkages between small enterprises and multi-national companies.

Approximately 90% of businesses worldwide are small, medium and micro enterprises. Enterprise development relies on skilled talent to sustain entrepreneurs and grow the small businesses they create. In the majority of instances, small and medium enterprises (SME) owners require management training, business advice, finance and investment in local infrastructure before they can service multi-national companies. And because it is businesses that set the standards and expectations, they are best placed to provide appropriate resources to SMEs.

The key benefit of such a programme is that it assists companies to realise the opportunity for extending their value chains to those living at the 'base of the economic pyramid' – to buy from, distribute through or market to the poorest communities.

In November 2009, IBLF hosted an event signalling the launch of their programme of work on Employability and Enterprise Development. This included an influential piece of work initiated around the challenges and opportunities facing businesses in enterprise development. 'The Business of Jobs: Developing Employability & Enterprise through Collaboration' – which formed the basis for the forum.

Businesses require a skilled talent pool from which to recruit their future employees and to strengthen the overall competitiveness of the local economy. The emphasis is not only on vocational or technical skills, but also on business acumen, leadership and life skills, financial inclusion and corporate culture.

Developing Employability ●●●

The IBLF identified corporate projects focusing on developing employability that currently include the following.

- **Retention of human capital** - by avoiding lay-offs to protect historical investment in knowledge and skills. Companies invest, not only in training their employees, but also in developing retention strategies which benefit employees and the employer. These include performance-related pay, offering clearly defined career pathways and opportunities to track personal development which enables businesses to attract and retain talent.

  Many companies are finding innovative ways of keeping people employed whilst still cutting costs. 'Creative downsizing' measures include pay freezes, bypassing raises, shortening the working week and eliminating bonuses.

- **Vocational training** - through investment in training programmes to develop a talent pool and recruitment pipeline of technically trained and skilled potential employees. Across the world, companies looking for new talent to develop a robust recruitment pipeline find that, while there are many educated graduates in the market, few of them have the requisite technical skills they are looking for. To address this gap many companies are collaborating within sectors and/or with other stakeholders to develop vocational training. Often these are focused on skills required for specific industries.

- **Basic skills development** - by participating in external programmes to develop non-technical, personal and managerial skills. Companies are also investing in basic skills for the broader community such as literacy, numeracy and IT. Frequently this takes the form of corporate social investment, philanthropic donations, in-kind support and volunteering to support colleges and universities to train students in these skills. The most effective programmes deliver face-to-face training with students, rather than using e-platform learning. The business role may be better suited to 'training-the-trainer' and then relying on existing teaching institutions to deliver the final training to end beneficiaries.

Companies go beyond investment in their own employees by supporting employability development among job-seekers and the wider community. This takes various forms, including financial and product donations and employee volunteering in partnership with academic institutes and governments. The main benefits are an increase in productivity and innovation, motivation and retention of employees and an enhanced reputation.

Case Study[1]

Deloitte's ambitious programme to transform the 'work readiness' of school and college leavers across the UK has earned the business advisory firm the 'Best for Engaging with Schools and Colleges' Award in 2009, sponsored by the Edge Foundation, at the prestigious Sunday Times Best Companies Awards.

The award recognises Deloitte for the exceptional breadth and depth of its support in education and in particular its flagship Employability Skills Initiative. Deloitte aims to train a total of 800 teachers to deliver employability courses, reaching 40,000 students across the UK helping them to develop the skills, attitudes and behaviours needed to secure and sustain employment. The firm has invested £2.6 million in the initiative to date, with a further £1.2 million planned to 2012. Deloitte's total commitment to educational projects exceeds £1 million each year.

This year's Sunday Times rankings, based on a survey of more than 200,000 employees at 997 companies, recognised Deloitte as one of the UK's Top 10 'Best Big Companies to Work For', and also named the firm as the UK's 'Best Big Company for Work and Home Balance'.

More than 600 Deloitte staff and partners volunteer for educational projects across the UK each year, including running skills workshops in Further Education colleges, mentoring secondary school students and helping children with literacy or numeracy. Deloitte provide work-placements for older students and encourage school partners to visit Deloitte offices, helping raise the aspirations and widen the horizons of young people from diverse cultural and social backgrounds.

1 Deloitte. (2010, January 29). Deloitte named 'Best Big Company for Engaging with Schools and Colleges'. Retrieved March 21, 2010, from deloitte.com: http://www.deloitte.com/view/en_GB/uk/press-release/d9cea68c4d101210VgnVCM100000ba42f00aRCRD.htm

The key principles to keep in mind when designing a collaborative approach on the topics of employability and enterprise development are:

- base the project on a clear business need
- build in sufficient time to allow the partnership to be formed, a robust approach developed and implemented, and next steps determined
- in planning and delivering a programme, consider the spheres of influence in which a company operates, so as to be clear on which stakeholders to involve in the project
- seek diverse stakeholders to bring in the needed expertise and resources. Work with local partners to build on their local knowledge, networks and experience
- consider vulnerable sections of society such as women, minority groups and marginalised communities
- define social and business performance metrics and collect data
- share learning and experience widely.

Successful businesses and sustainable development for communities are mutually dependent. Since 2000, IBLF has taken an active role in developing the concept of economic development and promoting the critical role business can play in supporting job creation and creating environments where entrepreneurship can thrive.

To them, the role of business in increasing prosperity is clear - the private sector is the principal engine for creating jobs and wealth for billions of poorer people through enterprise development. Businesses are best at finding the market-based solutions required to create sustainable livelihoods and tackle development challenges[2].

The economic slowdown forced businesses to think harder about how to develop their workforce and during the downturn businesses had to become much more innovative. Companies were offering packages in the downturn rather than making layoffs which gave employees the chance for a period working in a non-profit operation which in turn was a creative way of transferring company skills into the community as well as developing people for the business's benefit.

Volunteering programmes make good business sense for businesses, allowing them to demonstrate their commitment to the communities in which they operate while deploying a powerful staff development tool. For volunteering activities not only give employees skills they might not acquire in the workplace. Working jointly on community projects also builds teams and internal networks, and helps employees learn to collaborate after the merger of business units or the acquisition of a rival company.

2 IBLF. (2009, December). THE BUSINESS OF JOBS:Developing Employability & Enterprise. Retrieved March 21, 2010, from iblf.org: http://www.iblf.org/~/media/Files/Resources/Publications/BusinessOfJobs.ashx

Jobs for the Future

Given the skills gaps that remain in the UK, the pressure to broaden talent searches will only become greater. According to government research, between 2004 and 2014 an estimated 650,000 construction workers, 500,000 IT workers, and 300,000 science and engineering workers will be required. To fill these positions, companies will need to invest in training schemes designed for those beyond their own workforce and outside their traditional talent pools. By employing people who have limited qualifications or training, and building their skill base, businesses can help improve future employability.

In July 2009 the CBI and Siemens plc published a report – Jobs for the Future[3] – which outlined a business vision for how this can be done. The report suggested that the UK starts with important advantages, but advantages are not guarantees. The employment trends survey expressed a note of caution in that the findings would suggest that the UK must continually reinforce the attractiveness of its labour market if it is to win investment in a globalised economy. Worryingly the survey showed that half of firms think the UK is now a less attractive place to invest and do business than five years ago. The CBI say that these problems must be addressed if the UK is to create and sustain employment for the future.

Key findings from the survey highlight that:

- nearly half (49%) of employers think the UK is a less attractive place to invest and do business compared with five years ago, but business leaders are more optimistic that this can be reversed
- over two thirds (67%) of firms feel employment regulation has become a serious burden, threatening labour market flexibility
- employers are concerned the agency workers directive will further reduce flexibility. It will also cut work opportunities for labour market entrants
- UK retention of the working time individual opt-out is important, with over a third (35%) of employers saying the impact of losing this flexibility would be significant or severe
- rises in the national minimum wage continue to bite – despite the economic downturn, over a third (37%) of affected firms are planning to pass on this year's cost in higher prices.

3 CBI. (2009, August). Employment Trends Survey 2009. Retrieved March 21, 2010, from cbi.org.uk: http://www.cbi.org.uk/ndbs/positiondoc.nsf/1f08ec61711f29768025672a0055f7a8/C5C5449D6970F56F802576C50057A132/$file/20091101-cbi-employment-trends-survey.pdf

Business in the Community's vision[4] is similar to that of the IBLF in that they see all cities and towns will have a growing number of businesses contributing to the health and wealth of their communities. BITC say that this vision will be achieved through local employment, supporting local enterprise and tackling relevant social issues.

Business in the Community's campaign for economic renewal focuses on specific regions or business sectors in which they provide support and advice on key social issues such as crime, health and skills development. They develop forums and channels for knowledge sharing, and undertake cutting-edge research.

The economic renewal campaign currently has three areas of focus:

- to increase business engagement with local partners through business brokerage
- to promote responsible community investment and development in the property and construction sectors through their work on property-led regeneration, including our under-served markets, property and construction forums
- to work with business to remove barriers to work by increasing employment opportunities for those living in the most disadvantaged neighbourhoods and other socially excluded groups. Their work in this area includes a focus on employability, social housing partnerships and unlocking talent.

Business in the Community engages, inspires, supports and challenges businesses to understand the unique contribution that corporate responsibility makes to social issues. They continually develop briefing notes for members and contribute actively to BITC's wider public policy work.

Their work guides businesses to invest, recruit, buy, sell and work collaboratively in a way that generates business benefits and makes economic and social impact in the community. BITC is working with business to support those who are homeless or at risk of homelessness, and other socially excluded groups, who require skills and opportunity to gain and sustain employment and currently they are working on:

- Business Action on Homelessness (BAOH) which aims to help homeless people to gain and sustain employment and live independently
- engaging businesses with prisons in order to develop programmes for ex-offenders
- Project Compass which is a programme for ex-services individuals as a significant proportion of homeless people are from the ex-services personnel community.
- the Backing Young Britain campaign.

4 BITC. (2010, April 9). Economic renewal strategy. Retrieved April 9, 2010, from bitc.org.uk: http://www.bitc.org.uk/community/economic_renewal/strategy_and_vision/index.html

The Backing Young Britain Campaign

In the last quarter of 2009 almost 900,000 16-24 year olds were not in Education, Employment or Training (NEET). The need to support young talent has never been more pressing and in response to this need and recognising that business needs to do all it can to help people during this recession, Microsoft UK launched its campaign to help 500,000 people into work by 2012. Through a combination of a new national apprenticeship scheme, targeted skills and employability training and a new job matching service, Microsoft will work with its partners, NGOs and local government to deliver this ambitious target.

British businesses, charities and voluntary organisations joined young people and government ministers in London in July 2009 to discuss how 16-24 year olds who are new to the jobs market could be supported to find jobs, work experience or training to use their talents and reach their potential.

Launching the Backing Young Britain[5] campaign, Ministers announced £40 million to fund over 20,000 additional internships, meaning graduates and non-graduates can access higher quality work experience and a new mentoring network to help young people find their feet in a tough jobs market.

The campaign also points people towards more support for young people who do become unemployed. Right from day-one, this will be provided through job clubs and – for those leaving education this summer – one-to-one support in Job Centre Plus offices.

It was announced that 117 bidders have been given the green light to create up to 47,000 innovative jobs for young people and the long-term unemployed through the UK government's Future Jobs Fund. These jobs will include sports coaches, education assistants and roles in the green and social care sectors.

Organisations can make a commitment to support young people in at least one of the following ways:

- work with a partnership to bid for one of the 100,000 jobs for young people from the Future Jobs Fund
- offer a volunteering place or a volunteer mentor for school or university leavers;
- provide work experience places to help young people learn about work, make contacts and fill their CV
- consider a young person for a job through a work trial
- offer an internship for a graduate
- provide an apprenticeship for 16-24 year olds
- join a Local Employment Partnership to make sure job vacancies are advertised to local unemployed people.

5 BIS. (2010, April 9). Backing Young Britain. Retrieved April 9, 2010, from bis.gov.uk: http://interactive.bis.gov.uk/backingyoungbritain/

The number of organisations supporting the campaign has grown significantly and rapidly meaning that the volume of opportunities being created for young people in the workplace has also grown and by April 2010 1,000 organisations from all across the country were creating more opportunities for 16 -24 year olds.

The national launch of the IT apprenticeship scheme for smaller businesses also took place in summer 2009. It was successfully trialled in the Black Country and the aim is to have more than 700 IT apprentices by September 2010 and more than 3,000 over the three year period of the campaign.

At the launch it was predicted that the number of people unemployed would top 2.5 million for the first time since 1995 and it was also identified that there are thousands of people who do not have the appropriate skills that businesses need in today's IT led economy. Businesses still need these people, and so a significant part of the campaign will focus on making "Skills for Business" training vouchers available to people who want to give themselves an extra chance when going for interviews. Digital skills are crucial for the knowledge economy and this campaign will go a long way to helping people benefit from the new opportunities that technology brings.

"Skills for Business" training will be primarily delivered through Microsoft partners and NGOs, including UK Online Centres, The Wise Group and Leonard Cheshire Disability. Training is also available for more technical IT skills in addition to the apprenticeship scheme. A new job matching and training service for those engaged in the IT industry, MSEmploy also launched in 2009 and will help match vacancies amongst Microsoft's partner network of 32,000 companies with people seeking employment. Jobcentre Plus is on board to help point job seekers towards the new support available as well.[6]

6 Microsoft. (2009, July). Microsoft launches its campaign to create 500000 new jobs by 2012. Retrieved March 21, 2010, from microsoft.com: http://www.microsoft.com/uk/press/content/presscentre/releases/2009/09/PR03932.mspx

Case Study[7]

Local - Tesco regenerating their communities

In the UK they have opened stores which revitalise disadvantaged areas, working in partnership with local agencies. One such example is the regeneration in Gorton, Manchester.

Gorton is an area that has suffered from the decline of traditional manufacturing. With 12% unemployment, a fragile local economy and high crime rate, the area badly needed a boost. Tesco provided the injection of money, jobs and hope to revitalise the local economy.

They worked with the local regeneration company New East Manchester Limited to develop plans for a Tesco Extra in Gorton to act as a catalyst for further investment. The scheme has provided work for 130 local long-term unemployed people between the ages of 17 and 62, most of whom were not registered jobseekers. Tesco recruited them by distributing thousands of leaflets door to door, as well as working with training and employment agencies.

The vision to create a new district centre – which includes a market hall and new retail units as well as the Tesco store – received planning consent in late 2006 and the store opened in October 2008.

Since 2000, when Tesco opened their first Regeneration Partnership store in Seacroft, Leeds, they have created jobs for the long-term unemployed in 20 stores. In 2008 they opened Regeneration Partnership stores in Aston (Birmingham), Gorton and Cheetham Hill (Manchester), providing almost 900 jobs, nearly 500 of which were for long-term unemployed people.

These areas have often suffered neglect for many years and can appear unattractive commercially. Other retailers may be reluctant to invest there. However, by providing what customers want and by operating their business efficiently, Tesco have been able to develop successful stores in deprived areas, and have helped to attract other businesses to these areas.

In their Regeneration Partnership stores as part of their recruitment process they target local people who have been unemployed for at least six months, including those with low levels of numeracy and literacy skills and people with disabilities. These new employees will attend a special life skills programme as well as job training. Unlike most other employment schemes, Tesco guarantees a job to the people they select for Tesco training.

Following the success of this approach, Tesco were one of the first companies to work with the UK government in Local Employment Partnerships, designed to provide jobs for the long-term unemployed. They are committed to a Local

7 Tesco PLC. (2010, March 21). Regenerating our communities. Retrieved March 21, 2010, from tescoplc.com: http://www.tescoplc.com/plc/corporate_responsibility_09/community/regenerating_our_communi ties/

Employment Partnership wherever they open a store. In 2008, Tesco won a Best Practice Recruitment award for their new store in Aston, Birmingham, where they hired almost two-thirds of the workforce through the Partnership. They also won two North West Local Employment Partnership Awards.

Case Study[8]

National - Barclaycard's Horizons, UK

"Horizons" is a pioneering scheme that helps lone parents to create a better future for themselves and their children. Barclaycard launched the Horizons programme in July 2005, seeking to develop its community programme to support people affected by debt problems. Research showed that lone parents were a group at risk of being in poverty. Since the programme's launch, Barclaycard has invested more than £3m in supporting 250,000 lone parents and their children in the UK. Horizons aims to improve the skills and confidence of lone parents, helping them to manage their finances, improve their education and job prospects, and support their children.

Using the skills of its charity partners, Horizons helps lone parents to improve their lives by giving them practical advice on money matters, providing grants towards training and education costs and helping lone parents to get back to work. The three elements to the programme are:

- Your Money - this is a free programme run by 12 Citizens Advice Bureaux across the UK. Lone parents can take part in a series of courses which cover a range of topics including basic household budgeting, choosing credit, managing debt, dealing with loans, Child Trust Funds and more.
- Your Education - The Family Action fund provides ongoing financial support to lone parents who are seeking to boost their skills and employment prospects by undertaking training. Providing such additional financial support can make a real difference in assisting parents to complete courses.
- Your Work - this is a unique, three-week, free programme run by lone parent charity Gingerbread. The programme is specifically designed to give lone parents valuable advice and support on all aspects of returning to work, as well as two weeks' work experience.

All Barclaycard's UK centres offer work experience placements to parents undertaking the course.

8 Barclays. (2010, March 21). Case studies: community workforce. Retrieved March 21, 2010, from group.barclays.com: http://group.barclays.com/Sustainability/Responsible-global-citizenship/Community-investment/CaseStudy/1231782003079.htmlcommunity/workforce-

Case Study[9 and 10]

International - with permission from Microsoft Microsoft creating employability globally

By working with partners to create relevant training opportunities and innovative tools for people who are underserved by technology Microsoft believe that they can help foster social and economic opportunities that change people's lives and transform communities. As part of the Microsoft Unlimited Potential commitment, their employability and workforce development programmes support organizations that work to ensure that individuals have the IT skills they need to succeed in the twenty-first-century workplace.

Unlimited Potential–Community Technology Skills Program Recipients

Since their Community Technology Skills Programme began in 2003, Microsoft has provided more than US$350 million in cash and software grants to more than 1,000 community partners. These donations have supported over 40,000 technology centres in more than 100 countries/regions.

Community Technology Centres

Microsoft supports non-governmental organizations (NGOs) that are focused on employability and workforce development. Many of these partners operate community technology centres (CTCs) which are found in various locations, from remote villages to major metropolitan areas. CTCs provide people of all ages and abilities free or low-cost access to resources that enable them to learn about computers, use the Internet, explore new careers, further their education, participate in community activities, and develop job-related technology skills. CTCs are expected to demonstrate a clear mission or a focus on delivering social benefits, and each centre's curriculum is driven by local demand.

Digital Literacy Curriculum

CTCs can use the Digital Literacy Curriculum, which teaches basic computer concepts and skills. Available in many languages, these e-learning courses and assessments help people learn such things as using the Internet, sending e-mails and being able to create a résumé.

Unlimited Potential Community Learning Curriculum

The Community Learning Curriculum provides a foundation for teaching basic-to-intermediate technical skills. Intended specifically for CTCs and telecentres,

9 Microsoft. (2010, March 21). Corporate Citizenship:Our actions in the community/workforce development. Retrieved March 21, 2010, from microsoft.com: http://www.microsoft.com/about/corporatecitizenship/en-us/our-actions/in-the-community/workforce-development.aspx

10 Microsoft. (2010, March 21). Our work on strengthening economies. Retrieved March 21, 2010, from microsoft.com: http://www.microsoft.com/about/corporatecitizenship/en-us/our-focus/strengthening-economies/development.aspxent

the content is designed to help people develop skills that apply to real-world challenges and opportunities. Available in 21 languages, the curriculum is provided free of charge for non-commercial use in non-profit CTCs and telecentres worldwide.

Expanded Job Skills Training Programs

Working closely with community and government partners, Microsoft offers training resources for adult learners. These include e-learning courses for office productivity tools and advanced technology professional training through programs such as Elevate America and Britain Works.

Partners in Learning

Microsoft provides IT training through their Partners in Learning program. Since 2003 they have reached more than 121 million students and 5.5 million educators in over 100 countries through Partners in Learning. By 2013 they plan to have invested $500 million in the program and have reached 250 million students.

Students to Business

Microsoft helps to connect businesses with students through their Students to Business programme. Through this programme they have connected over 300,000 students with companies, providing skills training, industry insight, and job placement services.

Their Strategic Partners

Microsoft accomplishes its workforce development goals by working closely with partners around the world. Examples of key partnerships include telecentre.org and Boys & Girls Clubs of America. (Microsoft, 2010)

Microsoft's contribution to strengthening economies also leads inevitably to the creation of employability as their long-term commitment to R&D and their investment in a partner-based business model - with nearly 700,000 partners worldwide - have directly and indirectly created millions of jobs and new businesses. The research firm IDC recently estimated that the launch of Windows 7 in late 2009 will account for 7 million jobs, or about 20 per cent of the global IT industry, in 2010; and that for every US$1 of windows 7 revenue that will go to Microsoft in 2010, companies working with Microsoft will make US$18.52.

As is the case with other chapters in this section of the book the case studies presented should provide sufficient insight into the benefits to responsible and sustainable businesses of working within their community whether local, national or global. As before there are many other inspirational examples that could also have been included. The case studies also provide proof that systemic thinking has to be an integral part of the process.

SECTION 6

Environment

- Climate Change
- The Energy Issue
- Natural Capital
- Waste
- Environmental Management and Reporting
- Legislation

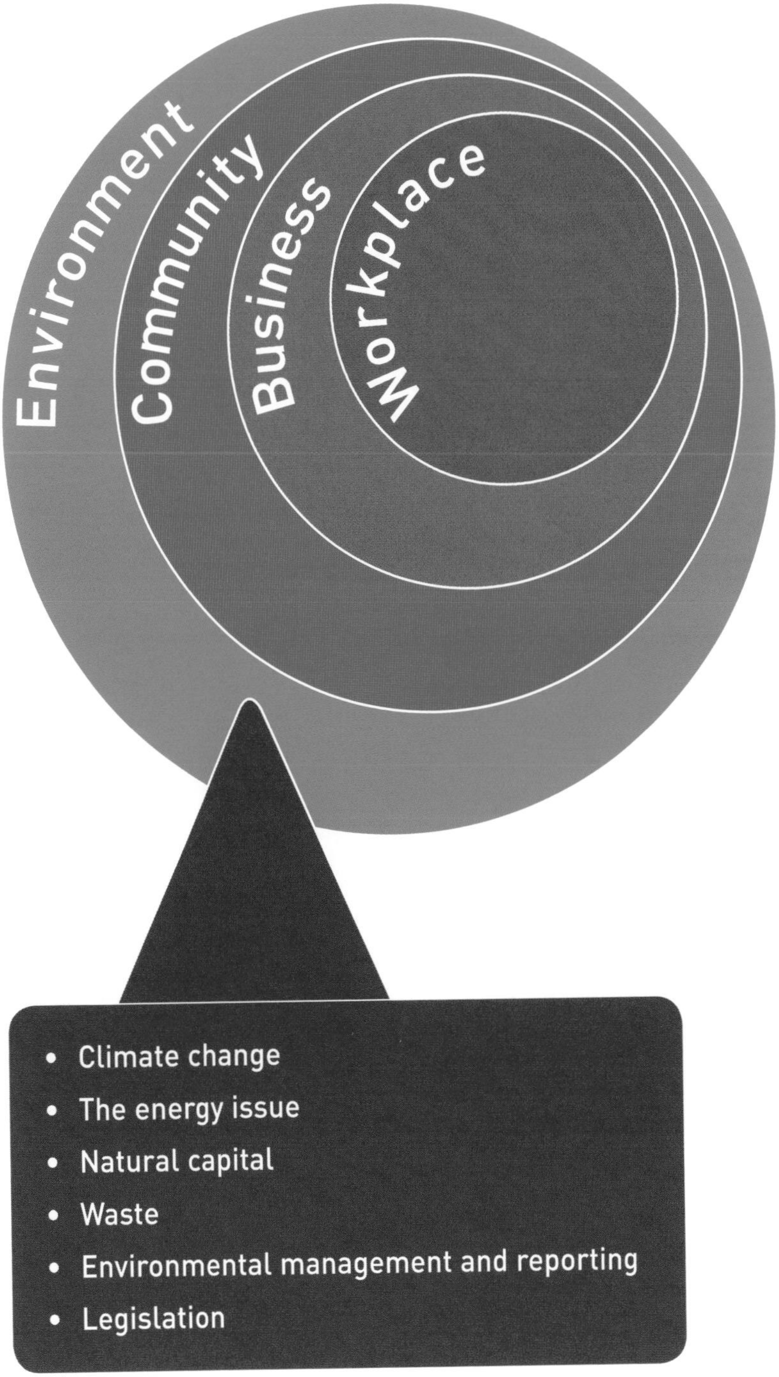
Environment
Community
Business
Workplace
Climate change
The energy issue
Natural capital
Waste
Environmental management and reporting
Legislation

Environment

Recycling at 100%

Energy use is monitored

Sustainable development

People, Planet, Profit

Over consumption eliminated

Natural Capital is valued

Scarce resources are replenished

ISO14001

Biodiversity is protected

Low-carbon emissions/carbon neutral

Ecosystems are not affected

The popular BBC programme "Dragons Den" is loosely based around the idea of Business Angels who will lend up to £100,000 for a share of the business and its profits. The programme is very enjoyable to watch but the "Dragons" only seem to be concerned about the financial bottom line and do not seem too concerned about people and planet, unless the proposal itself is "green". For them the return on their investment seems to be the only motivation for lending and natural capital and the environment plays no part in their thinking. But the trouble with "Dragons" is ....

Let me tell you where I am. I'm out!

The trouble with dragons is**.....** Dragons make dragons
And they make some more till there are wall-to-wall Dragons
making dragons galore.
The Dragons start spreading all over the place.....
Soon their houses and roads take up all of the space
Dragons eat all the food and drink all the drink
And use everything up without stopping to think
They also throw parties and make loads of noise
And leave a huge mess after playing with their toys.
Dragons chop down the forests which melts both the Poles
And puncture the atmosphere full of big holes.
Dragons blowout hot air which makes everything hotter
And hotter.......
And hotter.....
Until all the snow melts and the ice turns to water.
Then the seas start to rise and the deserts expand,
Until everything's covered in water and sand.
Say goodbye to the world into which you were born.
Soon everyone else will have packed up and gone
Everyone.......
Except the dragons
Poor dragons.
Imagine a world with no birds and no bees
Just Dragons as far as a Dragon can see
"Don't go," wailed the Dragons. "Don't leave us alone
A world without wildlife is no kind of home
If you stay, we all promise to do what it takes
To look after the planet for all of our sakes."
As waters rose higher right over their knees
A voice said, "OK start by not chopping down trees."
Then all of the animals chimed in with advice
From the greatest of elephants to the smallest of mice
Eat food that is grown much closer to home
And leave the wild places and ice caps alone
Stop blowing all that hot air but instead choose to walk
And put less of our world at the end of you fork
Respect all earth's creatures and cherish the land
Recycle, reuse and reduce your demands.
So – if you know a dragon and most of us do
Ask if it thinks that this story is true
For if we can't see that our stories are linked
Then sadly, like dragons, we'll soon be extinct.[1]

1 Gliori, D. (2008). The Trouble with Dragons. London: Bloomsbury Publishing plc.

CHAPTER 24

Climate Change

- The Impact of Climate Change
- Carbon Budgets
- Business Risk or Opportunity?
- Carbon Reduction Strategies

Pause & effect: Hesitation by organisations to make real changes may be because they are waiting for government to take the lead. Lack of action may also be because the risks of climate change are beyond the normal planning horizons for most organisations, with many people believing that that we still have decades before impacts will affect us. Climate change tends to sit off the radar, creating a risk that it falls into a strategic blind-spot.

CIMA Excellence in Leadership, July 2008

The 2006 Stern Review suggested that climate change could shrink global economies by up to 20% if no action is taken to curb emissions. Originally suggested to be 1% of GDP the cost to take action, by mid-2008, had risen to 2% of GDP, but it was also predicted to save £1.32 trillion globally in the long term[1].

The associated benefits are expected to include better energy security, protecting consumers from oil price spikes, new employment in green industries, more productive agriculture and lower air pollution, cutting health costs.

The Intergovernmental Panel on Climate Change (IPCC) predicted that climate change will have a substantial impact globally, and in Europe lead to increased risk of inland flash floods, more frequent coastal flooding, and increased coastal erosion. Climate change is also projected to increase the frequency of wildfires and health risks due to heat waves. These substantial inter-related social, environmental and economic impacts are why climate change is now one of Business in the Community's (BITC) top campaigning priorities[2].

The UK is the first country in the world to set itself legally binding 'carbon budgets' which were introduced in the Climate Change Act 2008. Carbon budgets set limits on the total greenhouse gas emissions allowed from the UK in successive five year periods.

The first budget started in 2008, setting the trajectory to the long-term target of an 80% reduction in emissions by 2050 on 1990 levels. The government announced the levels of the first three budgets in April 2009, requiring the UK to cut emissions by 34% on 1990 levels by 2020.

1 The Guardian. (2008, June 26). Cost of tackling global climate change has doubled, warns Stern. Retrieved April 9, 2010, from guardian.co.uk: http://www.guardian.co.uk/environment/2008/jun/26/climatechange.scienceofclimatechange

2 IPCC. (2007, November 17). Climate Change 2007-The IPCC fourth assessment report. Retrieved April 15, 2010, from ipcc.ch: http://www.ipcc.ch/press_information/press_information.htm#5

A 34% reduction represents 266.8 million tonnes less of greenhouse gases in 2020 than in 1990. The UK has already achieved a reduction of about 21% since 1990, equivalent to cutting emissions entirely from four cities the size of London.

Put another way, it is equivalent to a reduction of almost six tonnes of greenhouse gases per person in 2020 compared to 1990. Six tonnes of CO2 is equivalent to driving an average car from London to Manchester over 45 times, or boiling a kettle for more than 340,000 cups of tea.

The UK government's Transition Plan set out the policies and proposals for meeting their first three carbon budgets. The plan would deliver emissions cuts in all sectors through a varied set of policies, ranging from the EU ETS capping emissions from heavy industry, supporting innovative new low-carbon technologies, as well as helping people make low-carbon choices in their homes, their workplaces and when they travel.

Which sectors will savings come from?

- Power and heavy industry (50% of reductions)
- Transport (20% of reductions)
- Homes (15% of reductions)
- Workplaces (10% of reductions)
- Agriculture (5% of reductions)

The reduction of emissions internally is seen as a vital part of achieving carbon neutrality. Reductions in emissions through energy efficiency measures or cutting back on business travel can deliver cost savings as well as helping the UK to meet its emission reduction targets.

Businesses may wish to set an internal reduction target to be achieved over a given time-frame, however it is important for businesses to realise that reducing emissions internally is a continuous process, not least because innovation is likely to increase the ways in which it will be able to make internal emissions reductions over time. Recognising the need to take internal action as much as possible if UK targets are to be met, and the fact that there is a wide range of cost-effective reduction measures available, it is recommended that any internal reductions or reduction plans be as ambitious as possible.

Internal emissions reduction measures include:

- carrying out/completion of projects such as energy efficiency measures, through, for example, behaviour change programmes and supplier engagement strategies
- generation and consumption of electricity from renewable sources backed by Renewable Energy Guarantees of Origin (REGOs) certificates
- the purchase of green tariffs which comply with OFGEM's Independent Certification Scheme[3].

3 BBC News. (2009). Carbon Budget Factsheet. Retrieved April 9, 2010, from news.bbc.co.uk: http://news.bbc.co.uk/1/shared/bsp/hi/pdfs/15_07_09_lowcarbon.pdf

Many businesses may be tempted to think that taking action on climate change is an add-on to be dispensed with in tougher economic conditions. However, tackling climate change offers a number of business opportunities in the short term which will position businesses to survive any adverse economic climate. Those businesses that realise these opportunities now and embed low-carbon activities throughout their business will be best placed to flourish in the longer term as the UK moves towards a low-carbon economy.

Business activities account for about half of all emissions in the UK. Large companies have a significant impact on climate change. The Carbon Trust has estimated that 16,000, or 2%, of firms account for 80% of emissions from industrial processes and business use of buildings. SMEs individually have only a small carbon impact, but collectively they account for the remaining 20%.

Firms of all sizes and in a variety of sectors have the ability not only to curb emissions from their own operations but also to drive wider improvements in the UK and abroad. Business also has a critical responsibility to design new low-carbon products and solutions and in helping employees and customers make choices, which can in turn reduce their own emissions. They will need to incorporate climate change policies into their DNA. In a low-carbon future, companies will have to be green to grow.

The UK's ambition to improve energy efficiency and security will also be influenced by business, both in providing low-carbon energy sources and improving the country's energy efficiency. Business will need to redouble its efforts to become more energy efficient, by focusing on areas such as transport and buildings.

The foundation to any carbon reduction claim is calculating emissions in an accurate, consistent and transparent way. The most common and internationally accepted approach to categorising emissions is through the Greenhouse Gas (GHG) Protocol. The GHG Protocol groups emissions into three different 'scopes' which are as follows.

Scope 1 (Direct emissions) - Activities that are owned or controlled by the business that release emissions straight into the atmosphere are direct emissions. Examples of scope 1 emissions include emissions from combustion in owned or controlled boilers, furnaces, vehicles (owned or controlled), emissions from chemical production in owned or controlled process equipment.

Scope 2 (Energy indirect) - Emissions being released into the atmosphere associated with consumption of purchased electricity, heat, steam and cooling. These are indirect emissions that are a consequence of activities which occur at sources not owned or controlled by the business.

Scope 3 (Other indirect) - The final category is all other activities that release emissions into the atmosphere as a consequence of actions taken, which occur at sources that are not owned or controlled by the business and which are not classed as scope 2 emissions. In other words, they do not result from the purchase of electricity, heat, steam and cooling. Examples of scope 3 emissions are business travel by means which are not owned or controlled by the business, waste disposal, and the actual usage of the sold products or services.

Carbon Budgets ●●●

When looking to achieve a low-carbon or carbon neutral business the first step is to set the boundary for the emissions which are going to be addressed and to which any carbon reduction declaration will be related.

The scope of the emissions included in the footprint is decided by the business to some extent but the business should avoid claims' being misinterpreted and should therefore clearly communicate information on what emissions have been included in any declaration.

In line with government guidance for organisations, it is recommended that, as a minimum, emissions within scopes 1 and 2 should be included in any calculation of emissions. In addition, it is recommended that organisations include their significant scope 3 emissions. Calculating scope 3 emissions will mean developing a more complete understanding of the total impact on climate change. However it is acknowledged that it can be difficult to measure and calculate scope 3 emissions. The following criteria have been set out in the government's guidance for organisations to help identify those scope 3 emissions that are significant.

- **Scale** - What are the largest indirect emissions-causing activities with which the business concerned is connected?
- **Importance to business/activity** - Are there any sources of GHG emissions that are particularly important to the business/activity in question or that increase climate change risks (for example, electricity consumption in the case of consumer use of energy using products or emissions from vehicle use for motor manufacturers)?
- **Importance to stakeholders** - Which emission causing activities do interested parties such as customers, suppliers or investors expect to see reported?
- **Potential for reductions** - Where is there potential to influence or reduce emissions from indirect emission activities?

In some instances, it may be difficult to identify whether emissions should be categorised as scope 1 or scope 3. This may be because your emissions sources come from outsourced activities, leased assets or tenanted buildings. By calculating its scope 3 emissions, a business will get a more complete understanding of the business's total impact on climate change. Identifying the business's scope 3 emissions will also help increase its awareness of where its business sits within the supply chain and enable it to engage with other businesses in the supply chain. However the guidance provided has acknowledged that it can be difficult to measure and calculate scope 3 emissions so it is recommended that the focus should be on 'significant' scope 3 emissions.

The business community will need to become flexible in order to adapt to a changing climate. It will have to adjust to risks internally and down-supply chains within investments. The nature of climate change dictates that all businesses take ownership of climate risks. Those that are most resilient will have an implicit lead over their competitors.

Business Risk or Opportunity?

Business, like people, need information and incentives to take action on climate change. UK businesses on average waste 30 per cent of the energy they buy and improvements to commercial buildings, adoption of efficient appliances and better use of transport would save costs.

Climate change presents a whole range of new business opportunities for UK plc. Across the world a number of corporations are already taking steps to develop the capabilities to capture these opportunities[4].

Taking action on climate change will position businesses to ride any future economic storm by providing the following benefits:

Cost savings - A key way for businesses to reduce carbon emissions is by reducing their use of energy and transport. Cutting carbon in this way also cuts costs – a "win-win" situation. Simple, cheap or cost-free measures such as insulating buildings, re-setting heating timers so buildings are only heated when occupied, and coordinating deliveries so less travel is required, could help businesses make substantial costs savings. The Carbon Trust predicts that taking action on climate change could save UK businesses up to £1m a day collectively.

Retain existing and win new business - By adopting the simple energy and transport measures described above, businesses can pass on cost savings to customers, so helping to retain existing, and win new, business. They can also win new business by helping customers to reduce their own carbon emissions and costs.

Improved reputation and trust - In the current economic climate, establishing trust in a business' brand will be particularly important in retaining and winning new business. Businesses that take action on climate change and communicate it to their customers will be better placed to retain their loyalty and win new customers. Recent research from the Carbon Trust Standard shows that 66% of consumers say it is important to buy from environmentally responsible companies.

Short term opportunities of climate change

- Cost savings
- Retaining and winning new business
- Improved reputation and trust
- Increased morale

4 CBI. (2010, April 9). Climate Change. Retrieved April 9, 2010, from cbi.org.uk: http://climatechange.cbi.org.uk/business/

Longer term opportunities of climate change

- Improved financial performance
- New income streams
- Improved recruitment and retention of talent
- Acquiring skills for the future
- Keeping ahead of international competition
- Responding to upcoming legislation

The Institute of Chartered Accountants in England and Wales (ICAEW)[5] also state that climate change mitigation entails finding ways to reduce the greenhouse gas emissions that cause climate change. They suggest ways of mitigating climate change include reducing demand for emissions-intensive goods and services, increasing efficiency gains, increasing use and development of low-carbon technologies, and reducing non-fossil fuel emissions.

They recommend that companies consider the future impact of bigger changes driven by regulation, technology or consumers. They point out that with the UK's commitment to challenging and legally binding carbon emissions-reduction targets, climate change is now a key strategic issue. As this new business revolution unfolds, it is clear that there will be winners and losers, and that companies that adopt a flexible but proactive approach now are most likely to benefit.

The ICAEW suggests that a critical starting point for many businesses in assessing their role in climate change mitigation is the realisation that this is not just an ethical obligation, but a fantastic business opportunity. The challenge is, they say, to understand how this opportunity can be realised.

They highlight that the bottom line is that saving energy and saving carbon also saves money. The challenges presented by the economic environment are understandably front-of-mind for businesses that are struggling with the tightening of credit markets. In these circumstances, implementing energy efficiency measures is now more essential than ever. Indeed the pressures of the global economy have made energy saving and carbon reduction more important than ever.

To cut carbon a business does not have to invest large sums of capital. Most businesses could save up to 20% on energy bills by taking simple low-cost or no-cost action on energy efficiency. The first step to cutting their carbon emissions is to understand their carbon footprint.

Taking the next step on the low-carbon, low-cost journey requires investment in new, more energy-efficient equipment for businesses. From essential heating and lighting systems to core manufacturing equipment essential business equipment represents a drain of £3.3 billion a year on the bottom lines of smaller and mid-sized businesses (SMEs).

5 ICAEW. (2010, April 9). Climate Change and Corporate Responsibility. Retrieved April 9, 2010, from icaew.com: http://www.icaew.com/index.cfm/route/164289/icaew_ga/en/Technical_and_Business_Topics/Topics/Corporate_responsibility/Resources/Climate_change_and_corporate_responsibility

A lack of available credit through traditional mechanisms need not, however, be an obstacle for SMEs that want to invest in more energy-efficient equipment. For example, in the UK, the 2009 Budget announced £100m of new funding for interest-free Energy Efficiency loans, which allow businesses that have an energy electricity spend below £500,000 a year, or with fewer than 250 employees and a turnover of less than £43m, to replace old, inefficient equipment with new energy saving models.

The ICAEW note that the risks of climate change to business include the following.

- Adverse impacts on business activity due to an increase in the frequency and severity of extreme weather events like droughts, storms and floods. This will result in higher operational costs, for example, insurance, staff health and infrastructure maintenance.
- Regulations aimed at limiting carbon emissions can constitute a risk to businesses that engage in energy-intensive operations. These regulatory frameworks will affect businesses of all type and sizes.
- Businesses face heightened risks from litigation and reputation damage by failing to reduce carbon-intensive activity. In order to maintain competitive advantage, companies need to be prepared for climate risks. The ability to utilise and produce climate-friendly products and services will be a key driver in the competitiveness of companies.
- Global climate change has created new business opportunities arising from increased demand for adaptation products, services and strategies.

  These include:

  - Carbon trading
  - Carbon-offsetting
  - Consultancy
  - Product innovation

The ICAEW believes that cost savings can be achieved through the implementation of emission-reduction schemes and strategies.

BITC offer a brief guide for businesses[6] on how to adapt to climate change, giving practical advice and actions that a business can take to make the business more resilient to the unavoidable impacts of climate change, and improve its ability to recover from severe weather events.

6 BITC. (2010, April 9). Adapting to climate change. Retrieved April 9, 2010, from bitc.org.uk: http://www.bitc.org.uk/environment/the_princes_mayday_network_on_climate_change/the_mayday_journey_on_climate_change/adapting_to_climate_change/adapting_to_climate.html

Severe weather - A recent Chartered Management Institute survey, found that nationally 29% of organisations were affected by extreme weather in the last year, it is estimated that 80% of businesses affected by a major incident never re-open or cease trading within 18 months. Setting up a simple system to record and track the impacts is a useful means of measuring the risks over time.

High temperatures - Prepare for the effect of heat wave conditions on staff comfort, by allowing more flexible working or making simple modifications such as adding blinds to reduce direct sunlight.

Flooding - There has been a major flood every year in the UK for the past decade: this risk is predicted to increase in future years. If your business is located in a flood plain, it has been estimated that you are twice as likely to flood as have a fire. Many actions can be taken to improve your resilience and resistance to flooding. Flooding may not come from rivers. Surface water flooding, caused by ineffective drainage or blockages, may present a serious risk to your business. Check regularly to ensure local drains are not blocked with debris.

Insurance - The average cost of business interruption has increased nearly 60% in 4 years to £35,000. Despite this fact however 33% of small businesses have no business interruption cover and an insurance company sample of over 2,400 businesses established around 90% were under insured. Many smaller businesses are leaseholders of their premises and as such are only required to have contents insurance. Any modifications made by the lease holder may well have to be covered by the contents insurance.

Markets - Many companies may find the weather can impact sales or influence market size either negatively or positively as some products or services could be exploited.

Business Continuity - Companies that have a business continuity plan are statistically far more likely to remain in business following a major incident. Whether this incident comes from fire, flood, equipment failure or key staff incapacitated, a business continuity plan will ensure that the business can function in the event of an emergency. Many insurance companies, local authorities and other organisations provide free guides and templates to assist a business in preparing a plan.

Internal temperatures - If business premises suffer from high internal temperatures from direct sunlight or hot weather, as well as affecting staff comfort, this may also impact on productivity and health and safety. Flexible working arrangements may help reduce the impact this can have on your business, measures include home working and having more flexible working hours.

Travel - Research carried out by the Highways Agency revealed, that 50% of road users would continue with a journey after hearing a severe weather warning. In addition, research found that around a third of road users would not carry out any checks on their vehicles before heading out. Businesses should regularly check their vehicles for road worthiness, even an incorrect tyre pressure can cause extra consumption of fuel.

Utilities - Unlike domestic customers, water companies have no legal requirement to supply companies with water. In the event of shortages - you may find yourself without water. In the event of a widespread severe weather event, supplies may be lost so a business should identify the implications of such an event. Also what would be the implications to the business if it lost its electricity supply?

Suppliers - A business should also Investigate the possibility of having a reciprocal agreement with key suppliers to ensure cooperation in the event of a major incident happening to either party. These include cancelling, delaying or changing delivery addresses. The business should also ensure that it has a sufficient buffer stock to reduce risk in the event of the supply chain breaking down.

Maintenance - A business should ensure that its premises are well a maintained. The risk of a severe weather event impacting your premises will be reduced if regular proactive maintenance schedule is employed.

Assets - Where possible the business should move critical assets from the ground floor (or high off the floor), including paper archives, central IT and communications equipment. It should also incorporate future climate change into capital investment projects.

Data - The business should ensure that it has a reliable and effective archive system, either from a third party or an internal procedure. The business is at risk if all electronic data is not backed up regularly and archived off site. If there is a flood risk important records should not be kept on the ground floor but preferably in a specialist storage facility.

Risk Assessment - Severe weather and future climate change represent a risk to a business just like any other risk. It is important to identify possible hazards that may impact the business, and then assess their risk.

In April 2009 the Trades Union Congress (TUC) recommended that people with management skills should develop strategies to protect their staff from the effects of climate change. The union group published a new report on how organisations in both the public and private sector were responding to the threat of climate change. It found that only one out of 134 organisations interviewed had considered how their staff might be affected.

The report stated that some companies are planning for how they need to change to stay ahead of the competition, but few have given any thought to how climate change could dramatically alter the lives of their employees and have a huge impact on the way they work.

Employers who take the challenge posed by climate change seriously and consider the welfare of their staff as they adapt will reap the benefits with a more motivated, highly skilled and well-equipped workforce the report claimed[7].

Climate change is no longer the preserve of a relatively small number of large companies. Regulation, such as the new CRC Energy Efficiency Scheme, is increasingly making it necessary for more businesses to make carbon management a core function. But businesses are increasingly going the extra mile. A recent CBI member survey showed that 84% of respondents had adopted emissions reduction measures over and above regulatory requirements, because there is a solid business case to do so. This is encouraging. But their analysis also shows there is still more progress to make.

Businesses should more routinely report their emissions, engage their employees in managing office energy use, assess the risks of a changing climate and innovate to exploit new low-carbon opportunities.

To help to address these issues the CBI Climate Change Board[8] was set up in 2008 to deliver the commitments set out in the CBI 2007 climate change taskforce report Climate change: everyone's business. This report recognised that government, business and consumers all have a role to play in making the shift to a low-carbon economy.

The board brings together senior business leaders from a range of sectors to demonstrate business commitment to managing the risk of climate change by:

- promoting business-led policy solutions to realise carbon savings
- showcasing business opportunities for green growth
- leading by example on corporate commitments to manage carbon footprint
- monitoring progress by government and business in realising the UK's carbon targets
- influencing a post-2012 international climate change agreement.

A survey of international finance and sustainability professionals carried out by the Chartered Institute of Management Accountants (CIMA)[9] and Accounting for

7 TUC. (2009, April 24). Employers must do more to protect staff from climate change. Retrieved April 23, 2010, from tuc.org.uk: http://www.tuc.org.uk/economy/tuc-16338-f0.cfm

8 CBI. (2010, April 9). Climate Change Board. Retrieved April 9, 2010, from cbi.org.uk: http://climatechange.cbi.org.uk/cbi-climate-change-board/

9 CIMA. (2009, October 1). Climate change sliding off the corporate radar warns CIMA and Accounting for Sustainability. Retrieved April 9, 2010, from cimaglobal.com: http://www.cimaglobal.com/About-us/Press-office/Press-releases/Press-releases-2009/October/Climate-change-sliding-off-the-corporate-radar-warns-CIMA-and-Accounting-for-Sustainability/

Sustainability, two years on from the Stern Review, found that nearly nine out of ten senior business professionals believed that business has an important role to play in managing the effects of climate change (88%). Despite this, over half of the 900 surveyed believed that their organisations did not see climate change as a strategic priority, with one in five stating that climate change is not on their organisation's agenda at all.

This survey showed that while respondents were aware of the need to engage with the issue of climate change, not enough was being done about it, with a significant proportion saying more could be done to reduce their organisation's environmental impact (63%). Despite nearly three quarters of respondents believing that actively engaging in tacking climate change offers significant business opportunities, nearly half of the respondents either had or planned to scale down environmental initiatives as a result of the economic downturn.

CIMA[10] has long emphasised the key role finance professionals have to play in ensuring organisations consider climate change in a strategic context and integrating sustainability issues into their long-term decision making processes. An encouraging 80% of respondents agreed that the finance function should be engaged in climate change initiatives, although only one third were involved in this area on a formal basis. Reasons given for the finance team's lack of involvement include insufficient communications taking place between different teams (56%) and not having time to get involved in climate change initiatives (40%).

For many businesses, the question of how best to address the challenge of climate change remains largely unanswered. Some businesses have started to report on corporate responsibility matters and many have focused on environmental activities such as increasing their recycling efforts and reducing energy usage. But are organisations really taking the right steps now, to ensure that they can survive in an uncertain future? A future where resources that we take for granted may be scarce or unavailable, and where we will be facing other consequences of climate change, such as droughts, floods and rising sea levels. A number of recent surveys indicate that the answer to this is generally no.

CIMA suggest that the risks and opportunities presented by climate change are beyond normal planning horizons for most organisations. It tends to sit off the radar, creating a risk that climate change falls into a strategic blind spot.

CIMA also state that research has shown that one of the most important reasons why companies fail is that they "miss colossal external changes". Climate change is one such external event that will challenge the survival of businesses. Some organisations will not respond in time and those entities risk corporate failure.

In order to survive, organisations need to adapt their strategy to embed climate change issues into normal business life before it is too costly or too late. CIMA recommend that attention must be focused on the potential impact of climate change on the business, as well as the impact of the business on its environment.

10 CIMA. (2008, March). Sustainability and Climate change. Retrieved April 9, 2010, from cimaglobal.com: http://www.cimaglobal.com/Documents/ImportedDocuments/tech_dispap_Sustainability_climate_change_Mar_2008.pdf

CIMA believes that sustainability is an Enterprise Governance issue, having both conformance and performance aspects. It is about taking a long term view of the organisation's activities in order to create both shareholder and stakeholder value.

The long term risks and opportunities presented by climate change should be addressed when determining strategy, and then in performance management, so that outputs such as environmental metrics and corporate responsibility reporting are aligned to achieving this strategy. With regard to climate change, organisations that want to be successful should be prepared to make changes now, with inspiration, rather than later in desperation.

CIMA has put together a list of actions, split into the dimensions of conformance and performance. These actions are aimed at boards, management accountants and the wider management team working together to incorporate the climate change aspect of sustainability into their organisations' strategy.

CIMA admit that some of these actions will be more challenging to implement than others but generally a business should build on its current activities and skill sets. CIMA suggest that It is a matter of broadening the organisational mind set to encompass climate change issues, applying existing skills to address new challenges.

CIMA suggest the following actions on conformance and performance.

Conformance

- Ensure compliance with environmental legislation, regulations and standards.
- Calculate and track your carbon footprint with the aim of reducing the impact your organisation has on the environment.
- Conduct a risk assessment in relation to the impact climate change could have on your organisation.
- Prepare a stakeholder analysis focusing on climate change and tailor reporting to meet stakeholder needs.

Performance

- Identify opportunities arising from climate change and prepare a business case to develop the organisation's strategy.
- Continuously look for areas that can provide long-term cost savings and efficiency improvements.
- Determine whether your organisation can establish internal charges for energy costs.
- Consider the complete value chain and life-cycle costing when investing in new technologies and processes and exploiting new product opportunities.
- Introduce Key Performance Indicators linked to climate change to drive performance in this area.
- Identify the environmental management information needed to influence long term decision making with regard to climate change.

It should be seen that tackling climate change is not just a question of 'doing the right thing'. Businesses have a duty to their customers, employees and crucially, their shareholders to deliver long-term value and to manage risk. In other words, sustainability has always been a fundamental strategic goal. Managing and mitigating climate change must be embedded into business decision making. When it comes to capital expenditure and investment decisions, for example, it is vital that the principles of sustainable procurement are applied and long-term implications are considered. In other words the financial, environmental and social costs rather than just short-term costs.

Experience has shown that one of the most important reasons companies fail is that they 'miss colossal external changes'. That's a definition that can easily be applied to climate change. Like any risk, however, there are ups and downs and demonstrating a return on investment in climate change management can be difficult. Strategic, long-term goals also play an important part in ensuring continued commitment to long-term sustainability.

Climate risk management needs to be incorporated into mainstream business management strategies and procedures. A 'climate risks champion' with support from senior management, can also assist in driving forward the climate impacts and adaptation agenda throughout the business.

The "Lean and Green" report 2009 from the Chartered Management Institute identified that senior management commitment was the most important driver of environmental management practices, regarded as important or very important by 82% of respondents. Other key factors driving organisations to examine this agenda include cost savings (78%) and regulatory compliance (75%).

Carbon Reduction Strategies

Organisations looking to reduce their carbon impact can take a number of practical steps. The most common 'green' initiative is recycling, which 85 per cent of organisations have introduced with a further 8% likely to introduce it within the next three years.

Over the next three years however, many managers expect to introduce more efficient technologies, including replacing high energy-consuming equipment or introducing energy-efficient IT as well as more video-conferencing, more remote working, and less international travel.

The top three areas that organisations are targeting to cut carbon dioxide emissions are energy usage, followed by recycling measures and fuel usage. More complex management activities, such as managing carbon dioxide emissions from products and services or along the supply chain, are much less common.

The report "Lean and Green: leadership for the low-carbon future" from the Chartered Management Institute identified four cluster or groups of managers.

- **Business Greens (36%)** – managers who seek to integrate sustainability into their business processes on the basis of the benefits to the business. They are proud of their organisation's environmental performance and have a clear understanding of their environmental impact. Notably, this group was significantly better-represented in rapidly growing organisations.

- **Ethical Greens (25%)** – managers who are characterised by strong ethical environmental values rather than market-based or customer-driven business strategies. They, more than any other group, have a deep personal commitment to climate change issues.
- **Customer-focused (21%)** – focused primarily on customers and meeting their expectations. As such, they are sensitive to the potential for changes in consumer choices.
- **Non-Greens (18%)** – follow market trends regardless of the environmental impact of their actions and are very sceptical about climate change. Managers in this cluster were particularly predominant among smaller owner-managed or sole trader companies[11 and 12].

The FTSE4Good Index[13] states that, "The impact of climate change is likely to have an increasing influence on the economic value of companies, both directly, and through new regulatory frameworks. Investors, governments and society in general expect companies to identify and reduce their climate change risks and impacts, and also to identify and develop related business opportunities."

11 CMI. (2009, December 2). UK businesses lack motivation to go green. Retrieved April 15, 2010, from managers.org.uk: http://www.managers.org.uk/news/uk-businesses-lack-motivation-go-green

12 http://www.managers.org.uk/news/behind-times-boardrooms-hold-back-younger-generation%E2%80%99s-bid-go-green.

13 FTSE4Good. (2006, August). Climate Change Consultation. Retrieved April 9, 2010, from ftse.com: http://www.ftse.com/Indices/FTSE4Good_Index_Series/Downloads/FTSE4Good_Climate_Change_Consultation_Aug_06.pdf

Case Study[14]

DuPont was one of the early leaders with regard to climate change as a decade ago they pledged to cut carbon emissions to 65% below their 1990 levels by 2010. That is a little bit more ambitious than the US, which yet refuses to ratify the Kyoto protocol agreeing to cut emissions 7% below 1990 levels by 2010.

The company made its announcement in the name of increasing shareholder value and it has delivered on that promise. The value of DuPont stock increased 340% while the company reduced global emissions by 67%. DuPont's programme has now reduced emissions 80% below 1990 levels. Doing this created a financial saving for the company between 2000 and 2005 of $3 billion. The company's climate protection program showed it costs less to implement energy savings measures than it does to buy and burn fuel, and emit other gasses. In 1999, DuPont estimated that every ton of carbon it displaced saved it $6. By 2007, DuPont's efforts to squeeze out waste were saving the company $2.2 billion a year. The company's profits that year were also $2.2 billion as it is a company that is profitable because it is protecting the climate. The company continues to be profitable.

14 Dupont. (2010, January 26). DuPont Reports Fourth Quarter 2009 EPS of $.48; Increases 2010 Guidance Results Reflect Improving Volumes in all Regions. Retrieved April 15, 2010, from onlinepressroom.net/Dupont/: http://onlinepressroom.net/DuPont/NewsReleases/

CHAPTER 25

The Energy Issue

- A Controllable Cost
- Site Inspection
- Saving Energy and Saving Costs
- New Sources of Energy

A Controllable Cost

Energy is one of the largest controllable costs in most organisations. Because there is usually considerable scope for reducing consumption in buildings, identifying where the saving opportunities lie is often a good way to save money. Being energy efficient is proven to lead to improved profitability. Whether a business takes low-cost actions, or invests in long-term solutions, all cost savings go straight onto the 'bottom line', that is, these savings are pure profit.

Most businesses could use a lot less energy. Energy costs can usually be reduced by 10-20% through simple actions that produce quick returns. A 20% cut in energy costs represents the same bottom line benefit as a 5% increase in sales in many businesses.

A business should endeavour to develop an energy culture and it could do this by employing an energy manager but if it cannot afford one full-time then it should appoint 'champions' to take responsibility for energy. These champions should put energy on the map by checking meters and energy bills and monitor trends, develop an energy-management policy, and report to other senior managers on progress in improving energy efficiency and reducing costs.

The business should also promote understanding as every employee needs to know why energy efficiency is important. The energy champions should communicate that energy saved means money that can be usefully put back into the business, giving the business a valuable advantage. The champions should stress that the business's reputation and sales can be enhanced through active management of energy and carbon emissions and they should also make it clear that acting now will help the business take future regulatory requirements in its stride.

Energy management is not a vague idea as it can have significant benefits for a business, not least in safeguarding profits and employment. When a business raises the issue of energy efficiency among staff it should make sure that it reminds them that it is:

- **good for the bottom line** - all energy savings represent money that would otherwise be wasted. This money can be reinvested in the business
- **good for the business's reputation** - consumers and business customers increasingly expect suppliers to be environmentally responsible. Managing energy use is an excellent demonstration of this
- **good for the environment** - most of the carbon dioxide and other greenhouse gases released in the UK come from energy generation and use. A business that cuts its energy consumption will ultimately help reduce the threat posed by climate change
- **good for the future** - as the need to cut carbon emissions becomes increasingly urgent, it is likely that there will be more regulations even for the smallest businesses. By preparing now, a business can safeguard its operations against forthcoming legislation.

It is important for the business to raise awareness amongst its staff about how much energy they are using. If employees are not aware of the energy they use they are unlikely to save it and if it is easier to waste energy then that is just what they will do. A business should remind its employees that everyone can make a difference. Better training for staff will also help as ultimately employees control the equipment which uses the energy (a fact which is often overlooked by energy managers who look at the equipment only).

A business can communicate its energy saving objectives and targets through the use of posters, e-mails, stickers, events and reward schemes to bring energy efficiency to colleagues' attention. It is often useful to combine a drive for energy efficiency with other environment and health & safety campaigns. An approach that reinforces good working practices or provides incentives for achieving energy efficiency targets is often the best way to convince staff to save energy.

Case Study[1]

Businesses Target Own Employees in Home Insulation Campaign

In an excellent example of the utilisation of the sphere of influence a group of companies joined forces with the UK government in March 2010 as part of a new campaign to get their employees to insulate their homes. Launched by four companies (Sainsbury's, Accenture, Aviva and HSBC) and the UK government through its ACT ON CO2 campaign and the Energy Saving Trust, 'Insulate today' is a pilot project. It aims to incentive 250,000 employees to get their homes insulated and help the government meet its target of getting all lofts and cavity walls in the UK insulated by 2015. If successful, the scheme will be rolled out as larger-scale nationwide employee engagement programme.

Home insulation plays a key part in the government's 'Green Homes, Warmer Homes' strategy, published in March 2010, which aims to get seven million British households benefiting from eco upgrades by 2020 and aims to secure up to 65,000 green jobs.

Government research shows that most homes can save around £160 every year by getting their loft and cavity walls properly insulated, reducing their carbon footprint in the process. But home insulation still remains a low priority for most householders, with less than one in 10 homes having the recommended amount. Last year, the government estimates British households wasted over £500 million in energy bills through poor insulation. Also if all 250,000 employees save £160 the total saving would be £40 million per year which would at least eliminate 8% of that wastage.

1 energy saving trust. (2010, March). Latest news. Retrieved April 23, 2010, from energysavingtrust.org.uk: http://www.energysavingtrust.org.uk/corporate/Corporate-and-media-site/Media-centre/Latest-news

Site Inspection ●●●

A basic physical site inspection is recommended by the Carbon Trust[2] as it helps a business to identify all kinds of energy saving opportunities. The following areas could be looked at and the business could try to answer the suggested questions.

Heating

- Are thermostats working and set to the lowest comfortable temperature?
- Are there any cold draughts from windows or doors?
- Are windows and doors open when heating or air conditioning is on?

Heating typically accounts for about half of the energy used in offices and forms a significant proportion of energy use in other areas of a business. It is a key area to target with energy saving measures. Many businesses are overheated which can cause discomfort and wastes money. For every 1°C that a business overheats in its premises, it adds 8% to its heating costs!

Lighting

- Are you still using traditional tungsten light bulbs?
- Are lamps, fittings and roof lights clean?
- Are lights switched off if there is sufficient daylight or rooms are not in use?
- Do you have any old large diameter fluorescent tube lights?

There are many simple and inexpensive ways to reduce the energy consumption and costs associated with lighting without compromising health and safety or comfort levels. Lighting in a typical office costs about £3/m^2 annually, but in the most efficient office only costs about £1/m^2 and lighting a typical office overnight wastes enough energy to heat water for 1,000 cups of tea.

In the office

- Are computers left on overnight?
- Are monitors switched off when not in use, such as during lunch breaks?

Businesses rely on a range of office equipment. From computers and photocopiers to teleconference facilities, these items have become integral to daily activity. However, it is not always appreciated how much this equipment can cost a company. A computer and flat screen monitor left on 24 hours a day will cost around £50 a year. Switching them off out of hours and enabling standby features could reduce this to less than £15 a year and prolong the lifespan of equipment. A photocopier left on overnight uses enough energy to make over 5,000 A4 copies. On average, 20% of the total energy bill in commercial offices is accounted for by office equipment – about half of this use stems from PCs and monitors.

2 Carbon Trust. (2010, April 12). Energy Management Factsheet. Retrieved April 12, 2010, from carbontrust.co.uk: http://www.carbontrust.co.uk/Publications/pages/publicationdetail.aspx?id=GIL136

In the Factory

- Are pumps, fans or compressed air switched off when the equipment they serve is not in use?
- Can you hear compressed air leaks?

If you spot any of these, take action.

There are some excellent opportunities for energy saving that can be made on the factory floor or in the warehouse. The exact equipment used and the processes will be unique to each business, however it is possible to highlight a few common areas in which opportunities can often be found.

Firstly, compressed air. Many factories run their compressor for most of the day, even when compressed air is not needed, and are unaware of how much this is costing them. Staff should be encouraged to switch the compressor off when not in use.

Is electrical equipment left running when it is not being used? Conveyor systems, machine tools and other equipment should be switched off when not in use. Higher Efficiency Motors now cost no more than normal ones and can save 3-5% of the running cost. In many cases, using a Variable Speed Drive (VSD) to reduce the speed of a pump or fan by just 20% can halve its running cost. Refrigeration motors can consume their purchase price in energy costs in just a few weeks!

Monitoring Energy

Metering and monitoring are at the heart of energy management as the business needs the information to tell when and where it is saving money. With metering, a business can account for costs, assess performance and quickly spot the cause of expensive problems, such as faulty or ageing equipment.

The business should try to use real numbers as energy bills can often be estimated and so cannot be relied upon for accuracy. The business should check every bill as soon as it comes in and compare it with the meters on its premises to gain actual figures and it may even spot expensive mistakes on its bills. The business should also use bills and meter readings to find out how its energy is being used. It should try to identify patterns, such as cold weather and changes in operating practice to explain differences in energy consumption. It is always useful to compare bills from previous years to provide a benchmark and help gauge progress. Looking at energy bills and taking regular meter readings helps to track how energy is being used and to take control of energy costs. Using a meter to help monitor your energy typically identifies energy savings of more than 5%.

Case Study[3 and 4]

Barclays PLC - Working with Energy on Climate Change

Barclays' Climate Action Programme has given the company the structure to tackle climate change and access new markets. To achieve this, Barclays has developed a five step Climate Action Programme.

1. **Reduce CO2 emissions by improving energy efficiency** – Barclays has committed to multi-million pound investment in energy efficiency.
2. **Buy renewable energy** – EDF Energy provided Barclays with 300 GWh of renewable energy each year for the next three years.
3. **Make UK operations carbon neutral by offsetting remaining emissions** – Barclays has made its UK operations carbon neutral by offsetting 223,000 tonnes of CO2 emissions in 2006 and is now working progressively towards overall carbon neutrality across worldwide operations.
4. **Develop products and services that help customers reduce their own climate change impacts** – Barclays is a market leader in carbon trading, is one of the largest providers of long-term finance for the Western European renewable energy sector and has launched the UK's first carbon-neutral debit card, issued to all 11 million users.
5. **Engage with key stakeholders and contribute to the debate on climate change action** – Barclays has engaged with government, NGOs, employees, media and investors.

To support this Programme, Barclays produced 'The Rough Guide to Saving Energy', distributed to 60,000 employees, launched a website with information on Barclays' climate change activities and a joint website with Climate Care to allow customers to offset their air travel emissions.

Impact

- In the UK in 2006, Barclays reduced CO2 emissions from offices and buildings by 3% per full-time equivalent employee and reduced overall carbon intensity by 4%.
- Barclays' carbon footprint was reduced by up to 125,000 tonnes of CO2 per year over the next three years through the purchase of renewable energy.

3 BITC. (2010, April 12). Barclays PLC - Working with energy on climate change. Retrieved April 12, 2010, from bitc.org.uk: http://www.bitc.org.uk/resources/case_studies/afe1348_icc06_barc.html

4 Barclays. (2009). Reducing emissions from buildings. Retrieved April 12, 2010, from group.barclays.com: http://group.barclays.com/Sustainability/Citizenship/Environment/Reducing-our-environmental-impact/Editorial/1225802843269.htm

- Barclays' energy-efficiency investments in 2006 delivered financial savings of £500,000 p.a.
- Half of Barclays UK electricity consumption now comes from renewable sources, compared with 3 per cent previously.
- If everyone who receives the 'Rough Guide to Saving Energy' saves one tonne of CO2, the equivalent of taking 16,000 cars off the road each year would be saved in emissions.

In 2009 Barclays invested more money to improve energy efficiency throughout the business. The benefits were two-fold as reducing wasted energy not only yields environmental benefits but it also results in cost savings through reduced energy use.

The "powerPerfector" device optimises the energy supplied to a building, reducing consumption and in turn reducing carbon emissions. Following a successful pilot scheme in 2008 where the technology was introduced to five high street branches, in 2009 the trial was extended to nine branches of Barclays. Results demonstrated an average energy saving of 13% per site. Annually this equates to 166 tonnes of carbon dioxide and cost savings of more than £30,000 across the branches. Proposals to introduce powerPerfectors at 30 further Barclays sites were being considered for 2010. As well as its environmental benefits, the powerPerfector also helps prolong the life of electrical equipment, by protecting it from energy surges.

Saving Energy and Saving Costs

Rising energy prices and higher taxes are the biggest worries facing British businesses in 2010 after the state of the economy, according to research released in January 2010 by the Carbon Trust. The research showed that 61% of respondents in the survey of 700 businesses said they were worried about the unstable economy while around half (49%) said they worry about energy price rises. The same number admitted to worrying about rises in tax.

Concerns about energy prices are highest in industries with high energy use such as construction (55%), manufacturing (53%) and hospitality (52%). Far fewer businesses are worried about a possible change in government (20%) or complying with environmental legislation (13%).

The extent of business worries over energy prices was revealed as the Carbon Trust initiated a drive to persuade British businesses to stop wasting over £3bn of energy every year. Over 40% of the businesses interviewed said that one of their New Year resolutions was to reduce the amount of energy their business uses.

The "Best Advice" campaign, launched by the chairman of the Kingfisher group which includes B&Q, calls on businesses to take the first step to cutting their energy wastage through a free Carbon Survey from the Carbon Trust. The Carbon Survey, available free of charge to all businesses that spend between £50,000 and £3million on energy each year, provides the services of an energy expert on site and a tailored energy-saving action plan. It typically identifies possible savings on energy costs of between 20% and 30%.

Businesses that have already taken advantage of the service and cut their energy bills as a result include organic food supplier Abel & Cole, The Lowry Hotel in Manchester and landscaping product manufacturer Marshalls (who will be featured more extensively in Chapter 30). B&Q has significantly cut its energy costs and made a carbon saving of 10,000 tonnes of CO2 by working with the Carbon Trust since 2008. The company has engaged staff to save energy and improved heating and lighting, as well as through improvements to buildings.

Case Study[5]

In September 2006 B&Q launched its energy campaign "Energy efficiency made easy at B&Q" bringing wind turbines to the UK mass market for the first time and energy efficient advice booklets, TV advertising and an online advertising campaign to raise awareness.

B&Q has also improved its energy management in stores, introducing automatic energy use monitoring systems, high frequency energy efficient lighting, automatic dimming controls and 15% roof lights. B&Q has also set up performance league tables to enable comparison of site energy use.

In addition the company is working to increase climate change awareness amongst employees through environmental road shows attended by some 4,000 employees in 2006 and a discounted rate for home energy monitors for staff.

To extend its impact further, B&Q is working with its supply chain. QUEST audits and evaluates vendor understanding and performance of Quality, Environmental and Ethical issues and includes requirements contained in the Energy Using Products Buying Standard.

Impact

- Reduction in electricity usage 18.8GWh; resultant cost saving £1.3m.
- Reduction in store emissions for comparable periods 7,246 tonnes CO2; percentage reduction 4.1%.
- TV advertising resulted in over 5 million energy-saving brochures being requested.

5 BITC. (2010, April 12). B&Q plc - Energy efficiency made easy at B&Q. Retrieved April 12, 2010, from bitc.org.uk: http://www.bitc.org.uk/resources/case_studies/afe1473_icc07_bq.html

- It was estimated that the store energy-use monitoring system would help to reduce B&Q's CO2 emissions by 7,000 tonnes in the year 2006/07.
- The 2006 energy efficiency campaign reached a potential audience of 143 million people.

B&Q was the only retailer in the top five most visited sites after searches for 'wind turbines' and diy.com was one of only two retailers in the top five.

The Carbon Trust's Best Advice survey also asked business people who had given them the best piece of business advice they ever received and which famous business person they would turn to for advice given the chance. Only 16% of respondents said their bank manager or accountant had given them the best business advice. Far more said it had been a colleague (38%), a good friend (36%) or their boss (32%).

Since 2006, the Carbon Trust has delivered over £180m in energy savings to British businesses through its Carbon Surveys. The Carbon Trust estimates that British businesses currently spending between £50,000 and £3m on their annual energy bills could reduce their collective energy spend by more than £3bn by implementing energy saving actions of the type specified in Carbon Trust surveys[6].

In May 2009 a new Carbon Trust map showing potential for £2.5 billion in cost savings across the UK was released as part of its 'One Million A Day' campaign which urged businesses of all sizes to prioritise actions to kick-start immediate energy savings, reduce carbon emissions and make significant direct cost savings.

Backed by a Dragons' Den entrepreneur, the campaign's target is to help save the UK economy £1 billion over the following three years and reduce the UK's carbon emissions by at least 17m tonnes of CO2 - the equivalent to annual emissions from heating nearly 5.5 million average UK homes. The estimated national total of savings is thought to be £2.53bn with a range of cost savings from £124.6m to £276.8m per region[7].

6 Carbon Trust. (2010, January 27). British businesses feel the heat of rising costs. Retrieved April 12, 2010, from carbontrust.co.uk: http://www.carbontrust.co.uk/news/news/press-centre2010/2010/Pages/british-businesses-feel-heat-rising-costs.aspx

7 Carbon Trust. (2009, May 1). Ed Milliband encourages businesses to go green with new funding for business to save energy. Retrieved April 12, 2010, from carbontrust.co.uk: http://www.carbontrust.co.uk/news/news/press-centre/2009/Pages/UK-Cost-Map-News.aspx

In September 2009 the Carbon Trust announced the launch of the "Big Business Refit" campaign which aims to help thousands of small and medium sized businesses drive down their costs by as much as £40m through this new initiative. The Big Business Refit will offer SMEs expert advice and financial support to slash their energy costs by scrapping old inefficient equipment and replacing it with new energy efficient models.

In the first six months of 2009, hundreds of SMEs from bakeries to plastics factories were given loans at zero-interest to equip their businesses with the latest energy-saving technology. As a result, they are saving an average of £14,000 each on their annual energy bills – a collective total of almost £6m a year.

The top choices among the small and medium businesses that took a Carbon Trust loan in the first six months of 2009 were:

- new energy efficient lighting and lighting controls, a key way for any business to save money, (provided annual savings of nearly £1m)
- replacement air compressors, used for powering pneumatic tools, (provided annual energy savings of £400,000)
- mechanised materials handling equipment, such as cranes, which are used to load heavy equipment, (provided annual savings of £400,000)[8].

By the end of March 2010 the Carbon Trust confirmed that through the Big Business Refit campaign it had funded £60m of energy efficient equipment upgrades for Small and Medium Sized Enterprises (SMEs) through its interest-free loan scheme. Since April 2009 more than 1,847 businesses in the UK have used the scheme to replace old energy equipment and to cut back on energy costs. By making the switch to the new energy efficient equipment these SMEs collectively save £20m per year as well as 130,000 tonnes of CO2.

8 Carbon Trust. (2009, August 26). Small businesses flick the switch on £6m of wasted energy. Retrieved April 12, 2010, from cabontrust.co.uk: http://www.carbontrust.co.uk/news/news/press-centre/2009/Pages/big-business-refit.aspx

Case Study[9]

Local Councils Join Forces to Cut Carbon and Slash Energy Bills

In September 2009 the Carbon Trust launched the "East Midlands Carbon Management Programme" supported by the East Midlands Improvement and Efficiency Partnership meaning that ten local authorities in the East Midlands joined a new programme which could help them to reduce their carbon emissions by 13,000 tonnes a year and cut their annual energy bills by £2million or more. The ten authorities worked together over the next three months to develop clear action plans to save both cash and carbon.

The Carbon Trust has already supported over 260 local authorities – more than half the UK's total - in reducing their carbon emissions, identifying annual savings of more than £120 million and 1.2 million tonnes of carbon dioxide per year. The participants in the East Midlands Carbon Management Programme can expect to reduce their energy bills by up to 25 per cent as a result of implementing energy efficiency projects.

9 Carbon Trust. (2009, September 28). Local Councils join forces to cut carbon and slash energy bills. Retrieved April 12, 2010, from carbontrust.co.uk: http://www.carbontrust.co.uk/news/news/press-centre/2009/Pages/local-councils-join-forces.aspx

New Sources of Energy

The government's Renewable Energy Strategy outlines its plans to decarbonise the UK's energy supply by sourcing 15% of all energy from renewable sources by 2020 and by providing incentives to invest in renewable electricity, heat and transport fuel. In addition most electricity generation is subject to emissions caps and carbon pricing via the EU Emissions Trading Scheme.

For energy intensive operations, including fossil fuel electricity generation, the EU Emissions Trading Scheme (EU ETS) puts a cap on carbon dioxide emissions and creates a market and price for carbon allowances.

The Renewable Energy Strategy defines how the UK aims to increase the amount of energy it sources from renewables from 1% to 15% of total energy use by 2020[10].

The Association of Chartered Certified Accountants (ACCA)[11] highlighted the importance of the move to a low-carbon economy in their "Mitigation: Climate Change Briefing Paper" published in September 2009. They identified the growing

10 Carbon Trust. (2010, April 12). Energy supply. Retrieved April 12, 2010, from carbontrust.co.uk: http://www.carbontrust.co.uk/policy-legislation/energy-supply/pages/low-carbon-energy.aspx

11 ACCA. (2009, September). Mitigation: Climate Change Briefing Paper. Retrieved April 12, 2010, from accaglobal.com: http://www.accaglobal.com/pubs/general/activities/subjects/climate/projects/briefing_papers/tech-ccb-mit.pdf

propensity of consumers to 'buy green' which in turn highlights the business opportunity that the move to a low-carbon economy will create for businesses in all sectors.

One of the most fundamental changes that ACCA say needs to be seen, both in the UK and internationally, is the emergence of a new, low-carbon energy industry with significantly reduced reliance on fossil fuels. To meet the EU targets of generating 15% of its total energy supply from renewable resources by 2020, up from less than 5% in 2009, the UK will need to take a giant step forward in enabling key renewable technologies, such as offshore wind and marine energy, to reach commercial maturity.

The paper states that, fortunately, the UK is in a strong position to accelerate the development of these technologies. With Europe's largest wind, wave and tidal resources, as well as extensive engineering expertise, exploiting these resources will offer major economic development opportunities for UK-based companies.

In fact, analysis has shown that by taking a bold new approach to commercialisation of clean technologies, the UK could generate up to £70 billion for the economy and almost 250,000 jobs in offshore wind and wave power alone. This same offshore wind and wave alone could also provide at least 15% of the total carbon savings required to meet the UK's 2050 targets.

The ACCA paper also reported that recent research indicates this 'clean tech' revolution has begun and some green roots have been planted. United Nations Environment Programme data released in 2009 showed that overall, renewable energy investment in 2008 was more than four times greater than in 2004. Global investments in renewable energy overtook those in carbon-based fuels for the first time in 2008 with the overall market for clean technologies that year valued at some £3 trillion.

ACCA hopes that this new policy framework will now drive the action and investment needed from business as this will create an environment where sustainable economic growth can be a reality. Critically, it will also mean that organisations globally can not only contribute to the fight against climate change but also benefit from doing so in both the short and long term.

In line with this desire to find solutions in new technology, The Carbon Trust realise that substantial CO2 reductions in industry will only be made possible by getting to the very heart of manufacturing processes, which can account for between 50-90% of a manufacturing company's energy consumption. That is why they have been working directly with a number of industry sectors in a unique collaboration known as the "Industrial Energy Efficiency Accelerator". By bringing together key players in each sector, they are driving innovation in process control and the uptake of low-carbon technologies to deliver a step-change reduction in emissions.

Industry is responsible for 25% of the UK's total CO2 emissions. At the Carbon Trust, their experience suggests that with the right technologies and support, some industry sectors could go further than they have to date and make energy savings of more than 20%. To achieve this, they will be working with a diverse range of large and medium scale industry sectors. For any organisation, energy savings equate to cost savings, so the benefits to business, industry sectors and the UK as a whole are many.

The Carbon Trust's Industrial Energy Efficiency Accelerator works by first identifying, and then addressing the barriers to implementation of opportunities for emissions reduction in industrial processes in a three stage approach.

- **Step 1** – Examination of specific processes in depth to understand energy use and interfaces with other systems falling into three themes product strategy, processes and equipment.
- **Step 2** – Gathering evidence to support a business case for implementing energy-efficiency opportunities.
- **Step 3** – Promoting the uptake of their demonstrated solutions.

In 2008/09 they completed Stage 1 with three pilot industry sectors: Animal Feed Milling, Asphalt Manufacture and Plastic Bottle Blow Moulding. They are now taking these sectors on to Stages 2 and 3 and rolling out Stage 1 to a further 20 sectors including Bakeries, Brick Manufacturing, Confectionery, Dairies, Maltsters, Microelectronics and Paper[12].

The Carbon Trust's "Technology Accelerators" aim to accelerate deployment of technology sectors that are on a path towards full commercialisation but where there are significant barriers to uptake. They identify and address market and regulatory barriers to deployment, and this often involves large-scale monitored demonstrations and widespread dissemination of findings to industry and government. Current areas of work are as follows[13].

Industrial Energy Efficiency Accelerator	Step-change reduction in emissions from industrial processes through innovation in process control
Marine Renewables Proving Fund	Accelerating the leading and most promising marine devices
Offshore Wind Accelerator	Initiative with five international energy companies that aims to reduce the cost of energy from offshore wind by 10%+
Biomass Heat Accelerator	Engaging identified sites to install up to 30 optimised systems
Marine Energy Accelerator	Accelerating progress in cost reduction of marine energy (wave and tidal stream energy) technologies
Buildings Accelerators	Refurbishments of existing stock and new low-carbon buildings

12 Carbon Trust. (2010, April 12). Industrial Energy Efficiency Accelerator. Retrieved April 12, 2010, from carbontrust.co.uk: • http://www.carbontrust.co.uk/emerging-technologies/current-focus-areas/IEEA/Pages/industrial-energy-efficiency-accelerator.aspx

13 Carbon Trust. (2010, April 12). Technology Accelerator. Retrieved April 12, 2010, from carbontrust.co.uk: http://www.carbontrust.co.uk/emerging-technologies/current-focus-areas/Pages/Technology%20Accelerators.aspx

Industrial Energy Efficiency Accelerator	Step-change reduction in emissions from industrial processes through innovation in process control
Micro Combined Heat and Power Accelerator	Large scale trial into the use of micro-CHP units
Advanced Metering Accelerator	Completed study on the use of advanced metering
Marine Energy Challenge	Development and increased understanding of wave and tidal stream energy technologies

Case Study[14]

Sainsbury's Finds Way to Grow Without Adding to Carbon Footprint

Sainsbury's has found a way to address the conflict of commercial expansion without adding to its carbon footprint – by building an extension to an existing store that has the effect of reducing the overall energy used by the larger site. Sainsbury's Durham store, adds 50 per cent more space to the building, but energy required to run the larger store, because of introduction of energy efficiency measures and on-site renewable technologies, will fall by 10 per cent. Sainsbury's says this means the carbon generated in building the extension will be neutralised after just two years.

The development is significant, because research shows that despite having environmental policies in place, most of the UK's leading retailers have increased their absolute carbon footprint because of commercial expansion in recent years. The report, published last October by market research company Mintel, looked at 12 leading retailers and found that most of them had increased their absolute carbon footprints due to expansion of their square footage and/or increasing their opening times.

The 'carbon negative' impact of the new extension has been brought about in part by a first among leading UK retailers in onsite renewable power generation – a biomass boiler that burns wood pellets made from waste wood that would otherwise have been sent to landfill sites.

The Durham store extension is also the first Sainsbury's building to use CO2 refrigeration, a move first announced by the retailer in November 2009 in a bid to phase out F gas refrigeration in favour of the more environmentally responsible CO2. This measure will help reduce the company's carbon footprint by around a third.

14 J Sainsbury plc. (2010, March 29). Sainsbury's "carbon-negative" store extension. Retrieved April 23, 2010, from jsainsbury.co.uk: http://www.jsainsburys.co.uk/index.asp?PageID=424&section=&Year=2010&NewsID=1267

New legislation means all new commercial developments will have to be zero carbon by 2019 and the extension to the Durham store helps to address this upcoming regulation. However, it also addresses the problem of how to reduce the carbon footprint of existing buildings and for this reason has been welcomed by the UK Green Building Council.

"Existing buildings account for 17 per cent of the UK's total carbon emissions and need to be in the front line of our efforts to tackle climate change," said Paul King, chief executive of the UK Green Building Council.

Sainsbury's ground-breaking Durham store shows that it is possible to grow your business – in this case increasing the size of the store by 50 per cent – and still reduce net carbon emissions. While it is essential that we build the most efficient new buildings, the real challenge lies in the 98 per cent that are already in use.

The Mintel report suggested that the quickest way to address the conflict between commercial expansion and reducing an organisation's carbon footprint was through the introduction of renewable energy.

Case Study

Offshore Wind-farms to be Used for Air Defence

As a possible example of the benefits of systemic or "linking thinking" it was announced in May 2010 that offshore wind farms will double as radar defence systems in a pioneering deal involving the Ministry of Defence, which previously opposed the erection of almost 1,000 wind turbines off the UK's eastern seaboard because of fears over their ability to scramble defensive radar.

Wind energy projects across Britain have been held up for years because of planning disagreements, some concerned with interference from turbines that can baffle air-traffic control and defence systems, creating blind spots or "blackout zones" in coverage.

The wind-driven turbine blades can rotate at up to 200mph, mimicking on-screen the appearance of slow-moving aircraft and showing up as a blur of images. Simply discounting the clutter is dangerous because the images obscure patches from which planes could suddenly emerge; there are fears that hijacked airliners or bombers could evade detection.

But now the wind farm industry will spend at least £16m on advanced radar defence systems to be integrated into new offshore wind farms, clearing the way for a significant boost in the UK's supply of renewable energy.

CHAPTER 26

Natural Capital

- Scarce Resources
- Peak Oil and Peak Water
- Economics and Biodiversity
- Natural Capitalism

> *A 'perfect storm' of food shortages, scarce water and high-cost energy will hit the global economy before 2030. Factor in accelerating climate change and this lethal cocktail leads to public unrest, cross-border conflict and mass migration – in other words, an economic and political collapse that will make today's economic recession seem very tame indeed.*

The UK government's chief scientific adviser, John Beddington in March 2010.

Scarce Resources

Natural capital consists of the earth's natural resources and the ecological systems that support society and life itself, many of which have no known substitutes. Despite this, current business practices often fail to take into account the value of these assets – which increases with their scarcity.

This leads to natural capital being eroded by the wasteful use of resources such as energy, materials, water, fibre and topsoil.

As the UK's financial debts have built up so have its debts to nature in terms of the unsustainable depletion of natural resources. Businesses know that liquidating capital assets to fuel consumption is a problem but they do not seem to know how to stop it. It has been suggested that the self-same abuses of debt-driven 'casino capitalism' that have caused the global economy to collapse also lie behind the impending collapse of the natural capital on which society ultimately depends.

Case Study[1]

Big Business Leaves Big Forest Footprints

Consumers around the globe are not aware that they are "eating" rainforests as many every-day purchases are driving the destruction of the vital tropical ecosystems. Burning tropical forests drives global warming faster than the world's entire transport sector; there will be no solution to climate change without stopping deforestation.

A report published in 2010 by Forest Footprint Disclosure revealed for the first time how global business is driving rainforests to destruction in order to provide things for consumers to eat. It also revealed what businesses are doing to try to lighten their forest footprint which at the moment is not very much.

Consumers "eat" rainforests each day in the form of beef-burgers, bacon and beauty products but without knowing it. Because of growing demand for beef, soy and palm oil, which are in much of what we consume, as well as timber and bio-fuels, rain forests are worth more cut down than standing up. Governments, which claim to own 70% of them, create prosperity for their nations through this process, but poor forest communities need their forests for energy and food.

The report shows that the EU is the largest importer of soy in the world, much of it coming from Brazil and it also shows that after China, the EU is the biggest importer of palm oil in the world. Soy provides cheap food to fatten pigs and chickens, while palm oil is used in everything from cakes and cookies, to fine skin moisturisers.

Some of the farms in Brazil can boast 50 combines abreast at harvest time, marching across prairies where once the most diverse ecosystem on Earth stood. Further north, thousands of square miles of rainforest natural capital is going up in smoke each year, often illegally, to provide pastureland for just one cow per hectare to supply beef hungry Brazilians or more prosperous mouths in China and India. Many of the hides from these cattle then go into the designer trainers, handbags or luxury car upholstery that wealthy markets have such an appetite for. Few Europeans know that their fine steak or choice after dinner mints might have an added expense on the other side of the world that unknown to them, is altering life on Earth.

All of this matters for three reasons. Firstly, evolution is being changed forever and secondly, burning tropical forests drives global warming faster than the world's entire transport sector. Finally, losing forests may undermine food, energy and climate security whilst it is estimated that saving them could reduce environmental costs by $3-5 trillion per year.

1 BBC News. (2010, February 16). Big business leaves big forest footprints. Retrieved April 12, 2010, from news.bbc.co.uk: http://news.bbc.co.uk/1/hi/sci/tech/8516931.stm

The impact global business has on deforestation will be a key factor in halting deforestation in the future. This was why the Forest Footprint Disclosure project was launched in 2009 to invite companies to first recognise their impact on forests and then disclose what they were doing about it...

In 2009 the report “Time to Pay the Bill” and also Greenpeace's “Slaughtering the Amazon” highlighted the cattle industry as a driver of climate change responsible for the bulk of Brazil's greenhouse gases through deforestation and methane emissions from 180 million cows. This resulted in the withdrawal of a $60m loan from the World Bank's International Finance Corporation to Brazil's largest exporter of beef. In June 2009, Brazil's major supermarkets all announced they would no longer accept beef from ranches involved in deforestation and in July 2009 sportswear manufacturer Nike said it would not accept leather in its products from Brazil if it came from deforested areas. Consumers and businesses can play their part by demanding that their suppliers know where their "Forest Risk Commodities" come from.

Curbing emissions from deforestation, which was the outsider in the UN negotiations just two years ago, has moved to become the front-runner. It is now widely recognised that forests offer the quickest, most cost-effective and largest means of curbing global emissions between now and 2030.

Conservation will never out-compete commerce with a global population rising toward nine billion. Feeding and fuelling our growing world is one of the greatest opportunities of the 21st century, but sending natural capital up in smoke and squandering ecosystems that support wealth creation in the process will, ultimately, be counterproductive. Businesses that understand this will be the rising stars of the future. Investors will want to spot them.

If the world wishes to overcome the financial crisis, avoid the next collapse, and lift its people out of poverty, the way business is done must change. Reducing environmental damage and restoring intact ecosystems is the essential basis if society is to create future prosperity. Businesses and governments can either drive change in ways that allow companies and economies to flourish or they will be forced respond to resultant crises and hope for the best.

The CBI's report “The Shape of Business: the next ten years”[2] warns that In addition, growing tensions over potential scarcity and distributional problems for many primary resources (for example, food, water, land and oil) will put pressure on business costs and operating models. In extreme circumstances they also fear that some of the environmental and population-driven changes such as those affecting food supplies are likely to lead to a rise in protectionism, social unrest and political instability. This

2 CBI. (2009). The Shape of Business: the next ten years. London: CBI.

will limit access to markets and some key resources and this will restrict business's freedom to operate and could put a brake on further development of globalisation trends that have been important for business over the past two decades. Volatility in the oil price over the next ten years will also be disruptive for business at the very least, affecting companies' ability to plan and invest.

In some sectors, the cost and availability of key minerals in the next ten years will be a major driver of innovation and change. For example, world lithium demand was approximately 80,000 tonnes in 2002, was 110,000 tonnes in 2009 and is projected to reach nearly 300,000 tonnes per year by 2020, driven predominantly by the demand for electric and hybrid vehicle batteries. But, while lithium sources are relatively plentiful and the challenge is mainly to produce material of sufficient quality, supplies of neodymium and other rare earth elements required for the high strength magnets used in electric motors has now become seriously restricted. This is because China has placed an export ban on the raw material. Again, the consequences are increased cost and uncertainty for business.

The report also highlights that at home the UK also faces serious challenges in energy security and supply with 42% of the country's power generating capacity due to reach retirement age between 2009 and 2020. This may influence business decisions about the location of certain activities and supply chain elements.

Peak Oil and Peak Water ●●●

A group of leading business people in February 2010 called for urgent action to prepare the UK for "Peak Oil". The second report of the UK Industry Taskforce on Peak Oil and Energy Security (ITPOES)[3] found that oil shortages, insecurity of supply and price volatility will destabilise economic, political and social activity potentially by 2015. Peak Oil refers to the point where the highest practicable rate of global oil production has been achieved and from which future levels of production will either plateau, or begin to diminish. This means an end to the era of cheap oil.

The report, "The Oil Crunch - a wake-up call for the UK economy", urged the formation of a coalition of government, business and consumers to address the issue. The Taskforce stated that the impact of Peak Oil will include sharp increases in the cost of travel, food, heating and retail goods. It found that the transport sector will be particularly hard hit, with more vulnerable members of society the first to feel the impact. The Taskforce warned that the UK must not be caught out by the oil crunch as it was with the credit crunch and states that policies to address Peak Oil must be a priority for any government.

Having assessed the systemic changes caused by the global economic recession, coupled with the projected growth from non-OECD countries, ITPOES predicts Peak Oil will occur within the next decade, potentially by 2015 at less than 95 million barrels per day. (In 2008, production levels were 85 million barrels per day.) The study finds that the recession has delayed the oil crunch by two years. This provides

3 ARUP. (2010, February 10). Business calls foraction on 'oil crunch' front. Retrieved April 23, 2010, from arup.com: http://www.arup.com/News/2010-02_February/10_Feb_2010_Action_On_Peak_Oil_Crunch_Threat_To_UK_Economy.aspx

invaluable time to plan for a future which will see structural increases in oil prices coupled with shortages and increased market volatility. The UK will be particularly badly hit by these factors with a tightening of supply leading to greater oil import dependency, rising and volatile prices, inflationary pressures and the risk of disruption to the transport system.

Key recommendations from the report included the acceleration of the "green transport revolution" to see the ongoing introduction of lower carbon technology and trials of sustainable bio fuels. This would cover private vehicles, but will also extend to the general transport network, with the government urged not to cut investment in public transport. A focus on new clean technologies should be combined with wide scale behavioural change promoted through incentives and education to produce a modal shift to greener modes of transport.

The Taskforce recognises that oil demand in the OECD area (developed countries) is now flat or declining but also recognises that demand in non-OECD (developing countries) continues to expand rapidly, having already recovered from the recession. Demand in the non-OECD areas already accounts for 45% of global oil demand and is expected to reach 50% by the middle of the decade.

The report issued a range of recommendations including the following.

General policies

- Government, local authorities and business must face up to the Peak Oil threat and put contingency plans in place.
- A package of policies is required to deal with the economic, financial and social impact of potential high oil prices.
- There is a need to accelerate the green industrial revolution.

Transport

- Government support should be boosted for alternative technological solutions and associated infrastructure, such as electric vehicles.
- Policies and fiscal measures to support and incentivise a shift from the traditional car to more fuel- and carbon-efficient modes of transport to be established.
- Government investment in public transport must be maintained.

Power generation and distribution policies

- Government must provide a stable pro-investment regulatory and political climate.
- The nation's power generation and transmission distribution infrastructure must be changed to adapt to new demand patterns, price spikes and supply interruption.

Retail and agriculture

Measures must be taken to protect the public, particularly the most disadvantaged, from the impact of rising fuel costs on food and other consumer goods prices.

> *As we reach the maximum rate of oil extraction, the era of cheap oil is behind us. We must plan for a world in which oil prices are likely to be both higher and more volatile and where oil price shocks have the potential to destabilise economic, political and social activity.*

Philip Dilley, Chairman of Arup.

However, contradictory reports published in the media in March 2010 showed that green fuels potentially cause more harm than fossil fuels and using fossil fuel in vehicles is better for the environment than so-called green fuels made from crops. The findings show that the Department for Transport's target for raising the level of biofuel in all fuel sold in Britain will result in millions of acres of forest being logged or burnt down and converted to plantations. A government study concludes that some of the most commonly-used biofuel crops fail to meet the minimum sustainability standard set by the European Commission.

Under this standard, each litre of biofuel should reduce emissions by at least 35 per cent compared with burning a litre of fossil fuel. Yet the study shows that palm oil increases emissions by 31 per cent because of the carbon released when forest and grassland is turned into plantations. Rape seed and soy also fail to meet the standard. The Renewable Transport Fuels Obligation requires that 3¼ per cent of all fuel sold should come from crops in 2010. The proportion is due to increase each year and by 2020 is required to be 13 per cent.

Water is also in danger of becoming an even more scarce resource than it already is and there is a growing concern that "Peak Water" is also a very strong possibility and although China and India are rapidly developing as major industrial powers they may yet be thwarted in this growth by a shortage of water.

Access to water supply and sanitation is a fundamental human need. Water is vital for the well-being and health of humankind and nature, yet it is an increasingly threatened resource. The growing pollution of global water reserves and more widespread water scarcity due to human activities, an increasing world population with a greater demand for water and climate change will create major threats to food production, human health, the natural environment and economic development at a global level.

Oil and Water Compared

Oil	Water
Finite resource	Literally finite, but could be unlimited in we were prepared to pay the cost
Non-renewable resource	Renewable overall, but could be non-renewable in some areas
Long-distance transport is economically viable	Long-distance transport is not economically viable
Almost all petroleum is consumed, converting high-quality fuel into lower quality heat	Overall, water is not "consumed" from the water cycle, although some uses of it are consumptive.
Flows as withdrawal from finite pool of resources	Water cycle will renew natural flows
Energy can be provided by a wide range of alternatives other than the combustion of oil	Water has no substitute for a wide of functions and purposes
Limited availability, so substitution will be inevitable by a renewable source or sources	Locally limited but globally unlimited after substitute sources such as desalination of oceans are economically and environmentally developed.

Case Study[4]

Drought experts met in Brussels in February 2010 to attend a conference on supporting drought policies in Europe. The conference brought together planners, water resource experts, environment specialists, climatologists, and economists to discuss the challenges of drought identification and characterisation, the environmental and socio-economic impacts of drought, and management choices and policy options for drought.

Drought affects water quantity and quality. As streams and rivers dry up organic matter becomes more concentrated in the water which also becomes warmer due to higher air temperatures. This not only puts stress on our water systems designed to deliver drinking water but also those designed to clean water for drinking and for treating wastewater.

Droughts can also have less immediate and direct impacts on our environment. Forests can often suffer during drought due to lack of water, the build up of dry matter in large quantities, and episodes of insect and disease outbreaks. The risk of forest fires increases often started by lightning from developing rainstorms. Rain falling on areas following forest fires can also wash toxic carbon and nitrate concentrations in drainage flows into rivers and streams.

Droughts may also reduce water in the soil. This in turn can reduce soil fertility and structure, affecting water holding capacity of the soil for plants and growing crops. Fertile topsoil may also be lost where dry soil is blown away where wind speed increases during hot and dry drought conditions. Drought conditions can impose limitations on the productivity of terrestrial ecosystems such as their ability to cycle essential chemicals such as carbon, especially where forests and other vegetation die and peatlands dry out.

Major impacts of drought on biodiversity may include changes in seasonal timings, shifts in the distribution of species, changes in habitat composition and structure as species move northwards, including the expected increase in invasive species and diseases, and the impact of changing land use as agriculture, water, forestry and other countryside industries and interests react to water stress.

In 2010 World Water Day focused on Clean Water for a Healthy World and raised awareness of the importance of water quality for human health and the environment.

4 IUCN. (2010, February 25). Supporting Drought Policies in Europe. Retrieved April 23, 2010, from iucn.org: http://www.iucn.org/about/work/programmes/water/wp_news_events/wp_news2007/?4954/Supporting-Drought-Policies-in-Europe

Case Study[5]

Every business depends and impacts on water resources. Some use it to process raw materials and manufacture goods. Some use it for cooling and cleaning. For others, it is a central ingredient in the goods they produce, or it is required to consume the product they sell. The future of business depends on the sustainability of water resources, which are increasingly under pressure. Globally, per capita availability of freshwater is steadily decreasing and the trend will inevitably continue as the world's population swells towards 9 billion, emerging economies increase consumption levels and climate change unfolds.

For the global economy to carry on expanding at the same pace without improvements in efficiency, worldwide annual water consumption would have to rise from 4,500 km3 today to 6,900 km3 in 2030 – that is 40% above current accessible, reliable supply. Some of the key questions facing business today include: How might water availability and allocations restrict my company's supply chain? What effects will the lack of water security have on my markets? Will my customers have enough water to enable them to use my products or services? Can I justify my water consumption with regard to other users, including environmental requirements? And also: Can I boost my revenues by providing solutions?

The global business community increasingly recognizes the water challenge, but to respond effectively it needs guidance, tools, standards and schemes to enable change to more sustainable practices. The World Business Council for Sustainable Development (WBCSD) has been actively working on water issues for over 10 years and has helped move water up everybody's business agenda. The WBCSD recently produced a set of tools intended to help member companies integrate water issues in their strategic planning. The Global Water Tool launched in August 2007 and updated in 2009, helps companies map their water use and assess risks relative to their global operations and supply chain. It is now being used by some 300 corporations worldwide and is increasingly being recognized as a critical and practical tool by non-business stakeholders too.

5 WBCSD. (2010, April 29). Ever-increasing Interest in the Global Water Tool . Retrieved May 1, 2010, from wbcsd.org: http://www.wbcsd.org/Plugins/DocSearch/details.asp?DocTypeId=251&ObjectId=MzgzMTY&URLBack=%2Ftemplates%2FTemplateWBCSD2%2Flayout%2Easp%3Ftype%3Dp%26MenuId%3DMzcx%26doOpen%3D1%26ClickMenu%3DRightMenu%26CurPage%3D1%26SortOrder%3Dpubdate%2520desc%2C%2520sect

Case Study[6]

A world-famous carpet manufacturer in Devon has officially opened a new water recycling plant which the company claims will reduce its carbon output. The carpet company has spent £2m on the process plant at its mill where the wool is spun and dyed.

Water from the River Dart is used to wash the wool, but in the past it cost £700,000 a year to treat and dispose of the contaminated water. With the new plant, the water can be reused 40 times. The process also keeps the water warm so it does not have to be reheated each time. Eventually what residue remains will be used as fuel and a spokesman for the company stated that, "It's more cost effective for us to be green and it's the more responsible thing to do."

6 BBC News. (2009, November). Axminster Carpets axes dirty water. Retrieved April 12, 2010, from news.bbc.co.uk: http://news.bbc.co.uk/1/hi/england/devon/8383750.stm

Economics and Biodiversity

The Economics of Ecosystems and Biodiversity (TEEB)[7] recognises that natural capital underpins economies, societies and individual well-being. The values of its benefits are, however, often overlooked or poorly understood. They are rarely taken fully into account through economic signals in markets, or in day to day decisions by business and citizens, nor indeed reflected adequately in the accounts of society.

The steady loss of forests, soils, wetlands and coral reefs is closely tied to this economic invisibility. So too are the losses of species and of productive assets like fisheries, driven partly by ignoring values beyond the immediate and private. Business and society is running down the natural capital stock without understanding the value of what they are losing. Missed opportunities to invest in this natural capital contribute to the biodiversity crisis that is becoming more evident and more pressing by the day. The degradation of soils, air, water and biological resources can negatively impact on public health, food security, consumer choice and business opportunities. The rural poor, most dependent on the natural resource base, are often hardest hit.

TEEB recommends that under such circumstances, strong public policies are of the utmost importance globally. These policy solutions need tailoring to be socially equitable, ecologically effective, and economically efficient. Solutions are already emerging from cooperation between economists and scientists and they point to four urgent strategic priorities.

- To halt deforestation and forest degradation as an integral part of climate change mitigation and adaptation focused on 'green carbon' and to preserve the huge range of services and goods forests provide to local people and the wider community.

7 TEEB . (2009). TEEB – The Economics of Ecosystems and Biodiversity. TEEB .

- To protect tropical coral reefs and the associated livelihoods of half a billion people through major efforts to avoid global temperature rise and ocean acidification.
- To save and restore global fisheries and related jobs, currently an underperforming asset in danger of collapse and generating US$ 50 billion less per year than it could.
- To recognise the deep link between ecosystem degradation and the persistence of rural poverty and align policies across sectors with two related challenges ahead. The first is to understand the values of natural capital and integrate them into decision-making and the second is to respond efficiently and equitably.

TEEB also point out that unlike economic and human capital, natural capital has no dedicated systems of measurement, monitoring and reporting. This is astonishing given its importance for jobs and mainstream economic sectors as well as its contribution to future economic development. TEEB recommend that as part of good governance, decision-making affecting people and the use of public funds needs to be objective, balanced and transparent. Access to the right information at the right time is fundamental to coherent policy trade-offs. They also say that better understanding and quantitative measurement of biodiversity and ecosystem values to support integrated policy assessments are a core part of the long-term solution.

As already stated, society depends on the environment for the supply of its basic needs such as air to breathe, water to drink, food to eat and the physical world to sense. Business constantly draws upon the products of this 'natural capital' but how can it be valued in a way that usefully informs policy, planning and development processes? The benefits which are derived from natural capital are often called 'ecosystem services', and the 'ecosystem approach', which aims to value different elements of natural capital, has been proposed as a framework for development decisions, policy-making and delivery.

The Natural Capital Initiative (NCI)[8] was formed by the Institute of Biology, the Centre for Ecology & Hydrology and the British Ecological Society to create a forum for constructive discussion about ecosystems and the services they provide, in order to find ways to connect the needs of business and communities with the sustainability of their resource use. NCI aims to involve the natural, social and economic sciences as well as the public, private and non-governmental sectors, and to bring relevant debates into the public domain. They believe that whole ecosystems and all the valuable services they provide can be considered in decision-making.

The NCI propose a range of options and issues for policymakers, communicators, researchers and business to consider. Those aimed at business are outlined below.

- There is good reason to think that consumers, business and government all desire better resource management. Business should not be reluctant to take the initiative, and government should not fear a lack of public will.
- Businesses can benefit by taking responsibility ahead of waiting for government to do so. By taking the initiative a business can gain strong customer loyalty.

8 Centre for Ecology and Hydrology. (2009, April 29). Major event aims to protect and enhance natural capital . Retrieved April 23, 2010, from ceh.ac.uk: http://www.ceh.ac.uk/news/news_archive/2009_news_item_17.html.

- There are multiple benefits from agriculture but farmers are motivated by their markets. UK businesses need to find ways to measure and communicate the value of those other benefits to their marketplace.
- The unpredictability of supply associated with unsustainable exploitation of natural resources is a risk to business.
- Society needs entrepreneurs who create and promote opportunities for sustainability and are seen to be earning as a result of it.

It is recommended therefore that putting a value on nature could set the scene for a true "green economy". By recognising that much environmental damage has been caused by the way business is done it may also lead to the realisation that there might be a way of changing economic models from being part of the problem into part of the solution. This was raised in early 2010 by the Economics of Ecosystems and Biodiversity (TEEB) highlighting that the living fabric of this planet and its ecosystems and biodiversity are in rapid decline worldwide. It was suggested that this is probably due to a combination of commercial over-exploitation, population pressures or unhelpful policies. Is economics part of the problem of ecosystem degradation and biodiversity loss and can it be part of the solution?

It was suggested that the economic invisibility of nature in our dominant economic model is both a symptom and a root cause of this problem. Business values what it can price, but nature's services such as providing clean air, fresh water, soil fertility, flood prevention, drought control and climate stability are not traded in any markets and not priced. These so-called "ecosystem services" are all "public goods" provided free. The tendency is to value private wealth creation over improving public wealth.

TEEB say that businesses cannot manage what they do not measure and they are not measuring either the value of nature's benefits or the costs of their loss. Instead they seem to be navigating the new and unfamiliar waters of ecological scarcities and climate risks with faulty instruments. TEEB articles suggest that replacing an obsolete economic compass could help economics to become part of the solution to reverse the declining ecosystems and biodiversity loss. This thinking ties in with the messages put forward in chapter 6.

Business leaders should engage in a new vision for a new economy with new policy directions which change incentive structures, reduce or phase out perverse subsidies, and help create a new era of "holistic economics" or economics that recognises the value of nature's services and the costs of their loss to set the stage for a new "green economy".

TEEB have assembled a library of suggestions for policy-makers on how to use good economics to conserve wild nature (TEEB for Policy-Makers, November 2009). In July 2010 TEEB will publish a parallel document on what role business can play in changing the rules of the game and herald a society that profits and progresses yet lives in harmony with nature[9].

9 TEEB. (2009, November 13). Launch of TEEB Policy makers report. Retrieved April 23, 2010, from teebweb.org: http://www.teebweb.org/InformationMaterial/PressCentre/tabid/1052/language/en-US/Default.aspx

Case Study[10]

Restoring Natural Capital in Degraded Landscapes

Fuelling the growing demand for food, fuel and fibre, 13 million hectares are converted annually for agricultural use, mostly from forests. Together, crops and pasture make up more than any other land use - over 40% - and are projected to grow by another 15% over the next 50-100 years. The conversion into agricultural lands is perhaps one of the greatest single impacts on the Earth. These impacts include the greenhouse gas emissions that make up a third of global emissions since 1950, the 70% of freshwater used for irrigation, and growing loss of biodiversity, among others.

The scope and scale of agriculture and the projected growth in demand for food, biofuels and other commodities puts it on a crash course with identified pathways for environmental sustainability. With a growing awareness of the value of the goods and services that nature provides, governments and institutions are looking for ways to both decrease per capita demand and increase the efficiency of current land use practices.

But how can agricultural landscapes produce more with less impact? Incentives are evolving, including certification standards such as Fair Trade and the newly developing payments for ecosystem services like those for water, or the trading of carbon. Developing an understanding of the relationships and trade-offs among forests, soil, biodiversity, water, and food production, among other key ecosystem components, is driving a new paradigm for applied scientific research.

Coffee is one of the top five traded global commodities. A hundred million people depend on it for their livelihoods and the evolving models provide insight into the opportunities and challenges for sustainable agriculture. Pollinating insects help with the production of over 65% of the world's crops. Recent declines in native and managed bee colonies have created concern about food production.

An ongoing project by Earthwatch illustrates the connection of these pollinators to the landscape and how different stakeholders come together to identify potential solutions. Using teams of volunteers and the project found that wild and domesticated bees enhanced both the yield and quality of coffee berries in Costa Rica. Wild bees and other pollinators were in turn attracted by plants, other than coffee, which the farmers had grown around their fields. Recognising the value of these other management practices in boosting yields helps farmers understand the benefits of biodiversity in the landscape.

10 BBC News. (2010, March 23). Restoring natural capital in degraded landscapes. Retrieved April 12, 2010, from news.bbc.co.uk: http://news.bbc.co.uk/go/pr/fr/-/1/hi/sci/tech/8583015.stm

Earthwatch are expanding on this work in another coffee region of Costa Rica by working with farmers and volunteers are identifying the value of nearby forests in boosting bee populations and coffee production. These volunteers and other citizen scientists are helping to collect and analyse field data as it relates to bee activity and coffee plant growth. These diverse teams of volunteers are also exploring the financial mechanisms that help recognise and reward the goods and services that farmers and forests provide to local and global communities.

New sustainable techniques are needed to mitigate the negative consequences of intensive agriculture. Rebuilding healthy, diverse soils requires great effort to yield not only nutritional, healthy food, but also to mitigate erosion, capture carbon, and act as a sponge to prevent flooding, among other benefits.

The "TEEB for Business report"[11] was to be released at the first Global Business of Biodiversity Symposium in London on 13 July, 2010. The report recognises that business and enterprise have a huge role to play in how they manage, safeguard and invest in natural capital. The report is aimed squarely at this sector and will provide practical guidance on the issues and the opportunities created by the inclusion in mainstream business practices of ecosystem- and biodiversity-related considerations. The report is for a wide array of enterprises, including those with direct impacts on ecosystems and biodiversity, such as mining, oil and gas and infrastructure; for those businesses that depend on healthy ecosystems and biodiversity for production, such as agriculture and fisheries; for industry sectors that finance and underwrite economic activity and growth, like banks and asset managers, as well as insurance and business services; and for businesses that are selling ecosystem services or biodiversity-related products such as eco-tourism, eco-agriculture and bio-carbon.

The TEEB report for business aims to:

- offer practical guidance for business on how to measure and manage the risks of biodiversity and ecosystem losses
- explore innovative economic tools for adapting production to produce in more biodiversity-friendly ways, including avoidance, mitigation and offsets
- help business leaders to identify and grasp new market opportunities linked to the conservation and sustainable use of biological resources
- provide business managers with the tools to inform themselves and others about the wider impacts of business activities, not only in terms of financial and human capital, but also natural capital.

11 TEEB. (2009, March). Introduction and call for contributions. Retrieved April 12, 2010, from teebweb.org: http://www.teebweb.org/LinkClick.aspx?fileticket=y_KfQ5lJNh8%3D&tabid=1021&language=en-US

Natural Capitalism

For over decade it has been suggested that the next industrial revolution, like the previous ones, will be a response to changing patterns of scarcity. It will create upheaval, but more importantly, it will create opportunities. The term "natural capitalism" is a new business model that enables businesses to fully realise these opportunities. The journey to natural capitalism involves four major shifts in business practices, all vitally interlinked.

- Radically increase the productivity of natural resources.
- Shift to biologically inspired production models and materials.
- Move to a "service-and-flow" business model such as providing illumination rather than selling light bulks.
- Reinvest in natural capital by restoring, sustaining and expanding it.

The next Industrial Revolution is already being led by companies that are learning to profit and gain competitive advantage from these four principles. Not only that, their leaders and employees are feeling better about what they do. Shortages of work and hope, of satisfaction and security, are not mere isolated pathologies, but result from clear linkages between the waste of resources, money, and people. The solutions are intertwined and synergistic: firms that downsize their unproductive tons, gallons, and kilowatt-hours can keep more people, who will foster the innovation that drives future improvement[12].

2010 has been declared the International Year of Biodiversity (IYB) by the United Nations. [13].

Case Study[14]

The Organic Herb Trading Company based in Somerset imports and distributes a diverse range of organically certified raw materials, some of these produced from the organic farm on which they are based. Established over 20 years ago they are the leading supplier of organic herbal raw materials to the UK market and are also a major player in Europe. The Managing Director of the company is an active speaker and participant in many initiatives including being a board member of the Union of Ethical Bio-Trade. Ethical Bio-Trade is a set of business practices that follow the Ethical Bio-Trade Principles and Criteria that contribute to ethical sourcing of biodiversity and the Union for Ethical Bio-Trade is a non profit association that promotes the 'Sourcing with Respect' of

14 http://www.organicherbtrading.co.uk/

12 Rocky Mountain Institute. (1999, September 30). Natural Capitalism. Retrieved April 23, 2010, from natcap.org: http://www.natcap.org/images/other/NCpressreleaseBP.pdf

13 Natural History Museum. (2010, April 12). 2010 International Year of Biodiversity. Retrieved April 12, 2010, from biodiversityislife.net: . http://www.biodiversityislife.net/

ingredients that come from native biodiversity. Members commit to gradually ensuring that their sourcing practices promote the conservation of biodiversity, respect traditional knowledge and assure the equitable sharing of benefits all along the supply chain.

One new venture for the company is trading in the new "superfruit" from the baobab tree which has twice as many antioxidants as goji berries, more calcium than milk and more iron than red meat. African people call the baobab the "Tree of Life". Living for a thousand years or more, baobabs dominate parts of the African landscape with their root-like branches and massive trunks that can reach 25 metres or more in circumference.

The baobab's velvety green fruits grow from beautiful white flowers that are pollinated at night by bats. Inside the hard coconut-like shell are the seeds which are coated in a pale powder that is sharp and tangy to the taste. It is this fruit powder that is used in food and drinks. African people have been eating baobab for centuries. From Senegal to South Africa people use it in different ways, many of them mixing the fruit powder with water and sugar to make a refreshing drink.

It is not only delicious but popular as a boost to health, especially among pregnant women, children and the elderly. Baobab fruit is also said to help fight fevers and settle the stomach. The Kung San bushmen of the Kalahari eat it to ward off winter colds and 19th century seafarers ate baobab jam to protect themselves against scurvy.

As well as an impressive range of nutritional properties it is suitable for use in a wide variety of food and drink products including:

- smoothies, juices, juice drinks and flavoured waters
- cereals, cereal bars and snacks
- ice creams, yoghurts and dairy desserts
- jams, sauces, marinades and condiments
- speciality teas
- health supplements.

Baobab can be supplied to food manufacturers in two formats.

- **Baobab Fruit Powder -** Baobab fruit grows as a natural powder within a hard shell. Baobab fruit powder is exceptionally rich in antioxidants, calcium, potassium, iron and magnesium. It is free-flowing, milled and sifted, has a high pectin content useful for binding and thickening, and is high in dietary fibre.
- **Baobab Fruit Extract -** The suppliers have developed an extract with all the unique flavour of baobab but without the pectin. It is clear in solution and ready for formulation, ideal as a flavouring for soft drinks, juices and other products.

Ethical Trade and Sustainability

Baobab not only offers a unique taste of Africa and powerful nutritional properties, it can also provide life-changing income to millions of poor rural people in Southern Africa.

Many of these families exist on $100 or less per year and cannot buy the tools, seeds and supplies they need to earn more from agriculture. By harvesting baobab, which is abundant in Southern Africa, these people can substantially increase their income at no cost to themselves. This helps them pay for family healthcare and their children's education as well as household necessities.

A 2006 report by the UK's Natural Resources Institute estimated that, if fully commercialised, baobab can deliver new income to over two and a half million poor families. What's more, when communities earn money from baobab, they have an incentive to protect the trees. This helps to conserve the environment and its biodiversity and ensure the natural regeneration of baobab woodlands.

The Organic Herb Trading Company and its partner PhytoTrade Africa are committed to the ethical and sustainable development of the baobab trade. As well as paying communities a fair price for their baobab fruit, their producers return part of their sales income to the villages to fund community projects. They also use forestry techniques based on European best practice, identifying and monitoring every producing baobab tree and putting in place appropriate measures to ensure long term sustainable production.

CHAPTER 27

Waste

- Business Waste
- Waste a Business Opportunity
- Business Waste by Type
- Zero Waste

Business Waste ●●●

Business waste represents over 60 per cent of England's waste, compared to municipal waste which is only 10 per cent. Over 280 million tonnes of waste were produced in England in 2006.

Business waste comprises commercial and industrial waste (76 million tonnes in 2006) and construction, demolition and excavation waste (102 million tonnes). By comparison, municipal waste, which mainly comes from households, amounted to 28 million tonnes in the same year.

The UK government introduced a landfill tax in 1996 to encourage greater recycling and other methods of disposal. The tax rate was increased by £3 per tonne each year between April 2005 and March 2007 and part of this additional tax revenue was ring-fenced to help the business community make more efficient use of resources. This resulted in the Business Resource Efficiency and Waste Programme.

A report produced by the National Audit Office (NAO) for Defra in March 2010[1] showed that the amount of harmful business waste sent to landfill had fallen but they were not able to confirm whether this was due to the government's £240m Efficiency and Waste programme which ran from March 2005 until April 2008 so no conclusion as to value for money could be drawn. Other factors such as the increase in landfill tax and the recession may also have reduced the amount of waste sent to landfill.

1 National Audit Office. (2010, March 5). Defra reducing the impact of business waste through the Business Resource Efficiency Programme. Retrieved April 20, 2010, from nao.org.uk: http://www.nao.org.uk/whats_new/0910/0910216.aspx

Case Study[2]

Small builders working in challenging economic conditions could unlock valuable cost benefits by using a new waste-saving guide from sustainable business experts Envirowise, launched in 2010.

The free guide outlines a step-by-step review process which can help businesses identify the main causes of waste around their site and save as much as 40% on waste disposal costs.

With around 89.6 million tonnes of construction waste generated across England alone each year, the cost saving potential for the UK runs into millions of pounds.

Savings can be achieved by making simple low-cost or no-cost changes such as segregating waste at source. For example, reducing waste by 20% can cut a business's waste disposal costs by 40% and waste to landfill by 60%.

The Federation of Master Builder's most recent State of Trade survey showed that economic conditions for small builders in the UK continues to be very challenging. However, reducing waste costs is a straightforward, effective way to help improve the bottom-line.

2 Envirowise. (2010, April 15). New guide could help builders cut waste costs. Retrieved April 15, 2010, from envirowise.gov.uk: http://www.envirowise.gov.uk/uk/Press-Office/Press-Releases/UK-Press-Releases/New-guide-could-help-builders-cut-waste-costs-by-as-much-as-40.html

The NAO report concluded that Defra's approach to tackling business waste is not as developed as its approach to dealing with municipal waste, where there are binding targets in place. It stated that Defra did not have up to date information on how much business waste there is, or how much is being recycled, which makes it difficult for it to target its activities.

Earlier in 2010 MPs had criticised the government's 'vague' waste plans and they recommended that the government should toughen its approach to cutting landfill issuing firm targets for companies and food waste recycling for homes. The MPs also pointed out that policies focused on household waste which makes up only 9% of the 330m tonnes England produces a year (based on Defra statistics). Their report also suggested that firm plans to deal with business waste must replace "vague ambitions and rhetoric". However, the report did find that 23% less waste went to landfill in England and Wales in 2007 compared with 2001. The use of disposal plastic carriers has also dropped - from 13bn in 2007-8 to 10bn in 2008-9.

The wide-ranging paper also looked at the government's Waste Strategy for England. It said some progress had been made getting homes to recycle more - with nearly 37% being recycled or composted in England. Household waste also reduced by 3% in 2008 and fly tipping dropped by 9%. But it says more effort should be made to reduce waste thrown away in the first place.

The report also pointed to an increase in "textile waste" sent to landfill - which waste operatives had dubbed the "Primark effect", assuming that people throw away cheap clothing more quickly. The committee also felt that the government should set "more ambitious" targets to recycle 50% of household waste by 2015 and 60% by 2020.

The committee also stated that the government has failed to address waste from the industrial and commercial sectors sufficiently - expressing only an "expectation" that their waste levels would be reduced by 20% over six years from 2004. Apart from a target to halve total construction, demolition and excavation waste sent to landfill by 2012, there were "few firm targets" for "non-household" waste, which accounts for 90% of total waste. There was a "significant gap" in details of what businesses were doing to tackle waste because it was not being properly surveyed.

> *At the same time it must encourage companies to take a completely new view of waste and see it as a valuable source of raw material.*
>
> **Michael Jack Committee chairman**

The report stated that a third of all food bought is thrown away - about 6.7m tonnes a year generating more carbon dioxide than four million cars - and says more needs to be done to persuade people to change their behaviour. Institutions such as schools, hospitals and Parliament should be encouraged to compost food waste[3].

Waste a Business Opportunity ●●●

A common theme throughout this book has been the idea that climate change can provide opportunities for business as well as risks and to echo this notion the report, 'Less is More': Business Opportunities in Waste and Resource Management[4] published in March 2010 outlines opportunities for business across the product supply chain, from design through to waste management.

Defra and BIS joined forces to take a close look at business's use of material resources and waste and their report suggests that British business can tap into the growing waste and recycling sector to support economic growth and create jobs,

The report stated that money can be saved by cutting waste during production processes and applying new business models. Huge environmental and economic benefits can be delivered when products are designed and made to last longer, rather than being thrown away and replaced. There are also opportunities for new markets in recovered materials, ranging from mixed plastics to food waste and coloured glass.

3 BBC News. (2010, January 19). MPs criticise 'vague' plans to reduce business waste . Retrieved April 20, 2010, from news.bbc.co.uk: http://news.bbc.co.uk/1/hi/uk_politics/8466883.stm

4 Defra. (2010, March 16). New opportunities for British business. Retrieved April 20, 2010, from defra.gov.uk: http://www.defra.gov.uk/news/2010/100316a.htm

> *What's good for the environment can be good for business. There are real opportunities for British companies who can lead the way in innovative product design and supply systems. We need to be smarter about re-using and recycling waste, getting the full value from our resources rather than simply dumping it in landfill.*

In order for the waste management sector to have a real opportunity to use its expertise to deliver new services in resource efficiency and management, the report stated that Defra and BIS will join forces to work with industry to transform the perception of waste from a problem which has to be dealt with, to an opportunity to be exploited.

In the report they set out to understand the barriers and incentives to more efficient resource use, the business opportunities if those barriers were overcome and the potential for government action. They have identified opportunities for British businesses across the supply chain, from product design and manufacture, through to management, recovery and re-use of materials. In all of these areas they argue, economic and environmental benefits go together. These are opportunities which will support a healthy natural environment and the sustainable use of resources.

This work has identified that the areas of greatest business opportunity lie in:

- **reducing or eliminating waste at source**, when materials have most value and none of the costs of disposal or treatment have been incurred. These opportunities occur throughout the supply chain and across all businesses. For the waste management sector, it is a chance to use their expertise to deliver higher value-added services and share knowledge in resource efficiency from the design stage onwards.
- **applying new business models to existing markets.** These include improving the efficiency of material use and the durability of products at the design stage, process improvements in manufacturing and the development of product service systems ("goods to services") that facilitate repair and refurbishment rather than outright replacement.
- **the improved collection and sorting** of waste from smaller companies and commercial premises, allowing the value in these materials to be recovered.
- **the development of new markets for recovered products** so that materials currently seen as waste come to be seen as a valuable resource for another process or sector of industry. There are mature markets in several products already, including most metals, paper and glass, and significant opportunities in areas such as plastics, coloured glass and food waste.

The report states that over the coming years, the separate collection of recyclable material from households and businesses will become even more important than it is today. While the priority should always be to prevent waste arising in the first place, over the coming decade, there will nevertheless be significant business opportunities in collecting a higher percentage of the recyclates produced by households and businesses. These materials must be treated as a valuable resource, rather than a waste for disposal. For high-value materials such as metals, or those such as paper where collection and recycling processes are already in place, well-established international markets exist. For materials that are not commonly recovered, market development is required. Once a transparent market exists, firms have the information they need to invest in collection and processing.

There is potentially a role for government in setting specific market standards, facilitating transparency, collating information, or even helping to create a pilot market for a greater range of materials.

Business Waste by Type ●●●

The following four key waste streams – food, paper/card, plastics and glass – provide examples of the potential actions which can support market development.

Food waste

The WRAP report "Household Food and Drink Waste in the UK" published in 2009 identified that UK households throw away 8.3 million tonnes of food and drink every year. Most of this is avoidable and could have been eaten if only consumers had planned, stored and managed it better. Less than a fifth is truly unavoidable – things like bones, cores and peelings.

The report noted that households throw away food for two main reasons: of the avoidable food and drink waste, 2.2 million tonnes is thrown away due to cooking, preparing or serving too much and a further 2.9 million tonnes is thrown away because it was not used in time.

For example, of the avoidable food and drink thrown away:

- 860,000 tonnes of fresh vegetables and salads
- 870,000 tonnes of drink
- 500,000 tonnes of fresh fruit
- 680,000 tonnes of bakery
- 660,000 tonnes of home-made and pre-prepared meals
- 290,000 tonnes of meat and fish
- 530,000 tonnes of dairy and eggs
- 190,000 tonnes of cakes and desserts
- 67,000 tonnes of confectionery and snacks.

As the report notes, all this wasted food is costly. In the UK consumers spend £12 billion every year buying and then throwing away good food. That works out at £480 for the average UK household, increasing to £680 a year for households with children – an average of just over £50 a month. Food waste is also harmful to the environment. Throwing away food that could have been eaten is responsible for the equivalent of 20 million tonnes of carbon dioxide emissions every year – that's the same as the CO2 emitted by one in every four cars on UK roads[5]. Responsible food and drink manufacturers/retailers should consider packaging food in smaller quantities and also more information of proper storage of their products.

Food waste represents both a waste of resources and a major contributor to the UK's greenhouse gas (GHG) emissions. According to a recent report published by the University of Surrey 'Cooking up a storm', the food system as a whole contributes around 19% of the UK's GHG. Food waste in landfill degrades and produces methane (CH4), generating an estimated 0.3% of the UK's GHG emissions. More significantly the embedded emissions associated with production, processing, transport and retailing of food that ends up as waste adds around 18 million tonnes' worth of CO2, equivalent to 2% to the UK's production-related emissions.

Food waste reprocessing provides an opportunity to reduce waste, save money and improve environmental performance. There are two main opportunities. The first is around development of commercial collections, which are currently isolated and small scale. The other lies with augmenting anaerobic digestion (AD) capacity to generate biogas. AD is now an established technology and every tonne of food waste treated through AD rather than placed in landfill saves between 0.5 and 1 tonne of CO2 equivalent.

The UK government is also obliged to reduce biodegradable (e.g. vegetables) municipal waste going to landfill by 25% by July 2010 (from 1995 levels). This is because decomposing wastes generate methane which is a potent greenhouse gas and is also highly explosive. Around 68% of English municipal waste is biodegradable.

5 WRAP. (2009, November). Household Food and Drink Waste in the UK. Retrieved April 20, 2010, from wrap.org.uk: http://www.wrap.org.uk/retail/case_studies_research/report_household.html

Case Study[6]

Businesses and local authorities are being offered help to turn food, farm and other organic waste into energy and fuel. Defra has published a plan to boost biogas production from anaerobic digestion (AD) to help tackle climate change and produce renewable energy.

'Accelerating the Uptake of Anaerobic Digestion in England: an Implementation Plan' sets out actions to help businesses, local authorities, farmers and food producers to adopt the technology, which transforms organic material like manure and waste food into fuel. The measures include financial incentives such as grants, a £10 million programme of demonstration sites across the country, and a new research unit to test out the latest technology.

Anaerobic digestion has fantastic potential because it uses organic material that would otherwise be thrown away and converts it into renewable energy.

This announcement emphasises the important role this technology can play in reducing greenhouse gas emissions and managing organic waste. It also sets out how the use of AD will increase to produce biogas from organic materials such as livestock manures and slurries, sewage sludge and food wastes - to generate heat and power, and become a transport fuel, either locally or injected into the gas grid. The treated residues from the AD process can also be used in agriculture as a bio-fertiliser.

The number of anaerobic digestion plants has grown significantly. Three years ago, there were an estimated three facilities processing municipal and commercial food waste. Today, there are ten in operation with the same number under construction. The number of digestion plants on farms has also grown, with around 25 currently in operation and at least 15 more planned.

6 Defra. (2010, March 25). Food and farm waste canhelp power the nation, says Benn. Retrieved April 20, 2010, from defra.gov.uk: http://www.defra.gov.uk/news/2010/100325b.htm

Paper and Board

There is a strong domestic and international market in recovered paper and board. Close to 9 million tonnes of paper and board were recovered in the UK for recycling in 2008 with just over half sent overseas for recycling. However recovery from some groups and sectors is patchy – these include the hospitality and event sectors and smaller commercial premises.

The UK produces only 5 million of the 12 million tonnes of paper it consumes, reflecting the global nature of the paper industry, the relatively high costs of manufacturing in the UK and the overcapacity which prevails for some grades in Europe. Business opportunities in the sector are actively explored by market participants, with new newsprint capacity added in 2009 through inward investment. Additional capacity of containerboard production is also currently being planned.

Current market rates for mixed papers £53-55 per tonne

Case Study[7]

Saving Energy Through Print Processes

A Barclays Wealth programme to save paper, energy and costs from printing was named one of 2009's top environmental initiatives in a prestigious poll. The managed print scheme, which reduced the number of printers across the UK business from 1,400 to 420 energy-efficient devices, was named Environmental Initiative of the Year at the 2009 Financial Sector Technology Awards.

The new multi-function machines use approximately 60 per cent less energy than the old equipment, and include features such as an automatic sleep mode, double-sided printing, and a setting which uses 30 per cent less toner.

A 'PIN to collect' option also avoids wasted paper through forgotten print-outs, as recipients have to enter a code number at the collection point before their document is printed. Through 2009, the project saved 20 million sheets of paper – a 25 per cent reduction on the previous year. It also saved the business £200,000 through reduced energy, paper and toner costs, reducing energy use to 73,000 kWh (kilowatt hours) annually.

Based on the success of the UK pilot, Barclays Wealth is now seeking to deploy its managed print service across other areas of the business.

Barclays also aims to reduce the amount of waste produced from its operations and to increase the proportion of waste that is recycled.

In the UK, with the help of its suppliers, its improved the waste removal and recycling services in 46 of our corporate offices in 2009. It also introduced improved recycling services, with increased collections for aluminium cans and plastic cups and bottles. That year, 63 per cent of waste from its UK offices was recycled, an improvement of 28 per cent on 2008.

Recycling in its UK branch network is more challenging due to the small volume of waste produced at each site. In 2009, it carried out a successful trial of a mixed recycling service at a small number of branches. These schemes were coupled with employee engagement programmes to encourage colleagues to recycle at work.

In total 90 per cent of paper waste from Barclays branches in the UK was recycled in 2009.

7 Barclays. (2010, April 20). Reducing waste. Retrieved April 20, 2010, from group.barclays.com: http://group.barclays.com/Sustainability/Citizenship/Environment/Reducing-our-environmental-impact/Editorial/1231783991446.html

Glass

The UK collected 1.6m tonnes of packaging glass for recycling in 2008. Of this, 1.3m tonnes were recycled domestically but less than 800,000 tonnes of cullet (crushed recovered glass) were recycled by UK container and glass wool manufacturers. The rest was used in other markets such as aggregates.

While this avoids landfill, the CO2 benefits are significantly inferior to those from remelt applications.

The economics of sorting mixed-colour cullet to make it suitable for use by the UK glass container industry, and issues surrounding the quality of cullet, have resulted in a falling proportion of glass going to remelt (the most environmentally beneficial option) and an increase in glass going to aggregates.

The report concluded that opportunities therefore lie in either developing viable capacity for sorting this glass or developing markets for closed loop recycling using mixed colour glass. Defra is currently consulting on proposals to set higher packaging waste recycling targets for 2011 to 2020 and for glass the proposals are intended to help promote closed loop recycling.

Current market rates for glass (clear) are £33-36 per tonne

Plastics

In 2008 the UK recovered in excess of 500,000 tonnes of plastic packaging. Most of this is exported for recycling overseas but domestic reprocessing capacity is increasing. Rapid expansion in plastic bottle collection has allowed investment in UK reprocessing with more than 260,000 tonnes of capacity planned by the end of 2011. Each tonne of PET recycled back to a PET application saves 1.5t CO2 emissions.

Recycling of "mixed plastics" (i.e. plastics other than bottles) is less well developed. Most of the 1 million tonnes of mixed plastics in the UK household waste stream is land filled. Mixed plastics have traditionally been considered too difficult or of too low value to warrant recycling. However, WRAP has found that a combination of increasing landfill tax and decreasing costs of sorting technology now means that the recycling of mixed plastics can be viable. This is an area with great potential for growth. Another area of opportunity lies with commercial and industrial plastics packaging collection (packaging film, returnable transit packaging and plastic pallets).

Current market rates for plastic bottles (clear PET) £179-184 per tonne

Clothing

Clothing is one of the ten pilots Defra has established to understand the lifecycle impacts of a range of products and to consider social and economic sustainability alongside the main focus on environmental improvements[8]. The UK consumes two million tonnes of textiles each year and over half of this is clothing. The waste related business opportunity lies in the fact that only 500,000 tonnes of textiles is collected for re-use and recycling each year, with an estimated 615,000 tonnes per year going to landfill. At over £300 per tonne there is significant value that could be generated by liberating these resources from storage, or diverting them from landfill each year.

Each year the average person in the UK spends about £650 on 50 or so items of clothing and what people wear accounts for a surprisingly large amount of their carbon footprint. When they are manufactured, transported, washed and thrown away clothes are responsible for significant greenhouse gas emissions. It has been calculated that if a person sourced all their clothes second hand or simply did not buy it would save 70kg of CO2 but it is still unknown as to how much could be saved through recycling them.

It takes ten times more energy to make a tonne of textiles than it does a tonne of glass and when wool and cotton are thrown into landfill they produce methane and yet people happily recycle bottles but only think of recycling clothing. Possibly clothing manufacturers and retailers should follow the example of Marks and Spencer's Plan A which encourages their customers to place discarded clothing with Oxfam.

Current market rates for mixed textiles £300-318 per tonne

The joint Defra and Welsh Assembly Government publication 'Consultation on the Introduction of Restrictions on the Landfilling of Certain Wastes[9]. published in March 2010 considered the case for restrictions on sending the following types of waste to landfill: paper and card, food, textiles, metals, wood, garden waste, glass, plastics, and electrical and electronic equipment.

They want to make the most of the materials and waste flowing through the UK economy at every step of the way. By thinking much more carefully about what they do with waste instead of sending it directly to landfill UK business can expect to see new markets for recycled products and recovered materials. For example, a tonne of aluminium cans is currently worth £819-850 and 100,000 tonnes of aluminium packaging are currently put into landfill each year. This can potentially generate revenue of between £82m and £85m for existing or new businesses to exploit. One objective of the "Less is more" report referred to earlier is to create new jobs as the waste sector gets bigger over time. Making one aluminium can from scratch uses nearly 20 times more energy than making it from a recycled can.

8 Defra. (2010, April 23). Product Roadmaps:Clothing. Retrieved April 23, 2010, from defra,gov.uk: http://www.defra.gov.uk/environment/business/products/roadmaps/clothing/index.htm

9 Defra. (2010, March 18). Benn:stop sending waste to landfill needlessly. Retrieved April 23, 2010, from defra.gov.uk: http://www.defra.gov.uk/news/2010/100318c.htm

Also launched in the same month was a consultation on how the UK can meet the EU Landfill Directive targets to reduce the amount of biodegradable municipal waste sent to landfill and a " Strategy for Hazardous Waste Management in England", which will help drive hazardous waste away from landfill, and promote prevention, recycling and recovery. It should also help the provision of infrastructure for the management of this waste by providing clarity on the principles that should apply.

6.2 million tonnes of hazardous waste are produced in England and Wales each year. This comes from: chemicals, oils, construction and demolition, waste and water treatment, and household/commercial activity. There are currently 461 permitted operational landfill sites in England and Wales. Of these operational sites 24 are for hazardous waste, 265 are for non-hazardous waste and 172 are for inert waste.

In 1996 Landfill Tax was introduced as an incentive to reduce the amount of waste going to landfill. Recent years have seen a sharp rise in landfill with current levies at £32 per tonne rising to £48 tax per tonne by 2010 - that's on top of the actual cost of disposal. This tax is paid to the UK government from which most of the money is used to offset employers' National Insurance contributions with a smaller portion going to environmental projects.

By **2013** landfill tax per tonne will be **£72** bringing actual costs to **£172/tonne** typically 4% of turnover and in many companies it can be as high as 10%. With waste disposal costs continuing to rise, there is more pressure on businesses to look at the areas where they generate most waste and reduce it. The benefits to a business are increased turnover through improved resource efficiency. This in turn can help it to maintain or improve its competitiveness.

In Chapter 24 the high percentage of businesses recycling was highlighted in the "Lean and Green" report by the CMI. In addition, it seems that UK consumers have embraced recycling - fewer than 10% of adults claim to be "confused" about what can and cannot be recycled. Also, some 44% of adults state a willingness to return reusable drinks bottles to supermarkets or other collection points. On packaging, 74% think that retailers use too much and 78% of consumers say they recycle as much packaging as they can. But whether you reuse your carrier bags seems to depend partly on your sex and age. While older people (over 80%) have embraced reusable bags, younger people are lagging behind (only 59% among pre-family adults). Some 82% of women have adopted reusable bags compared to 65% of men. For most people being greener is a 'nice to do' rather than a 'need to do' aspect of their lifestyles[10].

However, it is imperative that cross-contamination is avoided as this reduces the financial value and recyclability of the resource. For instance can banks are purely for cans and no other metals (including aluminium foil) and it takes only 2% contamination to completely ruin a consignment.

10 Mintel. (2009, October). Consumers want greener living but not at any cost. Retrieved April 23, 2010, from mintel.com: http://www.mintel.com/press-centre/press-releases/405/consumers-want-greener-living-but-not-at-any-cost

Research carried by Which? magazine in 2009 found that rejection rates for recycling varied greatly depending on which part of the country was being looked at. In 2007-2008 two-thirds of councils rejected less than 1% of items collected for recycling but some rejected more than 10%. Those councils with the highest rejection rates are shown below[11].

Local Authority	Rejects 07-08	Reject rate 07-08	Cost to send to landfill
Hertsmere Borough Council	3,361 tonnes	22%	£178,116
Manchester City Council	8,133 tonnes	16%	£431,036
Newcastle-under-Lyme	1,877 tonnes	12%	£99,486
Watford Borough Council	1,466 tonnes	12%	£77,684
Tynedale District Council	869 tonnes	11%	£46,031

Obviously individuals or businesses would be mortified to discover that their recycling efforts were in vain and probably due to carelessness. A study into certain types of "degradable" plastics also found there was uncertainty about their impact on the natural environment. The research by Loughborough University found that certain carrier bags, bin bags and flexible packaging, made from common plastics with small amounts of chemicals to speed up their breakdown were not suitable for recycling with other plastics, reuse or composting. As a result the Co-operative said it would not be using carrier bags made from that type of plastic in its stores in future[12].

So far this chapter has looked at waste as some form of physical residue that is either disposed of in landfill or ideally recycled. Waste however, can take other forms. In Chapter 25 the amount of energy being wasted by UK businesses was explored. It also highly likely that many manufacturing businesses are constantly trying to eliminate wastage brought about through inefficiency on the factory floor as part of their quality control systems. There is one other area of wastage that many businesses simply overlook and that is the wastage of water.

11 Which? (2009). The truth about recycling. Which? , 31-33.

12 Loughborough University. (2010, March 18). Research questions the environmental credentials of 'degradable' plastics. Retrieved April 23, 2010, from lboro.ac.uk: http://www.lboro.ac.uk/service/publicity/news-releases/2010/52_degradable_plastics.html

Water

Sustainable business experts Envirowise suggest that UK businesses are collectively missing out on combined cost savings of as much as £10 million per day by failing to maximise the potential of water efficiency as highlighted in a recent survey of UK businesses. Almost two thirds of respondents said they did not measure or monitor their water use at all, and a huge 85% did not have any water reduction targets in place. However, Envirowise[13] estimates that businesses could reduce their water bills by as much as a third if they were to take steps to manage their water use more effectively.

Envirowise notes that more than 9.8 billion cubic metres of water are being used nationally each year so there is significant potential for businesses to save money and reduce their environmental impact by taking action on water efficiency. Envirowise are encouraging companies to join "Rippleffect", a national initiative offering online advice and support to cut water waste and costs. More than 500 UK businesses registered for Rippleffect in 2008. New features for 2009 included water efficiency advice in areas such as rainwater harvesting, vehicle washing and boiler & cooling tower operation.

Envirowise also provide advice on waste minimisation and have identified the "waste hierarchy" so that businesses can make savings in their waste costs and also reduce their impact on the environment by helping them to identify different options by ranking them in order of environmental impact. Businesses should start at the top of the hierarchy to eliminate all waste where possible.

13 Envirowise. (2009, August). UK Businesses sitting on untapped cost saving of around 10million per day. Retrieved April 23, 2010, from envirowise.gov.uk: http://www.envirowise.gov.uk/uk/Press-Office/Press-Releases/UK-Press-Releases/UK-Businesses-sitting-on-untapped-cost-saving-of-around-10million-per-day.html

The Waste Hierarchy[14]

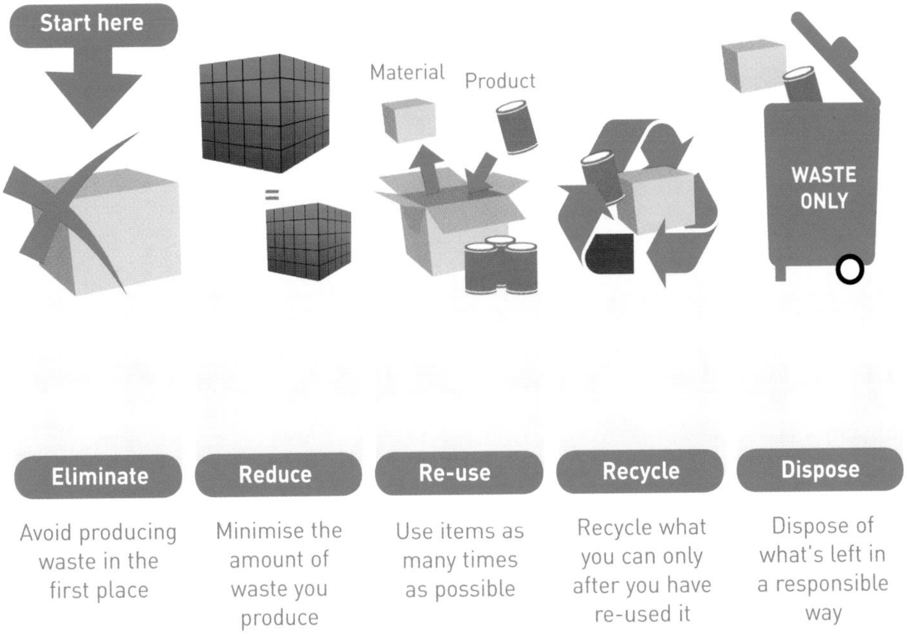
Start here
Material
Product
WASTE ONLY
Eliminate
Avoid producing waste in the first place
Reduce
Minimise the amount of waste you produce
Re-use
Use items as many times as possible
Recycle
Recycle what you can only after you have re-used it
Dispose
Dispose of what's left in a responsible way

Figure 1

Eliminate

Eliminating waste entirely may not always be possible, but by not creating it in the first place reduces costs of raw materials.

Reduce

Reducing the amount of waste produced can be achieved in a number of ways, by reducing the amount of packing used, by reducing off-cuts and rejects, by sending information electronically, by purchasing material in bulk and by using returnable containers.

14 Envirowise. (2010, April 23). Introduction to the waste hierarchy. Retrieved April 23, 2010, from envirowise.gov.uk: http://www.envirowise.gov.uk/uk/Our-Services/Publications/EN504-Introduction-to-the-waste-hierarchy.html

Re-use

To limit extra costs of buying items in, many can be re-used to reduce waste.

For example:

- packaging - boxes can be re-used many times
- printer toner cartridges - choose a supplier that has a returns policy so that they can be re-filled and used again
- paper - re-use paper from misprints and drafts as scrap paper
- drums - many raw materials are delivered in drums that can be washed and returned to the supplier, or re-used on site as waste containers
- furniture and textiles - waste furniture and textiles may be of use to charities or to waste exchange groups.

Recycle

Recycling is an increasing requirement through legislation in order to reduce the impact on the environment. Many items can now be recycled and a business should speak to its local recycling centre or waste management contractor to find out what they are and how they should be segregated.

Disposal

Disposal is the last resort when the other hierarchy options have been exhausted. There are legal obligations that all producers and handlers of waste need to comply with, so it is important that the business contacts its waste management contractor to discuss options like recycling to make waste disposal more efficient and save money.

Case Study

The manufacturing facilities of a major soft drinks company in the United Kingdom, including the firm's largest factory in the country, have gone zero waste and no longer send rubbish to landfill.

In keeping with the firm's goal to shrink its footprint worldwide, seven plants had become zero-waste sites by the close of 2009. Five plants had hit the target by early December.

The company cited two key ingredients in their plants' success, the enthusiasm of employees and the appointment of four "waste marshals". The waste marshals were in charge of making sure that waste was correctly sorted and stored - and that all their co-workers were educated about how to separate and recycle and the reasons for doing so.

At the start of 2008, the company's largest manufacturing plant was sending 32.3 tonnes of waste to landfills each month. The campaign to reduce waste brought that down to 1.5 tonnes week by the end of 2008. From there, workers brought the figure to zero in 2009. Based on 2010 figures, that is an overall saving in actual costs of £4,393 per month or £52,716 per year.

Electrical equipment

A study in 2009 on recycling suggested that Britons are the worst in Europe when it comes to recycling electrical equipment. The computer manufacturer Dell found that fewer than half of UK residents regularly recycled old hardware, compared with more than 80% of Germans. Within the UK, the Welsh are the worst when it comes to recycling technology; almost 20% have never done so. It is thought the UK creates enough electrical waste each year to fill Wembley Stadium six times over. An environmental consultant said that lack of awareness was a serious issue. The percentage of people who did not recycle e-waste ranged from 7% in Northern Ireland to 19% in Wales.

A Dell spokesperson said that governments in every country need to make the disposal of old electrical equipment as accessible and commonplace as recycling old paper, plastics and glass.

In early May 2009, mobile operator 0_2 looked at what electrical equipment was inside a typical home. It found that there was an average of 2.4 TVs, 1.6 computers, 2.4 games consoles, 3 mobile phones, and 2.2 MP3 players[15 and 16].

15 BBC News. (2009, May 22). UK 'worst electrical recycler' . Retrieved April 23, 2010, from news.bbc.co.uk: http://news.bbc.co.uk/1/hi/technology/8063115.stm

16 Dell. (2009, May 22). British Public sitting on a mountain of technology waste. Retrieved April 23, 2010, from content.dell.com: http://content.dell.com/uk/en/corp/d/press-releases/2009-05-09-mountain-uk.aspx

Electrical waste includes digital watches, fridges, TVs, computers and toys. Not only is this waste stream disparate in function but in addition the materials of which they are comprised vary considerably. For example an average TV contains 6% metal and 50% glass whereas a cooker is 89% metal and only 6% glass. Other materials used include plastics, ceramics and precious metals. The complex array of product types and materials make waste electrical and electronic equipment difficult to manage.

The main component of waste electronic equipment is large household appliances known as white goods, which make up 43% of the total. The next largest component is IT equipment which accounts for 39%. Much of this is made up from computers, which rapidly become obsolete. Televisions also represent a large proportion, with an estimated 2 million TV sets being discarded each year.

There is a growing problem associated with e-waste as the following case study shows.

Case Study[17]

Threat from E-waste 'Mountains'

Urgent action is needed to tackle the "mountains" of e-waste building up in developing nations, says a UN report as huge amounts of old computers and discarded electronic goods are piling up in countries such as China, India and some Africa nations. India could see a 500% rise in the number of old computers dumped by 2020 and unless dealt with properly the waste could cause environmental damage and threaten public health, the report states.

The report gathered information about current levels of e-waste in 11 nations and also looked at how those totals might grow in the next decade. Globally, e-waste is growing at a rate of about 40 million tonnes per year as consumers, in both developed and developing nations buy new gadgets and discard their old ones. Many of the older items end up in developing nations. By 2020, China and South Africa could see e-waste generated by old computers rise by 400% over 2007 levels.

The report estimated that e-waste from mobile phones will be seven times higher in China and 18 times higher in India in ten years' time. (Some nations are happy to take in e-waste to use in order to extract some of the precious materials and metals that go into making modern consumer electronics.)

In an average year the report stated global production of mobile phones and computers uses 3% of the silver and gold mined, 13% of the palladium and 15% of the cobalt. However, it found, in some places efforts to extract these metals are inefficient and do not do enough to handle the hazardous materials recovery produces. For example, it said that e-waste treatment in China

17 BBC News. (2010, February 22). 'Mountains' of e-waste threaten developing world . Retrieved April 23, 2010, from news.bbc.co.uk: http://news.bbc.co.uk/1/hi/technology/8528066.stm

typically involved back yard incinerators which were a wasteful and polluting way to recover precious materials.

"China is not alone in facing a serious challenge," said Achim Steiner, executive director of the UN Environmental Programme (UNEP) which issued the report. "India, Brazil, Mexico and others may also face rising environmental damage and health problems if e-waste recycling is left to the vagaries of the informal sector."

The report said Bangalore in India was a good example of how local initiatives could reform the gathering and treatment of e-waste. It urged nations such as Brazil, Colombia, Mexico, Morocco and South Africa to set up state-of-the-art e-waste treatment centres now, while the amounts they produced were relatively small.

Zero Waste does not mean that waste disappears. Instead, it means eliminating the unnecessary use of raw materials, using sustainable design, resource efficiency and waste prevention, re-using products where possible, and recovering value from products when they reach the end of their lives either through recycling, composting or energy recovery, in accordance with the waste hierarchy.

Zero waste strategies mean that everyone – business, householders and the public and voluntary sectors – needs to reflect on how to reduce the amount of waste that is produced, how they can reduce unnecessary consumption and how they can improve recycling rates.

If the same strategy was adopted by every business in England, a 60% reduction of the 330 million tonnes of waste per year to landfill would save English business nearly £27bn per year. At an average market rate for recyclates of £213 it could generate a possible maximum revenue for recycling businesses of over £42 bn per year. These figures may be somewhat fanciful but they do indicate that the concept of zero waste is well worth pursuing.

CHAPTER 28

Environmental Management and Reporting

- Guidance from Defra and DECC
- Small Business User Guide
- Standardisation Needed

Guidance from Defra and DECC

This section summarises with extracts Defra's guidance (2009) on measuring and reporting greenhouse gas (GHG) emissions[1].

Defra state that companies that measure, manage and communicate their environmental performance are inherently well placed. They understand how to:

- improve their processes
- reduce their costs
- comply with regulatory requirements and stakeholder expectations
- and take advantages of new market opportunities.

Failure to plan for a future in which environmental factors are likely to be increasingly significant may risk the long-term future of a business. Good environmental performance makes good business sense. Environmental risks and uncertainties impact to some extent on all companies, and affect investment decisions, consumer behaviour and government policy.

Narrative Reporting Requirements

The Companies Act (2006) recently made changes to the narrative reporting requirements for UK companies. All companies, other than small, are already required to produce a business review. In the case of quoted companies, the directors will be required – to the extent necessary for an understanding of the business – to report on environmental matters, employees and social/community issues.

Amendment to Pensions Act (2001)

In 2001, a new mandatory requirement was introduced for UK Pension fund trustees to disclose how they have considered social, economic and environmental matters. Those companies that disclose this information, for example in environmental reports, are therefore in a stronger position to be considered in investment decisions by trustees.

Sustainability Indices

The emergence of ethical indices such as the Dow Jones Sustainability Index and the FTSE4Good index have also helped drive environmental reporting as companies reporting on their environmental performance are in a better position to be considered for inclusion in the index.

1 Defra. (2009, September). Guidance on how to measure and report your greenhouse gas emissions. Retrieved April 25, 2010, from defra.gov.uk: http://www.defra.gov.uk/environment/business/reporting/pdf/ghg-guidance.pdf

Global Reporting Initiative (GRI)

In 2000, the GRI produced broader sustainability reporting guidelines for organisations to report on the economic, social and environmental dimensions of their activities products and services. This provides stakeholders with a universally-applicable, comparable framework in which to understand disclosed information.

Defra, in partnership with DECC (Department of Energy and Climate Change), published guidance for UK businesses and organisations on how to measure and report their greenhouse gas (GHG) emissions in September 2009. The guidance explains how businesses and organisations can measure and report their GHG emissions as well as set targets to reduce them. The guidance is aimed at all sizes of business as well as public and third sector organisations.

The guidance is part of the UK government's implementation of the Climate Change Act 2008. Organisations using this guidance will not be required to submit reports or make data available to government. Reporting on emissions is voluntary.

Amongst other things the Climate Change Act 2008 requires the government to:

- carry out a review by December 2010 to evaluate the contribution that reporting on GHG emissions is making to the achievement of its climate change objectives
- introduce regulations requiring the mandatory reporting of GHG emissions information under the Companies Act 2006 by the 6th of April 2012 or lay a report to Parliament explaining why this has not happened. There will be a further consultation on this guidance before a decision is made on mandatory reporting requirements.

The guidance sets out broad general principles on how to measure and report greenhouse gas emissions. It is based on the GHG Protocol, the internationally recognised standard for the corporate accounting and reporting of GHG emissions. This means it aligns with many widely used national and international voluntary measuring and reporting schemes such as the International Organisation for Standardisation (ISO) 14064-18 and the Carbon Trust Standard. The guidance also complements both PAS 20509 and ISO 1404010 which can be used to measure the carbon footprint of products.

Some organisations already report emissions data for regulatory schemes such as the EU Emissions Trading System (EU ETS) (see Chapter 29) and Climate Change Agreements (CCAs). Others will need to do so as part of the forthcoming CRC. These schemes only cover some of an organisation's GHG emissions, whereas this guidance covers an organisation's total GHG emissions (also known as its corporate carbon footprint) as illustrated in the following diagram.

Corporate Carbon Footprint

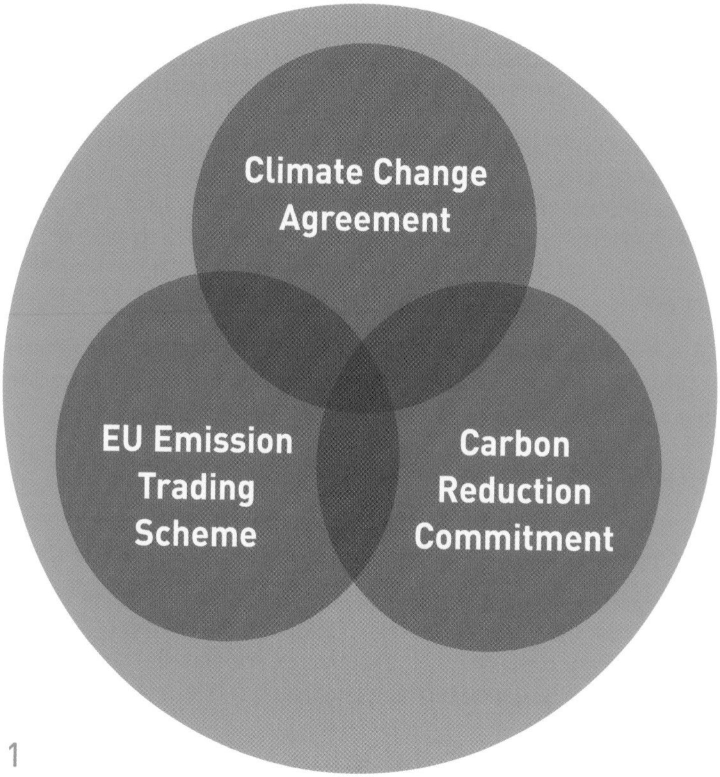

Figure 1

If the business has a simple organisational structure and it owns 100% of its operations it needs to identify activities that release greenhouse gases. To calculate its total GHG emissions it needs to identify from which parts of the organisation it needs to collect information. Organisations vary in structure from sole traders to complex multi-nationals with large numbers of subsidiaries and joint ventures. The more complex the structure of the organisation, the more difficult it is to identify who has responsibility for the emissions produced by these different operations.

If the business owns less than 100% of the operations in which it has some business involvement, it will need to identify the operations or share of operations for which GHG emissions need to be calculated. The business can do this by reference to one of four established approaches.

- **The equity share approach** – under which a company accounts for GHG emissions from operations according to its share of equity in the operation.
- **The control approach** – under which a company accounts for 100% of the GHG emissions from operations over which it has control. It does not account for GHG emissions from operations in which it owns an interest but has no control. Control can be defined in either financial or operational terms.

- **The financial control approach** – a company has financial control over an operation if the company has the ability to direct the financial and operating policies of the operation with a view to gaining economic benefits from its activities.
- **The operational control approach** – a company has operational control over an operation if the company or one of its subsidiaries has the full authority to introduce and implement its operating policies at the operation.

Recommendation 1

Apply your chosen approach consistently and for most organisations this will be the financial control approach.

The financial control approach is the recommended approach because it is the approach which aligns most consistently to financial accounting but it may be the case that the equity share approach or operational control approach is more appropriate for some businesses and they may wish to use either of these approaches instead.

Many UK organisations have operations and businesses overseas and therefore to get an understanding of their total emissions they should include emissions related to their overseas activities. It may be challenging to collect data from these overseas operations so they may wish to initially focus on measuring and calculating emissions from UK operations. However, Defra suggest that businesses should make best endeavours to collect data from overseas operations to give a complete picture of their operations in line with their financial reports. Businesses will need to make it clear when reporting their total global greenhouse gas emissions as to any geographical areas they have not included.

Recommendation 2

Measure or calculate your total emissions on a global basis.

The most widely accepted approach is to identify and categorise emissions-releasing activities into three groups known as scopes. The three scopes already seen in Chapter 24 are:

- **Scope 1 (Direct emissions)** - Activities owned or controlled by your organisation that release remissions straight into the atmosphere.
- **Scope 2 (Energy indirect)** - Emissions being released into the atmosphere associated with your consumption of purchased electricity, heat, steam and cooling but which occur at sources you do not own or control.
- **Scope 3 (Other indirect)** - Emissions that are a consequence of your actions, which occur at sources which you do not own or control and which are not classed as scope 2 emissions.

Carbon dioxide produced from the combustion of biomass/biofuels should be reported separately to emissions in scopes 1, 2, and 3. Carbon dioxide produced from biomass/biofuels not as a result of the combustion of biomass/biofuels (e.g. industrial fermentation) should be reported within the scopes.

In some instances, it may be difficult to identify whether emissions should be categorised as scope 1 or scope 3 emissions. For example, this may be because the business's emissions sources come from outsourced activities, leased assets or tenanted buildings.

For some organisations, emissions within scope 3 may be the largest proportion of their total emissions. By calculating their scope 3 emissions, they will get a more complete understanding of their organisation's total impact on climate change. Identifying an organisation's scope 3 emissions will also help increase its awareness of where it sits within the supply chain and enable it to engage with other organisations in the supply chain. However it is acknowledged that it can be difficult to measure and calculate scope 3 emissions so it is recommended that a business focuses on its 'significant' scope 3 emissions.

Recommendation 3

Measure or calculate emissions that fall into your scopes 1 and 2.

Discretionary: Measure or calculate your significant scope 3 emissions in addition to your scopes 1 and 2.

The six greenhouse gases covered by the Kyoto protocol are:

- Carbon Dioxide CO2
- Methane CH4
- Nitrous oxide N2O
- Perfluorocarbons PFC
- Sulphur Hexafluoride SF6
- Hydrofluorocarbons HFC.

Recommendation 4

Measure or calculate emissions from the six GHGs covered by the Kyoto Protocol (See chapter 29).

Defra suggest that the most common approach used to calculate GHG emissions is to apply documented emission factors to known activity data from the organisation.

Activity Data x Emission Factor = GHG emissions

Activity data is information used to calculate GHG emissions from combustion and other processes, for example, this could be litres of fuel consumed by the organisation's vehicles. Most activity data is easy to obtain, relatively accurate and can be found on bills, invoices and receipts.

It is best to collect activity data by volume or mass (e.g. litres of petrol used) as emissions can be calculated more accurately. There are a number of ways to collect and manage this activity data at a corporate level. For example, this could include direct entry of activity data by operational staff onto secure Internet or Intranet databases, or standard spreadsheet templates completed and emailed to a central point where data can be processed. Ideally, GHG reporting should be integrated into existing reporting tools and processes of your organisation.

When collecting data at a corporate level, using a standardised reporting format is recommended to ensure that data received from different business units and operations is comparable. A business may wish to establish a quality management system to ensure that it produces a high quality corporate carbon footprint. A quality management system provides a systematic process for preventing and correcting errors in your organisation's GHG emissions data. If it is not possible for you to calculate your emissions from known activity data, you will need to estimate.

Estimated Activity Data x Emission Factor = GHG emissions

Where the organisation already reports GHG emissions data for regulatory schemes such as EU ETS or CCAs, the new CRC and regulatory schemes in other administrations, it may wish to use this emissions data for the purposes of reporting its total GHG emissions. Defra recommend that as there are some differences in approach between the regulatory schemes and their reporting guidance the business should provide information on the calculation approach and conversion factors used for those emissions reported for regulatory purposes.

Where GHG emissions data reported for existing regulatory schemes does not cover all the emissions sources or greenhouse gases that the organisation is responsible for, it should use the approach outlined in Defra's guidance to measure or calculate those remaining emissions. The organisation should also use the recommended format in Defra's guidance for reporting its emissions data. However, given the differences in approaches between the regulatory schemes and Defra's reporting guidance, a business may wish to measure, calculate and report all its total global GHG emissions, for purposes other than reporting for the regulatory schemes, using the approach in the guidance.

Defra recommend that the reporting period of a business should be for 12 months. The emissions year should ideally correspond with the business's financial year, but where they are different, the majority of its emission reporting year should fall within the financial year.

Which Conversion Factors should the Business use?

The methodology behind the calculations of a variety of emissions needed is too complicated and lengthy to include in this chapter but all the necessary information is available on the Defra website. Below is an indication of which annex holds the relevant information for each type of emission.

Annex 1	Emissions from combustion of fuels
Annex 2	Emissions from Combined Heat and Power (CHP) where the business is the generator
Annex 3	Emissions from the consumption of Electricity
Annex 4	To understand which industrial processes lead to GHG emissions
Annex 5	To convert greenhouse gases into carbon dioxide equivalents
Annex 6	To calculate emissions associated with Passenger Transport
Annex 7	To calculate emissions associated with Freight Transport
Annex 8	To calculate emissions from the use of Refrigeration and Air Conditioning Equipment
Annex 9	To calculate life-cycle emissions from the use of Water, Biomass and Bio-fuels, and from Waste Disposal
Annex 10	To calculate emissions from the use of Overseas Electricity
Annex 11	For the typical Calorific Values and Densities of UK Fuels
Annex 12	To convert between common units of energy, volume, mass and distance
Annex 13	To estimate emissions from your supply chain

The purpose of the greenhouse gas (GHG) conversion factors is to help businesses convert existing data sources (e.g. utility bills, car mileage, refrigeration and fuel consumption) into CO2 equivalent emissions by applying relevant conversion factors (e.g. calorific values, emission factors, oxidation factors). These greenhouse gas conversion factors should be used alongside guidance on how to measure and report greenhouse gas emissions to help measure and report on the greenhouse emissions that the organisation is responsible for. The 2009 Guidelines to Defra/DECC's GHG Conversion Factors for Company Reporting can be found on:

http://www.defra.gov.uk/environment/business/reporting/pdf/20090928-guidelines-ghg-conversion-factors.pdf

Recommendation 5

Where your organisation is using standard emission factors, you should use the Defra/DECC GHG conversion factors for UK emissions. If you require other emission factors you should refer to the emission factors in the GHG Protocol calculation tools.

A business should report its GHG emissions as a gross figure in tonnes of CO2e (CO2 equivalent). Gross emissions are its total GHG emissions before accounting for any emission reductions that have been purchased or sold. This should be the business's reported headline figure.

Recommendation 6

Report total GHG emissions as a gross figure in tonnes of CO2e.

Where an organisation has purchased or sold emission reductions (i.e. carbon credits and green tariffs) that meet certain 'good quality' emission reduction criteria, Defra recommend that it reports on all purchased or sold emissions reductions – either for the purposes of compliance or offsetting. Defra recommends that organisations account for these emissions reductions against their gross figure to report a net figure in tonnes of CO2e. This net figure should be additional to its gross figure and should not replace it.

Recommendation 7

Report purchased or sold emissions reductions that meet the 'good quality' emission reduction criteria. Then report a net figure in tonnes of CO2e, in addition to the gross figure.

Organisations should normalise their total global scope 1 and 2 emissions using an intensity ratio.

Intensity ratios compare emissions data with an appropriate business metric or financial indicator, such as sales revenue or square metres of floor space. Using an intensity ratio allows you to compare your performance over time and with other similar types of organisations.

Recommendation 8

Report on total scopes 1 and 2 emissions using an intensity ratio.

It is recommended by Defra that a business should report a summary table of its GHG emissions data for the chosen annual reporting period, the previous year's performance and the base year. An example Corporate Carbon Footprint provided in the guidance showing GHG emissions data for period 1 January 2010 to 31 December 2010 is shown below.

Base Year

	2010 Tonnes of CO2e	2009 Tonnes of CO2e	2006 Tonnes of CO2e
Scope 1	17,100	17,500	13,120
Scope 2	14,500	15,100	10,000
Scope 3	9,410	10,415	12,990
Total gross emissions	**41,010**	**43,015**	**36,110**
Carbon offsets	(5,000)		
Green tariff	(7,250)	(9,800)	
Total annual net emissions	**28,760**	**33,215**	**36,110**

Defra/DECC recommends organisations report on emission reduction activities (i.e. carbon offsets and green tariffs) that meet Defra's good quality criteria.

Defra/DECC also recommend that the business provides some written explanation on how these figures have been calculated and provide context for the data for its stakeholders. They further recommend that these supporting explanations are provided as notes to its reported emissions data.

Recommendation 9

Provide supporting explanations.

An example reporting template can be found in Annex 1 (see summary above) to help clarify the reporting format expected of companies using the guidance.

Where should a Business Report this Information?

Quoted companies already report information on environmental matters (to the extent it is necessary for an understanding of the development, performance or position of the company's business) in their business review which forms part of their Annual Report and Accounts. They will want to consider if they wish to follow this guidance there.

Defra/DECC encourage organisations to publish their GHG emissions data and supporting explanations. Where the business reports its data is a matter of choice. For some companies it may be their annual report/business review or it may be in a separate corporate responsibility/sustainability report. Organisations which do not publish such external reports may wish to publicly disclose this information on their website. To help to maintain a meaningful and consistent comparison of emissions over time, the business will need to choose and report on a base year.

Recommendation 10

Choose and report on a base year. Your base year should be:

- the earliest year that verifiable emissions data is available for
- either a single year or a multi-year average (e.g. 2006-2008).

For consistent tracking of performance over time, the business may need to recalculate its base year so that it can compare its current emissions with historic emissions. The business should develop a base year recalculation policy which clearly explains the basis and context for any recalculations. If applicable, the business should state any significance threshold applied for deciding on historic emissions recalculation. It should consider recalculating its base year emissions in the following cases.

- Structural changes that have a significant impact on the company's base year emissions, such as the transfer of ownership or control of emissions–releasing activities or operations from one company to another. While a single structural change might not have a significant impact on the base year emissions, the cumulative effect of a number of minor structural changes can result in a significant impact. Structural changes include:
  - mergers, acquisitions, and divestments
  - outsourcing and insourcing of emitting activities.
- Changes in calculation methods or improvements in the accuracy of emission factors or activity data that result in a significant impact on the base year emissions data.
- Discovery of significant errors, or a number of cumulative errors, that are collectively significant.

Base year emissions do not need to be recalculated in the following cases.

- Economic growth or decline – refers to changes in production output, and closures and openings of operating units owned or controlled by the organisation.
- Outsourcing or insourcing of emitting activities – structural changes due to "outsourcing" or "insourcing" do not trigger base year emissions recalculation if the organisation is reporting its other indirect (scope 3) emissions from relevant outsourced or insourced activities. Only where the emitting activities move outside the scope of its reported GHGs, or emitting activities move within the scope of its reported GHGs, should you include them.
- Operations acquired or sold that did not exist in the base year – the business should not recalculate its base year where it acquires (or insources) and divests (or outsources) operations that did not exist in the base year. Once the organisation has developed its policy on how it will recalculate base year emissions it should apply this policy in a consistent manner.

Recommendation 11

Develop a base year recalculation policy. Update your base year following significant changes that meet your significance threshold against the criteria outlined above.

Organisations that externally report their emissions data may wish to receive independent assurance over the reported GHG emissions. An independent firm would provide an assurance statement setting out their opinion on the accuracy, completeness and consistency of GHG emissions data reported based upon the evidence they have collected. There is no requirement for a business to obtain any level of assurance over its emissions data. Businesses choose to receive assurance because it can help to increase stakeholder confidence in the accuracy and completeness of GHG emissions data. There will be a cost associated with receiving any type of assurance. This is an evolving issue and there are many different levels of assurance so Defra/DECC recommend that the business talks to an assurance expert.

Why should the Business Set a Target?

Once a business has measured and calculated its total GHG emissions, setting an emission reduction target is the logical next step. There are a number of good business reasons to do this.

- To improve cost efficiency – cost savings can be made by identifying opportunities to increase resource and energy efficiency. This may help to improve competitive advantage.
- To demonstrate leadership – by setting ambitious targets, measuring, managing, reporting and reducing GHG emissions.
- To improve brand recognition in an increasingly environmentally conscious marketplace – consumers and employees have a greater awareness of corporate social responsibility and expect business to a take a leadership role in the management of GHG emissions.

What Kind of Target Should a Business Set?

Organisations can set:

- an absolute GHG reduction target which compares total GHG emissions in the target year to those in a base year; or
- an intensity target based on a decrease in GHG emissions intensity using an appropriate normalising factor (e.g. tonnes/gross CO2e per tonne of product, floor space or Full Time Equivalent). This takes into account increases or decreases in production over time.

The advantages and disadvantages of both types of target are outlined below:

Absolute Targets

Advantages	Disadvantages
• Designed to achieve a reduction in a specified quantity of GHGs emitted to the atmosphere	• Target base year recalculations for significant structural changes to the organisation will be necessary. These add complexity to tracking progress over time
• Environmentally robust as it entails a commitment to reduce GHG emissions by a specified amount	• Does not allow comparisons of GHG intensity/efficiency
• Transparently addresses potential stakeholder concerns about the need to manage absolute emissions	• May be difficult to achieve if the company grows unexpectedly or growth is linked to GHG emissions

Intensity Targets

Advantages	Disadvantages
• Reflects GHG performance improvements independent of organic growth or decline	• No guarantee that GHG emissions will be reduced – absolute emissions may rise even if intensity goes down and output increases
• Target base year recalculations for structural changes are usually not required	• Companies with diverse operations may find it difficult to define a single common business metric
• May increase the comparability of GHG performance amongst companies	• If a monetary variable is used for the business metric, such as £ million of sales, it must be recalculated for changes in product prices and product mix, as well as inflation, adding complexity to the process

The business should consider whether targets should be:

- organisation-wide (including all UK and overseas emissions)
- inclusive of all emissions (scope 1, 2 and 3) that it measures and reports on
- based on the most recent base year data that it has available
- achieved over 5 to 10 years.

Recommendation 12

Set a reduction target and choose the approach to use.

Small Business User Guide

Defra and DECC have also published a "Small Business User Guide"[2] to encourage SMEs to also start to collect data and to record their GHG emissions because legislation aimed at the larger businesses is often eventually applied to SMEs.

2 Defra. (2009, September). Small Business User Guide. Retrieved April 25, 2010, from defra.gov.uk: http://www.defra.gov.uk/environment/business/reporting/pdf/ghg-small-business-user-guide.pdf

They indicate why a small business should measure its greenhouse gas emissions by highlighting that it would:

- **save money** – by helping the business to identify which of its activities use a lot of energy and so helps it to reduce energy and resource use
- **generate new business** – if the business reduces its costs it can become more competitive and bring in new customers
- **meet the information demands of its customers** – it helps the business to meet customer requests for information on greenhouse gas emissions. This is becoming an increasingly important element of the procurement process
- **do your bit** – a business should understand the contribution it is making to climate change and reduce it.

In the same way that larger businesses need to identify which greenhouse gas emissions are released as a result of their operations the same is true of the smaller business.

The main activities from a smaller business which release greenhouse gases may include

- electricity/gas use
- waste disposal/recycling
- business travel
- owned or controlled vehicles
- employee business travel
- staff commuting.

The business needs to collect and then convert the gas emissions data using the same methodology as that expected of the large business. Further information for small business can be found on the Defra website.

Case Study[3]

Tesco's Carbon footprint

Share of emissions by country for 2008/9

UK	54%	Hungary	4%	Slovakia	1%
Thailand	10%	Republic of Ireland	3%	US	1%
South Korea	7%	Czech Republic	3%	Japan	1%
Poland	6%	Malaysia	3%	India	>1%
China	5%	Turkey	2%		

Group emissions by source for 2008/9

- Grid Electricity 62%
- Refrigerant 20%
- Diesel/Oil 11%
- Natural Gas 6%
- Business Travel 1%

3 Tesco PLC. (2009). Our Direct Carbon Footprint. Retrieved April 25, 2010, from tescoplc.com: http://www.tescoplc.com/plc/corporate_responsibility_09/environment/climate_change/leading_by_example/carbon_footprint/

	2008/9 emissions	% change since 2007/8	% change since 2006/7
Total Direct Carbon footprint over 52 weeks	4.92mtCO2e	+3.7%	+12.5%
Total Direct Carbon footprint over 53 weeks	5.02mtCO2e	+5.7%	+14.7%
Carbon intensity/net sales area	55.1 kgCO2e/ft2	-10.9%	-16.2%
Existing stores and distribution centres: energy consumption for fixed floor area (excluding refrigerant)	32.0 kgCO2e/ft2	-9.1%	-12.6%
New stores: average emissions	34.8kgCO2e/ft2	-10.5%	-20.8%
Distribution emissions per case delivered	0.17 kgCO2e/ case delivered	-3.6%	-11.5%

mtCO2e = million tonnes of carbon dioxide equivalent

kgCO2e/ft2 = kilograms of carbon dioxide equivalent per square foot of floor area

Tesco was commended for its carbon management and reporting approach in the 2008 global Carbon Disclosure Leadership Index, and was the highest scoring retailer. This index assesses the approaches taken by the FTSE 500 companies.

Tesco calculated its carbon footprint according to the World Business Council for Sustainable Development (WBCSD) greenhouse gas protocol, which is the internationally recognised standard for corporate carbon reporting, and updated guidelines produced by the UK government (Defra) in 2008.

Case Study[4]

Morrisons

Key performance indicators

Since our 2005 baseline year we've made an absolute saving of over 240,000 tonnes of CO2e. Despite significant growth over that time, our emissions remain on a downward trend.

Tonnes of carbon emissions (CO2e)

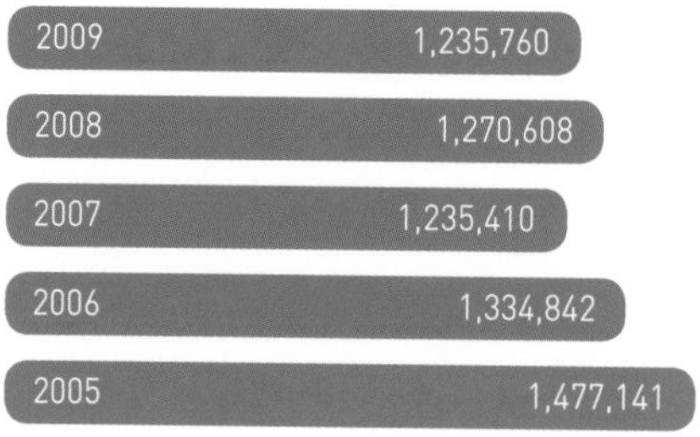

Emissions by type (Percentage %)

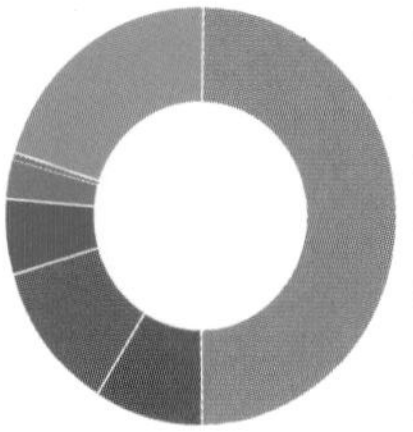

Morrisons are focusing on cutting carbon and preventing waste. These closely linked issues are key material impact areas for their business.

Energy efficiency and performance

Target	Progress	
Reduce carbon footprint cumulatively by 36% by 2010 (saving of 533,304 tonnes, based on 2005 emissions).	Cumulative saving of 56% (831,943 tonnes) since 2006 or an absolute saving of over 240,000 tonnes.	Achieved
Reduce Group energy use by 8% per square metre by 2010 (based on 2005 emissions).	Reduced by 5.2% compared to 2005.	Not achieved due to new manufacturing facilities, higher volume of production and the increase in store numbers.

4 Morrisons. (2010, April 25). Our performance 2009/10. Retrieved April 25, 2010, from morrisons.co.uk: http://www.morrisons.co.uk/Corporate/Corporate-Social-Responsibility-200910/Performance-200910/Environment/

Refrigeration management

Target	Progress	
Replace HCFCs with HFCs by the end of 2010.	146 stores completed (72% of total programme).	On Target
Extend CO2 refrigeration system technology to five stores in 2008.	20 stores completed and 20 more scheduled for 2010.	Achieved
Apply new heat reclaim technology to 40 stores by the end of 2008.	Technology installed into 45 stores by the end of 2009.	

Water conservation

Target	Progress
15% reduction in water use by 2010 (saving of 686,592 cubic metres, based on 2005 baseline).	19.4% reduction (886,640 cubic metres).

Transport efficiency

Target	Progress	
Save 8% of our haulage CO2e by 2010, through mileage reductions and increased efficiencies.	8% reduction compared to 2005.	Achieved
Reduce road kilometres travelled per pallet of stock by 6% by 2010.	11.7% reduction compared to 2006.	Achieved
Achieve an 8% reduction in empty road miles travelled.	22.8% reduction compared to 2006.	Achieved

Case Study[5]

Asda

It is their intention to update and compare their carbon footprint every calendar year.

Asda's Carbon Footprint 2009

Their current carbon footprint is 1.2 million tonnes (carbon equivalent) which represents a 5.0% absolute reduction from the previous year. This has been calculated using Defra's October 2009 emission factors (ie the recommended good practice):

	2009 emissions	2008 emissions	Change since 2008
Carbon intensity	65.68 tCO2e/£m	74.72 tCO2e/£m	-12.0%
Total Direct Carbon Footprint	1.199 mtCO2e	1.258 mtCO2e	-5.0%

mtCO2e = million tonnes CO2 equivalent

tCO2e/£m = tonnes CO2 equivalent per million pounds sales

Asda has grown successfully over the past few years and increased both market share and sales. Notwithstanding this growth, in the past 2 years the company has made a 7% absolute reduction in its carbon footprint which equates to a 21% reduction in carbon intensity (per £m sales).

Continuing the focus from 2008, in 2009 Asda made significant reductions in key areas which would reduce carbon emissions most effectively, namely energy efficiency, refrigerant gas leak reductions and diverting waste from landfill.

	2009 emissions	2008 emissions	Change since 2008
Refrigerate	180,115.2	192,623.4	-6.5%
Electricity	749,106.8	778,230	-3.7%
Waste to landfill	25,198.4	29,700	-15.2%

5 Asda. (2010, February 25). Asda's Carbon Footprint 2009. Retrieved April 25, 2010, from asda.com: http://your.asda.com/assets/2010/2/25/Asda_carbon_footprint_2009.pdf

2008

Emissions from energy usage (mainly electricity) and refrigerant gas usage: site energy and activity was 87%, transport of goods 12% and employee business travel 1%.

In addition to making reductions in its carbon footprint, Asda has also increased the accuracy of its model with AEA. This leads AEA[6] to conclude that the improvements made in our direct footprint since 2007 'are likely to be independent of data recording issues and due to energy saving initiatives or cut backs made by ASDA.

6 AEA: energy and climate change consultancy: http://www.aeat.co.uk

Standardisation needed

It is interesting to note that two of the three supermarkets are using Defra's guidance and quoting carbon intensity targets whereas the other is not. Also Tesco is using a carbon intensity figure related to "sales area" but Asda have used "per £m of sales" so ultimately standardisation of these figures is necessary. As with other accounting ratios this is likely to evolve over time.

Benchmarking, league tables and clear reporting enable businesses to show exactly how they are doing in terms of reducing their carbon footprints on the grounds that that "if you don't measure it, you can't manage it". Better accuracy takes away all the debate about whether energy management needs to improve. Measurement is critical and many businesses are already well versed in applying targets key performance indicators (KPIs) and scorecards to ensure their organisation's sustainability strategy is delivering results. Asda for example, via their finance team, not only produce environmental targets, but disseminate them via portals to each store and use them as part of performance reviews allied to individuals' targets on climate change and bonuses.

Many companies are required to include environmental performance reporting alongside their financial disclosures but by using voluntary targets, businesses have an opportunity to reduce emissions on their own terms. These targets must be credible and meaningful enough to satisfy and ideally exceed regulatory requirements. Any disclosures on climate change and emissions should be as credible and robust as possible. This can be achieved by a number of mechanisms, including the independent verification/assurance of GHG-emissions data and claims, and the use of standards and guidance such as the GRI G3 environmental indicators, the Defra/DECC guidance, WBCSD GHG Protocol and ISO 14064 standards, to ensure that the information is credible, accurate and comparable.

CHAPTER 29

Legislation

- Energy Acts 2008 and 2010
- Climate Change Act 2008
- CRC Energy Efficiency Scheme
- Other Relevant Legislation

Energy Acts 2008 and 2010 ●●●

Understanding the regulatory picture will be very important to all business because invariably what is expected of the large companies today will eventually filter down to SMEs. Cutting carbon can deliver significant financial benefits but businesses also need to be aware that their environmental performance is subject to growing regulatory scrutiny. This chapter can only include an outline of the main areas of legislation relevant to a responsible business concerned about climate change.

Legislation[1]

The Department of Energy and Climate Change (DECC) works to ensure that the right legislative framework is in place to let the government meet its policy objectives: reducing greenhouse gas emissions in the UK, confirming global commitments to tackle climate change and ensuring secure, affordable energy supplies.

They have successfully taken three Bills through Parliament, which are now the Energy Act 2008, the Climate Change Act 2008 and the Energy Act 2010. The Climate Change Act 2008: Impact Assessment was updated in March 2009 to reflect the Act's final contents.

On 8 April 2010, the Energy Bill received Royal Assent becoming Energy Act 2010. It implements some of the key measures required to deliver DECC's low-carbon agenda. It includes provisions on delivering a new financial incentive for carbon capture and storage, implementing mandatory social price support, and introducing a package of measures aimed at ensuring that the energy markets are working fairly for consumers and delivering secure and sustainable energy supplies.

In November 2008, the government introduced the Planning Act 2008 which is of considerable importance for energy infrastructure projects. Also in November 2008, the Planning and Energy Act 2008, a Private Member's Act, was introduced.

Energy Act 2008

The Energy Act 2008 was given Royal Assent on 26 November 2008. It implements the legislative aspects of the Energy white paper 2007: 'Meeting the energy challenge'.

The Energy Act updated energy legislation to:

- reflect the availability of new technologies (such as Carbon Capture & Storage (CCS) and emerging renewable technologies
- correspond with the UK's changing requirements for secure energy supply (such as offshore gas storage)
- protect the environment and the tax payer as the energy market changes.

Along with the Planning Act 2008 and Climate Change Act 2008, the Energy Act ensures that UK legislation underpins its long-term energy and climate change strategy.

1 DECC. (2010, April 25). Legislation. Retrieved April 25, 2010, from decc.gov.uk: http://www.decc.gov.uk/en/content/cms/legislation/legislation.aspx

The Act covers the following.

- **Offshore gas supply infrastructure** – strengthening regulation to allow for private sector investment to help maintain the UK's reliable energy supplies. This is crucial, as the government expects to have to rely on imported gas to meet up to 80 per cent of the energy demands by 2020.
- **Carbon Capture & Storage (CCS)** – creating regulation that enables private sector investment in CCS projects. CCS has the potential to reduce the carbon emissions from fossil fuel power stations by up to 90 per cent.
- **Renewables** – strengthening the renewables to increase the diversity of the UK'S electricity mix, improve the reliability of energy supplies and help lower carbon emissions from the electricity sector.
- **Feed-in tariffs** – enabling the government to offer financial support for low-carbon electricity generation in projects up to 5 megawatts (MW). The aim is for generators to receive a guaranteed payment for generating low-carbon electricity.
- **Decommissioning offshore renewables and oil and gas installations** – strengthening the government's statutory decommissioning requirements to minimise the risk of liabilities falling to the government.
- **Improving offshore oil and gas licensing** – improving licensing to respond to changes in the commercial environment and enable DECC to carry out its regulatory functions more effectively.
- **Nuclear power** – ensuring new nuclear power station operators build up funds to meet the full costs of decommissioning and their share of waste management costs.
- **Offshore transmission** – amending powers so that Ofgem is able to run offshore transmission licensing more effectively.
- **Smart metering** – allowing the Secretary of State to modify electricity and gas distribution and supply licences, so the licence holder has to install, or help install, smart meters to different customer segments, including private households.
- **Renewable Heat Incentive** – allowing the Secretary of State to establish a financial support programme for renewable heat generated anywhere, from large industrial sites to individual households.
- **Housekeeping** – various other points covering nuclear security and the transfer of some regulatory functions to DECC.

Energy Act 2010

The Energy Bill received Royal Assent in April 2010, becoming the Energy Act 2010.

The main elements of the Act are as follows.

- **Carbon capture and storage (CCS)** – delivering a new financial incentive to bring forward four commercial scale demonstration projects on coal-fired power stations and to support the retrofit of additional CCS capacity to those projects should it be required at a later date.

- **Mandatory social price support** – creating a framework to mandate energy companies to provide support to the fuel poor, including powers to give greater guidance and direction on the types of households eligible for future support and the type of support they should be given.
- **Clarifying Ofgem's remit** – making it clear that Ofgem must include the reduction of carbon emissions and the delivery of secure energy supplies in their assessment of the interests of consumers and step in proactively to protect consumers as well as considering longer term actions to promote competition.
- **Tackling market power exploitation** – giving Ofgem additional powers to tackle market exploitation where companies might take advantage of constraints in the electricity transmission grid.

Other measures are as follows.

- Requiring the government to prepare regular reports on the progress made on the decarbonisation of electricity generation in Britain and the development and use of CCS.
- Extending the time limit from 12 months to 5 years within which Ofgem can impose financial penalties on energy suppliers for breaches of licence conditions.
- Allowing the government to set the period within which energy companies must inform customers of changes to their gas and electricity tariffs.
- Enabling action to be taken against unfair cross-subsidy between gas and electricity supply.

Climate Change Act 2008

The UK has passed legislation which introduced the world's first long-term legally binding framework to tackle the dangers of climate change. The Climate Change Bill was introduced into Parliament on 14 November 2007 and became law on 26 November 2008.

The Climate Change Act creates a new approach to managing and responding to climate change in the UK, by:

- setting ambitious, legally binding targets
- taking powers to help meet those targets
- strengthening the institutional framework
- enhancing the UK's ability to adapt to the impact of climate change
- establishing clear and regular accountability to the UK Parliament and to the devolved legislatures.

In March 2009, the Climate Change Act Impact Assessment was updated to reflect the final contents of the Act.

Two key aims of the Act

- To improve carbon management, helping the transition towards a low-carbon economy in the UK.
- To demonstrate UK leadership internationally, signalling a commitment to sharing responsibility for reducing global emissions in the context of developing negotiations on a post-2012 global agreement at Copenhagen in December 2009.

Key provisions of the Act

- A legally binding target of at least an 80 per cent cut in greenhouse gas emissions by 2050, to be achieved through action in the UK and abroad. Also a reduction in emissions of at least 34 per cent by 2020. Both these targets are against a 1990 baseline.
- A carbon budgeting system which caps emissions over five-year periods, with three budgets set at a time, to help keep on track for the 2050 target. The first three Carbon budgets run from 2008-12, 2013-17 and 2018-22 and were set in May 2009. The government must report to Parliament its policies and proposals to meet the budgets, and this requirement was fulfilled by the UK Low Carbon Transition Plan.
- The creation of the Committee on Climate Change (CCC) - a new independent, expert body to advise the government on the level of carbon budgets and on where cost-effective savings can be made. The Committee will submit annual reports to Parliament on the UK's progress towards targets and budgets. The government must respond to these annual reports, ensuring transparency and accountability on an annual basis.
- The inclusion of international aviation and shipping emissions in the Act or an explanation to Parliament why not - by 31 December 2012. The Committee on Climate Change is required to advise the government on the consequences of including emissions from international aviation and shipping in the Act's targets and budgets. Projected emissions from international aviation and shipping must be taken into account in making decisions on carbon budgets.
- Limits on International credits. The government is required to "have regard to the need for UK domestic action on climate change" when considering how to meet the UK's targets and carbon budgets. The independent Committee on Climate Change has a duty to advise on the appropriate balance between action at domestic, European and international level, for each carbon budget. The government must set a limit on the purchase of credits for each budgetary period – for the first budgetary period a zero limit was set in May 2009, excluding units bought by UK participants in the EU Emissions Trading System.
- Further measures to reduce emissions, including powers to introduce domestic emissions trading schemes more quickly and easily through secondary legislation – the first use will be the Carbon Reduction Commitment Energy Efficiency Scheme, measures on bio-fuels, powers to introduce pilot financial incentive schemes in England for household waste, powers to require a minimum charge for single-use carrier bags (excluding Scotland).

- A requirement for the government to report at least every five years on the risks to the UK of climate change, and to publish a programme setting out how these will be addressed. The Act also introduces powers for government to require public bodies and statutory undertakers to carry out their own risk assessment and make plans to address those risks.
- An Adaptation Sub-Committee of the Committee on Climate Change, providing advice to, and scrutiny of, the government's adaptation work.
- A requirement for the government to issue guidance by 1 October 2009 on the way companies should report their greenhouse gas emissions, and to review the contribution reporting could make to emissions reductions by 1 December 2010. A requirement also for the government to use powers under the Companies Act 2008 to make reporting mandatory, or explain to Parliament why it has not done so, by 6 April 2012.
- New powers to support the creation of a Community Energy Savings Programme, as announced by the Prime Minister on 11 September 2008 (by extending the existing Carbon Emissions Reduction Target scheme to electricity generators).
- A new requirement for annual publication of a report on the efficiency and sustainability of the government estate. The first report was published in June 2009.

Carbon Reduction Commitment Energy Efficiency Scheme[2] ●●●

The Carbon Reduction Commitment Energy Efficiency Scheme (CRC) is a new mandatory emissions trading scheme started in April 2010 that aims to reduce the amount of carbon dioxide (CO2) emitted in the UK.

CRC will affect large, non-energy intensive organisations in both the public and private sector ranging from large national businesses to local authorities, large hospitals and educational establishments. Organisations that meet the qualification criteria, which are based on how much electricity they consumed in 2008, will be obliged to participate in CRC. In practice, this will include many organisations with annual electricity bills of around £500,000 and over. Those involved will have to monitor their emissions and purchase allowances, sold by government, for each tonne of CO2 they emit. All energy other than transport fuels will be covered, such as:

- electricity
- gas
- fuel
- oil.

Government estimates indicated that around 20,000 commercial and public sector organisations will be required to participate in CRC in some way. The majority of

2 DECC. (2010, April 25). CRC. Retrieved April 25, 2010, from decc.gov.uk: http://www.decc.gov.uk/en/content/cms/what_we_do/lc_uk/crc/crc.aspx

these will simply be required to disclose their carbon footprint information once every few years, assisting the scheme administrator to monitor their electricity usage. Of these, around 5,000 organisations will be required to participate fully in CRC. This means they must not only record and monitor their CO2 emissions, but also purchase allowances.

Since the 2010 CRC seeks to capture only UK emissions, organisations with multi-national interests and subsidiaries need to consider which parts of the corporate group needs to participate. Landlords and tenants should also carefully consider their requirement to participate in the 2010 CRC. The government has decided that the counterparty to an electricity supply contract will have the obligation to participate, so this could apply to a landlord even where it leases to a third party.

During the introductory phase, allowances will be sold by the government at a fixed price of £12 per tonne of CO2. On one estimate, the threshold of 6,000MWh annual electricity consumption would require allowances under the CRC costing £38,000. Following the initial sale period, participant organisations can buy or sell allowances by trading on the secondary market. This enables organisations that have reduced their energy consumption more than they expected to sell some allowances, while those that have higher emissions than anticipated can purchase extra allowances. In the event that total demand for allowances exceeds supply, the CRC administrator will have powers to purchase additional allowances from the EU Emissions Trading Scheme. Such allowances may attract a higher price than £12 per tonne of CO2.

The key priorities for participating organisations are as follows:

- September 2009 - qualification packs were sent to all addresses that had a half-hourly meter settled on the half-hourly market
- April 2010 to September 2010 - all qualifying organisations must register using the online 2010 CRC registry
- April 2010 to March 2011 - first year requiring CRC reporting
- April 2011 to March 2012 - first full "compliance year", requiring the purchase of allowances to off-set emissions
- April 2011 - sale of allowances to cover emissions of the first compliance year (April 2011 to March 2012, inclusive)
- July 2011 - footprint report and annual report due; allowances to be surrendered

CRC is a key element of the government's climate change policy and is intended to ensure that participant organisations contribute to UK targets to reduce greenhouse gas (GHG) emissions including:

- the legally-binding carbon budgets, defined under the Climate Change Act, requiring GHG emissions by 2020 to be reduced by between 34% and 42% relative to a 1990 baseline; and
- the target to reduce GHG emissions by 2050 by at least 80% compared to the 1990 baseline; and
- the EU Directive requiring EU-wide reductions in GHG emissions by 2020 of at least 20% compared to a 1990 baseline.

As can be seen, the CRC represents a carbon reduction scheme designed to ensure that less energy intensive organisations contribute to UK efforts to meet multiple greenhouse gas emission reduction targets by reducing emissions by 1.2 million tonnes of carbon per year by 2020.

The CRC has the following key features.

- It is based on mandatory emissions trading and is a carbon reduction scheme designed to capture emissions that currently fall outside existing initiatives like the EU Emissions Trading Scheme (ETS) and Climate Change Agreements (CCA)
- Early adopters and those that make the biggest carbon emission reductions stand to benefit from (relative) financial benefits and reputational enhancement, since the publication of a performance league table, revised annually, is an inherent element of the carbon reduction scheme. In the first year, organisations at the top of the table who have done the most to reduce their emissions will get a bonus of up to 10% of their base recycling payment.
- The provision of revenue recycling, where monies raised through the purchase of allowances will be recycled to reflect relative performance as determined by the league table. In the event of excessive allowance prices within the CRC, a "Safety Valve" mechanism allows EU Emissions Trading Scheme (ETS) allowances to be purchased via the Environment Agency for use in the scheme.
- The CRC is intended to be 'revenue neutral' to the Exchequer. All money raised from the sale of allowances will be recycled back to the participants in proportion to their relative performance in the scheme.
- It is a carbon reduction scheme designed to provide flexibility and it avoids being prescriptive on how participating organisations should meet their own, specific performance commitment. Organisations are free to choose the best solution(s) for their circumstances, using one or more of energy efficiency (for example, high efficiency lighting) and/or buying additional allowances from organisations that have surplus allowances and/or on-site renewable energy generation (for example, a wind turbine).
- Penalties will apply to organisations that break the rules of CRC and there will be annual, published performance league tables showing the relative performance of participating organisations in respect of CRC compliance but also the extent to which such organisations use renewable energy.

If an organisation fails to submit a footprint report by the deadline, it will have to pay a fixed fine of £5,000. Then for each subsequent working day it fails to submit a report, it will be fined at a rate of £500 per working day up to a maximum of 40 working days.

What is the Climate Change Levy?[3]

The levy is part of a range of measures designed to help the UK meet its legally binding commitment to reduce greenhouse gas emissions. It is chargeable on the industrial and commercial supply of taxable commodities for lighting, heating and power by consumers in the following sectors of business:

- industry
- commerce
- agriculture
- public administration
- other services.

The levy does not apply to taxable commodities used by domestic consumers, or by charities for non-business use. All revenue raised through the levy is recycled back to business through a 0.3 per cent cut in employers' National Insurance contributions, introduced at the same time as the levy.

The levy is charged on taxable supplies. Taxable supplies are certain supplies of the following taxable commodities:

- electricity
- natural gas as supplied by a gas utility
- petroleum and hydrocarbon gas in a liquid state
- coal and lignite
- coke, and semi-coke of coal or lignite
- petroleum coke.

The following are not taxable commodities for levy purposes:

- oil
- road fuel gas
- heat
- steam
- low value solid fuel with an open market value of no more than £15.00 per tonne
- waste as defined in statute.

Some supplies are excluded or exempt from the levy. Others have a reduced or half-rate.

3 HMRC. (2010, April 25). What is Climate Change Levy? Retrieved April 25, 2010, from customs.hmrc.gov.uk: http://customs.hmrc.gov.uk/channelsPortalWebApp/channelsPortalWebApp.portal?_nfpb=true&_pageLabel=pageExcise_InfoGuides&propertyType=document&id=HMCE_CL_001174#P1_34

How is the levy calculated?

The levy is applied as a specific rate per nominal unit of energy. There is a separate rate for each category of taxable commodity:

- electricity = £0.0043 per kilowatt hour
- gas supplied by a gas utility or any gas supplied in a gaseous state that is of a kind supplied by a gas utility = £0.0015 per kilowatt hour
- any petroleum gas, or other gaseous hydrocarbon supplied in a liquid state = £0.0096 per kilogram
- any other taxable commodity = £0.0117 per kilogram.

Does a business need to register for the levy?

A business making or intending to make taxable supplies needs to contact HM Revenue & Customs and register for the Climate Change Levy. The date it needs to register from is the date of making the taxable supply or intention to make the supply. Unlike VAT there is no registration threshold. If a business has to register but does not do so HMRC can register it compulsorily. The business may also have to pay a penalty.

Other Relevant Legislation ●●●

Defra is responsible for setting legislation, policy, regulations and guidance for a number of environmental issues[4]. There are also several European and international laws and policies that apply.

Air and water quality, and flooding

- Air quality regulations
- Water legislation
- Water framework directive (European Commission)
- Marine and Coastal Access Act 2009
- Marine strategy framework directive (European Commission)
- Flood and Water Management Bill

Biodiversity

- Natural Environment and Rural Communities Act 2006
- EU Habitats and Birds Directives
- Planning Policy Statement 9 on Biological and Geological Conservation

4 Defra. (2010, April 25). Legislation, policy, regulation and guidance. Retrieved April 25, 2010, from defra.gov.uk: http://www.defra.gov.uk/environment/policy/index.htm

Local environment and noise

- Local environmental quality
- The Noise Act

Chemicals and genetic modification

- UK chemicals policy
- EU chemicals policy
- International chemicals policy
- Genetic modification

Waste and recycling

- Waste and recycling

Climate change

- Climate Change Act

A business must comply with environmental legislation designed to reduce the harm it may cause to the environment. Full explanations of these areas covered by Defra can be found on their website.

EU Emissions Trading Scheme[5]

The EU Emissions Trading Scheme (EU ETS) puts a cap on the carbon dioxide (CO2) emitted by business and creates a market and price for carbon allowances. It covers 45% of EU emissions, including energy intensive sectors and approximately 12,000 installations.

How it works currently

The scheme is now in Phase II, which runs from 2008 until 2012. During this phase, every EU member state:

1. **Developed a National Allocation Plan (NAP)**
   - Member State proposed a limit ('cap') on total emissions from relevant installations.
   - The plans were approved by the European Commission, in many cases after some revision.
2. **Distributes Allowances**
   - The 'cap' is converted into allowances, known as EUAs (1 tonne of Carbon Dioxide = 1 EUA).
   - The Member States distribute these allowances to installations in the scheme in their country according to their approved plan.

5 Defra. (2010, April 25). EU Emissions Trading Scheme. Retrieved April 25, 2010, from defra.gov.uk: http://www.defra.gov.uk/defrasearch/index.jsp?query=EU+Emissions+Trading+Scheme

- Up to 10% of the allowances may be auctioned instead of being given for free. These auctions will be largest in the UK and in Germany.

3. **Operates the Scheme**

- Installations must monitor and report verified carbon emissions.
- At the end of each year, installations must surrender sufficient allowances to cover their emissions and can buy additional allowances or sell any surplus.
- Joint Implementation (JI) and Clean Development Mechanism (CDM) credits can be used within the scheme, through the 'Linking Directive', agreed in 2004).

How it will work in the future - Phase III

Phase III will start in 2013 and run until 2020. The biggest changes in Phase III will be as follows:

- **Design**

  The Scheme will be designed at a European level, rather than by each country individually.

- **'Cap' will reduce over time**

  The 'cap' will decline by at least 1.74% a year, so that emissions in 2020 will be at least 21% below their level in 2005.

- **More will be covered**

  The scheme will include the production of all metals (including Aluminium) and potentially aviation. For some sectors it will include the emission of other greenhouse gases in addition to carbon dioxide.

- **Allowances**

  Much greater proportion of allowances will be auctioned (rather than given to installations).

  Use of Clean Development Mechanism (CDM) allowances will be more tightly restricted.

- **Background**

  The scheme started in 2005 in order to help the EU meet its targets under the Kyoto Protocol (8% reduction in greenhouse gas emissions from 1990 levels).

  The scheme is the world's largest carbon-trading scheme. It provides an incentive for installations to reduce their carbon emissions, because they can then sell their surplus allowances.

Installations are included in the scheme on the basis of their Carbon Dioxide (CO2) emitting activities. Industries that are covered include:

- electricity generation
- iron & steel
- mineral processing (for example: cement manufacture).
- pulp and paper processing.

The UK Low Carbon Transition Plan[6]

The UK Low Carbon Transition Plan plots how the UK will meet the 34 per cent cut in emissions on 1990 levels by 2020. We have already reduced emissions by 21 per cent – equivalent to cutting emissions entirely from four cities the size of London.

The aim is that by 2020:

- more than 1.2 million people will be in green jobs
- 7 million homes will have benefited from whole house makeovers, and more than 1.5 million households will be supported to produce their own clean energy
- around 40 per cent of electricity will be from low-carbon sources, from renewables, nuclear and clean coal
- we will be importing half the amount of gas that we otherwise would
- the average new car will emit 40 per cent less carbon than now.

The UK Renewable Energy Strategy[7]

Renewable energy is key to our low-carbon energy future. We need to radically reduce greenhouse gas emissions, as well as diversify our energy sources. As part of this move to a low-carbon economy, we need a dramatic change in renewable energy use in electricity, heat and transport.

The UK has signed up to the EU Renewable Energy Directive, which includes a UK target of 15 per cent of energy from renewables by 2020. This target is equivalent to a seven-fold increase in UK renewable energy consumption from 2008 levels.

The UK government suggested how much of the remaining energy might be generated from renewables sources across the 3 main sectors:

- **Electricity** - to be over 30%. It is currently less than 6%
- **Heat** - At 11%. It is currently less than 1%
- **Transport** - At 10%. It is currently less than 3%.

6 DECC. (2010, April 25). The UK Low Carbon Transition Plan. Retrieved April 25, 2010, from decc.gov.uk: http://www.decc.gov.uk/en/content/cms/publications/lc_trans_plan/lc_trans_plan.aspx

7 DECC. (2010, April 25). The UK Renewable Energy Strategy. Retrieved April 25, 2010, from decc.gov.uk: http://www.decc.gov.uk/en/content/cms/what_we_do/uk_supply/energy_mix/renewable/res/res.aspx

It is believed that offshore wind can deliver up to 4.5% out of the 15% overall renewable energy strategy target.

Meeting the UK's renewable energy targets are not just about preventing climate change and securing future energy supplies. Achieving the targets could provide £100 billion worth of investment opportunities and up to half a million jobs in the renewable energy sector by 2020.

UK Low Carbon Industrial Strategy[8]

The UK Low-Carbon Industrial Strategy, launched in July 2009, is intended to ensure that British businesses and workers are equipped to maximise the economic opportunities and minimise the costs of the transition to a low-carbon economy.

Key points

1. Up to £60 million to capitalise on Britain's wave and tidal sector strengths, including investment in Wave Hub – the development of a significant demonstration and testing facility off the Cornish coast – and other funding to make the South West Britain's first Low Carbon Economic Area.
2. Up to £15 million capital investment in order to establish a Nuclear Advanced Manufacturing Research Centre consisting of a consortium of manufacturers from the UK nuclear supply chain and universities.
3. A £4 million expansion of the Manufacturing Advisory Service, to provide more specialist advice to manufacturers on competing for low-carbon opportunities, including support for suppliers for the civil nuclear industry.
4. Up to £10 million for the accelerated deployment of electric vehicle charging infrastructure.
5. Up to £120 million to support the development of a British based offshore wind industry.

Low Carbon Transport[9]

Greenhouse gas emissions from transport represent 21 per cent of total UK domestic emissions, decarbonising transport must be part of the solution.

The strategy is based on the following themes:

- supporting a shift to new technologies and fuels
- promoting lower carbon transport choices
- using market-based measures to encourage a shift to lower carbon transport.

8 BIS. (2010, April 25). UK Low Carbon Industrial Strategy. Retrieved April 25, 2010, from interactive.bis.gov.uk: http://interactive.bis.gov.uk/lowcarbon/2009/07/low-carbon-industrial-strategy/

9 DFT. (2010, April 25). Low Carbon Transport Innovation Strategy (LCTIS). Retrieved April 25, 2010, from dft.gov.uk: http://www.dft.gov.uk/pgr/scienceresearch/technology/lctis/

As a result of concerns over land use for certain bio-fuels the UK government commissioned a review to recommend whether any policy changes were appropriate. Whilst the target of 10% renewable transport energy by 2020 has been retained, interim targets up to 2013/14 have been reduced to allow for a transition to more sustainable fuels.

Waste Strategy[10]

As shown in Chapter 27 all businesses generate waste and have to store, handle and recover or dispose of it. Defra outline legal requirements for managing your waste efficiently.

These laws are designed to prevent the environment from being polluted by business waste and to encourage more sustainable management of waste. Some legislation applies to all business waste, whilst some deals with particular types.

Businesses should comply with waste storage and disposal legislation as every business that produces (or imports, carries, keeps, treats, recovers or disposes of) waste is under a duty of care to ensure that they handle waste safely and in compliance with the regulations in this area.

Duty of Care

Waste management responsibilities under the Duty of Care should ensure the following:

- safe and secure storage
- a description of the waste, including where it came from and the amounts involved
- choosing a registered carrier or waste manager licensed to accept your waste or a waste collection authority (local council)
- completing and signing a transfer note including a description of the waste
- keeping a copy of the signed transfer note for two years
- ensuring that the waste is being dealt with properly, for example, tracking its disposal route.

Waste storage

The business must store waste securely in appropriate containers, such as skips or labelled drums. It should cover waste material if necessary to prevent it blowing away, and make sure that waste cannot leak into the ground or watercourses.

A business should consider whether different types of waste need to be separated - for example to prevent chemicals reacting together if they leak. You must not mix different types of hazardous waste, and you must not mix hazardous waste with non-hazardous waste or with materials that are not waste.

10 Defra. (2010, April 25). Waste Strategy. Retrieved April 25, 2010, from defra.gov.uk: http://www.defra.gov.uk/environment/waste/strategy/strategy07/documents/waste07-strategy.pdf

Waste recovery or disposal

When a business sends waste to be recovered or disposed of, it must ensure that it is handled by an authorised organisation - such as the local authority or a registered contractor - and taken to an authorised site.

WEEE

The Waste Electrical and Electronic Equipment Directive (WEEE) is the fastest growing part of the waste stream today. The Directive sets criteria for the collection, treatment, recycling and recovery of waste electrical and electronic equipment. Producers will be largely responsible for financing most of these activities (producer responsibility). Private householders are to be able to return WEEE without charge. The list of equipment includes:

- household appliances
- IT and telecommunications equipment
- audiovisual and lighting equipment
- electrical and electronic tools
- toys, leisure and sports equipment
- medical devices and
- automatic dispensers.

Business to Business (B2B) WEEE

B2B WEEE requires producers to be responsible for collection, treatment and recovery of WEEE for their products placed on the market after 13 August 2005. They are also responsible for products on the market before this date but only where old products are replaced on a like-for-like basis.

Under the arrangements, B2B WEEE Producers are responsible for the collection and treatment of EEE from the last user.

Strict rules on recycling all types of batteries are coming into force, including a complete ban on sending them to landfill. Virtually every business uses batteries, so they should be prepared for the changing legislation.

Breach of the duty of care is a criminal offence. In some circumstances this may be punishable on summary conviction (in the Magistrates court) by a fine of up to £50,000 or a conviction on indictment (in the Crown Court) by an unlimited fine or possibly imprisonment.

National Waste Strategy

The EU Framework Directive on Waste (75/442/EEC) amended by Directive 91/156/EEC, required all European Member States to produce a National Waste Strategy and was implemented in the UK through the Environment Act 1995 and the first National Waste Strategy was introduced in 2000. The Strategy has subsequently been amended but the hierarchy of waste management – prevention, reuse, recycling/compost, energy recovery and disposal remains central to the strategy. The strategy was revised in 2007 and now includes more ambitious objectives and targets including:

- putting more emphasis on waste prevention and re-use
- meeting and exceeding the Landfill Directive diversion targets for biodegradable municipal waste in 2010, 2013 and 2020
- increasing diversion from landfill of non-municipal waste and securing better integration of treatment for municipal and non-municipal waste
- increasing recycling of resources and recovery of energy from residual waste using a mix of technologies.

Regulation plays an important role in government efforts to improve environmental standards. The Chartered Management Institute's "Lean and Green"[11] report published in 2009 identified one internal barrier and one external barrier to improved compliance. The internal barrier was based on a lack of resources, which was seen as the single most important barrier. The report concluded that this is likely to be linked to the lack of commitment and strategic vision from directors which they felt was evident throughout the research. The external barrier was due to the complexity of the regulations (rather than the volume) and it was identified as a leading problem, particularly for smaller businesses.

The report also found two distinct groups in relation to attitudes to environmental regulation. Some 46% of respondents took a positive view, stating that environmental regulations help to drive higher standards of environmental practice, encourage innovation and create new markets. However, the second cluster of 54% perceived regulation as a barrier towards achievement of their strategic goals and warned that it can encourage an expensive, "bureaucratic tick-box compliance culture". The report also highlighted that managers in larger companies were more likely to have a positive view of regulation than smaller companies and it was directors who were particularly scathing about the impact of regulation, with 68% reporting a negative perspective. Managers working in organisations which were in decline also had a greater tendency to hold a negative view of regulation.

11 CMI. (2009). Lean and Green:Leadership for a low carbon future. Chartered Management Institute.

ISO 14000[12]

ISO 14000 is actually a series of international standards on environmental management. It provides a framework for the development of both the system and the supporting audit program.

ISO 14001 was first published in 1996 and specifies the actual requirements for an environmental management system. It applies to those environmental aspects which the organization has control and over which it can be expected to have an influence.

ISO 14004, also published in 1996, provides guidance on the development and implementation of environmental management systems and principles, and also their co-ordination with other management systems.

ISO 19011 offers guidelines for quality and/or environmental management systems auditing. It supersedes a number of standards, including ISO 14010, 11 and 12.

Despite these perceived barriers to compliance there are many examples of responsible and sustainable businesses that have utilised their sphere of influence to full effect by helping to form new legislation rather than reacting to it as it comes into place. Examples appear throughout this book. Earlier in this book we considered how crucial a good business reputation is and how financially devastating it can be if a business loses that reputation. Breaches of legislation causing fines or at worst imprisonment will only create negative publicity and loss of reputation, whereas compliance can be used to commercial advantage.

12 Environmental Management. (2010, April 25). ISO14000 SERIES ENVIRONMENTAL MANAGEMENT SYSTEMS . Retrieved April 25, 2010, from iso14000-iso14001-environmental-management.com: http://www.iso14000-iso14001-environmental-management.com/

SECTION 7

Bringing it Together

- Applying the Sphere of Influence Framework to Business
- Legal Sector Alliance Model

CHAPTER 30

Applying the Sphere of Influence Framework to Business

- Marshalls Workplace
- Marshalls Business
- Marshalls and its Community
- Marshalls and the Environment

Marshalls Workplace[1]

The key message of this book, which was first introduced in Chapter 1, is that a responsible and sustainable business has to recognise and take account of its actions and adopt a proactive approach in its strategies and policies rather than wait for legislation, consumer pressure, employee pressure, shareholder pressure or a failing reputation to force its hand. In other words be a leader and an innovator not just a follower. Help shape legislation rather than simply comply with it and become the market leader and innovator in sustainable products and services. All of this can be achieved if a business recognises and effectively utilises its sphere of influence. Marshalls is just such a business and justifiably should be regarded as an inspiration and a role model for other businesses from all sectors to follow.

Leading hard landscaping company Marshalls triumphed at 2010's PLC Awards by picking up the Achievement in Sustainability Award for the second year running. The group marketing director at Marshalls collected the award at the ceremony held in London's Grosvenor House Hotel. The event was attended by 1,500 guests including quoted companies, investment banks, fund managers, investment analysts, and corporate advisors. The PLC Awards dinner took place in March 2010. Marshalls' head of marketing said, "To win this award last year was fantastic, but to win it again this year is a real achievement". The judges said, "Nobody does it better than Marshalls and that's the reason they continue to lead in their industry in terms of sustainability." The head of marketing continued by saying that, "2009 wasn't the easiest year for anyone but sustainability is the only way to go if we want to tackle serious global issues like climate change. At Marshalls, sustainability is part of our DNA, it's the way we do business. It's only by adopting a sustainable approach that businesses can really start to make an impact on the triple bottom line."

The Triple Bottom Line

Marshalls is committed to developing both its business and its products in a sustainable manner, rather than just focusing on environmental performance. True sustainability is achieved by balancing the environmental, social and economic impacts of a business.

Marshalls' business decisions are made over the long term against a triple bottom line:

- effective protection of our environment
- social progress which recognises the needs of everyone
- maintenance of stable economic growth.

The Achievement in Sustainability award recognises accomplishments in one or more of the three key areas of the triple bottom line: economic, environmental and social sustainability. It also recognises companies that make their own operations more sustainable and play an important role in helping address wider issues such as the causes and effects of climate change. The Voting Panel looks for leadership, innovation and a lasting commitment to sustainability.

1 Marshalls. (2010, April 12). Sustainability. Retrieved April 12, 2010, from marshalls.co.uk: http://www.marshalls.co.uk/sustainability/

Sustainability at Marshalls is based on these three elements. In effect, this means operating a successful and profitable business whilst minimising impact to the environment and looking after the communities they work with in the UK and overseas.

Marshalls' carbon reduction programme is a key management focus. They have committed to reduce emissions of greenhouse gases by 80% by 2050 in line with government targets and they are well on their way. Broadly speaking, their programme looks at their carbon management and how they can reduce emissions at each site. Marshalls have energy plans for each site and now have energy champions who promote the company's carbon reduction policy throughout the organisation.

Established in the late 1880s, Marshalls is the UK's leading manufacturer of superior natural stone and innovative concrete hard landscaping products, supplying the construction, home improvement and landscape markets. They provide the product ranges, design services, technical expertise, innovative ideas and inspiration to transform gardens, drives and public and commercial landscapes.

The Group operates its own quarries and manufacturing sites throughout the UK, including a network of regional service centres and two national manufacturing and distribution sites. As a major plc, Marshalls is committed to quality in everything it does, including environmental and ethical best practice and continual improvement in health and safety performance for the benefit of its 2,400 strong workforce.

Marshalls' core values underpin the business as all take pride in their jobs and have respect for each other. Every individual is considered equally important and the company values the contribution that every one of their dedicated and skilled workforce makes. Innovation is critical to their strategy, in terms of technology, manufacturing and products, and allows them to deliver the highest quality goods. The company fosters a culture based on honesty and trust, where each and every individual is accountable for themselves, their role and the performance of the business.

Marshalls is committed to being a caring and sensitive neighbour and they operate their sites in accordance with all relevant legislation. Their programme of quarry restoration ensures that they return land back to nature wherever they can and that any restoration is in keeping with its surroundings. The company also, where possible, puts in place measures to protect land that is sold on to third parties by ensuring that part of the land is turned over to nature or used to create recreational and wildlife areas.

Marshalls believes in conducting its business in a manner which aims to achieve sustainable growth whilst incorporating and demonstrating a high degree of social responsibility. As a public limited company, Marshalls accepts legal compliance as an absolute minimum standard and where no legislation is in place, industry practice is used. The Board is ultimately responsible for ensuring the business operates in a socially responsible way including compliance with relevant legislation.

Marshalls' purchasing policy sets out the standards and ethics applied to its supply chain and operates management systems to manage its suppliers. The majority of products are sourced in the UK and where products are sourced from outside the UK an ethical risk assessment is completed and an appropriate action plan agreed – multi-stakeholder independent social audits are part of Marshalls' best practice.

Marshalls continues to focus on sustainability as an integral part of its culture. Marshalls' plan sets out to deliver benefits to the environment, recognise social progress and generate economic growth. The company has been recognised by many external organisations as being a leader in the area of ethical sourcing, carbon management, water use reduction and overall for its sustainable agenda delivering real change.

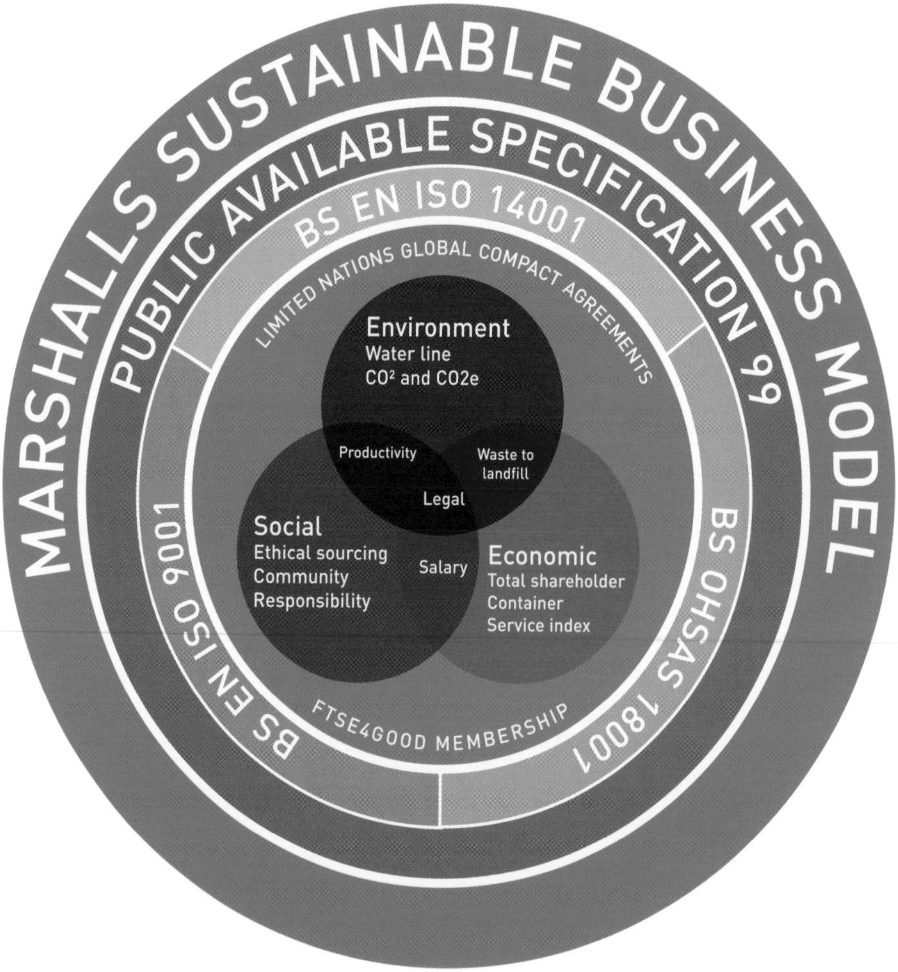

Figure 1

Workplace
2,464 employees

Energy Champions

As part of Marshalls' Energy Management Steering Group action plan, project groups are set up to look at specific areas of the business such as training, procurement and transport. These project groups are led by senior directors who take responsibility for their specific areas. The project groups mobilise resources by working with energy teams and champions within the business, which enables Marshalls to ensure sites and corporate departments are sharing best practice and working together to solve energy reduction problems. Energy champions are based on-site and they take part in energy reduction schemes and engage other employees in energy management.

It is enlightening to know that Marshalls is taking the commitment to reducing its CO2 emissions seriously. By informing our employees, training Energy Champions and supporting action plans, I believe we will be much better placed to achieve our reduction targets.

Ron Short, Works Engineer at Falkirk Works and Energy Champion, Marshalls Energy Champions

Payroll Giving

Giving something back is actively encouraged at Marshalls and employees are empowered to engage in activities they care about through volunteering and community projects.

During 2008, Marshalls' employees donated £26,355 to UK charities through payroll giving and in 2009 a further £27,991 was donated.

Employee Code of Ethics

All Marshalls' employees are encouraged and expected to adhere to the company's Statement of Values and Principles. The statement includes guidance on business practice, employee relations and equality of opportunity and is subject to regular review to ensure that it continues to set stretching standards in terms of excellence, trust, honesty and integrity. There is also a published process (the Serious Concerns Policy) through which employees can raise, in confidence, serious concerns about possible improprieties.

Marshalls Working in India

At the very heart of its sustainability drive, Marshalls is helping transform lives and entire communities for the better by creating and fostering long term partnerships.

Marshalls continues to be an active member of the Ethical Trading Initiative (ETI), a unique organisation bringing together global companies, trade unions and NGOs, and developing practical solutions to ethical trade that deliver real benefits for workers.

Marshalls' work with the ETI focuses on the ETI Base Code, which is based on the International Labour Organisation's conventions as follows:

- no-one should be forced to work
- workers should be able to join and form trade unions
- working conditions should be safe and healthy
- child labour should not be used
- working hours should not be excessive
- wages should be enough to live on and provide some discretionary income
- workers should be treated equally, regardless of their sex, ethnic group, religion or political opinions
- where possible, workers should be provided with regular employment
- workers should not be verbally, physically or sexually abused or disciplined.

Marshalls' employees have also been learning more about the company's ETI programme through training days designed to explain the ETI Base Code and to ensure that every member of staff is doing all they can to ensure that workers' welfare and rights are protected in Marshalls' supply chain.

Marshalls also continues to work with and finance Hadoti Hast Shilp Sansthan, an Indian non-governmental organisation (NGO) helping to improve the lives of vulnerable families working in the quarries around Bhundi and Kota in Rajasthan.

Marshalls' funding has helped to provide social insurance (in case of illness or injury) and health check camps for itinerant quarry workers, which offer immunisation for children and pregnant women and distribute free medicines for prevalent diseases. Marshalls committed to a 50% increase in funding in 2008 for more healthcare provision and social insurance, plus educational classes for the children of the quarry workers. And sometimes the simplest changes make the most difference. For example, Marshalls raised funds to buy shoes for local children so that more pupils could make the walk to school.

The insurance scheme has helped as follows:

- the number of beneficiaries has increased significantly as the labourers now understand and by March 2009, 46 labourers claimed on their insurance
- monthly insurance awareness camps for the labourers organised at Dabi and Gararda Education increased awareness
- three schools operating in Gararda, Gawar and Sutada have been supplied with well equipped classrooms and provision of a midday meal
- 133 students aged 6-14 years now attend these schools
- a fourth school was opened in February 2009 in Sutra Health Camps
- between January and March 2009, a total of nine health camps were held in Gararda, Gawar, Sutra and Sutada with 1,042 beneficiaries
- door to door visits (consultancy and free medicine distribution) to 323 families, in the first three months of 2009 alone.

In the UK several workplace initiatives were recognised in the company's Corporate Responsibility Report 2009.

- Marshalls' West Lane Works received a prestigious National Business Award in the category of The Health, Work and Well-being Award for Small Business. This was a new Award for 2008 covering places of work with less than 250 employees that could best demonstrate how they have improved the health and well-being of the workforce.
- Marshalls in Llay achieved both Investors in People status and the Basic Skills Employer Pledge Award. The Head of Basic Skills Wales, said, "Marshalls is to be congratulated on the way they have supported basic skills training for their employees. The Employer Pledge Award which they have received is only given to those who truly deserve the award. The respect shown to employees by providing them with the chances to be upskilled is an example to all employers. Those who have received the training are now role models for others both in the workplace and in their community."
- Stancliffe Stone scooped two awards at the Local Employment Partnerships Awards (LEP) for Recruitment Innovation and Commitment to Diversity. The Awards celebrate and recognise the achievements of companies and individuals in the North East and celebrate the vital role these partnerships play in getting people back to work, particularly in the challenging economic environment.

Marshalls Business

Business
Customers Suppliers
5,618 Shareholders

Marshalls announced its partnership with the Carbon Trust's Carbon Labelling Company in 2007 to develop carbon labels for its products. By being one of 13 pilot partners for the carbon labelling project, Marshalls helped shape PAS 2050 methodology by testing, fine tuning and proving the effectiveness of the standard. In 2009 Marshalls carbon labelled 503 domestic products which is the largest number by any company in the world. By committing to carbon labelling and showing an innovative approach, Marshalls also commits to reducing the carbon footprint of every labelled product. In order to raise awareness and increase understanding of carbon labelling, Marshalls produced the Marshalls Guide to Carbon Labelling.

Only by comprehending carbon labels can consumers make an informed decision about the products they want to buy. Marshalls has also trained its installers in the meaning of carbon labels and how to use them – they in turn communicate with homeowners. Marshalls has undertaken a range of continuous professional development (CPD) sessions for commercial architects and contractors as well as speaking at industry events throughout the UK and Europe.

Working with the Carbon Trust means that Marshalls can identify opportunities to reduce emissions across its supply chain and it gives them the ability to compare products across an entire range. Using the Carbon Reduction Label to communicate this gives Marshalls' customers the added benefit of factoring a product's carbon impact into their buying decisions.

Jonathon Porritt, Programme Director of Forum for the Future and Chairman of the UK Sustainable Development Commission said that he was extremely encouraged by Marshalls' commitment to carbon reduction, particularly as they have gone that one step further by labelling an entire product range, while others are initially only piloting a few products. He went on to say that, "this is exactly the kind of leadership we need to see a lot more of in this and other sectors."

Environmental Profiling of Products

A perennial problem in the construction industry is how to assess the environmental impact of a scheme. Accurate environmental profiling is vital in order to provide meaningful comparisons between using different products, e.g. natural v reconstituted stone. It is overly simplistic and subjective to measure the CO2 equivalent, without also assessing other environmental impacts such as freight transport, waste disposal and water extraction. This is why the Building Research Establishment (BRE) has developed Ecopoints, to provide a single score environmental assessment of different building materials. Ecopoints are based on a range of 13 different environmental impacts, which are then given percentage weightings based on the relative importance of different sustainability issues. Marshalls is now working with BRE to establish the Ecopoints rating of its products based on a complete Life Cycle Assessment.

Ecopoints are based on a range of 13 different environmental impacts, which are then given percentage weightings based on the relative importance of different sustainability issues.

1 Climate change
2 Water extraction
3 Mineral resource extraction
4 Stratospheric ozone depletion
5 Human toxicity
6 Ecotoxicity to freshwater
7 Nuclear waste (higher level)
8 Ecotoxicity to land
9 Waste disposal
10 Fossil fuel depletion
11 Eutrophication is when the environment becomes enriched with nutrients. This can be a problem in marine habitats such as lakes as it can cause algal blooms.
12 Photochemical ozone creation
13 Acidification.

Marshalls is working at the forefront of environmental profiling. They have given their customers a better understanding of how it all works and the opportunity to make comparisons that just were not possible a year ago. What's great about working with Marshalls is that they are happy to push the boundaries in their commitment to sustainability.

Dr Peter Bonfield, Chief Executive, BRE

Environmental Profiling

Being green is not all about opting for the simple life... Marshalls does not have an 'Eco-range'.

The company has taken action on all of its products and will continue to do so. To help customers understand the environmental impact of their landscaping choices, Marshalls has been working with the Carbon Trust to carbon label all of its domestic products and has developed a carbon calculator at www.marshalls.co.uk/sustainability which shows the CO_2 impact of different hard landscaping products. Meanwhile, Marshalls' industry-leading research and development also means that its products now use a higher content of recycled materials. For example, the CO_2e embodiment of Marshalls' concrete block paving has been reduced by up to 39% - a major result verified by independently approved data.

One of the big highlights for the company in 2009 was the introduction of "Noxer" paving to their commercial range. The great thing about Noxer is that it's been specially formulated to help improve air quality and reduce the risk of pollutants. In some cases, it can reduce up to 45% of nitrogen oxide in the atmosphere, most of which comes from vehicle traffic.

Shareholder analysis at 31 December 2009 showed that there were 5,618 shareholders in total but with 69% of the shareholders owning only 1.4% of the shares whereas at the other extreme 76% of the shares were owned by 1.5% of the shareholders.

Marshalls and its Community

Community
Charitable donations £41,574
Employees donating £27,991
50 Living Street Auditors

Marshalls takes its community relations seriously and contributes to the communities in which it operates, building goodwill and a reputation as a good neighbour and employer. Marshalls is proud of its community relations and keen to further develop its standing as a responsible business in the community:

- understanding and reacting to the needs of its communities
- building partnerships in the community which will enhance its reputation as an active contributor to local community development
- supporting local schools and local educational facilities to encourage pupils to develop and enjoy the landscapes of the future
- helping the local community with its products and services and encouraging its employees to add value to the local community

- consulting with local stakeholders and evaluating its performance as a positive contributor to the local community.

Marshalls has continued to demonstrate its commitment to a Corporate Responsibility agenda, engaging in many BITC programmes and initiatives throughout 2009. They remain active partners in Calderdale Cares, volunteering in their local community to support disadvantaged groups, and have hosted events including a Seeing is Believing visit and knowledge workshop, sharing their best practice on how to develop skills in the workforce. They have demonstrated leadership in the Corporate Responsibility field, spearheaded by Graham Holden, CEO, who sits on the BITC Regional Advisory Board, and their efforts have been rewarded by achieving a BITC Big Tick in 2009, and having a further two Big Ticks reaccredited.

Living Streets

Marshalls joined forces with Living Streets in 2009, a national charity, formerly known as the Pedestrians Association, which is working towards people-friendly public spaces. As part of this new partnership, over 50 of Marshalls' employees have been trained in Community Street Auditing – giving them an important insight into how the Living Streets agenda is applied to the streets and public spaces they help to create. The audits are designed to gather together street users, including the general public, residents and local authority representatives, and by listening to them to come up with better landscapes which will make a difference to their communities and communal areas. Audit trainees from Marshalls have found the training useful, giving them an insight into what street users would like and what street designers need to take into consideration when landscaping public areas.

> *Visiting the street and involving myself with others to decide what was good and poor in the existing street conditions was the best part. The day helped me have an understanding of what architects, planners, local authorities and engineers need to consider when engaging in street design.*

A Marshalls volunteer

Community Partnerships

Marshalls takes community responsibilities seriously, with many of its UK sites actively working with local communities. The business has also set targets for all manufacturing sites to establish a partnership with a local school or educational establishment close to their operation. In 2009, these partnerships will form part of an action plan to ensure Marshalls continues to contribute to the local community and makes a positive impact.

It is really important for them to work locally so their staff can take part in projects that matter to them. They work with local schools, colleges and communities on all sorts of different projects – restoration, environmental, education – whatever makes the biggest impact and adds the most value to the community. They take a partnership approach so that they work together to make it happen and for the company and its employees that's what's really great about the sites working at local level. They also work at a national level, by supporting such campaigns as Living Streets.

Here are just a few examples of the great work Marshalls' employees are doing in their spare time, fundraising or helping out with organisations throughout the UK.

- Marshalls' St Ives Works donated time and paving to Needingworth Primary School. The paving was provided to create a safe hard standing area around a small allotment in the school grounds. This will now help make the allotment more accessible throughout the year, enabling the children to grow their plants and vegetables as part of general lessons.
- In April 2009 Marshalls employees took part in Living Streets' Walk to Work Week – an initiative which aims to raise awareness of the benefits of walking and encourage the nation to fit more walking into their everyday lives. People from all areas of the company joined in by walking to work, walking on their lunch break or even organising a walking meeting.
- Employees at Marshalls' Eaglescliffe site donated paving and volunteers to create a patio at Teesside Hospice which provides respite and in-patient care for the critically ill as well as adult and children's bereavement counselling.
- Volunteers from the Sandy Works helped Sunshine Preschool in Great Barford to transform rough ground into a versatile play area. The project incorporated several elements recommended by Ofsted inspectors, including areas of hard landscaping along with sensory features to cater for the children's development needs. The children will be able to enjoy a newly constructed sand pit, mud pit and water feature along with a grassed area to accommodate their plastic play equipment.
- A Marshalls' corporate responsibility activity was acknowledged with an award from Yorkshire Forward at a ceremony at Leeds Town Hall. Marshalls' Brookfoot Works, in partnership with Pennine Housing 2000, Calderdale College, HBOS and RSA won recognition for providing support for 'Project Challenge', a six month programme for disadvantaged youths aged 16-24.

During 2009, the Group made charitable donations of £41,574.

Marshalls continues to support the Royal Horticultural Society's Campaign for School Gardening engaging children in the world of horticulture and basic landscape design. The aim is to ensure that, by 2010, 10,000 primary schools in the UK will have signed up to the Campaign for School Gardening. In 2009, they also donated the plants from their show garden at the RHS Chelsea Flower Show to a school in Hull.

These initiatives align with the Group's brand values and its focus on innovation.

Marshalls and the Environment

Environment

Compliance and Legislation

Marshalls regards compliance with relevant environmental laws and government directives, as well as adhering to responsible standards where no legislation exists, as an integral part of its business strategy.

Integrated Management Systems

Marshalls has introduced BSI Publicly Available Specification 99 (PAS 99) for Integrated Management Systems into its operations as a basis for sustainable development. Marshalls has a target to ensure that 90% of production output is manufactured at sites which have obtained IMS by the end of 2012. 83% of sites are accredited to ISO 9001 (Quality Management) 78% of sites are accredited to ISO 14001 (Environmental Management) 81% of sites are accredited to BS OHSAS 18001

Marshalls' policies, for Energy and Climate Change Policy, Environmental Policy, Integrated Management System Policy, Quality Policy, and Health & Safety Policy, are reviewed at least annually and are signed by Marshalls' Chief Executive on behalf of the board. In line with the government's targets, Marshalls has committed to reduce emissions by 80% by 2050.

Voluntary Disclosure

Marshalls' energy requirement is in excess of 6,000MWh and therefore it will be subject to the Carbon Reduction Commitment (CRC) introduced by The Department for Energy and Climate Change (DECC). Marshalls has prepared for the requirements of the scheme and was ready for the proposed starting date of April 2010.

Marshalls has also voluntarily joined Carbon Action Yorkshire, a think tank and learning group for CRC, and discloses information on its greenhouse gas emissions, risks, opportunities and plans via the Carbon Disclosure Project and The Prince's May Day Network.

Carbon Reduction Programme

Marshalls is committed to reducing the amount of carbon produced as a result of its operations and has put in place a carbon reduction programme incorporating a range of initiatives:

- carbon management programme
- carbon labelling
- energy champions for each site
- energy plans for each site
- retrofitting energy efficiency equipment
- switch off procedures
- driver training
- route planning software.

The focus for 2009/10 was:

- improved awareness and training
- improved procurement and design
- renewable energy review
- improved communications
- energy best practice teams and processes.

May Day Network

Marshalls is also proud to be a member of The Prince's May Day Network and is committed to every one of its pledges:

PLEDGE 1: Measure carbon emissions

PLEDGE 2: Report carbon emissions publicly or to Business in the Community

PLEDGE 3: Set an absolute target and take action to reduce carbon emissions

PLEDGE 4: Encourage employees to reduce their carbon emissions at home and at work

PLEDGE 5: Work in partnership with suppliers to reduce carbon emissions in the supply chain

PLEDGE 6: Mobilise customers to take action on climate change

Marshalls voluntarily discloses carbon emission information to The Prince's May Day Network and was asked to be featured as a case study.

Water

Marshalls has continued to invest in water recycling to reduce its dependence on mains and borehole water supplies, with investment at two further sites during 2008. The company remains committed to improving the balance between recycled and externally supplied water at its main production sites. Marshalls' overall target for water use is 0.05m3 per tonne of production of water from mains or boreholes by 2015.

Marshalls recognises that this target can only be achieved by harvesting and recycling, and the company continues to invest in product innovation, in order to help the government achieve its Future Water targets and provide permeable paving and driveway solutions to consumers following recent legislation on paving over front gardens. During 2008, use of treated water from mains sources declined by 14.9% overall.

New government legislation on the supply and use of water, Future Water, came into force in late 2008. With changes ranging from tap water metering to flooding countermeasures, the scale of impact for the hard landscaping industry was significant, with both landscapers and manufacturers being encouraged to provide water permeable solutions that comply with technical standards to eliminate water run-off. As a solution, the legislation introduced Sustainable Urban Drainage Systems, or SUDS. SUDS are hard landscaping products designed to allow an acceptable volume of surface water to permeate through into the ground below, helping to reduce surface run-off and limit the impact on street drains. As a result of Future Water and growing environmental concerns, Marshalls introduced a range of permeable paving solutions for the domestic market and converted every core domestic driveway product to a permeable version.

Marshalls' entire sales force has been trained on Future Water and training has also been provided for the Marshalls Register of Approved Installers on how to install SUDS professionally. During 2008/09, Marshalls has run 113 training sessions and trained 732 people.

As part of its Energy and Climate Change Policy, Marshalls has also committed to:

- begin the process with a 2,000 tonnes of CO_2 pa reduction year on year
- reduce specific emissions by 3% per annum (kg CO_2 /t finished material)
- audit all new businesses within one year of acquisition and bring them into Group targets within three years.

Campaign for Better Landscapes

In 2009, Marshalls launched its Campaign for Better Landscapes, calling for both public and private bodies, as well as individuals, to seriously consider the societal and individual benefits of creating 'better landscapes'. This communications campaign is looking to encourage those responsible for their own landscapes to consider the impact of their landscaping decisions on the environment and the community.

Biodiversity

Conserving natural habitats, encouraging wildlife and sympathetic restoration of quarry sites, is crucial to ensure that quarrying causes no lasting ecological damage. But to achieve definite environmental improvements, the quality of land management must be rigorously audited.

Marshalls' Maltby site received the Wildlife Trusts Biodiversity Benchmark for Land Management in 2007 and Maltby became the first active manufacturing site in the UK to be accredited with the benchmark. Marshalls went on to receive the National Gold Award at the International Green Apple Awards 2007 for Environmental Best Practice and in 2008 was awarded the Green Hero Award by the Green Organisation for sharing best practice on biodiversity.

Since achieving its Biodiversity benchmark, Marshalls has been invited to Doncaster Metropolitan Borough Council's Local Site Partnership meetings and is taking an active role in helping to protect and manage Sites of Scientific Interest for the future. Another Marshalls' site, Stoke Hall, has now registered with the Wildlife Trusts and passed an initial assessment with a final audit scheduled. Marshalls aims to have biodiversity action plans at every site by 2012.

Re-forestation in India

During 2009 Marshalls has been working with the University of Bangor on a research project to look at the restoration of quarry land in India. The research was carried out during a two month period in late 2008, in Kota and Bundi Districts which lie to the south of Jaipur, Rajasthan. These are areas well known for the extraction of different grades of sandstone. The research was designed to examine the feasibility and potential for quarry restoration schemes to bring both ecological and socio-economic benefits to areas that are no longer worked. Based on recommendations, Marshalls is now working on the ground with Indian partners.

Waste and Recycling

Marshalls' target for 2008 was to reduce the proportion of waste material going to landfill to under 15%, which they reached and exceeded. In 2008, 90% of Marshalls' waste was reused or recycled with only 10% going to landfill.

Case Study

Brookfoot Works – A Recycling Case Study

At Marshalls' Brookfoot site, an engineering intervention has reduced waste to landfill material and demand for aggregates by 1,350 tonnes per year. It has also reduced the requirement for pigment by 23,000kgs, increased recycling of aggregate waste by 29% on site and provided a business saving projected to be £63,000 per year.

Another engineering intervention in 2009 to the same system was expected to return a payback on capital investment in six months and provide annual savings of £90,000 per year in salvaged steel shot and additional heavy dust reintroduced to plant mixing processes.

The proximity of the manufacturing machines means that very little energy is used to recycle the materials and the material usage reduces the demand on transport, lowering the carbon footprint of the products.

Waste Reduction

Packaging

Reducing packaging is a major priority, while still ensuring secure transportation, safe handling and minimising product damage and wastage between manufacturing sites and point of use. Marshalls monitors suppliers of packaging products to ensure that supplies either are obtained from sustainable sources, for example, pallet timber, or from recycled materials wherever possible e.g. strapping.

Marshalls uses a single waste contractor to manage all waste activities to maximise opportunities for recycling waste streams. As a result, recycling both on and off site recovered 82% of the Group's waste for other uses. The remaining 18% was sent to landfill. Marshalls also uses waste from other industries in its own production. Innovative concrete mix ensures product quality, while using waste materials such as recycled concrete, china clay, slate, cement and steel slag.

Transport

Marshalls' transport emissions are being reduced by the specification of fuel efficient Euro 5 diesel vehicles, dedicated route planning software, vehicle tracking, and a full time driver trainer. Driver performance is also reviewed regularly.

Marshalls also actively looks into alternative forms of energy. Marshalls has already added a percentage of bio fuel to the diesel fuel used by its road transport fleet. 85% of Marshalls' transport fleet now uses Euro 5 diesel engines delivering both fuel efficiency and reduced greenhouse gas emissions. During 2008, the company increased the use of its own fleet against contracted hauliers.

In addition to this, Marshalls has also invested in logistics software for centralised planning and also operates its fleet in partnership with other companies so as to minimize the amount of journeys required to deliver Marshalls' products.

As a responsible and sustainable business Marshalls have also been very vocal on the issue of "Greenwash" and the company claims that there are a lot of companies making claims about being ethical or green that they cannot substantiate. These companies communicate their 'credentials' but with no data or real substance to back them up. Without independent third party verification, anyone can say anything. There's no proof. Marshalls wanted to shine a light on this Greenwash, because ultimately it is Greenwash that will seriously damage the already fragile consumer trust in business and products.

Marshalls' main priority for 2010 is to build on their successes and concentrate on the Marshalls Sustainable Business Model and the Campaign for Better Landscapes. They have revised their model to incorporate their membership of the United Nations Global Compact and FTSE4GOOD, along with their continued commitment to Integrated Management Systems. Their approach to sustainability will continue to run through the heart of the business and will play a key role in how they deliver their service to their customers. This commitment to responsibility and sustainability is best summed up in their own aims and objectives which state that:

- they manage their business with pride and integrity
- they are committed to full legal compliance in all that they do
- they aim to provide a safe, fulfilling and rewarding career for all their employees
- they will continue to develop community programmes which support their brand values and further promote their recognition as an active contributor to local community development
- they actively assess and manage the environmental impacts of all their operations
- they will further develop their standing as a responsible business in the community
- they will benchmark and evaluate what they do in order to constantly improve their competitive edge in the marketplace
- they will continually benchmark and evaluate what they do in order to improve their corporate responsibility performance.

We regard Corporate Responsibility as a journey in the course of which we aim to align our business values, purpose and strategy with the social and economic needs of our stakeholders, whilst embedding responsible and ethical business policies and practices in everything we do.

Marshalls, 2010

CHAPTER 31

Legal Sector Alliance Model

- The Legal Sector Alliance
- LSA Principles
- Impact Areas
- The 2009 Annual Report

The Legal Sector Alliance (LSA)[1]

Climate change is the greatest challenge facing mankind today and we only have a very small window of opportunity to act. The continued growth of the Legal Sector Alliance demonstrates that law firms recognise the urgency of the situation and are committed to taking a leadership position in this area. By collaborating to share best practices in sustainable business, the legal sector can make a positive contribution to combating climate change.

HRH The Prince of Wales

This book frequently touches on the notion that a business can gain substantial competitive advantage over its rivals if it is seen as a more "concerned" and "responsible" business. However it is also refreshing and inspirational to see a whole variety of small to large businesses in a particular sector agreeing to come together to fight in unison on a specific issue such as climate change. The Legal Sector Alliance is just such an example and it may well be the model for other industry sectors to follow.

The Legal Sector Alliance (LSA) is an inclusive movement of (currently 149) law firms and organisations committed to working collaboratively to take action on climate change by reducing their carbon footprint and adopting environmentally sustainable practices. It represents over a quarter of solicitors in private practice in England and Wales. LSA members vary significantly in size, from global organisations to small and regional law firms. This diverse knowledge-sharing environment enables the Alliance to ensure that they are providing guidance on key issues that is suitable to every type of law firm. It was launched in December 2008 by His Royal Highness the Prince of Wales and supported by the Law Society and Business in the Community.

The LSA believes that acting on climate change is in its collective interest and that a greater impact can be achieved through collaborative action and the sharing of knowledge and experience than could otherwise be achieved by the efforts of individual firms.

To act as a framework for individual and collective action, they have developed a set of principles, which cover members' own operations, as well as their wider influence on employees, suppliers, clients and policy makers.

1 LSA Annual Report 2009. (2009, December 2). Annual Report 2009. Retrieved January 11, 2010, from legalsectoralliance.org.uk: http://www.legalsectoralliance.org.uk/files/lsareport2009.pdf, page 4.

Their aims and objectives are to:

- raise awareness of climate change and the urgent need for action within the legal sector
- identify opportunities for the legal sector to collectively respond to climate change risks
- support the profession in capitalising on emerging business opportunities
- enable solicitors and law firms to adopt low-carbon and environmentally sustainable business practices
- use its influence to raise awareness and prompt action outside the profession.

To be achieved:

- by producing and signposting relevant tools and resources
- working with external stakeholders including government, clients and suppliers
- by facilitating knowledge sharing across the profession.

LSA Principles

These principles have been developed in consultation with the profession and leading environmental NGOs. They are intended to provide both a framework to support individual action by each member and an outline of the LSA's commitment to collective action.

They cover members' own operations, but also their wider influence on clients, suppliers, employees and policy makers. The initial focus of the principles is on UK activities, recognising that firms with operations elsewhere are likely to apply these or similar principles to their other operations in phases.

The LSA recognises that because of the different sizes and starting points of those within the sector, each member will need to apply the principles and take action in different ways. For this reason, they have provided some examples of how the principles might be applied, but they are not intended to be prescriptive.

The LSA intends to review the principles annually based on implementation experience, to reflect ongoing learning and emerging good practice, and to reflect the increased maturity of the sector and its collective contribution to climate change reductions.

Members of the Legal Sector Alliance commit to the following.

1. **Measure, manage and reduce the impact of our operations**

   Some examples of how this might be applied:

   - measure and monitor performance to help identify problem areas
   - measure the carbon footprint of a business using the LSA Carbon Footprint Protocol
   - set a target against which reductions will be measured
   - seek to reduce the environmental impact of the internal operations and physical assets under their control
   - reduce resource use, improve reuse and recycling of waste
   - modify operations and services to minimise impacts
   - adapt the workplace to cope with the climatic and other changes likely as a result of past and future CO2 emissions (eg flood defences)
   - undertake a review of printing and working practices
   - develop and implement a sustainable transport policy for business travel.

2. **Work with external stakeholders to reduce our indirect impact**

   Some examples of how this might be applied:

   - engage with clients about working in a way that reduces carbon footprints
   - work collaboratively with suppliers to minimise the end-to-end carbon footprint along the supply chain
   - include environmental considerations in procurement decisions
   - encourage/challenge suppliers to deliver more environmentally sustainable products
   - engage with their local community on climate change issues.

3. **Integrate awareness of climate change across the business**

   Some examples of how this might be applied:

   - develop and implement a climate change policy
   - ensure accountability/responsibility for environmental issues at the most senior level
   - review progress against the principles once a year at the most senior level
   - embed climate change issues into risk evaluation and strategic decision making
   - begin to communicate our commitment to the principles across any international offices
   - raise awareness among employees and empower them to take action.

4. **Advise clients on the opportunities and obligations arising from and under climate change law**

   Some examples of how this might be applied:

   - reflect their knowledge of the science and impacts of climate change in advice given
   - raise awareness of the possibilities of new and emerging markets developing across many sectors
   - anticipate and plan for compliance and regulation and help clients to do so
   - communicate the LSA's approach to climate change to clients.

5. **Work collaboratively to engage in the public debate on climate change and to develop, apply and promote best practice across the sector**

   Some examples of how this might be applied:

   - share best practice through case studies and peer networking
   - contribute to research and policy formulation in the field of climate change
   - highlight opportunities for more sustainable ways of practising law to the LSA
   - provide pro bono advice to environmental organisations working to combat climate change
   - actively engage in public debate on climate change and the regulatory response
   - identify opportunities to work in partnership with NGOs and government.

6. **Report on progress and be accountable**

   Some examples of how this might be applied:

   - report annually to the LSA on progress measured against the LSA principles
   - disclose greenhouse gas emissions using the LSA Protocol or a globally recognised standard
   - use annual reports, websites or intranets to report on progress.

The LSA recognises that the principles will apply to different members within the sector in different ways and that they will be at different stages of integrating climate change across their business. Therefore, it is natural that this would be reflected in their ability to implement the principles. Where it is impossible for a member to implement a particular principle they will be invited to explain why they are unable to do so in their annual report back to the LSA and this will be taken into account. Those adopting these principles are doing so voluntarily and independently.

The Legal Sector Alliance Principles are intended to provide a framework for action however it is up to individual members to decide how best to put them into practice.

Impact areas ●●●

By taking positive action in a few key areas, firms can individually demonstrate their environmental responsibility and collectively the legal sector can make a significant contribution to addressing climate change.

The identified priority areas are:

- carbon footprinting
- minimising resource use
- engaging employees
- working with suppliers
- carbon footprinting.

Des Hudson, chief executive of the Law Society, was reported in the Times as saying "You can't manage what you haven't measured, so calculation of your carbon foot print is absolutely crucial before you take action to reduce it"[2].

The first step for any business wanting to take action on climate change is to understand the impact of its activities on the environment and the most common way of doing this is to measure its 'carbon footprint'. The problem is that there are a number of ways that it can be calculated using various tools and methodologies and including a variety of activities within its scope.

For example, one firm might calculate its carbon footprint measuring only those things for which it is directly responsible, such as energy use and greenhouse gas emissions while another may include indirect impacts such as staff travel to and from work or the emissions of its suppliers. This not only makes it difficult for individual firms to benchmark their performance, it can also lead to unfair comparisons between firms.

In order to address this, the Legal Sector Alliance has developed a Protocol which, if adopted widely, will not only help firms to easily calculate their footprint, but will also improve transparency, consistency and comparability within the sector.

The Protocol comprises a spreadsheet-based measurement tool and accompanying guidance. The Protocol has been adapted from the existing measurement tools and developed in consultation with the Carbon Trust. The calculation methodology and technical content of the measurement tool have been verified by the Edinburgh Centre for Carbon Management.

Employee commuting is not measured within the LSA Protocol, however, they do encourage firms to promote green travel. Green travel is any form of transport that causes less damage to the environment and community than driving. The LSA has advised its members on its website that the main recognised forms of green travel are walking, cycling and using public transport. Other green alternatives mentioned

2 The Times Newspaper. (2008, April 29). The water cooler: What the legal world is buzzing about this week. Retrieved January 11, 2010, from timesonline.co.uk: http://business.timesonline.co.uk/tol/business/law/article3842059.ece

included car sharing, or driving a car that runs off cleaner fuel than petrol or diesel. Transport is a key focus area for the LSA in 2010, and the organisation will be producing guidance for members on how to minimise the environmental impacts of business travel.

The scope of the LSA's carbon footprint Protocol includes data on business travel, which can be obtained through analysis of internal information. This data can be analysed to ascertain whether more sustainable modes of travel can be used, or where travel can be reduced, for example by increased use of tele- or video-conferencing.

The LSA Protocol does not include employee commuting, because the data is very difficult both to gather and to verify. However, they do encourage firms to look at how their employees travel, so that they can consider how to support them in finding more sustainable alternatives, ideally through a travel plan. A travel plan is a term used to describe a co-ordinated package of strategies and measures aimed at promoting sustainable transport to, from and within a particular site. The plan is a dynamic process that evolves and should be reviewed and revised over time.

The LSA recommends that a travel survey is the ideal starting point for firms wanting to implement a travel plan. It can help to build up a picture of their staff, how they travel and how the firm can support them, for example by promoting flexible working or by providing more cycle racks and changing facilities. The LSA has developed an employee travel survey, based on samples of surveys which LSA members have used, and this is available to download from their website.

Minimising Resource Use

Once a business has set about assessing its environmental impact by measuring its carbon footprint, the LSA suggests that the next logical step is for a firm to find ways to reduce that impact.

The LSA website identifies a number of quick and easy steps that can help firms to get started and they can be found under the heading "Quick wins in the office". In addition, the Legal Sector Alliance is looking at whether they, as a profession, could change the way that they do business in order to reduce the sector's collective environmental impact.

Members of the LSA Task Force have prepared a discussion paper which looks at the three main areas where the legal sector's effect on the environment is arguably the greatest - energy usage in buildings, business travel and paper/resource usage. In addition, they have considered how to engage employees as that is a key factor in enabling a firm to reduce its environmental impact.

The LSA is continually developing further ideas around how firms can minimise their resource use and how the profession can reduce its collective impact in the future. The website encourages members to submit case studies highlighting how they were able to minimise their resource use so that others may follow their example.

Engaging Employees

Collectively the legal sector in England and Wales employs around 150,000 people. Therefore, engaging employees in climate change activities is a key way for firms to reduce their carbon emissions.

Likewise, firms are increasingly experiencing upward pressure from their employees to take action on climate change. Young people are frequently asking potential employers about their environmental policies. Employees are increasingly accepting responsibility for helping save money around the workplace according to new research released today by the Carbon Trust with the majority (87%) saying it is important for them to help their employer cut costs in the current climate, and 78% willing to be more energy efficient to save money[3].

Therefore, as well as being a key way of supporting firm-wide carbon reduction targets, there are a number of benefits of mobilising employees on climate change, including cost savings, increased staff morale and improved recruitment and retention. Ways of engaging employees include running awareness-raising campaigns, identifying "green champions" and providing incentives.

Case Study

One member of the LSA has taken practical eco-efficient steps and engaged employees on its environmental priorities, resulting in waste reductions and costs savings for the firm. A major UK law firm providing a full service to clients worldwide this LSA member made its environmental policy an integral part of its wider business strategy and has taken a two-strand approach to its environmental activities.

1. Taking practical eco-efficient steps centrally

To reduce energy use the company converted to 100% renewable electricity sources for its main office, installed movement detectors in meeting rooms, and programmed its air conditioning system to power down out of core office hours. To reduce and improve the impact of paper use the company has introduced e-filing and an electronic fax distribution system, and switched to paper which is FSC approved and has a minimum of 75% recycled content.

The company has also introduced on-site filtering and bottling of drinking water to eliminate the carbon emissions and waste associated with plastic bottled water, and replaced plastic cups and spoons in kitchen areas with metal spoons and glasses.

3 Carbon Trust. (2009, March 27). UK employees ready to cut costs around the workplace. Retrieved January 15, 2010, from carbontrust.co.uk: http://www.carbontrust.co.uk/news/news/press-centre/2009/Pages/employee_resource.aspx

2. Engaging employees on their environmental impact

The company recognised that to attract and retain the most talented individuals it needed to demonstrate its environmental credentials. To engage employees on environmental initiatives it created a network of 30 'eco-champions' tasked with encouraging colleagues to adopt more eco-friendly working practices, such as re-using travel wallets. It also held a firm-wide campaign to encourage staff to do "Three Simple Things" – turn off PC monitors, think before they printed and recycle. As part of this it arranged screenings of 'An Inconvenient Truth' and started a DVD loan scheme to allow employees to watch the film at home.

Impact

- On-site water bottling reduced use by 8,000 bottles per year and saved approximately £10,000.
- Plastic spoons reduced by 100% from 15,000 per year to zero.
- Re-use in rail ticket wallets has resulted in a 32% reduction in purchases and is estimated to save £1,000 per year.
- Over 200 staff attended screenings of 'An Inconvenient Truth' and 120 staff have taken a copy home.

Working with Suppliers

A legal services firm's most significant environmental impact is indirect – both upstream (the impact of its suppliers and their products) and downstream (the impact of transactions conducted by clients with the firm's advice).

The need to reduce carbon emissions in the procurement process has prompted the Legal Sector Alliance to develop a sustainable procurement guide for law firms. A sustainable approach to procurement means looking at the impacts of the product or service on the environment over its entire lifecycle from creation to disposal. Taking paper as an example, you would assess whether the paper is made from virgin pulp or a form of recycled product, its production process, how it is packaged, how it is delivered to you and whether you can recycle it.

Sustainable procurement is an approach to buying products and services that takes into account the economic, environmental and social impacts of what you buy. The LSA supports action on climate change and therefore the guide focuses solely on environmental impacts and particularly reducing carbon emissions in the supply chain - also referred to as "green procurement". The aim is to explore how sustainability considerations complement other key business criteria such as cost, value-for-money and stakeholder preference.

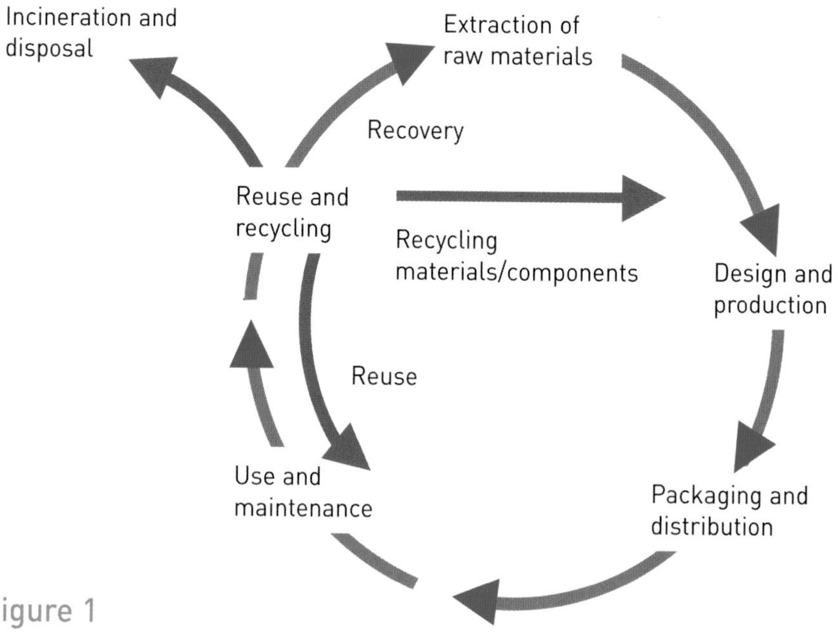

Figure 1

Identifying Priority Areas

The LSA website provides examples of products and services that are likely to be familiar to most law firms (for example, paper or energy). However, the examples are not exhaustive, and members may find the following framework useful for prioritising other categories when identifying whether the carbon impact of each stage in the product lifecycle is high or low.

Carbon usage - high or low?		
	Example: IT consulting	**Example: paper**
Extraction of raw materials	Low	High
Design and production	Low	High
Packaging and distribution	Low	High
Use and maintenance	High (travel)	Low
Incineration and disposal	Low	High
Overall	Low	High

Once the risk of a category is established as high or low, this can be contrasted with its volume of use within the firm, which can most easily be measured by annual spend. Firms should then prioritise effort in relation to those categories sitting in the top right hand quadrant. (See figure 2[4])

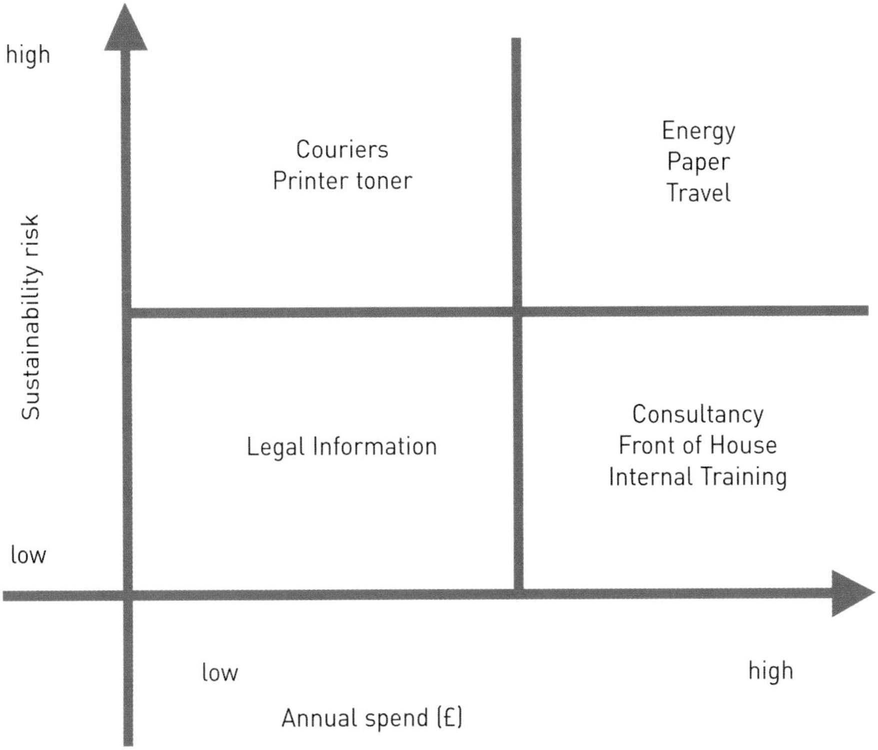

Figure 2

The 2009 Annual Report[5]

2009 is the first year that LSA members have reported performance against the LSA Principles. The report, which was launched in December 2009, details the results of the first ever survey of the LSA members' climate change performance and preparedness, and is a significant sustainability milestone for the legal sector. It provides a baseline for understanding members' strengths and seeks to ensure that LSA continues to provide the best possible support and resources to assist organisations in capturing improvement opportunities.

4 Legal Sector Alliance. (2010, January 11). Legal Sector Alliance. Retrieved January 11, 2010, from legalsectoralliance.comL: http://www.legalsectoralliance.com/

5 LSA Annual Report 2009. (2009, December 2). Annual Report 2009. Retrieved January 11, 2010, from legalsectoralliance.org.uk: http://www.legalsectoralliance.org.uk/files/lsareport2009.pdf

The key reasons for carrying out the self-assessment were to enable the LSA to:

- understand how the LSA principles are being acted on
- develop collective understanding of best practice
- assess the impact of the LSA
- identify areas of shared difficulty and opportunities for the development of further tools and resources
- provide a reporting structure for individual LSA members to use in their own communications
- forecast member activity for 2010.

Principle 1: Measure, manage and reduce the impact of our operations

The results of this year's survey show that 57 per cent of LSA members had calculated their organisation's carbon footprint and an additional 33 per cent were planning to do so in 2010. Of the members that calculated their carbon footprint, two-thirds had used the LSA Carbon Protocol to do so.

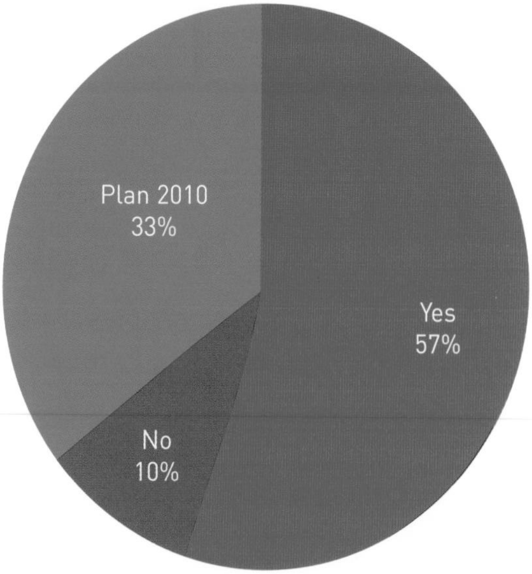

Figure 3

Members were asked whether targets had been set to reduce their energy, waste, water and travel. Organisations were more likely to have set targets for waste (42%) and/or energy (35%) than for travel (27%) or water (21%).

Around half of the members indicated plans for target setting in 2010 for each element.

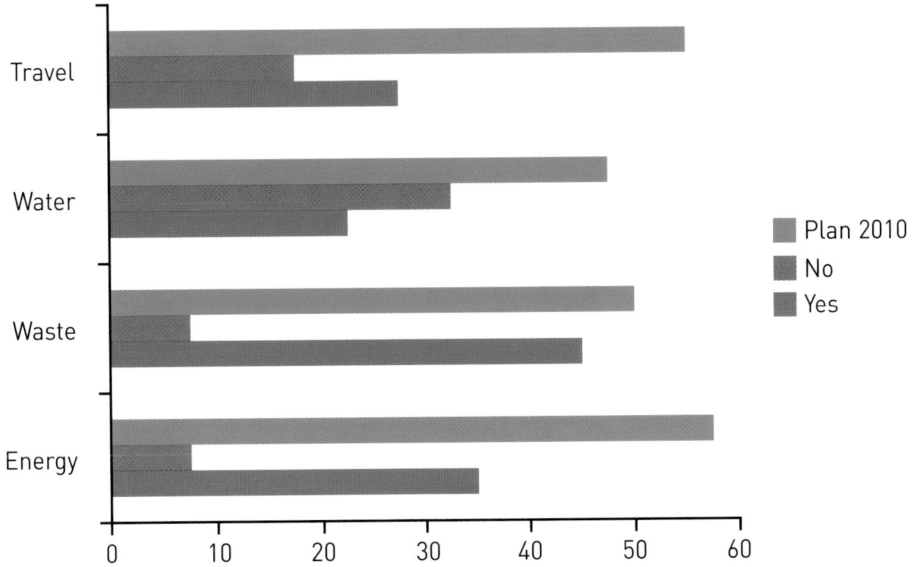

Figure 4

Principle 2: Work with external stakeholders to reduce our indirect impact

Forty per cent of respondents had developed a sustainable procurement policy and 50% planned to do so in 2010. Forty eight per cent indicated that they engaged in ongoing dialogue with suppliers to encourage improvement of sustainability and carbon performance. Almost a quarter of members frequently reviewed suppliers' environmental performance and around half planned to do so from 2010.

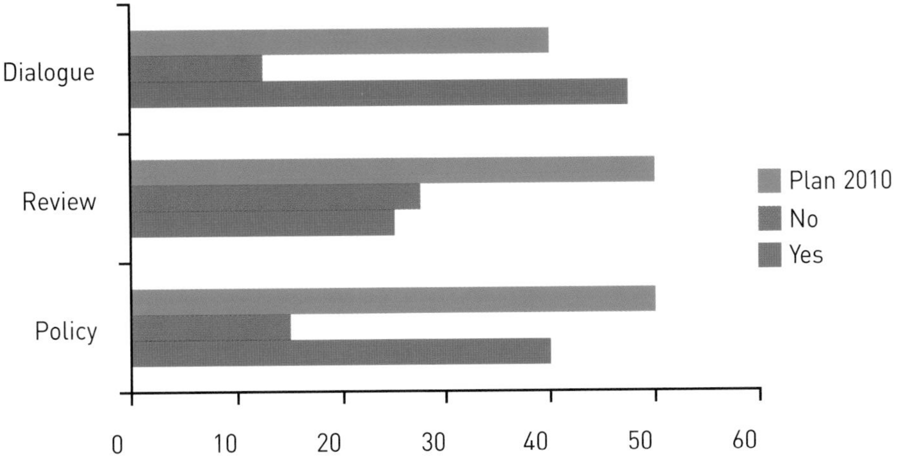

Figure 5

Principle 3: Integrate awareness of climate change across our business

Three quarters of the respondents reported senior level responsibility for environmental issues. Few members factored climate change risk into business continuity planning and strategic decision making with just 23% doing so and 33% having no plans to do so in the forthcoming year.

Two thirds reported regularly communicating with all employees on progress. Only 5% of respondents indicated that they did not communicate regularly and had no plans to do so during 2010. Nearly half of those members responding reported they had published environmental policies with high levels of awareness and employee involvement. By the end of 2010 over 90% of members will have published such policies.

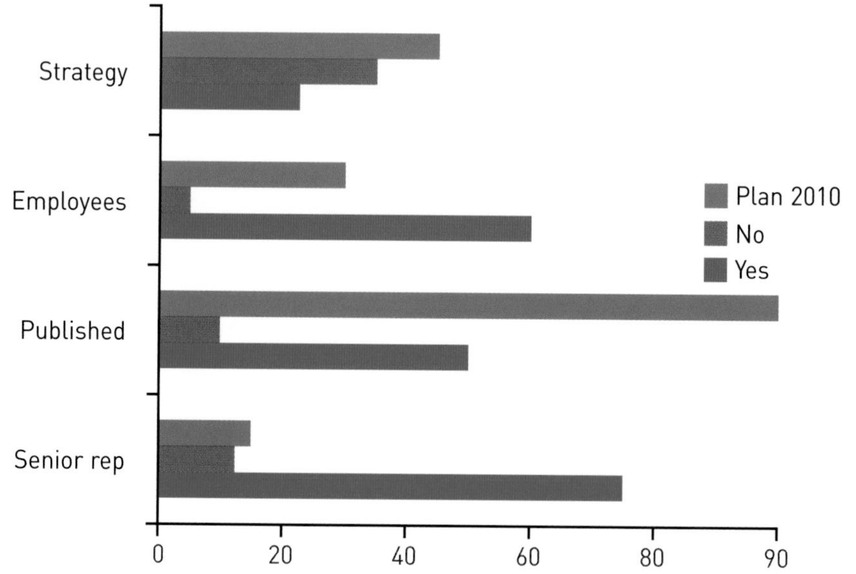

Figure 6

Principle 4: Advise clients on opportunities and obligations arising from and under climate change law

Forty three per cent of members advise clients on opportunities and obligations arising from and under climate change law whilst 39% provided proactive client communication on environmental and climate change issues. Only 29% offered any training in this area. Around one quarter of respondents felt that Principle 4 was not applicable to their organisation due to the nature of their practice.

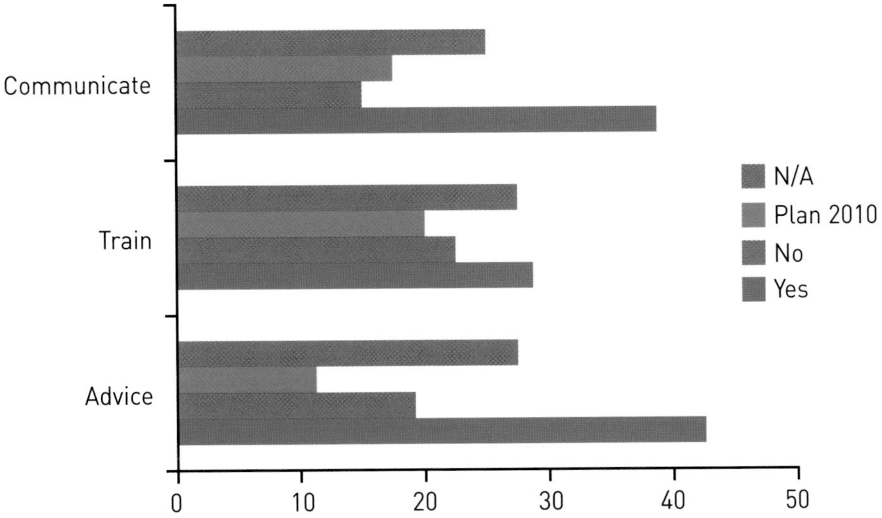

Figure 7

Principle 5: Work collaboratively to engage in the public debate on climate change and to develop, apply and promote best practice across the sector

The main avenue for engagement/collaboration for around half the members was through active participation in regional LSA events and other relevant climate change events. 10% stated that they had authored or contributed to relevant articles for the media, 21% had provided a case study for the LSA website and only 12% had completed the LSA survey on adaptation. A number of members, particularly smaller organisations, felt that beyond involvement in the LSA there were limited opportunities for law firms to participate in the climate change debate. They recognised that the LSA had a key role in promoting best practice across the sector.

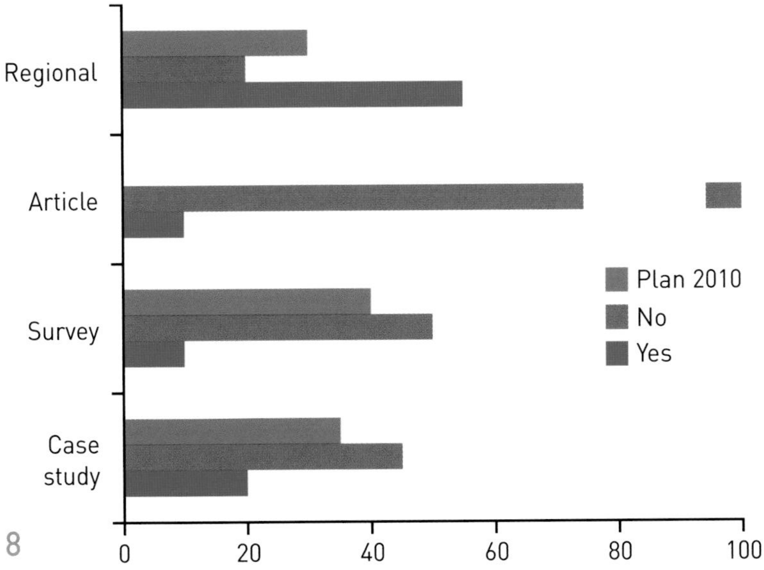

Figure 8

Principle 6: Report on progress and be accountable

80% of members either currently published their carbon footprint or planned to do so in 2010. 22% published environmental performance reports on an annual or more regular basis. Over half the members (53%) indicated that they had no plans to seek independent verification of publicly recorded data. A lack of financial and time resources was generally considered to be the most significant barrier to regular and robust reporting. The members recognised the benefit of the LSA's ability to facilitate knowledge-sharing across the legal sector.

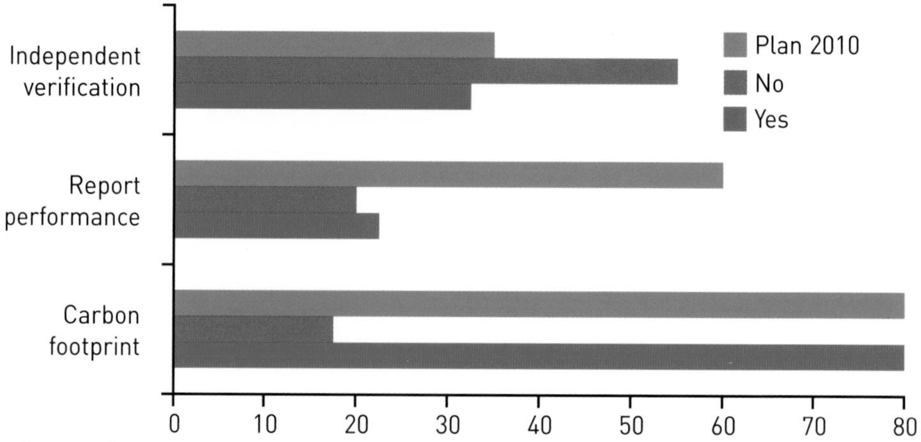

Figure 9

The report reflects some very positive movements in the legal sector and the LSA should be very proud of what it has achieved so far and more importantly what is still to come. There is a fair amount of modesty amongst the membership who indicate that individually they can have much less impact than the LSA as a whole. While there is some truth in this perhaps they need to be reminded that they each have a sphere of influence, which is where this book started. The majority of those responding are planning to implement much more in 2010 so overall the report leaves the LSA in a very favourable position to move the initiative forward.

On page five of the report the Chairman of the Legal Sector Alliance, Sir Nigel Knowles, said:

"This initiative is about collaboration within the legal profession to tackle climate change issues that specifically relate to us as a sector. By sharing our knowledge and experience we can also play an important role as influencers, working with our clients and suppliers to create a more sustainable supply chain going forward. Climate change is now a key issue for all businesses ...."

INDEX

T

U

V

W